The #1
New York Times
Bestseller

The #1 New York Times Bestseller

Intriguing facts about the 484 books
that have been #1 *New York Times* bestsellers
since the first list in 1942.

John Bear

Ten Speed Press
Berkeley, California

1☉

Ten Speed Press
P.O. Box 7123
Berkeley, California 94707

Illustrations on pages 5, 8, 24, 30, 32, 33, 35, 36, 40, 41, 42, 48, 54, 75, 79,
82, 88, 90, 99, 101, 102, 105, 122, 125, 129, 134, 135, 143, 144, 154, 156,
158, 162, 165, 175, 188, 199, 204, 205, 206, 221, 232, 237, 243, 248
© 1992 by Ellen Joy Sasaki

Design and production by John Bear, Nancy Austin, Nicole Geiger, and
Toni Tajima. Desktop publishing services: Canterbury Press, Berkeley

Thanks to the Berkeley Public Library for kind and generous assistance.

Permissions to reprint artwork begin on page v.

Library of Congress Cataloging-in-Publication Data

Bear, John, 1938
        The #1 New York Times bestseller / John Bear.
                P.   cm.
        Includes bibliographical references and index.
        ISBN 0-89815-484-7
        1. Best sellers—United States—Bibliography. 2. Books and reading—
United States—History—20th century. 3. Popular literature—United States—
History and ciriticism. 4. New York Times—History
I. Title.   II. Title: Number one New York Times bestseller.
Z1033.B3B43   1992   92-9706
016.381'45002'0973—dc20   CIP

First printing, 1992

1 2 3 4 5 6 - 96 95 94 93 92

continued on page 253

FROM THE AUTHOR

Thank you, John Milder. Ten years ago, in a discussion of unusual book titles, fellow author Milder suggested the title of this book as a likely attention-getter. At the time, neither of us could think of a book to write to that title. When the idea finally came (see next paragraph), John was gracious enough to relinquish his claim to the title.

Thank you, Jim Eason. When you brought up the subject of bestsellers on your KGO San Francisco talk show a few years ago, your enthusiasm and that of your callers planted the idea that matched the idea for a title, and grew into this book.

And thank you, Susannah Bear, for the immense amount of library research you did, and for your creative contributions.

This book is gratefully dedicated to these three people and, as always, to Marina.

HOW THE BOOK IS ORGANIZED

The book has two independent parts:

1. The left and right margins, which form a chronological history of all the #1 hardcover books from the inception of the list in 1942 through the fiftieth anniversary in 1992. Nonfiction books are listed on left pages, fiction books on the right.

2. The centers of the page may include:

a) charts and graphs relating to the phenomenon of #1 bestsellers;

b) reprints of articles and stories about best sellers;

c) sample text or illustrations from some of the #1 books; and/or

d) other stuff that seemed interesting and appropriate.

Date the book first reached #1 and number of weeks at #1(*)
*asterisk indicates a newspaper strike

Title

Author

Publisher

Text about the book, including a very brief plot outline, and/or information about the author and publishing history.

Chart showing the book's profile while on the list. The horizontal axis is the number of weeks; the vertical axis is the position on the list, with #1 at the top.

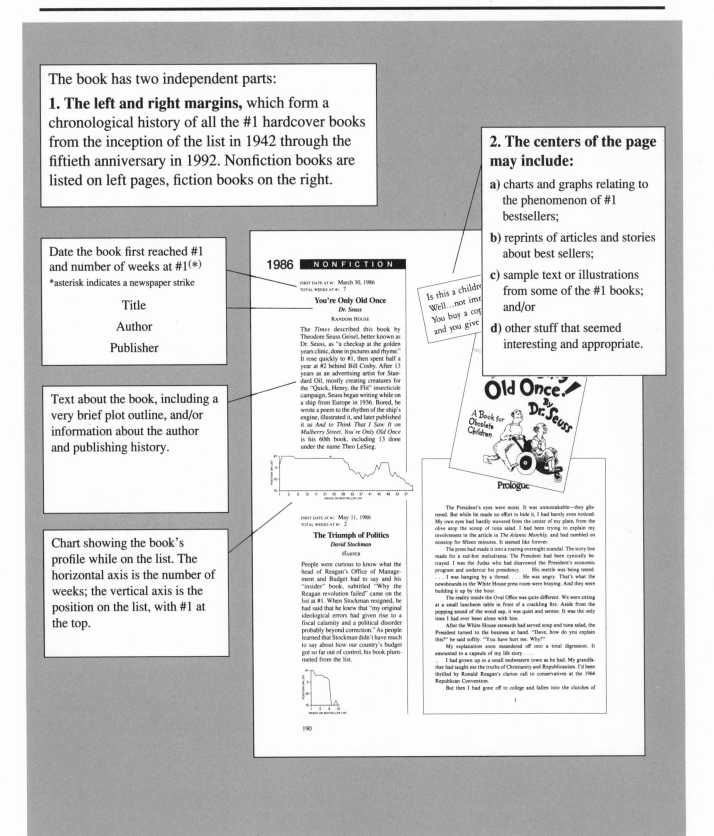

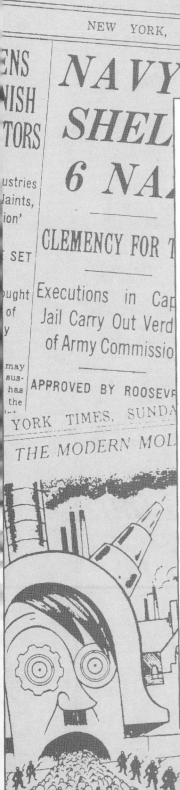

August 9, 1942

The war in Europe was not going well for the allies. The U.S. Navy was on the attack in the Solomons. Mahatma Gandhi was arrested again in India. The Yankees and the Dodgers had huge leads in the pennant races. The Dow Jones Industrial Average had just climbed to 105. Macy's was selling silk neckties for 94¢. Cigarettes were 15¢ a pack, $1.29 a carton. The filet-mignon dinner at Longchamps was $1.25. Paul Robeson's *Othello* opened on Broadway and *Bambi* was at Radio City Music Hall. A 5½-room apartment in Manhattan was renting for $64 a month. Teachers were earning $40 a month.

And on Sunday August 9th, with no prior announcement and no fanfare, the *New York Times* published a list called "The Best Selling Books, Here and Elsewhere." Without exception, that list has appeared in every Sunday edition of the paper for 50 years. The list has varied in length, from fewer than 10 books to more than 20; the criteria for making the list have changed from time to time, and been challenged more than once. But there has always been a #1, and the achievement of being a "#1 *New York Times* Bestseller" has taken on a life of its own. In 50 years, 247 fiction books and 237 nonfiction books have been #1 *New York Times* bestsellers. This book is about those books and the #1 phenomenon.

FIRST DATE AT #1: August 9, 1942
TOTAL WEEKS AT #1: 1

The Last Time I Saw Paris
Elliot Paul
RANDOM HOUSE

Elliot Paul lived for nearly 18 years on the Rue de la Huchette. His account of life on this small Paris street in prewar years gave readers something pleasant to reflect on as the Nazis occupied Paris. The first-ever #1 nonfiction bestseller lasted only one week in the top spot. It was shot down by Major de Seversky and his strategy for removing said Nazis from their strongholds.

FIRST DATE AT #1: August 16, 1942
TOTAL WEEKS AT #1: 4

Victory Through Air Power
Alexander de Seversky
SIMON & SCHUSTER

Within months after Pearl Harbor, this noted pilot, aircraft designer, and manufacturer issued his personal strategy for fighting and winning World War Two. After a month at #1, it was replaced by another aviation expert's personal strategy for winning the war. The author continued to write and reflect on war strategies through the Korean and Vietnam wars as well.

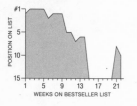

2. A Stairway Down to Antiquity

THE rue de la Huchette, in time and space, had a beginning, a middle and an ending. Centuries ago, when Paris was a walled city on the Ile de la Cité and cows were pastured in what is now the place St. Germain, some of the first Parisians to quit the fortified island area settled along the left bank of the Seine. The rue de la Huchette runs parallel to the river, just a few yards south of the quai. No one seems to be clear about the meaning of its name, least of all its modern inhabitants.

Most of the traffic moved through the little street in an easterly direction, entering from the place St. Michel. This consisted mainly of delivery wagons, make-shift vehicles propelled by pedaling boys, pushcarts of itinerant vendors, knife-grinders, umbrella menders, a herd of milch goats and the neighborhood pedestrians. The residents could sit in doorways or on curbstones, stroll up and down the middle of the way, and use the street as a communal front yard, in daylight hours or in the evening, without risk of life or
a pair
and f
when
rue d
again.
Th
Brasse

The Last Time I Saw Paris

BY ELLIOT PAUL

Random House · New York

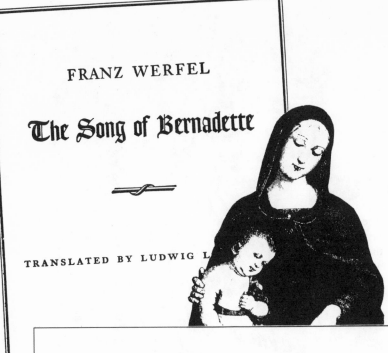

FRANZ WERFEL

The Song of Bernadette

TRANSLATED BY LUDWIG L

A Personal Preface

I<small>N</small> THE last days of June 1940, in flight from our mortal enemies after the collapse of France, we reached the city of Lourdes. The two of us, my wife and I, had hoped to be able to elude them in time to cross the Spanish frontier to Portugal. But since the consuls unanimously refused the requisite visas, we had no alternative but to flee back with great difficulty to the interior of France on the very night on which the National Socialist troops occupied the border town of Hendaye. The Pyrenean *départements* had turned into a phantasmagoria —a very camp of chaos. The millions of this strange migration of peoples wandered about on the roads and obstructed the towns and villages: Frenchmen, Belgians, Dutchmen, Poles, Czechs, Austrians, exiled Germans, and, mingled with these, soldiers of the defeated armies. There was barely food enough to still the extreme pangs of hunger. There was no shelter to be had at all. Anyone who had obtained possession of an upholstered chair for his night's rest was an object of envy. In endless lines stood the cars of the fugitives, piled mountain-high with household gear, with mattresses and beds; there was no gasoline to be had. In Pau a family settled there told us that Lourdes was the one place where, if luck were kind, one might still find a roof. Since the famous city was but thirty kilometres distant, we were advised to make the attempt and knock at its gates. We followed this advice and were sheltered at last.

It was in this manner that Providence brought me to Lourdes, of the miraculous history of which I had hitherto had but the

5

FIRST DATE AT #1: August 9, 1942
TOTAL WEEKS AT #1: 1

And Now Tomorrow
Rachel Field
M<small>ACMILLAN</small>

The first-ever #1 fiction bestseller told the poignant story of New Englander Emily Blair, the illness that left her deaf, and her fight to regain her hearing. Field, who was most famous for her earlier book, *All This and Heaven Too*, died five months before the *Times* bestseller list began. Like its nonfiction counterpart, this book was only #1 for one week before Ms. Blair was overtaken by the Holy Virgin.

POSITION ON LIST
1   5   9   13
WEEKS ON BESTSELLER LIST

FIRST DATE AT #1: August 16, 1942
TOTAL WEEKS AT #1: 13

The Song of Bernadette
Franz Werfel
V<small>IKING</small>

In 1858 a young French girl, Bernadette Soubirous, had a vision of the Holy Virgin at Lourdes. In June 1940, Franz Werfel, a founder of the expressionist movement in German literature, was in desperate flight from the Nazis. His path took him through Lourdes, where he vowed to write Bernadette's story. This is it. Not only was this novelized history #1 for three months, it miraculously remained on the list for nearly a year. Though Jewish, Werfel was drawn to Roman Catholicism.

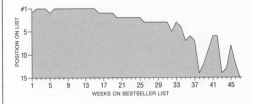

POSITION ON LIST
1   5   9   13   17   21   25   29   33   37   41   45
WEEKS ON BESTSELLER LIST

FIRST DATE AT #1: September 13, 1942
TOTAL WEEKS AT #1: 4

The Coming Battle of Germany
William B. Ziff
DUELL

The reading public was ready for encouragement about Germany's vulnerability. Ziff, a civilian aviation authority, zoomed to #1 with his detailed strategies for winning the war in Europe.

FIRST DATE AT #1: October 11, 1942
TOTAL WEEKS AT #1: 1

They Were Expendable
W. L. White
HARCOURT

He was a war correspondent and this was the first book of personal experiences and war exploits to make #1, albeit for only one week. Then the public was ready for some war humor.

FIRST DATE AT #1: October 18, 1942
TOTAL WEEKS AT #1: 15

See Here, Private Hargrove
Marion Hargrove
HOLT

A 23-year-old reporter's stories about becoming a soldier caught the public's fancy and became the first enduring #1 nonfiction bestseller, remaining at #1 for three months. Hargrove holds the record for the youngest person ever to reach #1 on the nonfiction list, and the second youngest overall (after Françoise Sagan). His book remained on the list for another four months and, after 50 years, is still in print and still selling.

Percentage of #1 Books that Are Now Out of Print

With the exception of the 1940s, there is clear evidence that nonfiction books are much less likely to stay in print than fiction books, which is hardly surprising, since the nonfiction subjects are likely to be more timely or topical. What, then, of the 1940s? More than likely, it is the number of war books, and the public's continuing interest in that period, possibly combined with a tinge of publisher's patriotism, reflected in the reluctance to drop someone like Ernie Pyle or Private Hargrove.

■ **FICTION**　　□ **NONFICTION**

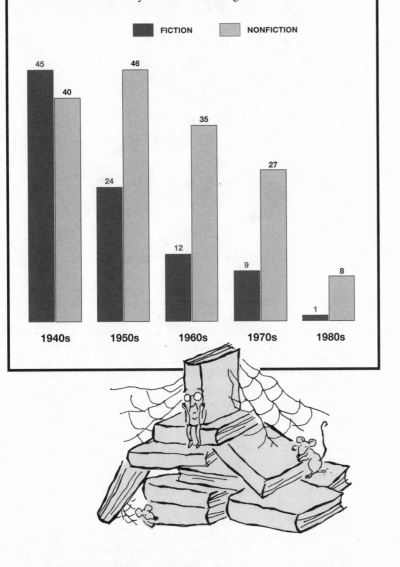

	1940s	1950s	1960s	1970s	1980s
Fiction	45	24	12	9	1
Nonfiction	40	46	35	27	8

FIRST DATE AT #1: September 6, 1942
TOTAL WEEKS AT #1: 1

Drivin' Woman
Elizabeth Chevalier
MACMILLAN

Chevalier's romantic novel of America Moncure, Kentucky plantation woman, and her struggles in the years following the Civil War, was only #1 for a week, but spent nearly three months in the #2 slot, usually behind the equally feisty Bernadette. Twenty years later, the author, who spent many years with the American Red Cross, would be considered by John Kennedy for secretary of the treasury.

FIRST DATE AT #1: November 22, 1942
TOTAL WEEKS AT #1: 46

The Robe
Lloyd Douglas
HOUGHTON MIFFLIN

The Reverend Douglas's story tells of a young Roman soldier, Marcellus, who was in charge of the crucifixion of Christ and won his robe gambling with other soldiers. *The Robe* spent nearly a year at #1 (with only a one-week hiatus due to Mrs. Parkington), the better part of a second year in the top five, and a third year elsewhere on the list. *The Robe* returned to the list at several times in the ensuing years, especially after the Hollywood epic movie. Douglas's book still holds the fiction record for longest time on the list, although several nonfiction books (*The Power of Positive Thinking, Peace of Mind,* and *A Light in the Attic*) have topped it. The author, a Lutheran clergyman, died in Las Vegas in 1951.

POSITION ON LIST

1　5　9　13　17　21　25　29　33　37　41　45　49　53　57　61　65　69　73　77　81　85　89　93　97　101　105　109　113　117　121　125　129　133　137　141　145　149　153　157
WEEKS ON BESTSELLER LIST

FIRST DATE AT #1: January 17, 1943
TOTAL WEEKS AT #1: 5

Our Hearts Were Young and Gay

Cornelia Otis Skinner and Emily Kimbrough

DODD, MEAD

A famous actress and a well-known essayist wrote wistfully of touring Europe in the years before World War One. Of her coauthor, Skinner wrote, "To know Emily is to enhance one's days with gaiety, charm, and occasional terror." This is one of only two #1 books that were written jointly by two independently successful writers. (The other is *The Talisman* by Stephen King and Peter Straub.) *Hearts* was the last #1 book Dodd, Mead would have for nearly forty years, until Agatha Christie's last two novels came out of the vault.

FIRST DATE AT #1: March 7, 1943
TOTAL WEEKS AT #1: 7

Guadalcanal Diary

Richard Tregaskis

RANDOM HOUSE

Bennett Cerf's Random House became the first publisher to have two #1 bestsellers with this book, a war correspondent's first-hand account of the first Allied World War Two offensive in the South Pacific. Tregaskis, who later wrote *JFK and PT-109*, was one of two newsmen to go ashore on Guadalcanal.

OUR HEARTS WERE YOUNG AND GAY

MOTHER decided one day that it would be part of our cultural education to go Old English and take the coach trip to Hampton Court. She had looked it all up in Muirhead's Guide Book and it sounded to be a thrill at once picturesque and distinguished. One rode on the swaying top of a tally-ho behind four spanking greys, or maybe they were bays, while Lord Somebody drove. This opportunity for displaying four-in-hand skill was, we learned, a pastime of the peerage and a few horsey American millionaires who, in the interests of tradition, kept up the old mail-coach service between London and Hampton Court. Two or three times a week the members of this sporting hierarchy took turns driving the romantic vehicle just for the hell of it, and the bourgeoisie, consisting chiefly of American tourists, could purchase places on it and go along for the ride. It was well known in advance who would drive, and if you were the sort who went in for such simple pleasures as getting into close, if not speaking proximity to nobility, you could ascertain in advance that if you made the trip of a Tuesday Lord Diddle-de-boom would drive you, while if you went on Friday your safe-conduct would be in the competent hands of the Earl of Whatsis. The Americans, I believe, weren't scheduled; they just served as subs, paid for the privilege and scrambled in whenever some nobleman's gout canceled his appearance.

I've forgotten what peer it was who drove the day we

104

Mrs. Parkington

❀❀❀❀❀❀❀❀❀❀❀❀❀❀❀❀❀❀❀❀

Oᴜᴛꜱɪᴅᴇ ᴛʜᴇ ꜱɴᴏᴡ ᴡᴀꜱ ꜰᴀʟʟɪɴɢ, ᴛʜɪᴄᴋʟʏ ɪɴ ɢʀᴇᴀᴛ ᴡᴇᴛ ꜰʟᴀᴋᴇꜱ, ꜱᴏ that the sound of the traffic on Park Avenue coming through the drawn curtains was muted and distant. Mrs. Parkington, seated before her mirror with a half-pint of champagne by her side, thought how nice it was to have a Christmas this year which seemed like Christmas. True, tomorrow the snow would be turned to slush, discolored by soot, and those great machines bought by the personable and bumptious mayor would be scooping it up and hauling it off to the North River; but snow—the mere idea of snow—was pleasant. Just the sight of it drifting down in soft white flakes through the bright auras of the street lights made you feel happy and content. And it summoned memories, very long memories, of the days when snow was not a nuisance in New York but brought out sleds and sleighs and there was racing in the park, and the sound of sleigh bells was heard everywhere in the city. Gus had loved the cutter racing; it suited his flamboyant nature. When one was eighty-four and in good health and spirits and had a half-pint of Lanson every evening just before dinner, one had a long memory. Long memories were perhaps common among widowed old ladies but memories so crammed with romance and excitement as that of Mrs. Parkington were rare.

She was doing her own hair, setting the waves exactly as they should be. She had always done her own hair ~~~~ four she had no i~~~~

FIRST DATE AT #1: March 14, 1943
TOTAL WEEKS AT #1: 1

Mrs. Parkington
Louis Bromfield
Hᴀʀᴘᴇʀ

Improbably, Bromfield's saga of the life of a New York *grande dame* from her teenage years to her 80s, dislodged *The Robe* from its lengthy reign at #1, if only for a week. It was the first of Harper's long line of #1 bestsellers. The author, whose lifetime ambition was to be a farmer, later established an experimental agricultural community, Malabar, in rural Ohio.

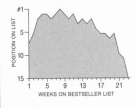

FIRST DATE AT #1: October 17, 1943
TOTAL WEEKS AT #1: 11

So Little Time
John P. Marquand
Lɪᴛᴛʟᴇ, Bʀᴏᴡɴ

World War Two looked potentially winnable for the first time, and American readers looked for some insight into how the nation had drifted towards war. Popular novelist Marquand's encompassing tale, with a hero who is outwardly successful but feels he has missed the way in life, caught the public's eye. It rose slowly to #1 during the winter, knocked *The Robe* from the top spot after nearly a year, and stayed #1 all spring. Although some critics likened Marquand to America's first Nobel laureate, he wrote, "I would hesitate to rank myself with [Sinclair] Lewis. I don't think I have nearly the same stature. But we are working in the same vineyard." He died in 1960, having written dozens of novels including the Mr. Moto series.

FIRST DATE AT #1: April 25, 1943
TOTAL WEEKS AT #1: 2

On Being a Real Person
Harry Emerson Fosdick
HARPER

The first "pop psychology" book to reach #1, this is a collection of Dr. Fosdick's essays, based on 20 years of experience in dealing with the personal problems of men and women who came to him for help. It rose quickly to #1 for a short visit, then stayed in the top five for an additional three months.

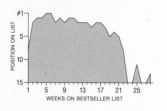

FIRST DATE AT #1: May 9, 1943
TOTAL WEEKS AT #1: 17

One World
Wendell Willkie
SIMON & SCHUSTER

In the midst of World War Two, this prominent Republican took a trip around the world, then wrote about his vision of the global unity that might emerge from the war. The book rose to #1 faster than any other to date, and remained there for four straight months. This was the first #1 book by a prominent politician, and it helped gain Willkie his party's presidential nomination the following year.

Authors Who Reached #1 Before They Were 35

AUTHOR	AGE	TITLE
Françoise Sagan	19.9	*Bonjour Tristesse*
Amy Wallace	22.0	*The Book of Lists*
Marion Hargrove	23.0	*See Here, Private Hargrove*
Bill Mauldin	23.8	*Up Front*
Norman Mailer	25.4	*The Naked and the Dead*
Richard Tregaskis	26.3	*Guadalcanal Diary*
Ralph Martin	26.4	*Jennie*
Joe McGinnis	27.0	*The Selling of the President 1968*
Kathleen Winsor	28.1	*Forever Amber*
James Jones	29.3	*From Here to Eternity*
David Wallechinsky	29.5	*The Book of Lists*
Michael Jackson	29.7	*Moonwalk*
Carl Bernstein	30.4	*All the President's Men*
Ken Follett	30.5	*Triple*
J	30.7	*The Sensuous Woman*
Ken Follett	31.4	*The Key to Rebecca*
Stephen King	32.1	*The Dead Zone*
Grace Metalious	32.2	*Peyton Place*
Gwethalyn Graham	32.3	*Earth and High Heaven*
John le Carré	32.4	*The Spy Who Came in from the Cold*
Germaine Greer	32.5	*The Female Eunuch*
Richard Simmons	32.7	*Never Say Diet*
Erich Segal	32.9	*Love Story*
Stephen King	33.0	*Firestarter*
Bob Woodward	33.1	*The Final Days*
Frederick Forsyth	33.2	*The Day of the Jackal*
André Schwarz-Bart	33.3	*The Last of the Just*
Stephen King	33.9	*Cujo*
Ross Lockridge	34.0	*Raintree County*
Maurice Herzog	34.1	*Annapurna*
Patrick Dennis	34.3	*Auntie Mame*
Douglas Casey	34.4	*Crisis Investing*
John Roy Carlson	34.4	*Under Cover*
Jean Kerr	34.6	*Please Don't Eat the Daisies*
Frederick Forsyth	34.6	*The Odessa File*
Leon Uris	34.8	*Exodus*
Stephen King	34.9	*Different Seasons*

Books with Half a Year or More at #1

WEEKS AT #1	TITLE	AUTHOR	FICTION OR NON
98	*The Power of Positive Thinking*	Norman Vincent Peale	NF
58	*Peace of Mind*	Joshua L. Liebman	NF
48	*Hawaii*	James Michener	F
48	*The Caine Mutiny*	Herman Wouk	F
46	*Gift from the Sea*	Anne Morrow Lindbergh	NF
46	*The Robe*	Lloyd C. Douglas	F
43	*The Egg and I*	Betty MacDonald	NF
42	*The Money Game*	Adam Smith	NF
41	*Love Story*	Erich Segal	F
39	*Iacocca: An Autobiography*	Lee Iacocca	NF
39	*The Rise and Fall of the Third Reich*	William Shirer	NF
39	*The Sea Around Us*	Rachel Carson	NF
38	*Jonathan Livingston Seagull*	Richard Bach	F
36	*The Source*	James Michener	F
36	*Trinity*	Leon Uris	F
35	*Brave Men*	Ernie Pyle	NF
34	*All I Really Need to Know I Learned in Kindergarten*	Robert Fulghum	NF
34	*The Spy Who Came in from the Cold*	John le Carré	F
33	*Kon-Tiki*	Thor Heyerdahl	NF
32	*Désirée*	Annemarie Selinko	F
32	*Jane Fonda's Workout Book*	Jane Fonda	NF
32	*The Complete Scarsdale Medical Diet*	Herman Tarnower	NF
31	*Markings*	Dag Hammarskjold	NF
30	*Advise and Consent*	Allen Drury	F
30	*Airport*	Arthur Hailey	F
30	*In Search of Excellence*	Thomas J. Peters	NF
29	*Anatomy of a Murder*	Robert Traver	F
29	*Centennial*	James Michener	F
29	*Herzog*	Saul Bellow	F
29	*Peyton Place*	Grace Metalious	F
28	*Doctor Atkins' Diet Revolution*	Robert C. Atkins	NF
28	*Under Cover*	John Roy Carlson	NF
28	*Valley of the Dolls*	Jacqueline Susann	F
27	*Only in America*	Harry Golden	NF
27	*The Agony and the Ecstacy*	Irving Stone	F
26	*Doctor Zhivago*	Boris Pasternak	F
26	*Fatherhood*	Bill Cosby	NF
26	*If Life Is a Bowl of Cherries, What Am I Doing in the Pits?*	Erma Bombeck	NF
26	*Inside U.S.A.*	John Gunther	NF
26	*Ship of Fools*	Katherine Anne Porter	F
26	*Travels with Charley*	John Steinbeck	NF

FIRST DATE AT #1: August 29, 1943

TOTAL WEEKS AT #1: 1

U.S. Foreign Policy

Walter Lippmann

LITTLE, BROWN

Lippmann was sandwiched between the left-wing Republican and the right-wing Republican in a nearly continuous year of #1 books on what the U.S. should be doing after the war. Lippmann got his start as the prominent muckraker, Lincoln Steffen's secretary. Later, he was a founder of the *New Republic* magazine and a famous television analyst. His book rose very briefly to #1 from a long-term #3 status. Lippmann died in 1966, having published more than 40 books.

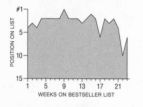

FIRST DATE AT #1: September 12, 1943

TOTAL WEEKS AT #1: 28

Under Cover

John Roy Carlson

DUTTON

The first major nonfiction bestseller of the *Times* list era, Carlson's report on alleged Communist subversive activity in America was #1 for more than half a year, and in the top five for three more months. Its success set the stage for the rise to power of one of Carlson's biggest fans, Senator Joseph McCarthy of Wisconsin.

CHAPTER IX

HITLER AND HIROHITO IN HARLEM

"If the United States is to include subject and ruler peoples, then let us be honest about it and change the Constitution and make it plain that Negroes cannot share the privileges of the white people. . . . If it [Democracy] is right, then let us dare to make it true."

PEARL BUCK

FANTASTIC AS IT SEEMS, Hitler's agents invaded Harlem—New York's Negro section. Despite its garishly lighted avenues and multitudinous taverns which are the scenes of noisy revelry until dawn, more than 350,000 Negroes live in tenements foul beyond description, and I regard Harlem as one of the most tragic "cities" in the United States; a blot on our Democracy.

Harlem Negroes had little to look forward to. Jobs for the men were few. Discrimination was rife. Streets teemed with young girls willing to sell themselves to passers-by.

New York newspapers periodically sensationalized a Harlem "crime wave." Mugging and robbery were committed in daylight—let alone at night. Negro youths started on their crime careers while still in their teens, giving Harlemites—the majority of whom were law-abiding—a black eye.

For want of anything better, vigorous young Negroes lounged around taverns, pool-rooms and hallways. Their days began at midnight. Discontented, frustrated, resentful, idle men were ideal material for fascism—and fascist agents knew it. And the Negro, oppressed, clannish, emotional, himself a victim of rac... ...ized by exhortations to violence.

It was on... ...Hitler" shoute... ...peakers with th... ...14th Street to ... ...natic speakers, s... ...per-

A girl named Betty Smith
has written a novel about Brooklyn
and it's enchanting all America

CHARMING, salty, warm and alive, the story of the Nolan family of Brooklyn, whose lives were as humanly gaudy as their background was inhumanly drab, has taken the country by storm. What makes it so extraordinary is the incredible richness of universal experience permeating every page.
$2.75

A TREE
GROWS IN BROOKLYN

STRANGE FRUIT
A NOVEL BY
LILLIAN SMITH

FIRST DATE AT #1: January 2, 1944
TOTAL WEEKS AT #1: 22

A Tree Grows in Brooklyn
Betty Smith
HARPER

Betty Smith's account of life in the slums of Brooklyn during the first years of the twentieth century, took half a year to rise to the #1 position, where it remained for four months. After being displaced by the only other #1 author with the name of Smith (Lillian), Betty remained on the list for several months, the first book by a woman to spend more than a year on the list.

FIRST DATE AT #1: May 14, 1944
TOTAL WEEKS AT #1: 15

Strange Fruit
Lillian Smith
REYNAL

Smith was one of the most outspoken and courageous white southern liberals of her generation to have a #1 bestseller. Her novel told the story of an educated black girl's love for a white man, and the murder and lynchings which were the strange fruit of that love. The book was the first #1 bestseller to be banned in Boston (as well as Detroit and, briefly, from the U.S. mails). It rose to the #1 spot and then was displaced seven times (mostly by Somerset Maugham) and finally sent packing for good by *Green Dolphin Street*. Reynal is one of the very few publishing imprints not to survive into the '90s. The author died in 1966.

FIRST DATE AT #1: March 26, 1944
TOTAL WEEKS AT #1: 12

Good Night, Sweet Prince
Gene Fowler

VIKING

The popular screenwriter's 10th book was about his friend, actor John Barrymore. It progressed steadily, week by week, from #5 to #4 to #3 to #2, but stayed there for a month before reaching #1, where it remained for the rest of the spring. Reviews were mixed. A few critics liked it, but *Theater Arts* called it "too sordid, repetitive, too full of trivia to be even mildly exciting."

FIRST DATE AT #1: June 18, 1944
TOTAL WEEKS AT #1: 7

Yankee from Olympus
Catherine Drinker Bowen

LITTLE, BROWN

The prominent author of more than 20 books had her only #1 appearance with this biography of Supreme Court Justice Oliver Wendell Holmes and his family. Of her career, Bowen wrote, "Love of cooking is thought by many to be a secondary female sex characteristic. So is the exercise of following little children interminably about the yard. If I had not been a writer, these moralistic conceptions would have defeated me before I reached the age of 30. Writing saved me. The housework still had to be done . . . , the children still had to be followed . . . , but these activities were no longer defeating because they were no longer the be-all and end-all of existence."

DOUBLEDAY,
DORAN
& COMPANY

announce
for publication
April 20, 1944

THE

Razor's Edge

by W.
SOMERSET
MAUGHAM

in the sincere belief that
it is a novel which will
rank with OF HUMAN
BONDAGE *and* THE
MOON AND SIXPENCE
as one of his greatest works.

DOUBLEDAY, DORAN

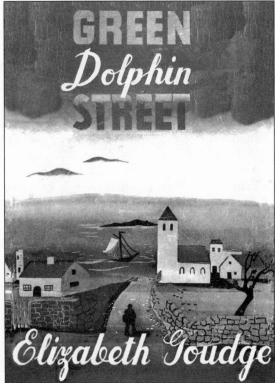

FIRST DATE AT #1: July 2, 1944
TOTAL WEEKS AT #1: 4

Razor's Edge
Somerset Maugham
DOUBLEDAY

Although it stayed on the list for nearly a year, Maugham's story of a young American flyer who returns home after World War One, then goes to Paris and India in search of personal peace, was only #1 for five weeks, never more than two in a row, and was displaced four times by *Strange Fruit.* Maugham, a medical doctor, was one of the best-known authors of his day, but this 38th book of his was his only visit to #1. Of his writing career Maugham wrote, "In my 20s, the critics said I was brutal. In my 30s, they said I was flippant. In my 40s, they said I was cynical. In my 50s, they said I was competent. In my 60s, they say I am superficial."

FIRST DATE AT #1: October 15, 1944
TOTAL WEEKS AT #1: 5

Green Dolphin Street
Elizabeth Goudge
COWARD-MCCANN

The first of many #1s with a color in the title, this long romantic novel was set in the Channel Islands and New Zealand. It tells the story of two sisters and the man they both fall in love with. Goudge spent four years writing the story that she called "hardly credible, and yet it was true." Of the book's war-time publication in England (where it was known as *Green Dolphin Country*) and the U.S., she wrote, "It says much for the courage of publishers that two brave men, one in England, one in America, were willing to take the risk of launching the Dolphin upon the seas of a turbulent and very nearly paperless world."

FIRST DATE AT #1: July 30, 1944
TOTAL WEEKS AT #1: 13

I Never Left Home
Bob Hope
SIMON & SCHUSTER

The end of the war was in sight and humor books began to appear regularly on the *Times* list. Around this time, books by Joe E. Brown, James Thurber, and Bennett Cerf, as well as philosopher George Santayana, all reached the top five, but only Bob Hope's first of eight books, an account of entertaining the troops at the front, made it to #1. Indeed, it was generally believed to be the best-selling book of 1944, and surely followed the most regular pattern, with its seven evenly spaced rises to #1.

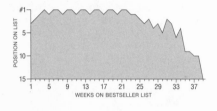

FIRST DATE AT #1: August 28, 1944
TOTAL WEEKS AT #1: 6

The Time for Decision
Sumner Welles
HARPER

Yet another "Now here's what we should do after World War Two" book, this one from the former under secretary of state. It seems as if the reading public kept switching from the serious to the humorous that summer. Welles was knocked out of #1 five consecutive times by Bob Hope, then decked for good by Ernie Pyle.

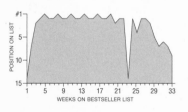

"I conducted a study (employing my usual controls) that shows the average shelf-life of a trade book to be somewhere between milk and yogurt. It is true that some books by Harold Robbins or any member of the Irving Wallace family last longer on the shelves, but they contain preservatives."
—Calvin Trillin

Number of #1 Titles for Each Publisher

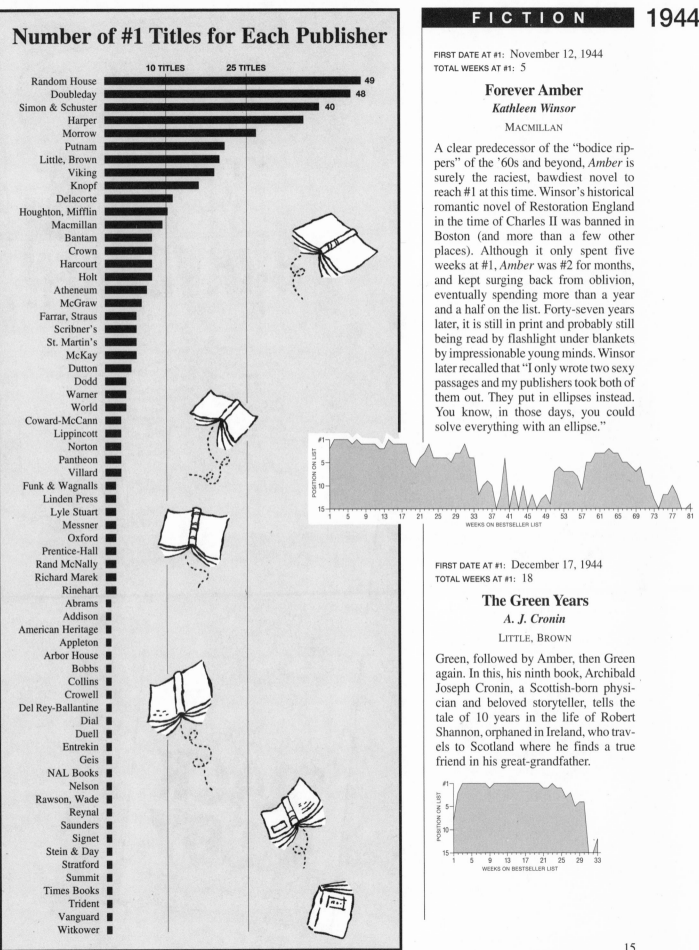

Publisher	Titles
Random House	49
Doubleday	48
Simon & Schuster	40
Harper	
Morrow	
Putnam	
Little, Brown	
Viking	
Knopf	
Delacorte	
Houghton, Mifflin	
Macmillan	
Bantam	
Crown	
Harcourt	
Holt	
Atheneum	
McGraw	
Farrar, Straus	
Scribner's	
St. Martin's	
McKay	
Dutton	
Dodd	
Warner	
World	
Coward-McCann	
Lippincott	
Norton	
Pantheon	
Villard	
Funk & Wagnalls	
Linden Press	
Lyle Stuart	
Messner	
Oxford	
Prentice-Hall	
Rand McNally	
Richard Marek	
Rinehart	
Abrams	
Addison	
American Heritage	
Appleton	
Arbor House	
Bobbs	
Collins	
Crowell	
Del Rey-Ballantine	
Dial	
Duell	
Entrekin	
Geis	
NAL Books	
Nelson	
Rawson, Wade	
Reynal	
Saunders	
Signet	
Stein & Day	
Stratford	
Summit	
Times Books	
Trident	
Vanguard	
Witkower	

(10 TITLES / 25 TITLES gridlines shown on chart)

FIRST DATE AT #1: November 12, 1944
TOTAL WEEKS AT #1: 5

Forever Amber
Kathleen Winsor
MACMILLAN

A clear predecessor of the "bodice rippers" of the '60s and beyond, *Amber* is surely the raciest, bawdiest novel to reach #1 at this time. Winsor's historical romantic novel of Restoration England in the time of Charles II was banned in Boston (and more than a few other places). Although it only spent five weeks at #1, *Amber* was #2 for months, and kept surging back from oblivion, eventually spending more than a year and a half on the list. Forty-seven years later, it is still in print and probably still being read by flashlight under blankets by impressionable young minds. Winsor later recalled that "I only wrote two sexy passages and my publishers took both of them out. They put in ellipses instead. You know, in those days, you could solve everything with an ellipse."

FIRST DATE AT #1: December 17, 1944
TOTAL WEEKS AT #1: 18

The Green Years
A. J. Cronin
LITTLE, BROWN

Green, followed by Amber, then Green again. In this, his ninth book, Archibald Joseph Cronin, a Scottish-born physician and beloved storyteller, tells the tale of 10 years in the life of Robert Shannon, orphaned in Ireland, who travels to Scotland where he finds a true friend in his great-grandfather.

FIRST DATE AT #1: December 17, 1944
TOTAL WEEKS AT #1: 34

Brave Men

Ernie Pyle

HOLT

Pyle died in action while his book was in the #1 position. The Pulitzer Prize-winning newspaperman whose reports from the front kept his book at #1 for two thirds of 1945 was killed by Japanese machine gun fire. Two other books of his stories challenged unsuccessfully for #1 soon after.

FIRST DATE AT #1: April 29, 1945
TOTAL WEEKS AT #1: 1

Black Boy

Richard Wright

HARPER

As a child, Wright was able to use the segregated Memphis public library by forging notes from a nonexistent white patron: "Will you please let this nigger boy have some books...." Wright's account of his early years, growing up poor and black in the South, became the first book by a black man to reach #1. It was only there for a week, although it did spend nearly half a year in the top five, never able to dislodge Ernie Pyle. Wright lived for many years in Paris, and he died there in 1960.

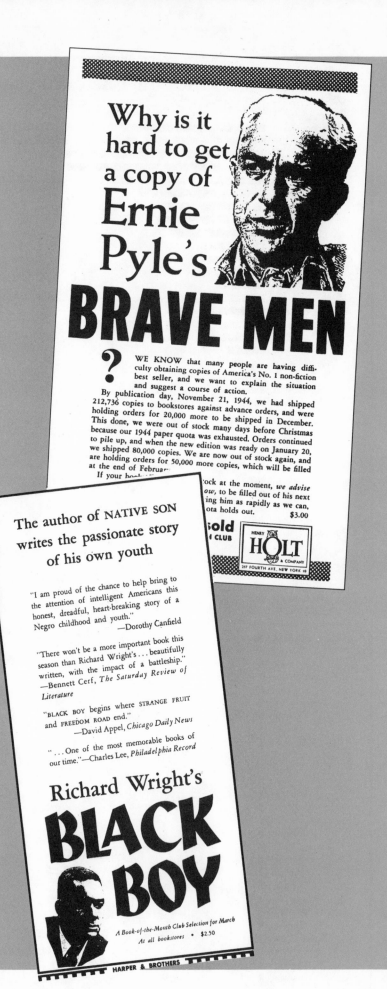

FICTION

FIRST DATE AT #1: April 22, 1945
TOTAL WEEKS AT #1: 2

Earth and High Heaven
Gwethalyn Graham

LIPPINCOTT

In one of the few Canadian books to reach #1 in the U.S., Graham tells the story of a young woman from a conservative Montreal family who falls in love with a Jewish soldier about to be sent overseas. Americans who feel that Canadians often move slowly and deliberately will note that this book had one of the slowest rises to #1 in history. It was in the top five for more than nine months before surging briefly to #1, then declining rapidly and falling off the list just before the one-year mark.

FIRST DATE AT #1: May 13, 1945
TOTAL WEEKS AT #1: 7

Captain from Castile
Samuel Shellabarger

LITTLE, BROWN

This historical novel of romance and action in sixteenth-century Spain and Mexico rose and declined quite symmetrically, but did remain in the top five for three months after its time at #1.

17

FIRST DATE AT #1: August 5, 1945
TOTAL WEEKS AT #1: 19

Up Front
Bill Mauldin

HOLT

As World War Two ended Americans were ready to laugh, and they laughed the Pulitzer Prize-winning cartoonist's war cartoons into first place for more than four months.

FIRST DATE AT #1: December 23, 1945
TOTAL WEEKS AT #1: 43

The Egg and I
Betty MacDonald

LIPPINCOTT

One of the most successful first books of all time, Anne Elizabeth MacDonald's reminiscences of life on a chicken farm in Washington and in mining towns of the West rose quickly to #1, where it remained for nearly a year. Even after being deposed by one of the all-time #1 bestsellers, it remained in the top five for another seven months and provided the inspiration for the Ma and Pa Kettle films. After a year in a tuberculosis sanitarium, the author (who was the only female labor adjuster for the National Recovery Administration) wrote a much less successful book, *The Plague and I.*

"*Just gimme a coupla aspirin. I already got a Purple Heart.*"

few combat COs tried to horn in on the dogfaces' entertainment.

Decorations are touchy things to talk about. The British kid us because we're overdecorated, and perhaps we are in some ways.

Civilians may think it's a little juvenile to worry about ribbons,

[133]

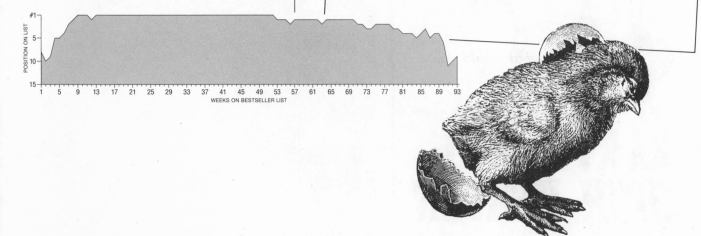

A
Novel
by
ADRIA
LOCKE
LANGLEY

A Lion is in the

I

FOR TWO days, ever since Hank's death, she had been in
a daze of numbness, held in a strange waiting on some
inner knowledge. Now she stood at her bedroom window in the executive mansion of the Magnolia State staring
across the tops of palms, live oaks and magnolias, at the high
tower of the magnificent Capitol which Hank had caused to be
built. The tower stood bright and gleaming, its windows and
marble reflecting the very sheen of midday, and the tall pole
with its flag at mourning mast let the sun run down its polished
roundness with bright little tongues of flame.

And then, Hank came alive to her as she heard again the
words with which he first admired the tower from this very
window:

"Lookit there, Sweetface—lookit there—ain't that purely a
thing a' beauty, though! There it is, Sweetface, the pinnacle
I been a-climbin' to, all marble 'n shinin'!" After a moment of
silent admiration, he added, "But now I look on it, I see it ain't
big enough nor high enough for t' satisfy Hank Martin." H
beat his chest with his fist, grinned broadly; then sobering,
dropped his voice to the tone of intimate confidence. "No,
Verity, I see now I gotta climb to that round glitterin' c
in Washington. I purely have."

But now Hank Martin, th-
of that pinnacle in the n
a silver casket guarante
maggots of the earth. (
which had been boug'

FIRST DATE AT #1: July 1, 1945
TOTAL WEEKS AT #1: 12

A Lion Is in the Streets
Adria Locke Langley
MCGRAW

The story of an American politician's
rise to the governorship of Mississippi
and subsequent fall, as seen through the
eyes of his wife. The book was generally
believed to be based on the life of Huey
Long. Langley taught writing in her
later years, and died in 1983.

FIRST DATE AT #1: September 23, 1945
TOTAL WEEKS AT #1: 1

So Well Remembered
James Hilton
LITTLE, BROWN

Hilton's account of 20 years in the life of
George Boswell, mayor of the small
English town he grew up in, spans the
time between the two world wars. Hilton
almost certainly would have had #1s
with his earlier pre-*Times* list novels,
Lost Horizon and *Good Bye Mr. Chips*.

FIRST DATE AT #1: October 27, 1946
TOTAL WEEKS AT #1: 58

Peace of Mind

Joshua L. Liebman

SIMON & SCHUSTER

The second-biggest #1 *New York Times* bestseller rose quickly to #2 where it remained for 14 weeks until *The Egg* had run its course. It then spent half a year at #1, another half year in the top five, months more at #1 (a total of 58 weeks), and then another year in the top five. The book is Rabbi Liebman's attempt to distill insights about human nature as discovered by psychologists and combine them with religious insight to help people improve themselves. The author died in mysterious circumstances while his book was still high on the list. What with Pyle and Smith before and Gunther after, this is a time in which four consecutive books totalled 161 weeks at #1. No other time period has come close.

POSITION ON LIST

#1

5

10

15

1 5 9 13 17 21 25 29 33 37 41 45 49 53 57 61 65 69 73 77 81 85 89 93 101 105 109 113 117 121 125 129 133 137 141 145 149 153 157

WEEKS ON BESTSELLER LIST

FIRST DATE AT #1: June 29, 1947
TOTAL WEEKS AT #1: 26

Inside U.S.A.

John Gunther

HARPER

As Americans tried to recapture and understand their identity in the postwar era, Gunther's fourth "Inside" book served as the guidebook, with facts about the country, who runs it, and the people who live in it. For a good part of the time that this book was #1, the #2 book (which never made it to the top) was, remarkably, Professor Arnold Toynbee's *A Study of History.*

POSITION ON LIST

#1

5

10

15

1 5 9 13 17 21 25 29 33 37 41 45 49 53 57

WEEKS ON BESTSELLER LIST

BY AND ABOUT #**1** AUTHORS:

"I am convinced that all writers are optimists whether they concede the point or not. . . . How otherwise could any human being sit down to a pile of blank sheets and decide to write, say two hundred thousand words on a given theme?"

—**Thomas Costain**

"There are three rules for writing a novel. Unfortunately, no one knows what they are."

—**Somerset Maugham**

An exciting, romantic novel by
THOMAS B. COSTAIN
author of RIDE WITH ME

THOMAS B. COSTAIN
Author of RIDE WITH ME

The Black Rose

A ROMANTIC NOVEL

"A grand historical novel that swashbuckles with the best of them." —ORVILLE PRESCOTT, N. Y. *Times.*

"A rousing swashbuckling historical romance with no ingredients missing . . . Mr. Costain writes brilliantly of those bloody, confused years when kings and barons struggled against each other, displaying a familiarity with the times worthy of a professional historian . . . the last hundred pages are superb, matching the best in any historical romance. What they contain cannot be whispered beyond a hint that they are based upon one of the most touching and appealing of all English legends." —CAPTAIN PETER JAMES SEARLES, U. S. N. (Ret.), N. Y. *Herald Tribune.*

"A full-measure picaresque drama . . . brims over with fascinating sidelights." WILLIAM DuBOIS, N.Y. *Times*

FIRST PRINTING: **650,000 COPIES**
A Literary Guild Selection

At your bookseller's, 403 pages, $3.00 • **DOUBLEDAY, DORAN**

FIRST DATE AT #1: September 30, 1945
TOTAL WEEKS AT #1: 18

The Black Rose
Thomas Costain
DOUBLEDAY

Canadian-born Costain was a long-time editor of the *Saturday Evening Post.* His first book was published when he was 57. This, his third, is the account of the adventures of the illegitimate son of a British Earl in thirteenth-century England and the Orient. It held off a strong challenge from Antoine St. Exupery's *Little Prince,* which remained at #2 for over two months, but never made it to #1.

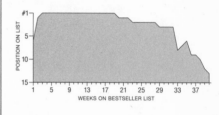

FIRST DATE AT #1: February 3, 1946
TOTAL WEEKS AT #1: 6

The King's General
Daphne du Maurier
DOUBLEDAY

Du Maurier's 11th book was her first to reach #1, although her 1938 bestseller, *Rebecca,* surely would have done so had there been a *Times* list. This historical novel of Cornwall during the Parliamentary wars is told by a crippled girl who is in love with the story's hero, Sir Richard Grenville.

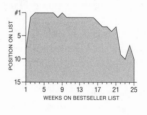

FIRST DATE AT #1: November 16, 1947
TOTAL WEEKS AT #1: 8

Speaking Frankly
James F. Byrnes
HARPER

Books by former presidential administration insiders telling what *really* happened typically have a fast rise to #1 and a relatively brief life there before descending to oblivion. Former Congressman, Senator, Supreme Court Justice, and Secretary of State Byrnes's memoirs of World War Two helped pave the way for the #1 works of H. R. Haldeman, Donald Regan, David Stockman, and others of their ilk.

FIRST DATE AT #1: May 23, 1948
TOTAL WEEKS AT #1: 1

Sexual Behavior in the Human Male
A. C. Kinsey, Wardell Pomeroy, and Clyde E. Martin
SAUNDERS

This scholarly account of the findings at a large Indiana sex research clinic was extremely popular; it appeared on the list for nearly a year, but it was up against the second biggest #1 of all time, *Peace of Mind*, for the first half of its run, and the perennially popular Dale Carnegie for the second, breaking through to #1 for just one week in the middle. It is the only #1 book with three main authors, and the only #1 to date for Saunders. (The sequel, on *The Human Female*, made the list briefly a few years later, but never came close to #1.) Prior to his human sexuality research, Kinsey wrote extensively on the zoology of the gall wasp.

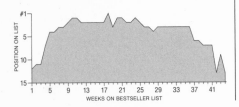

SEXUAL BEHAVIOR IN THE HUMAN MALE

ALFRED C. KINSEY
Professor of Zoology, Indiana University

WARDELL B. POMEROY
Research Associate, Indiana University

600   SEXUAL BEHAVIOR IN THE HUMAN MALE

Among married males, prostitutes provide about 11 per cent of the extra-marital outlet between ages 16 and 20, over 16 per cent of that outlet by age 30, and 22 per cent of the extra-marital outlet at age 55 (Tables 64, 65). This apparent increase, however, is not due to any increase in actual frequencies, but to the fact that the total outlet drops steadily through the years, while intercourse with prostitutes is maintained with more or less constant frequencies over a period of several decades.

The incidence and frequency figures vary tremendously for different segments of the population, and it is misleading to discuss the place of prostitution in the population as a whole. Contacts with prostitutes are most frequently had by males of the lowest social levels. By 25 years of

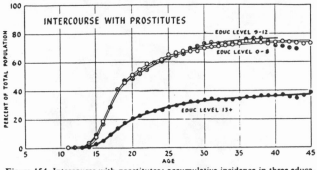

Figure 154. Intercourse with prostitutes: accumulative incidence in three educational levels

Showing percent of each population that has ever had intercourse with prostitutes by each of the indicated ages. All data based on total population, irrespective of marital status.

age, 74 per cent of the males who never went beyond grade school have had some intercourse with prostitutes (Table 87), while only 54 per cent of the males of the high school level, and only 28 per cent of the males of the college level, have had such experience. Among single males of the group that never goes beyond the eighth grade, as much as 6 per cent of the total sexual outlet is derived from prostitutes in the late teens, 14.3 per cent by the late twenties, and 23.4 per cent by the late thirties, if the male is not yet married by that time (Table 96). Among the boys who go to high school the figures start at 3 per cent in the late teens and climb to 10.3 per cent in the middle thirties. For males of the college level less than 1 per cent of the total sexual outlet is derived from prostitutes in the late teens, and only 3 per cent in the late twenties. This is one of the most striking differences between the patterns of college males and the patterns of all other groups.

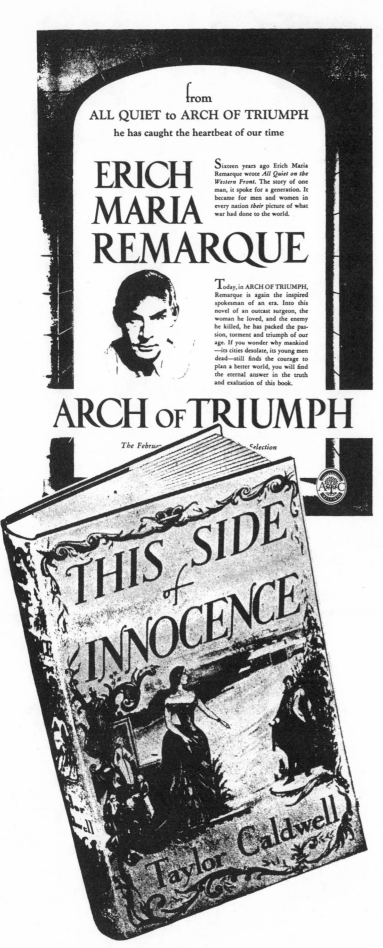

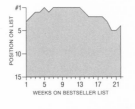

FIRST DATE AT #1: March 10, 1946
TOTAL WEEKS AT #1: 8

Arch of Triumph
Erich Maria Remarque
APPLETON-CENTURY

Near the end of his long and distinguished career, Remarque reached #1 for the only time with his story of a famous Berlin doctor who has escaped from the Nazis and is reduced to doing examinations of brothel inmates. The German-born author was exiled by the Nazis because his *All Quiet on the Western Front* was felt to be too powerful an anti-war statement. Authors typically have unusual employment to help support their writing habit, but few as curious as Remarque's earlier jobs as a tombstone salesman and organist in an insane asylum.

FIRST DATE AT #1: May 12, 1946
TOTAL WEEKS AT #1: 9

This Side of Innocence
Taylor Caldwell
SCRIBNER'S

Janet Miriam Taylor Caldwell's 10th book and first bestseller rose to #1 in its third week. After two months there, it dropped to #2 for over four months, but never again returned to #1. It is the history of a town in upstate New York, and the passions and hatreds of one family who lives there. Caldwell often commented that her books were reviewed unfairly because of her conservative political views. In a letter to *Newsweek,* she accused the *Times* of "monotonously vicious" reviews "when their reporters discovered how intensely I hated Communists." The book was Scribner's first #1 bestseller.

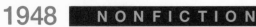

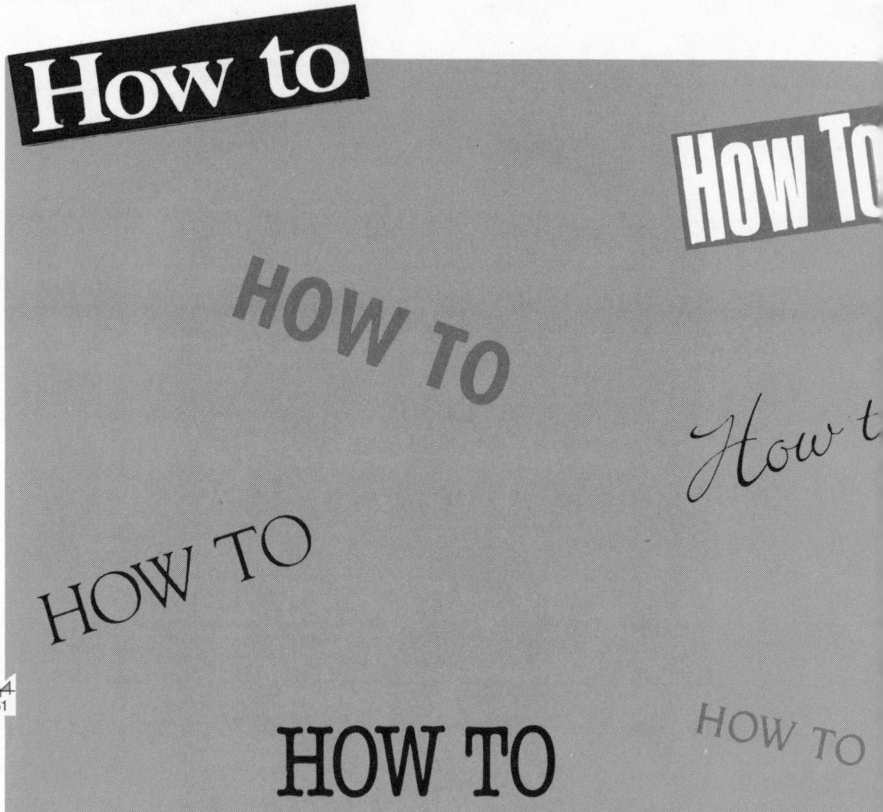

How to
How To
HOW TO
How to
HOW TO
HOW TO
HOW TO

FIRST DATE AT #1: August 2, 1948
TOTAL WEEKS AT #1: 14

How to Stop Worrying and Start Living

Dale Carnegie

SIMON & SCHUSTER

The sequel to Carnegie's huge pre-list success, *How to Win Friends and Influence People,* this inspirational self-help book spent more than three months at #1, and another six months in the top five.

#1
5
10
15
POSITION ON LIST
1 5 9 13 17 21 25 29 33 37 41 45 49 53 57 61
WEEKS ON BESTSELLER LIST

FIRST DATE AT #1: August 9, 1948
TOTAL WEEKS AT #1: 5

The Gathering Storm

Winston Churchill

HOUGHTON MIFFLIN

The British prime minister had an earlier bestseller with *Blood, Sweat and Tears.* All of his subsequent books in the World War Two series reached the list, but only this one rose to #1.

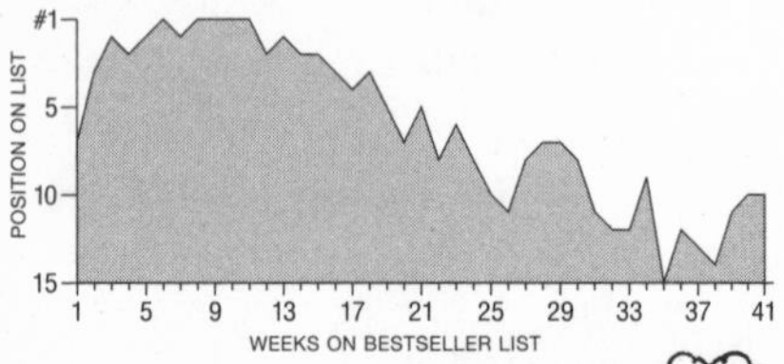

#1
5
10
15
POSITION ON LIST
1 5 9 13 17 21 25 29 33 37 41
WEEKS ON BESTSELLER LIST

THE ONLY THREE #1 "HOW TO" BOOKS

How to Stop Worrying and Start Living
How to Avoid Probate
How to Be Your Own Best Friend

How to
HOW TO
STOP WORRYING
AVOID PROBATE
BE YOUR OWN BEST FRIEND

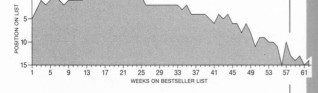

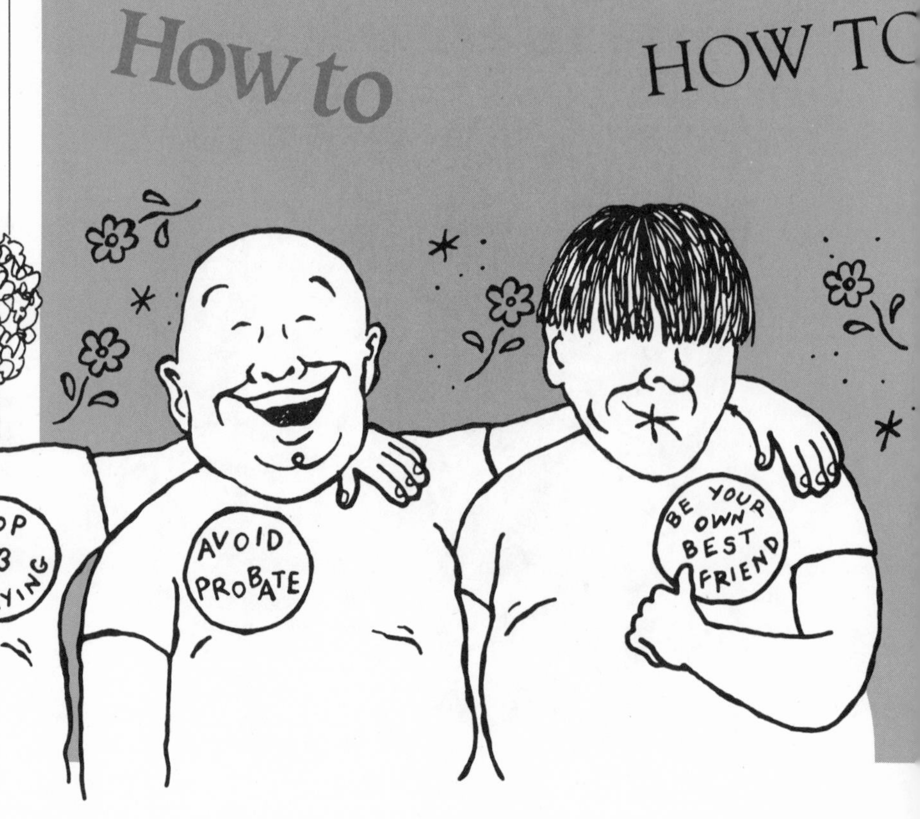

FIRST DATE AT #1: July 14, 1946
TOTAL WEEKS AT #1: 19

The Hucksters
Frederic Wakeman

RINEHART

The postwar public was fascinated by
the burgeoning world of advertising,
and for over four consecutive months
Wakeman's tale of greed and intrigue in
the agency business held on to #1, despite strong challenges from Orwell's
Animal Farm and Warren's *All the King's
Men,* neither of which ever reached the
top spot.

FIRST DATE AT #1: November 24, 1946
TOTAL WEEKS AT #1: 1

East River
Sholem Asch

PUTNAM

It is generally agreed that had the *New
York Times* list begun a few years earlier,
this would be Asch's third #1, as the first
two books of his controversial trilogy,
The Nazarene and *The Apostle,* were
both immensely popular. In *East River*
he chronicles life in a poor Jewish neighborhood in New York of the early 1900s,
focusing on a saintly shopkeeper and his
two sons. There is no apparent logical
explanation for the novel's one-week
disappearance from the list. Asch died in
England in 1957.

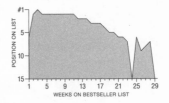

FIRST DATE AT #1: December 19, 1948
TOTAL WEEKS AT #1: 1

Roosevelt and Hopkins
Robert E. Sherwood
HARPER

This intimate history of FDR and his advisor Harry Hopkins, by an author who knew them both well, spent four months at #2 but only rose to #1 for one week. The manuscript was drawn from 40 cases of papers left by Hopkins. Sherwood is better known as a Pulitzer Prize-winning playwright, and author of the screenplay for *The Best Years of Our Lives*.

FIRST DATE AT #1: December 26, 1948
TOTAL WEEKS AT #1: 11

Crusade in Europe
Dwight D. Eisenhower
DOUBLEDAY

Ike's war memoirs rose to #1 in just four weeks, lasted about three months, then dropped off nearly as quickly as it had arrived. Only one book by a president or ex-president has ever been at #1 (Kennedy's *Profiles in Courage*), and this is the only #1 book by a future president.

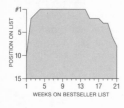

Harry L. Hopkins

ROOSEVELT AND HOPKINS
An Intimate History
BY
ROBERT E. SHERWOOD
Revised Edition

ILLUSTRATED

HARPER & BROTHERS
Publishers: New York

DWIGHT D. EISENHOWER

Crusade in Europe

A PERSONAL ACCOUNT OF WORLD WAR II

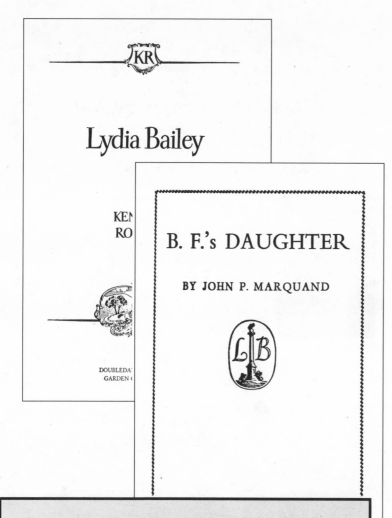

Authors with Two #1 Titles

AT LEAST 24 OF THE 46 ARE STILL WRITING.

(No one is sure about J. D. Salinger)

Jeffrey Archer

Jean M. Auel

Leo Buscaglia

Rachel Carson

Agatha Christie

Winston Churchill

Mary Higgins Clark

James Clavell

Bill Cosby

Lloyd Douglas

Allen Drury

Harry Golden

Elizabeth Goudge

David Halberstam

Ernest Hemingway

Thor Heyerdahl

Bob Hope

Lee Iacocca

John Irving

Kitty Kelley

Alexander King

Louis L'Amour

Jack Lait

William Manchester

Colleen McCullough

Joe McGinnis

John Naisbitt

Tom Peters

Mario Puzo

Andrew Rooney

J. D. Salinger

Erich Segal

Dr. Seuss

Samuel Shellabarger

Cornelia Otis Skinner

Martin Cruz Smith

John Steinbeck

Mary Stewart

William Styron

Gay Talese

Donald Trump

Scott Turow

Gore Vidal

Kurt Vonnegut

Irving Wallace

Thornton Wilder

FIRST DATE AT #1: December 1, 1946
TOTAL WEEKS AT #1: 9

B. F.'s Daughter
John P. Marquand

LITTLE, BROWN

Marquand's fourth bestseller (the first two published before the *Times* list) reached #1 in its second week; it follows the beautiful daughter of B. F., an industrialist, and her relationships with her father and the other men in her life.

FIRST DATE AT #1: February 2, 1947
TOTAL WEEKS AT #1: 12

Lydia Bailey
Kenneth Roberts

DOUBLEDAY

Roberts made #1 near the end of his career with this intricately plotted historical novel about a young Maine lawyer in Haiti who deals with Napoleon, Barbary pirates, the Jefferson administration, and the intrigues of the Tripolian war.

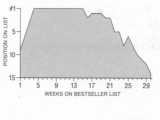

FIRST DATE AT #1: April 27, 1947
TOTAL WEEKS AT #1: 14

Gentlemen's Agreement
Laura Z. Hobson

SIMON & SCHUSTER

Hobson's novel is about a young journalist's discoveries and difficulties while posing as a Jew to gather materials for an article on anti-Semitism.

FIRST DATE AT #1: March 13, 1949
TOTAL WEEKS AT #1: 22

Cheaper by the Dozen

Frank B. Gilbreth, Jr. and Ernestine Gilbreth Carey

CROWELL

The Gilbreths' cheerful and humorous account of growing up in a 12-child family was the big nonfiction book of 1949. During its four months at #1, books by Carl Sandburg and Tennessee Williams, not to mention Arthur Miller's *Death of a Salesman* and George Orwell's *1984* all challenged for the top position but never made it (no other writings by these four gentlemen ever reached #1). During *Cheaper*'s reign, the American monk Thomas Merton occupied the #2 and #3 spots for a fair amount of time, with *The Seven Storey Mountain* and *Waters of Siloe*. While nearly all of Merton's books rose high on the *Times* list, he never made #1 either.

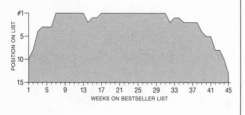

FIRST DATE AT #1: May 1, 1949
TOTAL WEEKS AT #1: 3

The Greatest Story Ever Told

Fulton Oursler

DOUBLEDAY

Following *The Big Fisherman*'s success, a number of stories based on the life of Jesus found a place on the bestseller list. This version by Oursler, a senior editor of *Reader's Digest*, rose quickly to #1 then declined slowly, after a brief time at the top. Oursler also wrote a very popular series of detective novels under the pseudonym Anthony Abbot.

---

22   *Cheaper by the Dozen*

Dad would ponder for a minute. Then, rearing back so those on the outskirts could hear, he'd say as if he had just thought it up:

"Well, they come cheaper by the dozen, you know."

This was designed to bring down the house, and usually it did. Dad had a good sense of theater, and he'd try to time this apparent ad lib so that it would coincide with the change in traffic. While the peasantry was chuckling, the Pierce Arrow would buck away in clouds of gray smoke, while the professor up front rendered a few bars of Honk Honk Kadookah.

Leave 'em in stitches, that was us.

Dad would use that same "cheaper by the dozen" line whenever we stopped at a toll gate, or went to a movie, or bought tickets for a train or boat.

"Do my Irishmen come cheaper by the dozen?" he'd ask the man at the toll bridge. Dad could take one look at a man and know his nationality.

"Irishmen is it? ... I might have known it. Lord love you, and it takes the Irish ... f red-headed Irishmen like that. The Lord Jesus ... 's that to pay toll on my road. Driv ...

"If he kne ...
around your ...

"He prob ...
And one ...

"Do my ...

"Dutch ...

"Have ...
who to ...
to see ...
ticket ...

FRANK B. GILBRETH, Jr. and
ERNESTINE GILBRETH CAREY

CHEAPER BY THE DOZEN

SINCLAIR LEWIS

KINGSBLOOD ROYAL

1

MR. BLINGHAM, and may he fry in his own cooking-oil, was assistant treasurer of the Flaver-Saver Company. He was driving from New York to Winnipeg, accompanied by Mrs. Blingham and their horrible daughter. As they were New Yorkers, only a business trip could have dragged them into this wilderness, and they found everything west of Pennsylvania contemptible. They laughed at Chicago for daring to have skyscrapers and at Madison for pretending to have a university, and they stopped the car and shrieked when they entered Minnesota and saw a billboard advertising "Ten Thousand Lakes."

Miss Blingham, whom they called "Sister," commented, "Unless you had a New York sense of humor, you would never be able to understand why that sign is so funny!"

When they came to their first prairie hamlet in Minnesota, six cottages, a garage, a store and a tall red grain elevator, Mrs. Blingham giggled, "Why, they've got an Empire State Building here!"

"And all the Svensons and Bensons and Hensons go up to the Rainbow Room every evening!" gurgled Sister.

Their laughter buoyed them f
to think of lunch. Miss Blingha
public, Minnesota. That seems
and it's quite a village—85,000 p

"Let's try it. They ought to l
yawned Mr. Blingham.

"All the best people there e
yelped Mrs. Blingham.

"Oh, you slay me!" said Siste
When, from the bluffs of the
the limestone shaft of the Bl

THE MONEYMAN

THOMAS B. COSTAIN

GARDEN CITY, N. Y.
DOUBLEDAY & COMPANY, INC.

FIRST DATE AT #1: July 6, 1947
TOTAL WEEKS AT #1: 2

Kingsblood Royal
Sinclair Lewis
RANDOM HOUSE

Thirty-five years after his first novel and 26 years after his first big bestseller, *Main Street,* America's first Nobel laureate in literature made #1 briefly for the only time in his life with his story of the dilemma faced by a white man who discovers he has some "Negro blood." The theme of the novel is racial intolerance in America.

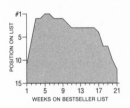

FIRST DATE AT #1: August 17, 1947
TOTAL WEEKS AT #1: 12

The Moneyman
Thomas Costain
DOUBLEDAY

Costain becomes the second author to return to #1 with this historical romance set in fifteenth-century France. The story of Jacques Coeur, a wealthy merchant and moneyman to King Charles VII, the book reached #1 in its third week on the list. Costain's daughter wrote of him that "He loves animals and won't even kill bugs, but his live and let live policy does not, alas, extend to his bridge partners."

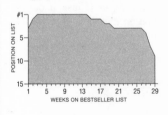

FIRST DATE AT #1: September 4, 1949
TOTAL WEEKS AT #1: 19

White Collar Zoo
Clare Barnes
DOUBLEDAY

The first #1 book that might, in some circles, be called a "non-book," *White Collar Zoo* is a collection of photographs of animals that look like humans. It rose quickly to #1 and stayed there nearly four months (all through the Christmas season), then spent another three months in the top five before dropping quickly. A sequel, *Home Sweet Zoo,* rose as high as #3, and *Campus Zoo* also did well, but neither was a #1.

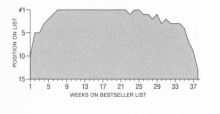

POSITION ON LIST
#1
5
10
15
1 5 9 13 17 21 25 29 33 37
WEEKS ON BESTSELLER LIST

FIRST DATE AT #1: January 15, 1950
TOTAL WEEKS AT #1: 7

This I Remember
Eleanor Roosevelt
HARPER

Books by first ladies have generally done better than those by their husbands, although only this one and Nancy Reagan's reached #1 (plus Barbara Bush's picture book, ostensibly by her dog, Millie). Mrs. Roosevelt was the most popular person in America, according to a 1949 magazine survey, and her reminiscences, written five years after she left the White House, had quite a fast rise and an even speedier decline following two months at #1.

POSITION ON LIST
#1
5
10
15
1 5 9 13 17 21
WEEKS ON BESTSELLER LIST

Another Classic by Josephine Artayeta de Viel

There was some serious speculation that the three best-selling nonfiction books of 1949 may have been ones written by

Josephine Artayeta de Viel

Ottilie H. Reilly

and Oswald Jacoby.

Remarkably, they were all on the same subject—a subject the *New York Times* apparently decided was unworthy of inclusion on its bestseller list. Nonetheless, the subject matter was one that might well have been called the hottest topic of that wild and crazy year. Triple score if you can identify the subject matter of all three books. (Answer at the bottom of the next page.)

FIRST DATE AT #1: November 9, 1947
TOTAL WEEKS AT #1: 15

House Divided
Ben Ames Williams
HOUGHTON MIFFLIN

Williams was one of the best-known and loved American authors of his time. While his *Leave Her to Heaven* never quite reached #1, this later Civil War novel about Southern aristocrats who are related to Lincoln but hate and distrust him, entered the list at #4, rose quickly to #1, and remained there from early November until the following spring.

FIRST DATE AT #1: February 8, 1948
TOTAL WEEKS AT #1: 2

East Side, West Side
Marcia Davenport
SCRIBNER'S

The daughter of opera diva Alma Gluck and stepdaughter of violinist Efrem Zimbalist, Davenport began her writing career with a biography of Mozart. Her fourth book, *East Side, West Side,* is a novel of New York City life in the years following World War Two: the story of a woman of mixed heritage (Jewish and Irish) married to a philandering man from a prominent family.

Marcia Davenport

MARCIA DAVENPORT'S first success as a writer was her first book, a life of Mozart, published in 1932. Hailed immediately by critics, it stands today as one of the eloquent biographies in the world of music. *Of Lena Geyer,* her first novel, was published in 1936. Here again she wrote about musicians and music, portraying the career of a great diva. Here too her critical and popular acclaim was unanimous. *The Valley of Decision* appeared in 1942. A monumental novel spanning nearly seventy years of American life, it soared to the top of best-seller lists all over the country at the same time that critics were heralding it as a literary achievement.

Born and raised in New York, Marcia Davenport is pre-eminently qualified to capture the varying guises and moods of this city which is itself one of the foremost characters in her new novel, *East Side, West Side.*

CHARLES SCRIBNER'S SONS, NEW YORK

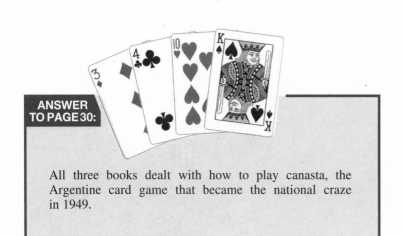

ANSWER TO PAGE 30:

All three books dealt with how to play canasta, the Argentine card game that became the national craze in 1949.

FIRST DATE AT #1: March 5, 1950
TOTAL WEEKS AT #1: 9

The Mature Mind
Harry Overstreet

NORTON

Remarkably similiar in content, scope, and bestseller pattern to Liebman's *Peace of Mind* (which was still on the list after two years), Overstreet's ninth book looked at the psychological foundations of maturity, evolved a definition of maturity, and then wrote about the forces that shape us (and what we can do about them). It was on the list for more than half a year both before and after its two months at #1. The author died in 1970.

POSITION ON LIST

#1
5
10
15
1 5 9 13 17 21 25 29 33 37 41 45 49 53 57 61 65 69 73
WEEKS ON BESTSELLER LIST

FIRST DATE AT #1: May 7, 1950
TOTAL WEEKS AT #1: 11

Worlds in Collision
Immanuel Velikovsky

DOUBLEDAY

In one of the most controversial books ever to make #1, Russian-born physicist Velikovsky suggested that a huge explosion on Jupiter in March, 1500 B.C. sent a comet smashing into Earth, briefly stopping its rotation and accounting for many of the Biblical "miracles." The book was almost universally denounced by the scientific community. Harvard astronomer Harlow Shapley called it "rubbish and nonsense." On the other hand, Clifton Fadiman compared Velikovsky to Darwin and Newton. The public was intrigued and made this the first of a very small number of so-called woo-woo books to make #1. (Strieber's *Communion*, decades later, is the most recent.) Velikovsky rose to #1 in four weeks, and stayed at either #1 or #2 for the entire summer and then some.

POSITION ON LIST

#1
5
10
15
1 5 9 13 17 21 25 29
WEEKS ON BESTSELLER LIST

Most Minimal Performance by a Publisher of #1s

While many publishers had only one book ever that was a #1 bestseller, in four cases, that one book only lasted one week:

Entrekin/Atlantic Monthly for *Parliament of Whores*
Abrams for *Gnomes*
Nelson for The Holy Bible, Revised Standard Version
Saunders for *Sexual Behavior in the Human Male*

Maximum Performance by a Publisher of #1s

Prentice-Hall specializes in textbooks and business books. They have had only two #1 bestsellers, but since one of them was the all-time champion, *The Power of Positive Thinking,* which was at #1 for 98 weeks, Prentice-Hall's average stay at #1 per book is 53 weeks. Next is Pantheon Books, which had only three #1s, but they were all big ones: *Gift from the Sea, Doctor Zhivago,* and *Born Free* with an average time of 28 weeks.

#1 Authors Whose First Names Do Not Appear in a Book of 3,500 Suggestions of What to Name the Baby

Adria (Langley)

Bel (Kaufman)

Germaine (Greer)

Gwethalyn (Graham)

Rosamunde (Pilcher)

Tallulah (Bankhead)

Chaim (Potok)

Dag (Hammarskjold)

Durk (Pearson)

Garrison (Keillor)

Gore (Vidal)

Haim (Ginott)

Ladislas (Farago)

MacKinlay (Kantor)

Mika (Waltari)

Quentin (Reynolds)

Ravi (Batra)

Salman (Rushdie)

Sholem (Asch)

Somerset (Maugham)

Thornton (Wilder)

Umberto (Eco)

VanWyck (Mason)

Whitley (Strieber)

Whittaker (Chambers)

Wil (Huygen)

BY AND ABOUT #1 AUTHORS:

"I do borrow from other writers, shamelessly! I can only say in my defense, like the woman brought before the judge on a charge of kleptomania, 'I do steal; but, You're Honor, only from the very best stores."

—Thornton Wilder

"Writing every book is like a purge; at the end of it one is empty . . . like a dry shell on the beach, waiting for the tide to come in again."

—Daphne du Maurier

FIRST DATE AT #1: March 7, 1948
TOTAL WEEKS AT #1: 5

Eagle in the Sky
Van Wyck Mason

LIPPINCOTT

The fourth and final volume in the author's tetralogy of American Revolution novels covers the years 1780 and 1781, and follows the adventures of three medical doctors. Mason wrote very fast, completing nearly 60 novels in 50 years before he drowned in Bermuda in 1978. After *Eagle in the Sky* was published, Mason announced that he would begin four Civil War novels and a biography. The *Times* marveled, "That is all, for the moment, that Mr. Mason plans, but this is only Sunday and there is a whole week ahead."

FIRST DATE AT #1: April 4, 1948
TOTAL WEEKS AT #1: 2

The Ides of March
Thornton Wilder

HARPER

Twenty years after his first major success, *The Bridge of San Luis Rey*, Wilder reached #1 with his fifth novel, a historical tale of Julius Caesar and other Romans during the month preceding Caesar's assassination. The narrative device is a series of fictitious objects: letters, documents, journal entries, and reports. Twenty-one years after *The Ides*, Wilder would once again have a #1 bestseller, *The Eighth Day*.

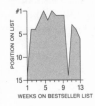

FIRST DATE AT #1: July 9, 1950
TOTAL WEEKS AT #1: 5

Roosevelt in Retrospect
John Gunther
HARPER

Perhaps if it had been called *Inside Roosevelt,* it would have had the success of Gunther's earlier "Inside" books. As it was, this portrait of FDR, with an analysis of events on both a personal and political level, had one of the shortest stays on the list, despite five weeks at #1.

FIRST DATE AT #1: August 27, 1950
TOTAL WEEKS AT #1: 4

Courtroom
Quentin Reynolds
FARRAR, STRAUS

The well-known lawyer and journalist reached #1 with his biography of Judge Samuel Leibowitz, told largely through cases he tried, including the Scottsboro case and the Lindbergh kidnaping.

FIRST DATE AT #1: September 3, 1950
TOTAL WEEKS AT #1: 1

The Little Princesses
Marion Crawford
HARCOURT

Princesses Elizabeth and Margaret were dear to many American hearts back then. This book by their Scottish governess was roundly condemned by most proper Britons as an invasion of royal privacy.

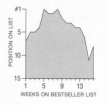

John Gunther

ROOSEVELT in RETROSPECT

Lady Who Became First Lady

193

No marriages proceed for forty years without occasional squabbles and fracases. Sometimes Mrs. Roosevelt would leave the Hyde Park table abruptly in the middle of a meal, because of some pressing engagement; the President and his mother would be hurt or angry. During one small dinner party she was curious about some talk going on at his end of the table and called out to be included in the tête-à-tête; he replied sharply, "The conversation remains at *this* end of the table!" But if anybody else rebuked her, he was furious. Robert E. Sherwood sat with him in the Oval Room one evening, listening to the radio; they heard a commentator bitterly attack Mrs. Roosevelt for her trip to the Pacific front. The President reached over and turned the radio off, an expression of acute pain and anguish on his face. It was as if he felt that perhaps she *was* open to criticism in some respects, and he could not bear to hear it.

During one of the worst periods of the war in 1942, when the Germans were at the gates of Cairo and the Japanese on the borders of India, Mrs. Roosevelt became obsessed by a case concerning a Negro named Waller, a tenant farmer who had been sentenced to death for the murder of his landlord. This was, it might have been thought, of absolute unimportance compared to Rommel's threat, the disastrous campaign in Burma, the U-boat menace, and a severe domestic crisis over man power. But not to Mrs. Roosevelt. She sought to intervene with the governor of the state where the murder occurred, and then asked the President to do so. Then FDR, though he had quite a lot else on his mind, wrote a "very strong letter" to the governor requesting him to commute Waller's sentence to life imprisonment.

The following memorandum from Harry Hopkins, which has not been published before, carries on the story:

The Governor had given six different reprieves and the President felt that he could not interfere again. He thought the Governor was acting entirely within his constitutional rights and, in addition to that, doubted very much if the merits of the case warranted the Governor's reaching any other decision.

Mrs. Roosevelt, however, would not take "No" for an answer and the President finally got on the phone himself and told Mrs. Roosevelt that under no circumstances would he intervene with the Governor and urged very strongly that she say nothing about it.

This incident is typical of things that have gone on in Washington between the President and Mrs. Roosevelt ever since 1932. She is forever

#1 Bestselling Authors Who Died Right Around the Time Their Book Was #1

Ernie Pyle was killed by Japanese machine gun fire at the time *Brave Men*, his first book of war dispatches, was in the #1 position.

Ross Lockridge committed suicide when his first and only novel, *Raintree County*, was at #3 on the list. It reached #1 a few weeks later.

Rabbi Joshua Liebman died at age 41 in unexplained circumstances while his book, *Peace of Mind*, was at #1, a position it held longer than any other book but one.

Agatha Christie wrote the final Miss Marple and Hercules Poirot mysteries in 1946, then stored them in a vault to be published posthumously. She changed her mind, and the Poirot book, *Curtain*, was published and reached #1 shortly before her death. The Marple book, *Sleeping Murder*, did appear posthumously and also reached #1.

Herman Tarnower offered profuse thanks to his companion, Jean Harris, for her help with *The Complete Scarsdale Medical Diet*. At a time when the book was still high on the *Times* list, Harris shot and killed Tarnower.

Gilda Radner died of ovarian cancer two months before her book about her life and her medical battle, *It's Always Something*, reached #1.

Dr. Seuss, Theodore Geisel, died in 1991 while his book *Oh, the Places You'll Go* was approaching the end of its second year on the *Times* list.

FIRST DATE AT #1: April 25, 1948
TOTAL WEEKS AT #1: 4

Raintree County
Ross Lockridge
HOUGHTON MIFFLIN

The book received rave reviews, and had reached #3 on the *Times* list the day that Lockridge committed suicide, March 6, 1948. It reached #1 a few weeks later. This epic novel describes one day in a man's life in a small Indiana town and, through a series of flashbacks, his life from his school days through the Civil War. Six weeks after Lockridge's suicide, the author of the current #1 nonfiction book, Rabbi Joshua Liebman, died suddenly at age 41 under mysterious circumstances.

FIRST DATE AT #1: May 23, 1948
TOTAL WEEKS AT #1: 3

Pilgrim's Inn
Elizabeth Goudge
COWARD-MCCANN

Goudge was the first woman to repeat as a #1 best-selling author, but had the misfortune to arrive just as *The Naked and the Dead* began its rapid surge to the top. Her novel continues the story of the Eliots, begun in an earlier, pre-list bestseller, *The Bird in the Tree*. Grandmother Lucilla continues to rule the family, several of whom buy an old pilgrim's inn, thus providing a title for the book. Called *The Herb of Grace* in England, this was Goudge's 15th novel.

FIRST DATE AT #1: October 8, 1950
TOTAL WEEKS AT #1: 34

Kon-Tiki

Thor Heyerdahl

RAND MCNALLY

All America seemed caught up in the Norwegian seaman's adventure, floating across the Pacific in a raft made of reeds and papyrus to prove that the ancient South Americans, with Stone Age technology, could have settled in Polynesia. The book reached #1, dropped down, then roared back to become one of the most successful nonfiction books ever.

FIRST DATE AT #1: October 15, 1950
TOTAL WEEKS AT #1: 1

Look Younger, Live Longer

Gayelord Hauser

FARRAR, STRAUS

German-born chiropractor and naturopath Helmut Eugene Gellert Hauser offered pointers on how to achieve the promise of the title through diet, exercise, and a good mental attitude. The book joined the list at the bottom and rose very slowly over the next six months. Sales in health food stores, not generally counted by the *Times*, might have kept Hauser at #1 longer had they been included.

SHANNON'S WAY
by A. J. Cronin

chapter 1

ON A DAMP evening in December, the fifth of that month, in the year 1919 — a date which marked the beginning of a great change in my life — six o'clock had struck from the University tower and the soft mist from the Eldon River was creeping round the Experimental Pathology buildings at the foot of Fenner Hill, invading our long work-room that smelled faintly of formalin, and was lit only by low, green-shaded lamps.

Professor Usher was still in his study — from behind the closed door on my right, with eardrums unnaturally attuned, I could hear his precise tones as he spoke, at length, upon the telephone. Surreptitiously, I glanced at the two other assistants who, with myself, made up the Professor's team.

Directly opposite, Spence stood at his bench, racking culture tubes, awaiting the arrival of his wife. She called for him regularly, every Friday night, and they went out together to dinner and the theatre. A slanting beam drew a cruel caricature of his broken profile upon the wall.

In the far corner of the laboratory Lomax had knocked off work and was idly tapping a cigarette upon his thumbnail — signal for a departure which he generally contrived to make easy and negligent. Presently, in a bored manner, surrounded by a languid cloud of smoke, he stood up, adjusting the wave in his hair at the mirror he kept over his sink.

FIRST DATE AT #1: June 20, 1948
TOTAL WEEKS AT #1: 19

The Naked and the Dead
Norman Mailer
RINEHART

The literary world was waiting for the first big book about World War Two, and they got it in Mailer's novel about an American platoon invading and occupying a Japanese-held island in 1944. Later Mailer would write that he had been "determined from the outset to hit the longest ball ever to go up into the accelerated hurricane air of our American letters." The book rose to #1 in four weeks, and stayed there all summer and into early fall, then remained in the top 10 for over six months. Mailer made the list again in 1991 with *Harlot's Ghost,* although not the #1 spot. The 43-year span between #1s would have been a record time between #1s.

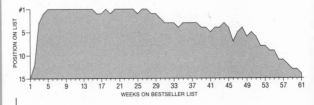

FIRST DATE AT #1: September 5, 1948
TOTAL WEEKS AT #1: 3

Shannon's Way
A. J. Cronin
LITTLE, BROWN

Cronin briefly dislodged Mailer from his long stay at #1, becoming the first author to make the top of the *New York Times* list three times. Cronin weaves together the story of a nation drifting toward war in late 1940 and the personal story of a man who, despite success according to any normal standards, feels he has missed the way in life. Cronin was very popular in Russia, where three million copies of his books were sold, but he got "not a nickel or ruble in royalties. I've tried even to get a pot of caviar from Khrushchev and he wouldn't even give me that."

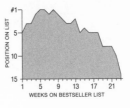

RACHEL L. CARSON

FIRST DATE AT #1: April 1, 1951
TOTAL WEEKS AT #1: 13

Washington Confidential
Jack Lait and Lee Mortimer
CROWN

As the McCarthy era crept in, people couldn't get enough inside news and gossip from the nation's capital, and Lait and Mortimer were there to provide an exposé that would propel them to #1 for a quarter of the year.

FIRST DATE AT #1: September 9, 1951
TOTAL WEEKS AT #1: 39

The Sea Around Us
Rachel Carson
OXFORD UNIVERSITY PRESS

The public loved Carson's poetic writing about scientific matters—the processes that formed the earth, moon, and stars, based on sound geologic evidence—and unexpectedly gave the venerable Oxford University Press its first and biggest bestseller. The book spent nine months at #1, and when finally displaced remained another six months in the top five. Four of Carson's eight books were written for and published by the U.S. Government Printing Office.

FIRST DATE AT #1: April 20, 1952
TOTAL WEEKS AT #1: 1

Mr. President
William Hillman
FARRAR, STRAUS

The first publication from the personal diaries, private letters, papers, and revealing interviews of Harry S. Truman.

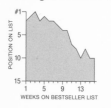

The Sea AROUND US

The Gray Beginnings

And the earth was without form, and void; and darkness was upon the face of the deep.
GENESIS

BEGINNINGS are apt to be shadowy, and so it is with the beginnings of that great mother of life, the sea. Many people have debated how and when the earth got its ocean, and it is not surprising that their explanations do not always agree. For the plain and inescapable truth is that no one was there to see, and in the absence of eyewitness accounts there is bound to be a certain amount of disagreement. So if I tell here the story of how the young planet Earth acquired an ocean, it must be a story pieced together from many sources and containing whole chapters the details of which we can only imagine. The story is founded on the testimony of the earth's most ancient rocks, which were young

3

Longest Average Time at #1 for All of an Author's #1 Books

Norman Vincent Peale holds the all-time record by a wide margin, since his only #1 book, *The Power of Positive Thinking,* was at #1 for 98 weeks. Joshua Liebman is a strong second with 58 weeks for his *Peace of Mind.* Among authors with more than one #1 book, Lloyd Douglas is first, with an average of 31 weeks per book. Here are the top ten in each category:

AUTHORS WITH "ONLY" ONE BOOK AT #1

Norman Vincent Peale	98
Joshua Liebman	58
Anne Morrow Lindbergh	46
Betty MacDonald	43
Adam Smith	42
William Shirer	39
Richard Bach	38
Ernie Pyle	35
Jane Fonda	32
Annemarie Selinko	32
Herman Tarnower/Samm S. Baker	32

AUTHORS WITH MORE THAN ONE BOOK AT #1

NAME	#1 BOOKS	AVERAGE WEEKS AT #1
Lloyd C. Douglas	2	31.0
Herman Wouk	4	25.0
Erich Segal	2	24.0
James Michener	9	23.0
Leon Uris	3	21.7
Rachel Carson	2	21.5
Lee Iacocca	2	20.5
Carl Bernstein	2	20.0
J. D. Salinger	2	18.0
John Steinbeck	2	18.0

AND JUST FOR COMPARISON, THE REST OF THE "BIG 9" AUTHORS:

John le Carré	7	11.1
Bob Woodward	6	10.3
Robert Ludlum	8	10.3
Daphne du Maurier	6	8.2
Sidney Sheldon	7	8.1
Tom Clancy	5	7.8
Stephen King	16	6.6
Danielle Steel	10	5.7

FIRST DATE AT #1: November 7, 1948
TOTAL WEEKS AT #1: 4

The Young Lions
Irwin Shaw
RANDOM HOUSE

Shaw's first novel (he was already well-known as a playwright), reached #1 very quickly, then began a long slow decline. In this book, Shaw traces the fortunes of three young men, one Jewish, one gentile, one Nazi, from 1938 through 1945 when they meet, with tragic results, at a concentration camp in a Bavarian forest.

FIRST DATE AT #1: December 19, 1948
TOTAL WEEKS AT #1: 16

The Big Fisherman
Lloyd C. Douglas
HOUGHTON MIFFLIN

The author of the hugely successful novel *The Robe* returned with another version of Jesus's life, and once again stayed on the *New York Times* list for more than a year, with the first four months at #1 and the next four months at #2.

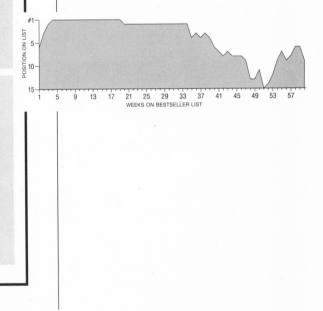

FIRST DATE AT #1: April 27, 1952
TOTAL WEEKS AT #1: 1

U.S.A. Confidential
Jack Lait and Lee Mortimer
CROWN

The success of their earlier *Washington Confidential* inspired the authors to expand the territory, but this book, a portrait of what it is like to live in America, was not nearly as successful.

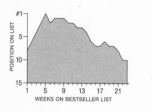

FIRST DATE AT #1: June 22, 1952
TOTAL WEEKS AT #1: 13

Witness
Whittaker Chambers
RANDOM HOUSE

The spy trial of Alger Hiss, former under secretary of state, caught the public's fancy, particularly witness Chambers' account of leaving secret documents for Hiss in a hollowed-out pumpkin. Chambers, a senior editor at *Time,* was first into print with his account (Hiss's came years later). Like most political inside stories, it had a quick rise and a quick decline, but spent the entire summer of '52 in the #1 spot.

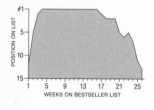

#1 Authors for Whom Writing Is Not the Primary Occupation

(They are listed chronologically, from the earliest author of a #1 book to the most recent.)

Victor de Seversky, aircraft designer

Marion Hargrove, soldier

Lloyd Douglas, clergyman

Cornelia Otis Skinner, actress

Wendell Willkie, politician

Bob Hope, comedian

Sumner Welles, politician

Bill Mauldin, cartoonist

Joshua Liebman, rabbi

James Byrnes, politician

Alfred C. Kinsey, sex researcher

Dwight D. Eisenhower, soldier

Winston Churchill, politician

Whittaker Chambers, editor

Tallulah Bankhead, actress

Norman Vincent Peale, clergyman

Morey Bernstein, business executive

Robert Traver, Supreme Court justice

Bernard Baruch, financier

J. Edgar Hoover, FBI director

Herman Taller, physician

Douglas MacArthur, soldier

Dag Hammarskjold, U.N. Secretary General

Bel Kaufman, high school teacher

Norman Dacey, financial consultant

Mark Lane, attorney

Sam Levenson, comedian

Haim Ginott, pediatrician

Robert Townsend, business executive

Alex Comfort, physician

Robert Atkins, physician

Richard Adams, British civil servant

James Herriot, veterinarian

Dan Rather, anchorman

Michael Korda, publishing executive

David Niven, actor

H. R. Haldeman, politician

Wil Huygen, physician

Lauren Bacall, actress

Herman Tarnower, physician

Phil Donahue, talk show host

Shelley Winters, actress

Carl Sagan, astronomer

Jeffery Archer, politician

Jane Fonda, actress

Edward Koch, politician

Lee Iacocca, business executive

Chuck Yeager, soldier

Priscilla Presley, actress

David Stockman, politician and businessman

Bill Cosby, comedian

Bernie Siegel, physician

Allan Bloom, college professor

Ravi Batra, college professor

Donald Trump, business executive

Michael Jackson, entertainer

Donald Regan, politician

Stephen Hawking, physicist

George Burns, comedian

Gilda Radner, actress

Barbara Bush, first lady

Charles Kuralt, anchorman

Julia Phillips, film producer

Nancy Reagan, first lady

Alan M. Dershowitz, law professor

Katherine Hepburn, actress

Oliver North, retired soldier

FIRST DATE AT #1: April 10, 1949
TOTAL WEEKS AT #1: 22

Point of No Return
John P. Marquand
LITTLE, BROWN

The third of Marquand's four #1 best-sellers was the most popular, rising to #1 in its fourth week and remaining there for four months. It follows several days in the life of a man waiting to learn if he will be promoted to the vice-presidency of his New York bank. While waiting, he returns to his Massachusetts home town on business and reviews his life.

FIRST DATE AT #1: September 18, 1949
TOTAL WEEKS AT #1: 6

A Rage to Live
John O'Hara
RANDOM HOUSE

For many years, writing was O'Hara's job. He would eat breakfast, put on his coat and tie, go in the next room, and write (with a lunch break) from nine to five, then remove his coat and tie and relax. Although O'Hara wrote 17 popular novels, only this—which he felt was his "big one"—reached #1 on the *Times* list. It is the story of a wealthy woman whose rage to live eventually destroys her marriages and leaves her an exile from her Pennsylvania town. When the *New Yorker* review called this book "one of those panoramic three-or-four generation novels that writers of the third and fourth magnitude turn out in such disheartening abundance," the enraged O'Hara refused to write for the *New Yorker* for more than 10 years.

FIRST DATE AT #1: September 21, 1952
TOTAL WEEKS AT #1: 5

A Man Called Peter
Catherine Marshall
MCGRAW-HILL

The biography of the late chaplain of the U.S. Senate, written by his widow, was one of the slowest rising *and* the slowest falling books, on either side of its brief span at #1. The author told *McCall's* that "Literature, if it is accurately to reflect life, must at times reach past the reader's intellect to the emotional level. In order to achieve that the writer has to feel something as he writes. There were times during the writing of *A Man Called Peter* when reliving... my life with Peter was almost too much for me....Particularly...the chapter on Peter's death. Not only did I have to reexperience every vivid detail...but there was...the necessity of holding that emotion in check. I am convinced that real communication in writing always has to be disciplined."

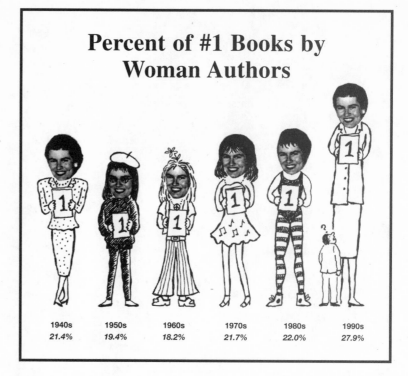

Percent of #1 Books by Woman Authors

1940s	1950s	1960s	1970s	1980s	1990s
21.4%	19.4%	18.2%	21.7%	22.0%	27.9%

FIRST DATE AT #1: October 26, 1952
TOTAL WEEKS AT #1: 16

Tallulah
Tallulah Bankhead
HARPER

Once a decade or so, the public seems ready for a "this is my story" book from a strong female celebrity. Tallulah's *Tallulah* was the first of the genre that later brought books by Lauren Bacall, Shelley Winters, and Katherine Hepburn. *Tallulah* had the fastest rise to date to #1, joining the list at #2 and reaching the top one week later for an uninterrupted stay of four months.

FIRST DATE AT #1: October 30, 1949

TOTAL WEEKS AT #1: 16

The Egyptian
Mika Waltari
PUTNAM

The one and only book by a Finnish author to become a #1 *New York Times* bestseller, *The Egyptian* was a huge success, remaining in the top 10 for half a year after being displaced from #1. Waltari's book (his translator, Naomi Walford, gets little credit) describes the religious, political, and everyday life in Egypt 1,000 years before Christ, as told by a physician who traveled extensively and was friend to both pharaohs and slaves. Waltari died in 1979.

●§ DAPHNE ᴅᴜ MAURIER

The Parasites

●§ CHAPTER ONE

IT WAS Charles who called us the parasites. The way he said it was surprising, and sudden; he was one of those quiet, reserved sort of men, not given to talking much or stating his opinion, unless upon the most ordinary facts of day by day, so that his outburst, coming as it did towards the end of the long wet Sunday afternoon, when we had none of us done anything but read the papers and yawn and stretch before the fire, had the force of an explosion. We were all sitting in the long low room at Farthings, darker than usual because of the rain, and the french windows gave very little light, chopped as they were in small square panes that added to the beauty of the house from without, but inside had all the appearance of prison bars, oddly depressing.

The grandfather clock in the corner ticked slowly and unevenly; now and again it gave a little cough, hesitating momentarily, like an old man with asthma, then ploughed on again with quiet insistence. The fire in the basket grate had sunk rather low, the mixture of coke and coal had caked in a solid lump, giving no warmth, and the logs that had been flung carelessly on top earlier in the afternoon smouldered in dull fashion, needing the bellows to coax them into life. The papers were strewn about the floor, and the empty cardboard covers of gramophone records were amongst them, along with a cushion that had fallen from the sofa. These things may have added to Charles's irritation. He was an orderly man, with a methodical mind, and looking back now with the realization that his mind was at that

●§ 1

FIRST DATE AT #1: February 19, 1950

TOTAL WEEKS AT #1: 5

The Parasites
Daphne du Maurier
DOUBLEDAY

Du Maurier's second #1 book is the story of three siblings, children of a famous theatrical couple who, accused of being parasites, attempt to reform and change their lives.

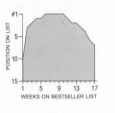

FIRST DATE AT #1: February 15, 1953
TOTAL WEEKS AT #1: 1

Holy Bible, Revised Standard Version

NELSON

The new translation in simpler (some said less eloquent) English, was the first of two Bibles to reach #1 on the *Times* list. It stayed on the list for over a year, but lasted only one week at #1, sandwiched between the actress and the mountain climber. As it happened, madam Polly Adler's book about her establishment, *A House Is Not a Home,* was in the #2 or #3 spot for quite a while, but never was able to displace the Bible.

FIRST DATE AT #1: February 22, 1953
TOTAL WEEKS AT #1: 12

Annapurna

Maurice Herzog

DUTTON

Herzog's first-hand account of climbing one of the highest mountains on earth moved quickly and steadily up to #1 in its fifth week. After being displaced by Dr. Peale three months later, it remained at #2 for another three months. During this period, Carl Sandburg, George Santayana, Thomas Merton, and Adlai Stevenson all had books in the top five, although none ever reached #1.

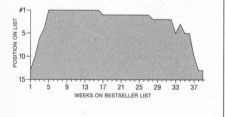

The Most Influential Books

In late 1991, the Library of Congress and the Book-of-the-Month Club conducted a survey, asking readers which book had most influenced their lives. Of the top thirteen, only two, possibly three, had ever been #1 bestsellers. Here is that list, with the #1 bestseller in boldface.

1. **The Bible** (no specific version was mentioned; two recent versions [RSV and New English] have been #1s.)
2. *Atlas Shrugged,* Ayn Rand
3. *The Road Less Traveled,* M. Scott Peck
4. *To Kill a Mockingbird,* Harper Lee
5. *The Lord of the Rings,* J. R. R. Tolkein
6. *Gone With the Wind,* Margaret Mitchell
7. *How to Win Friends and Influence People,* Dale Carnegie
8. *The Book of Mormon*
9. *The Feminine Mystique,* Betty Friedan
10. ***A Gift from the Sea,*** Anne Lindbergh (tie)
11. *Man's Search for Meaning,* Viktor Frankl (tie)
12. ***Passages,*** Gail Sheehy (tie)
13. *When Bad Things Happen to Good People,* Harold Kushner (tie)

EDITOR'S PROLOGUE

One sunny day in the summer after the end of the war, a search party found the Levinson Archive buried in seventeen iron boxes and a number of small parcels, the latter wrapped in rags and old clothes, under the sites of what had been, before the razing of the entire Warsaw ghetto, Nowolipki Street 68 and Swientojerska Street 34. Could but poor Levinson have been there himself that day!

The search party consisted of four survivors of the ghetto, including Henryk Rapaport and Rachel Apt, together with a team of surveyors from the Warsaw municipality, some city employees with digging implements, and a number of government people. Their search was as difficult as if they had been mariners hunting for some Atlantis under an uncharted sea. In hard fact, there was nothing left of the ghetto except the encompassing wall. Within, there was only an immense quadrangle of ruin: scores of city blocks reduced now to a plaza of thoroughly raked-over bits of mortar and crumbled brick, with here and there unaccountably untouched hills of rubble, like careless piles of husks and pollards left around after a threshing. For the most part, the wreckage had been cleared and everything but masonry carted away, as if even the down-pulled ruins of Jewry had been offensive. Among thousands of buildings that had once been ranked on this ground, only one—one building!—was left standing: fittingly, the Gensia Street Jail. Around the prostrate quarter was an eight-foot wall, into the rounded mortar at the summit of which bits of prohibitive glass had long ago been stuck, and Rachel Apt says the walltop sparkled that day in the summer sun, with glints of amber and blue and green.

Thus it was the task of the search party to go out into the huge wrecked space within the twinkling wall and try to find, not only the location of two specific nonexistent buildings, but also the exact ___ of their respective former courtyards, and inside those ___

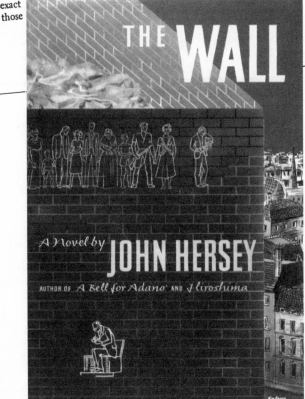

FIRST DATE AT #1: March 26, 1950
TOTAL WEEKS AT #1: 5

The Wall
John Hersey
KNOPF

The Nazis built a wall to confine the Jews of Warsaw in the ghetto. This is the story, allegedly based on diaries and other buried records, of the horrors endured by a few of the half million Jews enclosed behind that wall. The book reached #1 in its third week on the list; later, it stayed at #2 to *The Cardinal*'s #1 for more than three months.

FIRST DATE AT #1: April 30, 1950
TOTAL WEEKS AT #1: 24

The Cardinal
Henry Morton Robinson
SIMON & SCHUSTER

Robinson's novel follows the career of an American Roman Catholic priest from the beginning of the first world war to the beginning of the second. The cardinal is a composite, based on several priests the author knew. This was the first major book to be published in hard cover and paperback at approximately the same time.

FIRST DATE AT #1: May 17, 1953
TOTAL WEEKS AT #1: 98

The Power of Positive Thinking

Norman Vincent Peale

PRENTICE HALL

From the 17th of May in 1953 to the 17th of April in 1955, with the exception of a two-week hiatus, Dr. Peale's prescription for a happier, more fulfilling life spent an unprecedented 98 weeks as #1, forty weeks more than the runner-up, *Peace of Mind.* Only a two-week incursion by Elmer Davis interrupted the continuous reign. Among the main challengers, neither of which ever made it through to #1, were Polly Adler's *A House Is Not a Home,* and the Kinsey group's *Sexual Behavior in the Human Female.* Even after he was overtaken by another all-time leader, *A Gift from the Sea,* Dr. Peale remained in second place for more than six more months, before beginning a comparatively rapid descent. Peale disliked the manuscript for the book, then called *The Power of Faith* and threw it in the trash. His wife retrieved it and took it to Prentice Hall, where editor Myron Boardman changed "faith" to "positive thinking," and the rest is history.

If the 50 Years of the List Were Condensed into One Hour

Here's another way of looking at how the #1 spot is dominated by a very small number of authors. If the entire 2,600 weeks that the *New York Times* list has been in existence were condensed into one hour, then James Michener would have been in #1 for nearly five minutes. Eighteen authors account for half the time at #1, and the other 360 authors account for the other half.

FIRST DATE AT #1: April 17, 1955
TOTAL WEEKS AT #1: 46

A Gift from the Sea

Anne Morrow Lindbergh

PANTHEON BOOKS

A small book of essays in which the author represents herself sitting at the seashore dreaming and philosophizing. Each different shell she picks up turns her thought to different channels.

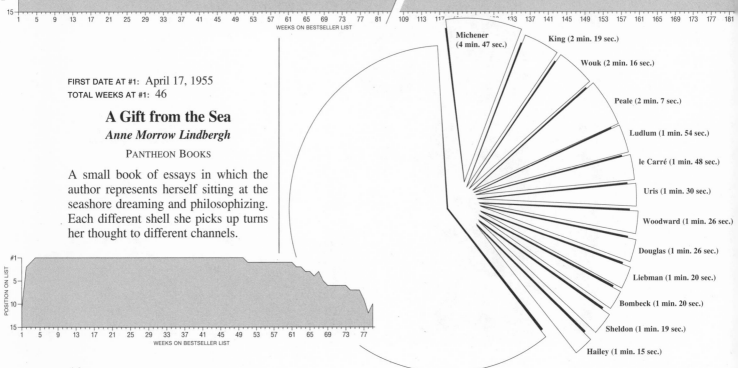

Michener (4 min. 47 sec.)
King (2 min. 19 sec.)
Wouk (2 min. 16 sec.)
Peale (2 min. 7 sec.)
Ludlum (1 min. 54 sec.)
le Carré (1 min. 48 sec.)
Uris (1 min. 30 sec.)
Woodward (1 min. 26 sec.)
Douglas (1 min. 26 sec.)
Liebman (1 min. 20 sec.)
Bombeck (1 min. 20 sec.)
Sheldon (1 min. 19 sec.)
Hailey (1 min. 15 sec.)

FIRST DATE AT #1: October 15, 1950
TOTAL WEEKS AT #1: 7

Across the River and into the Trees
Ernest Hemingway
SCRIBNER'S

Hemingway's only fiction appearance at #1 (he also made #1 in nonfiction) came near the end of his writing career and some critics felt "the Hemingway style degenerated into near self-parody." Others suggested that even bad Hemingway was pretty good stuff. The author once wrote that when he was having problems writing, "I would stand and look out over the roofs of Paris and think, 'Do not worry. You have always written before and you will write now. All you have to do is write one true sentence. Write the truest sentence that you know.' So finally I would write one true sentence and then go on from there." This book tells the story of an American officer who, realizing he has only a short time to live, makes one last visit to Italy, where he fought in two wars.

FIRST DATE AT #1: December 3, 1950
TOTAL WEEKS AT #1: 8

The Disenchanted
Budd Schulberg
RANDOM HOUSE

Although Schulberg's third book was written in the form of a novel, there were those who felt it was a thinly-disguised story of the life of F. Scott Fitzgerald, and should have been included among nonfiction books. The author insisted it was "a composite of the walking wounded of the time...." Schulberg would almost certainly have had a #1 book with his pre-list *What Makes Sammy Run.*

FIRST DATE AT #1: April 28, 1954
TOTAL WEEKS AT #1: 2

But We Were Born Free
Elmer Davis

BOBBS

In the midst of the McCarthy era, Bobbs had the courage to publish the news broadcaster's attack on those politicians who, under the guise of opposing Communism, were whittling away at the country's freedoms. It rose quickly to #2 where it spent nearly half a year, and briefly managed to divert Dr. Peale's steamroller.

FIRST DATE AT #1: March 4, 1956
TOTAL WEEKS AT #1: 12

The Search for Bridey Murphy
Morey Bernstein

DOUBLEDAY

Like Velikovsky's book earlier, and Whitley Strieber's *Communion* later, skeptics felt that this title might more logically have been on the fiction list. The Colorado hypnotist's account of "regressing" a patient into a past life as an Irish maiden, Bridey Murphy, had the shortest overall time on the list of any book that spent as long as 12 weeks in the #1 spot—a fast rise and a steep decline.

The Subject Matter of #1 Nonfiction Bestsellers

Putting the subject matter of a book into categories is a very subjective sort of thing. But the following categories seemed to make good sense for the kinds of books that appear at #1 on the *New York Times* list. The charts show the number of books in each category during the 1940s through the 1980s (which includes the beginning of the 1990s). Clearly celebrity memoirs and business books are the growth industry in nonfiction.

MEMOIRS	'40s	'50s	'60s	'70s	'80s+
Personal	2	2	2	3	7
Military	2	0	1	0	2
Political	0	1	0	0	1
Family	2	1	0	0	0
Celebrity	0	4	4	3	9
PUBLIC AFFAIRS					
Business	0	2	2	5	11
Politics	6	7	3	6	9
Life in America	1	4	5	6	5
History	0	1	0	3	1
The Kennedys	0	0	7	1	2
War	6	1	3	2	0
Crime	0	0	1	1	1
SCIENCE AND HEALTH					
Science	0	2	1	0	3
Medicine	0	1	2	0	1
Diet, exercise	0	0	1	2	3
Sex	0	1	0	2	2
Sports	0	0	0	2	3
Adventure	0	3	1	0	1
AND THE KEY TO THE SCRIPTURES					
Religion	1	3	1	0	0
New Age stuff	0	1	0	1	1
MISCELLANEOUS					
Animals	0	0	0	2	2
Biography	3	3	3	4	4
Humor	4	0	1	1	3

FROM

HERE TO

ETERNITY

BY

JAMES JONES

CHAPTER 1

WHEN he finished packing, he walked out on to the third-floor porch of the barracks brushing the dust from his hands, a very neat and deceptively slim young man in the summer khakis that were still early morning fresh.

He leaned his elbows on the porch ledge and stood looking down through the screens at the familiar scene of the barracks square laid out below with the tiers of porches dark in the faces of the three-story concrete barracks fronting on the square. He was feeling a half-sheepish affection for this vantage point that he was leaving.

Below him under the blows of the February Hawaiian sun the quadrangle gasped defenselessly, like an exhausted fighter. Through the heat haze and the thin mid-morning film of the parched red dust came up a muted orchestra of sounds: the clankings of steel-wheeled carts bouncing over brick, the slappings of oiled leather slingstraps, the shuffling beat of scorched shoesoles, the hoarse expletives of irritated noncoms.

Somewhere along the line, he thought, these things have become your heritage. You are multiplied by each sound that you hear. And you cannot deny them, without denying with them the purpose of your own existence. Yet now, he told himself, you are denying them, by renouncing the place that they have given you.

In the earthen square in the center of the quad a machine gun company went listlessly through the motions of its Loading Drill.

Behind him in the high-ceiling squadroom was the muffled curtain of sound that comes from men just waking and beginning to move around, testing cautiously the flooring of this world they had last night forsaken. He listened to it, hearing also the footsteps coming up behind him, but thinking of how good a thing it had been to sleep late every morning as a member of this Bugle Corps and wake up to the sounds of the line companies already outside at drill.

"You didnt pack my garrison shoes?" he asked the footsteps. "I meant to tell you. They scuff so easy."

"They're on the bed, both pair," the voice behind him said. "With the clean uniforms from your wall locker you didnt want to get

3

FIRST DATE AT #1: January 14, 1951
TOTAL WEEKS AT #1: 8

Joy Street
Francis Parkinson Keyes
MESSNER

A wealthy and aristocratic young Boston couple hope to bring people of various classes and nationalities together to live harmoniously in their house. Keyes's 29th book and only #1 was written in the renovated slave quarters of her New Orleans French Quarter mansion. Keyes (rhymes with *prize*) believed research was the key to her success. "People will discover what isn't authentic. They have a sort of sixth sense, and a feeling about whether or not the author's been there.... The writer must know the customs of the area...and the kind of furniture to use for his story. He must dress the character correctly and feed him properly."

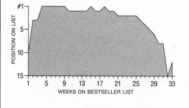

FIRST DATE AT #1: March 25, 1951
TOTAL WEEKS AT #1: 20

From Here to Eternity
James Jones
SCRIBNER'S

For 17 months, two of the big World War Two books fought their own battle. Eight weeks after Jones's tale of army life in Hawaii in the last months before Pearl Harbor reached #1, along came Wouk's *The Caine Mutiny.* Together, they held the #1 spot for 68 weeks, holding off challenges from Michener, Marquand, *Catcher in the Rye,* and Montserrat's *The Cruel Sea.* Later in his life, Jones wrote, "...that damn book has become the bane of my life. I've written at least three novels that are better than that, but everything gets compared to it, adversely, usually because it was such a huge bestseller....It's being compared by the notoriety it got rather than as a work of art."

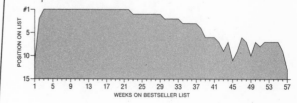

FIRST DATE AT #1: May 27, 1956
TOTAL WEEKS AT #1: 8

The Birth of Britain

Winston Churchill

DODD

The former prime minister returned to the #1 spot with the first volume of his four-volume history of the English-speaking peoples. Volume I covered the period from the Roman occupation to the end of the first century A.D. Subsequent volumes made the list, but none ever came close to being #1.

FIRST DATE AT #1: July 15, 1956
TOTAL WEEKS AT #1: 2

Arthritis and Common Sense

Dale Alexander

WITKOWER PRESS

Like Gayelord Hauser before him, Alexander's book of advice and nutritional suggestions for arthritis sufferers had very large sales in health food stores, and enough in traditional bookstores to keep it on the list for eight months, and in the top spot for a couple of weeks.

The Oldest Authors to Reach #1

AUTHOR	AGE AT #1	BOOK
George Burns	92.9	*Gracie*
Helen H. Santmeyer	88.7	*"…and Ladies of the Club."*
Bernard Baruch	87.2	*Baruch: My Own Story*
Agatha Christie*	86.2	*Sleeping Murder*
Dr. Seuss*	86.1	*Oh, the Places You'll Go*
J. R. R. Tolkein*	85.8	*The Silmarillion*
Agatha Christie*	85.3	*Curtain*
Douglas MacArthur	84.8	*Reminiscences*
Katherine Hepburn	83.9	*Me*
Rose Kennedy	83.9	*Times to Remember*
Dr. Seuss*	82.1	*You're Only Old Once!*
Winston Churchill	81.5	*The Birth of Britain*
James Michener	81.5	*Alaska*
Louis L'Amour	79.2	*The Haunted Mesa*
James Michener	78.7	*Texas*
Louis L'Amour	78.3	*Last of the Breed*
James Michener	76.7	*Poland*
James Michener	75.7	*Space*
Harry Overstreet	74.4	*The Mature Mind*
James Michener	73.8	*The Covenant*
Winston Churchill	73.7	*The Gathering Storm*
Sidney Sheldon	73.6	*Memories of Midnight*
Hedda Hopper	73.0	*The Whole Truth and Nothing But*
Sidney Sheldon	71.8	*The Sands of Time*
Peter Wright	71.6	*Spycatcher*
James Michener	71.5	*Chesapeake*
Lloyd C. Douglas	71.4	*The Big Fisherman*
Somerset Maugham	70.5	*Razor's Edge*
Thornton Wilder	70.2	*The Eighth Day*
Sidney Sheldon	70.0	*Windmills of the Gods*

*recently deceased

EACH YEAR, the Trustees of the Columbia University School of Journalism award the Pulitzer Prize to a work of fiction and one of nonfiction, which they judge to be the best of the year. Of more than 90 books so honored in the years since the *New York Times* list was established, only five books have both won the Pulitzer Prize and been a #1 bestseller.

Thirteen #1 authors have won a Pulitzer Prize for a book other than the one that made them #1:

Saul Bellow won a Pulitzer for *Humboldt's Gift*

James Gould Cozzens for *Guard of Honor*

Ernest Hemingway for *The Old Man and the Sea*

Pulitzer Prize Winners that Were also #1 Best Selling Books

The Caine Mutiny (Wouk)
Andersonville (Kantor)
Advise and Consent (Drury)
The Confessions of Nat Turner (Styron)
The Making of the President— 1960 (White)

John Hersey for *A Bell for Adano*

Sinclair Lewis for *Arrowsmith*

Norman Mailer for *The Executioner's Song* and *The Armies of the Night*

John P. Marquand for *The Late George Apley*

James Michener for *Tales of the South Pacific*

Katherine Anne Porter for *Collected Stories*

Carl Sagan for *The Dragons of Eden*

John Steinbeck for *The Grapes of Wrath*

John Updike for *Rabbit Is Rich* and *Rabbit at Rest*

Thornton Wilder for *The Bridge of San Luis Rey*

One conclusion is that Pulitzer Prizes are unlikely to go to "mass market" popular books. Another is that winning a Pulitzer may not help sales much. A third is that the Pulitzer is more than twice as likely to go to a non-#1 book of a given author than to a #1. A fourth is that a Pulitzer is much less likely to go to a woman: only 12 of the last 81 winners were women.

FIRST DATE AT #1: August 12, 1951
TOTAL WEEKS AT #1: 48

The Caine Mutiny
Herman Wouk

DOUBLEDAY

Had it not been for *From Here to Eternity,* Wouk surely would have had the only fiction book to hold the #1 position for more than a year. As it was, his story of the career of Willie Keith, from midshipman to captain of the minesweeper *The Caine,* shares the all-time #1 fiction record with *Hawaii,* and probably deprived William Faulkner of his only chance for #1 with his *Requiem for a Nun.*

FIRST DATE AT #1: March 30, 1952
TOTAL WEEKS AT #1: 8

My Cousin Rachel
Daphne du Maurier

DOUBLEDAY

Du Maurier's 13th novel and third #1 bestseller reached #2 in its third week, then temporarily interrupted the 48-week #1 run of *The Caine Mutiny.* Set in eighteenth-century Cornwall, the novel centers on a man living on his late uncle's farm with the widow, whom he suspects may have poisoned her husband. Some critics felt du Maurier never returned to the standard of *Rebecca*—the *Spectator* wrote that "her plots creak and depend on either outrageous coincidence or shamelessly contrived mood."

51

FIRST DATE AT #1: August 5, 1956
TOTAL WEEKS AT #1: 11

Eisenhower:
The Inside Story
Robert J. Donovan

HARPER

"Inside" papers and records of Eisenhower's first term were made available to Donovan, enabling him to write what some observers felt was virtually a campaign piece, issued to coincide with the president's decision to seek a second term. Like most political insider books, it had a steep rise to #1, and a steep decline, beginning right after Ike's landslide victory over Stevenson.

FIRST DATE AT #1: October 21, 1956
TOTAL WEEKS AT #1: 15

The Nun's Story
Kathryn Hulme

LITTLE, BROWN

Sandwiched between Eisenhower and Hoover we find a woman who entered a Belgian convent and remained a nun for 17 years before realizing that the inflexible authority of religious life was not for her. The book, by her friend and business partner, a long-time publicity director for the Ask Mr. Foster travel agencies, caught the public's fancy, rising quickly to #1 where it remained for nearly four months, then stayed an equal time at #2.

he decided on John Minor Wisdom, a New Orleans attorney and the Republican National Committeeman from Louisiana.

To give the group, which is called the President's Committee on Government Contracts, the maximum prestige Eisenhower named the Vice-President of the United States as its chairman. The vice-chairman was J. Ernest Wilkins, a Chicago attorney, who was later appointed by the President as Assistant Secretary of Labor, the first Negro ever to hold a sub-Cabinet post. (On August 18, 1954, Wilkins became the first member of his race ever to attend a meeting of the Cabinet when he substituted for Secretary Mitchell.)

Along with Wisdom the original list of public members included Reuther, Meany, John A. Roosevelt, son of the late President; Mrs. Helen Rogers Reid, director of the *Herald Tribune*; John L. McCaffrey, president of the International Harvester Company, and Fred Lazarus, Jr., president of the American Retail Federation.

The committee scored some noteworthy successes in the city of Washington. It persuaded the Capital Transit Company to end its ban on Negro bus drivers and streetcar operators. It also prevailed upon the Chesapeake & Potomac Telephone Company to drop segregation in its business offices. Through its efforts some four hundred Negroes were employed in the Savannah River plant of the Atomic Energy Commission in South Carolina.

In the meantime pressures being exerted from the White House brought great changes in customs in Washington. With the President's approval the Department of Justice filed a strong brief in the Thompson restaurant case, in which the Supreme Court ruled unanimously that restaurants may not draw the color line. This opened the doors of Washington eating places to Negroes. The hotels in the capital were persuaded to accept Negro guests, and the

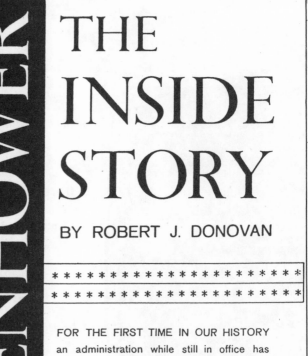

THE INSIDE STORY

BY ROBERT J. DONOVAN

EISENHOWER

* *
* *

FOR THE FIRST TIME IN OUR HISTORY an administration while still in office has permitted a distinguished journalist to compile an authentic, independent account of its conduct of affairs of state. In this sense this book is an inside story of Eisenhower in the White House. Here is a wealth of new and unpublished information

(continued on inside flap)

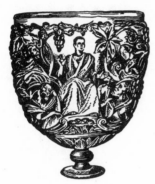

THE SILVER CHALICE

a novel by

THOMAS B. COSTAIN

Garden City, New York

DOUBLEDAY & COMPANY, INC.

FIRST DATE AT #1: September 7, 1952
TOTAL WEEKS AT #1: 15

The Silver Chalice

Thomas B. Costain

DOUBLEDAY

Costain became the first author to have four #1 novels with the story of Basil, the artisan who fashioned the chalice, a frame meant to hold the cup Christ drank from at the last supper. During one memorable week in late October, the top five titles on the *Times* list included Edna Ferber's *Giant,* Ernest Hemingway's *The Old Man and the Sea,* and John Steinbeck's *East of Eden.*

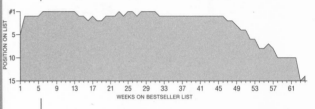

FIRST DATE AT #1: November 2, 1952
TOTAL WEEKS AT #1: 11

East of Eden

John Steinbeck

VIKING

Of Mice and Men, The Grapes of Wrath, and *The Moon Is Down* came too early, and *The Wayward Bus* reached the list, but just barely, so John Steinbeck first made #1 with this, his 15th book. The saga, set in Salinas, covers more than half a century in the lives of two American families, the tranquil and easy-going Hamiltons and the more turbulent Trasks. Not all Steinbeck fans or scholars know that he wrote poetry for the Monterey *Beacon* under the name of Amnesia Glasscock.

BY AND ABOUT #1 AUTHORS:

"The profession of book-writing makes horse racing seem like a solid, stable business."

"Little presses write to me for manuscripts and when I write back that I haven't any, they write to ask if they can print the letter saying I haven't any."

—John Steinbeck

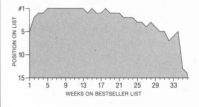

FIRST DATE AT #1: February 3, 1957
TOTAL WEEKS AT #1: 17

The F.B.I. Story
Donald Whitehead

RANDOM HOUSE

Written by a Washington-based reporter, this book was produced with the enthusiastic cooperation of J. Edgar Hoover, who wrote the foreword. It spent four months at #1 during the waning of the McCarthy era.

FIRST DATE AT #1: May 20, 1957
TOTAL WEEKS AT #1: 3

Day of Infamy
Walter Lord

HOLT

Lord's reconstruction of the events leading up to (and including) the Japanese attack on Pearl Harbor rose steadily to #1, then disappeared quickly from the list a few weeks later.

FIRST DATE AT #1: June 23, 1957
TOTAL WEEKS AT #1: 7

The Day Christ Died
Jim Bishop

HARPER

Reporter Bishop wrote about the crucifixion as if it were a newspaper story, a novel twist that sent him to #1 in weeks, and kept him in the top five for several months longer. Two of Bishops subsequent "*The Day...*" books made the list, but no other reached #1.

Publishers Who Have Had at Least One #1 Book Every Year

There are none. No one even comes close. The best record is Doubleday which had a #1 book in 31 of the 50 years. Random House had one for 30 of the 50 years, and Simon & Schuster for 27.

Every major publisher has had at least one long dry period, with no #1 books.

Delacorte went six years without one, from 1973 to 1979.
Doubleday went five years once, from 1963 to 1968.
Harper had three different four-year lean periods.
Knopf went fourteen years, from 1950 to 1964.
Little went seven years, from 1963 to 1970.
Morrow went ten years, from 1953 to 1963.
Putnam went nine years, from 1949 to 1958.
Random House had a five-year gap, 1960 to 1965.
Simon & Schuster went nine years, from 1950 to 1959.
Viking went eight years, from 1944 to 1952.

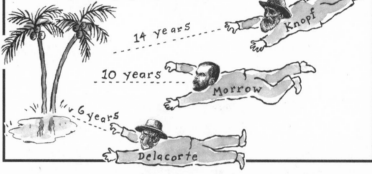

Last American President's Story Book of Life and Love

There was once a book about the publishing industry with the title *Lincoln's Doctor's Dog,* because it was believed those were the three most popular words to use in titles. As far as #1 bestsellers are concerned, once we have dealt with the obvious repeating words (like "the" and "and" and "of"), there are only nineteen more words that appear in five or more titles.

The (187)	From (8)	Book (6)
Of (71)	Story (8)	My (6)
And (29)	American (7)	President (6)
A (24)	For (7)	By (5)
Day(s) (12)	Last (7)	House (5)
I (9)	Love (7)	Life (5)
Time (9)	All (6)	This (5)

Incidentally, the words "Andy Rooney" and "Trump" appear in #1 titles more often (twice) than "about," "big," "can," "male," or "female" (once each).

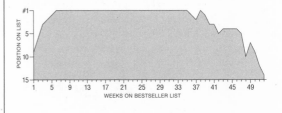

ANNEMARIE SELINKO

Désirée

Beyond This Place

A NOVEL BY

A·J·CRONIN

FIRST DATE AT #1: March 8, 1953
TOTAL WEEKS AT #1: 32

Désirée

Annemarie Selinko

MORROW

This relatively unknown and little-remembered book by a Viennese house-wife living in Denmark knocked off Steinbeck and Costain, reaching #1 in its sixth week, and it held off books by J. D. Salinger, Ernest Gann (*The High and the Mighty*), and Leon Uris (*Battle Cry*) to remain #1 for over seven months. It is the fictional diary of a silk merchant's daughter, once engaged to Napoleon, who marries his general, Bernadotte, later Marshal of France and King of Sweden.

FIRST DATE AT #1: October 11, 1953
TOTAL WEEKS AT #1: 6

Beyond This Place

A. J. Cronin

LITTLE, BROWN

The Scottish physician's third #1 book tells the story of a man who discovers that the father he believed dead is actually in prison, convicted of murder, and sets about to try to clear him of the charges.

FIRST DATE AT #1: August 4, 1957
TOTAL WEEKS AT #1: 6

The Hidden Persuaders
Vance Packard
MCKAY

Each of Packard's three #1 bestsellers was based on social science research, making it accessible for the layman. *The Hidden Persuaders* presents the use and misuse of social and psychological research by the advertising and public relations industries. Of Packard's career, Warren Bennis writes, "There is no denying that Vance Packard has got his...finger on one helluva issue—maybe *the* issue facing us in the last quarter of this century. It is true that [his] fingers tend to lack a subtlety, are not deeply nuanced and muck around a bit too much, but the important thing is that Packard's there...."

FIRST DATE AT #1: September 22, 1957
TOTAL WEEKS AT #1: 19

Baruch: My Own Story
Bernard Baruch
HOLT

The then-famous financier, philanthropist, and advisor to half a dozen presidents was one of a small handful of authors to put himself in the title. The book was extremely popular, rising very quickly and spending nearly five months at #1. The second volume of this two-volume autobiography was not nearly as successful. While Baruch was at #1, the children's book for adults, *Where Did You Go? Out. What Did You Do? Nothing.* was either at #3 or #2 for weeks, but never made #1.

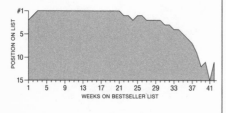

Vance Packard

THE HIDDEN PERSUADERS

What Makes Us Buy, Believe—And Even Vote—The Way We Do. An Introduction to the New World of Symbol Manipulation and Motivational Research.

Fake People in Titles

Amber
Aquitaine
B.F.
Bernadette
Bourne (3 times)
Désireé
Doctor Zhivago
Franny
Herzog
Iron John
Lydia Bailey
Mame
Marjorie Morningstar
Mary Anne
Matarese
Mistral
Mr. Goodbar
Mrs. Parkington
Nat Turner
Oliver
Portnoy

Rachel
Rebecca
Shannon
The Jedi
The Tommyknockers
Willis Wade
Zooey
Zoya

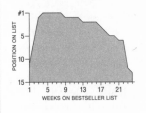

⋆ CHAPTER 1

The doctor came out of the house and he closed the door gently behind him. He looked up and there was a little boy.

"Hello, Luke," he murmured.

The little boy lowered his eyes humbly and when the doctor reached the top step of the porch the little boy turned and put out his hand, the doctor relaxed his grip on his bag and they walked down the steps together and across the sidewalk to the buggy.

The doctor got in on the driving side. The little boy held the doctor's bag with both hands. The doctor seated himself. He took up the reins. The little boy raised the bag and gently lowered it to the carriage floor.

"Thank you, Luke," the doctor said. He smiled absently. He nodded.

The boy looked silently up at the doctor. The doctor flipped the reins. The buggy drove off at a smart trot.

The boy watched the carriage disappear. When it was gone he took to his heels. He ran across town, never slacking, always as fast as he could go. He came to an empty street. When he saw that it was empty he slowed instantly. He walked directly to a wooden house in the middle of the street. In a window of the house was a porcelain sign, a rectangle of white, three and one-half inches high and fourteen inches long. On the sign was lettered severely and blackly, "Chester Kellogg, M.D."

The little boy sat down on the top step of the porch of this house. He waited a long time. He waited nearly two hours. He sat very still in the warm July afternoon, blinking a little sometimes and thinking his own thoughts. From far off, the air of the small town of Milletta brought to the porch occasional faint shouts of children at play. Once a door slammed. Once a trio of dogs burst into hysterical shrill yapping and their yelps died in the distance. The little boy heard everything and he heard nothing. The sounds funnelled into his ears and drained away. He was listening for something else.

1

"Writers should be read—but neither seen nor heard."

—Daphne du Maurier

F I C T I O N 1953

FIRST DATE AT #1: November 29, 1953
TOTAL WEEKS AT #1: 11

Lord Vanity
Samuel Shellabarger
LITTLE, BROWN

The adventures in love and war of the illegitimate son of a wealthy eighteenth-century nobleman.

FIRST DATE AT #1: February 16, 1954
TOTAL WEEKS AT #1: 25

Not as a Stranger
Morton Thompson
SCRIBNER'S

A dedicated young man struggles from boyhood to get his training and become a doctor. Then he must struggle to make a success of marriage to an unhappy and long-suffering wife.

FIRST DATE AT #1: August 1, 1954
TOTAL WEEKS AT #1: 11

Mary Anne
Daphne du Maurier
DOUBLEDAY

The fourth of du Maurier's six #1 bestsellers, *Mary Anne* is the fictionalized biography of Mary Anne Clarke, a famous courtesan and mistress to Frederick, Duke of York, son of George III.

57

FIRST DATE AT #1: February 2, 1958
TOTAL WEEKS AT #1: 13

Please Don't Eat the Daisies

Jean Kerr

DOUBLEDAY

The Erma Bombeck of the 1950s amused all of America with her account of the life, struggles, and troubles of a house-wife with four boys. After three months at #1, the book spent another three months in the top three before beginning its decline. Kerr recalls that when the family needed money, "I decided to write plays, spurred on by a chance compliment my father had paid years earlier. 'Look,' he exploded one evening over the dinner table, 'The only damn thing in this world you're good for is *talk*.' By talk I assumed he meant dia-logue—and I was off."

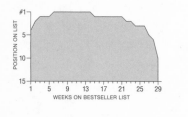

FIRST DATE AT #1: May 4, 1958
TOTAL WEEKS AT #1: 9

Masters of Deceit

J. Edgar Hoover

HOLT

We'll probably never know if the ru-mors that The Director secretly ordered F.B.I. agents everywhere to buy mul-tiple copies of his book, thereby pro-pelling him quickly into the #1 spot, are true. The files are unlikely still to exist. The book tells of the Communist threat to America and how best to fight it. It is Hoover's second book, the first: *Persons in Hiding* was published 20 years earlier.

Come to _____ _____ gave us the most trouble was a beag____ _____ Murphy. As far as I'm concerned, the first thing he did wrong was to turn into a beagle. I had seen him bouncing around in the excelsior of a pet-shop window, and I went in and asked the man, "How much is that adorable fox terrier in the window?" Did he say, "That adorable fox terrier is a beagle"? No, he said, "Ten dollars, lady." Now, I don't mean to say one word against beagles. They have rights just like other people. But it is a bit of a shock when you bring home a small ball of fluff in a shoe-box, and three weeks later it's as long as the sofa.

Murphy was the first dog I ever trained personally, and I was delighted at the alacrity with which he took to the newspaper. It was sometime later that we discovered, to our horror, that—like so many dogs—he had grasped the let-ter but not the spirit of the thing. Until the very end of his days he felt a real sense of obligation whenever he saw a newspaper—*any* newspaper—and it didn't matter where it was. I can't bring myself to go into the sordid details, ex-cept to mention that we were finally compelled to keep all the papers in the bottom of the icebox.

He had another habit that used to leave us open to a certain amount of criticism from our friends, who were not dogophiles. He never climbed up on beds or chairs or sofas. But he always sat on top of the piano. In the beginning we used to try to pull him off of there. But after a few noisy scuffles in which he knocked a picture off the wall, scratched the piano, and smashed a lamp, we just gave in —only to discover that, left to his own devices, he hopped

67

His head fell forward into her hands. He did not speak or open his eyes. She felt his body begin to sag. She wrapped her arms about him, held him upright in the chair. His head fell onto her shoulder. She held him to her breast so that he could not fall. She could scarcely feel his breathing. She heard Rathbone calling to the audience for a surgeon.

"Abraham, speak to me, tell me where you've been hurt."

The door to the box was opened. A man in uniform rushed to her side.

"Mrs. Lincoln, I'm Dr. Leale, surgeon from the General Hospital."

"Doctor, take charge of him."

Dr. Leale and Rathbone, bleeding profusely from an arm wound, lifted Abraham from the chair and laid him on the carpeted floor. She stood above them, her heart pounding so loudly in her ears that she had to strain to hear Dr. Leale.

". . . clot of blood on shoulder . . . may be a stab wound . . . slit the coat and shirt . . ."

The box filled with people: Laura Keene, trying to comfort her, another of the actors bringing water, a young man who introduced himself as Dr. Charles Sabin Taft, Julia's brother, still more doctors. She watched Dr. Leale trying to breathe air into Abraham's lungs, pour a little brandy down his throat.

"Can't we take him home?" she pleaded. "It would be so much better for him here."

"I'm afraid not, Mrs. Lincoln; the president would die before we got him to the White House."

Die! Abraham die?

She sank to her knees, put an arm under Abraham's head, raised him to her. Where her right hand held his head firmly against her, she felt something wet and sticky. She brought it up slowly, saw a blotch of blood. She stared at it in silence, uncomprehending, then raised her eyes to the doctors who were watching her. After a pause Dr. Leale said:

"I'm sorry, Mrs. Lincoln. The president was shot . . . in the back of the head."

Four soldiers who had been in the audience, ~~~~~~~ ~~~ ~~~~~ ~cked up Abraham, carried him ~~~~~~~~~~~~~ y Major ~~~~~~~~~~~~~~~~~~~~~~~~~~~~~~~~~~~~ family ~~~~~~~~~~~~~~~~~~~~~~~~~~~~~~~~~~~ with his ~~~~~~~~~~~~~~~~~~~~~~~~~~~~~ . More

~~~~~~~~~~~~ aham,
~~~~~~~~~~~~ vay of
~~~~~~~~~~~~ ading
~~~~~~~~~~~~ vith a

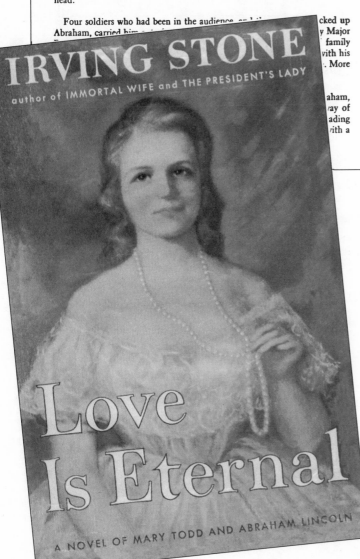

FIRST DATE AT #1: October 17, 1954
TOTAL WEEKS AT #1: 11

Love Is Eternal
Irving Stone
DOUBLEDAY

The first of Stone's three #1 appearances, *Love Is Eternal* is the story of the not-always-happy marriage of Abraham Lincoln and Mary Todd. "I decided early on," Stone wrote, "that I would read all the great tales that had been written, and those which had not yet been set down I would create myself."

FIRST DATE AT #1: December 19, 1954
TOTAL WEEKS AT #1: 14

The View from Pompey's Head
Hamilton Basso
DOUBLEDAY

Basso's only #1 was this very popular account of a New York lawyer who returns to the southern town of his birth, Pompey's Head, to settle a claim. He eventually clears up the case and settles some personal difficulties as well. After spending the entire winter at #1, it declined pretty evenly for 10 weeks.

FIRST DATE AT #1: April 10, 1955
TOTAL WEEKS AT #1: 6

Sincerely, Willis Wayde
John P. Marquand
LITTLE, BROWN

Marquand's fourth and last #1 book details the rise of an American industrialist, from his start as a mill hand to a tycoon running a huge corporation.

FIRST DATE AT #1: July 6, 1958
TOTAL WEEKS AT #1: 11

Inside Russia Today
John Gunther
HARPER

Gunther's third and last #1 book followed the successful formula of *Inside U.S.A.*: some politics, some travelogue, and an analysis of the current political situation in the post-Stalin years. The book remained at #1 all summer, when *Russia* gave way to *America*. During this time, Herbert Hoover's book on Woodrow Wilson was in the #2 spot for quite a while, the closest to #1 achieved by any living president or ex-president.

FIRST DATE AT #1: September 21, 1958
TOTAL WEEKS AT #1: 27

Only in America
Harry Golden
WORLD

The concept was unusual to begin with: a Jewish editor editing a Jewish newspaper in the deep south. But *The Carolina Israelite* had its fans, and this collection of short essays on the wonders of life in America became the biggest hit of 1958, rising steadily to #1 and remaining there for more than half a year. While the book was at #1, it became known that Golden, under a different name, had served a prison term for mail fraud. Carl Sandburg and Adlai Stevenson came to his defense, and sales seemed hardly affected at all.

122   ONLY IN AMERICA

wholly on the absence of racial segregation. The white and Negro stand at the same grocery and supermarket counters; deposit money at the same bank teller's window; pay phone and light bills to the same clerk; walk through the same dime and department stores, and stand at the same drugstore counters.

It is only when the Negro "sets" that the fur begins to fly.

Now, since we are not even thinking about restoring VERTICAL SEGREGATION, I think my plan would not only comply with the Supreme Court decisions, but would maintain "sitting-down" segregation. Now here is the GOLDEN VERTICAL NEGRO PLAN. Instead of all those complicated proposals, all the next session needs to do is pass one small amendment which would provide *only* desks in all the public schools of our state—*no seats*.

The desks should be those standing-up jobs, like the old-fashioned bookkeeping desk. Since no one in the South pays the slightest attention to a VERTICAL NEGRO, this will completely solve our problem. And it is not such a terrible inconvenience for young people to stand up during their classroom studies. In fact, this may be a blessing in disguise. They are not learning to read sitting down, anyway; maybe standing up will help. This will save more millions of dollars in the cost of our remedial English course when the kids enter college. In whatever direction you look with the GOLDEN VERTICAL NEGRO PLAN, you save millions of dollars, to say nothing of eliminating forever any danger to our public education system upon which rests the destiny, hopes, and happiness of this society.

My WHITE BABY PLAN offers another possible solution to the segregation problem—this time in a field other than education.

Here is an actual case history of the "White Baby Plan To End Racial Segregation":

Some months ago there was a revival of the Laurence Olivier movie, *Hamlet*, and several Negro schoolteachers were eager to see it. One Saturday afternoon they asked some white friends to lend them two of their little children, a three-year-old girl and a six-year-old boy, and, holding these white children by the hands, they obtained tickets from the movie-house cashier without a moment's hesitation. They were in like Flynn.

This would also solve the baby-sitting problem for thousands

FIRST DATE AT #1: May 22, 1955
TOTAL WEEKS AT #1: 12

Bonjour Tristesse
Françoise Sagan
DUTTON

At age 18, Françoise Quoirez had just failed the examinations that would have let her continue studies at the Sorbonne. To head off her parents' anger, she sat down to write a book. In three weeks, she was done. Using the pen name of Sagan, she became the youngest person ever to have a #1 bestseller, when *Hello, Sadness*, translated from the French, reached #1 before the author's 20th birthday. It tells the story of a young girl who, in her attempts to block her widowed father's remarriage, destroys her would-be stepmother and loses her own innocence.

FIRST DATE AT #1: July 3, 1955
TOTAL WEEKS AT #1: 2

Something of Value
Robert Ruark
DOUBLEDAY

The popular columnist based this novel on his experiences in Africa; it follows the fortunes of a white English boy and his native friend during the Mau Mau uprisings in Kenya. While only at #1 for two weeks, it remained in the top five for more than half a year, much to the displeasure of *Times* reviewer Orville Prescott who declared it to be the most loathsome book he had read in nearly 25 years of reviewing. Ruark, who once was an accountant for the WPA, said that "There was a time when I would go anywhere, eat airline food, use gin as a substitute for sleep, fight against the Mau Mau, chase elephants on horseback, slug athletes, enjoy being jailed, and wrestle with leopards, all for love of the newspaper business."

Peter McKenzie stood leaning against the bar in the dim cool malty-smelling taproom of the Norfolk Hotel in Nairobi and flicked his thumbnail twice against his glass. "I'll have a martini this time, please," he said to the steward. He turned toward his companion. "Pimm's is fine to cut the dust, but I need something a little sturdier after this last business. The same for you, Little John?"

"No, thanks, I'll have a martini too, please. Just what is it you call them?"

"Martini a maui mbile. American chap I had out last year thought it up. Seems they have some sort of drink called 'on the rocks' in the States, when it's just ice and double booze with no mixing. 'Martini twice on the mountain' was as close as we could come to it for Moussa's benefit. Right, Moussa?"

"Yas, Bwana. That other Bwana, he drinking very much. We call him the Bwana Ginni-Bottle here in the hotel."

Peter McKenzie was standing with John Thompson, another professional hunter, who had been second hunter with Peter on the safari from which they had just returned. John Thompson was a short, wiry, muscular blond man with bright monkey's brown eyes and a broken nose. He was Peter's best friend, and each was happy to defer to the other as second hunter on a big safari, although neither would serve as Number Two to any other hunter.

Peter was just twenty-five. He was a big man now, topping six feet. His black hair still curved down over his forehead, and a damp, white-dusty lock was visible under his tipped-back hat. His skin was burned so dark from the hot sun of the Northern Frontier that his teeth looked almost grotesque against his face. He had the strong sloping shoulders of a boxer, running smoothly into a corded column of neck. He was wearing a green short-sleeved bush jacket, faded nearly white, and green shorts. His legs, burned black as his face, were abnormally sturdy, enormously thewed, with the broad thick bands of the hard walker. Peter

FIRST DATE AT #1: November 11, 1959
TOTAL WEEKS AT #1: 19

Act One
Moss Hart

RANDOM HOUSE

The well-known playwright, New York stage director, and sometime television personality, saw his autobiography turn into a box office smash: 19 consecutive weeks at #1, and more than nine months on the list overall.

FIRST DATE AT #1: March 13, 1960
TOTAL WEEKS AT #1: 21

May This House Be Safe from Tigers
Alexander King

SIMON & SCHUSTER

In one of the rare instances where the sequel outperformed the original, volume two of the artist and author's anecdotes and reminiscences was the big hit of 1960, perhaps bolstered by King's television series, *Alex in Wonderland.*

THERE ARE certain crucial moments in life when the emotions one feels come perilously close to the mawkish, but the pain of those moments is not any the less acute because the moment itself happens to be a small or an unexalted one. I walked on, overwhelmed by a sense of sorrow and personal loss, and by the time I reached the New Amsterdam Theatre I knew that the dream of being an actor was behind me—that if I was to be a part of the only world I cared anything about, I must find some other way. And I knew now how bleak those prospects were.

As I waited for the elevator to come down, I wondered if it would not be wiser to walk out of the lobby and get the smell of the theatre out of my nostrils for good and all. But I remained standing there, watching the indicator as it marked the slow downward count of the floors. The elev[ator came down and a] young man stepped out into the lobby. H[...] one say that luck do[...] any career. There is [...] but I have seen the [...] all of our lives too [...] tion that portion of [...] able as fate itself an[...]

Would I not hav[...] stepped out of the [...] I am not suggesti[...]

[114]

ACT ONE

An Autobiography by **MOSS HART**

A RANDOM HOUSE BOOK

FIRST DATE AT #1: August 28, 1955
TOTAL WEEKS AT #1: 5

Auntie Mame
Patrick Dennis
VANGUARD

Edward Everett Tanner, writing under the name of Patrick Dennis, gave us one of the most enduring ladies of fiction. "Writing isn't hard; no harder than ditch digging," Tanner said. He began his career as a ghost writer and cherished his anonymity, but lost it with the huge success of *Mame*. *Mame* climbed slowly to #1 over four months, remained there only a month, but then spent an additional year and a half in the upper echelons of the list, finally fading away entirely after more than two years. Tanner died in 1976.

An Irreverent Escapade
AUNTIE MAME

With the patience of a class meant fifth grade.

"Oh, and where are you su[...]

"In the fifth class, but I was only nine while I was in it."

"Then you mean that you *are* precocious?"

"I beg your pardon?" I said.

"Precocious, darling. Bright for your age. Ahead of yourself in school."

"Yes," I said. "I was pre—what you said—all term long."

"Oh, I'm so glad, darling!" Auntie Mame trilled, writing something down on her pad. "We always *were* an intellectual family, although your father did everything possible to disguise the fact."

She returned to the will. "Now, your father says here that you're to be sent to *conservative* schools—he would! Tell me, was this Latin affair conservative?"

"I don't quite know what you mean," I said blushing.

"Was it dull? Tiresome? Tedious? Stuffy?"

"Yes, it was very stuffy."

"So like your father," she sighed. "By the way, I know the most divine new school that a friend of mine is starting. Coeducational and completely revolutionary. All classes are held in the nude under ultraviolet ray. Not a repression left after the first semester. This man I know is absolutely *au courant* with everything that's going on in Vienna—none of that dead-tired old Montessori system for *him*—and there's lots of nonobjective art and eurhythmics and discussion groups—no books or anything like that. How I'd love to send you there. Really give your libido a good shaking up."

I hadn't the faintest idea what she was talking about, but it sounded like a very unusual school, to say the least.

A tender, faraway look came over her face. "I just wonder," she said, "if it wouldn't be a ra-ther good idea to look into Ralph's school. Do you think you've got many repressions, dear?"

I colored painfully. "I'm afraid I don't understand a lot of the words you use, Auntie Mame."

FIRST DATE AT #1: October 2, 1955
TOTAL WEEKS AT #1: 13

Marjorie Morningstar
Herman Wouk
DOUBLEDAY

Wouk's only non-military #1 bestseller, this is an account of a beautiful "Jewish princess" from her teen years through many love affairs to her final destiny as a suburban matron with four children. The book spent nine months on the list, including three months in the top spot. Wouk told *Contemporary Authors* that he does all his writing in longhand. "I get the words down on impulse, and refine as I go in draft after draft. According to my wife—who is my agent and also types my early drafts—I revise and refine to tremendous excess. 'You can't leave a clean page alone.'"

Birthdays and Astrological Signs of #1 Authors

Some people will be annoyed at the devoting of this many pages to such a subject. Others will be annoyed because rising signs and moon locations are not included. So be it.

Louis L'Amour	3/22	Arthur Hailey	4/5
Elizabeth Chevalier	3/25	Joshua L. Liebman	4/7
Betty MacDonald	3/26	Julia Phillips	4/7
Bob Woodward	3/26	Donald F. Whitehead	4/8
Budd Schulberg	3/27	John Roy Carlson	4/9
Leo Buscaglia	3/31	David Halberstam	4/10
John Fowles	3/31	Quentin Reynolds	4/11
John Jakes	3/3	Scott Turow	4/12
Whittaker Chambers	4/1	Herbert Benson	4/14
Joan D. Vinge	4/2	Jeffrey Archer	4/15
Kitty Kelley	4/4	Thornton Wilder	4/17
William Manchester	4/4	Ernie Pyle	4/18
Robert E. Sherwood	4/4		

James Fixx	4/23	Theodore Sorensen	5/8
Vladimir Nabokov	4/23	Barbara Taylor Bradford	5/10
Elizabeth Goudge	4/24	Wayne Dyer	5/10
Ross Lockridge	4/2	Daphne du Maurier	5/13
Morris West	4/26	Katherine Anne Porter	5/15
Joseph Heller	5/1	Gayelord Hauser	5/17
James F. Byrnes	5/2	Merle Miller	5/17
George Will	5/4	Patrick Dennis	5/18
Douglas Casey	5/5	Samuel Shellabarger	5/18
Harry Golden	5/6	Richard Adams	5/19
Theodore H. White	5/6	Charles Reich	5/20
Thomas B. Costain	5/8		

continued on page 66

THE LAST HURRAH

By
EDWIN O'CONNOR

One

IT was early in August when Frank Skeffington decided — or rather, announced his decision, which actually had been arrived at some months before — to run for re-election as mayor of the city. This was a matter about which there had been public speculation for a good while: for, in fact, four years, ever since he had been inaugurated for what his opponents had fondly hoped was the last time. Since the beginning of the current year, however, the speculation had increased, not alone because the deadline was drawing nearer, but also because there were no other elections of importance coming up — the municipal elections took place in off years politically and so did not have to share the spotlight with national or state contests. Thus interest had mounted, and as it had, so had the hopes of Skeffington's opponents. For while he was admittedly among the most durable of politicians, he was just as admittedly getting older, and in recent speeches and press conferences he had expressed little interest in continuing his long political career. On one memorable occasion he had gone so far as to speak with a certain dreaminess of the joys of retirement, of the quiet time of withdrawal which would follow a lifetime spent in the service of the public.

"Far from the madding crowd," he had said, gazing at the reporters expressionlessly. "The declining years spent in solitude and contemplation. Possibly in some rustic retreat."

This hint had not been received without a measure of cynicism; one reporter from the chief opposition paper had led the questioning which followed.

"Tell us, Governor," he had said (for, as Skeffington had twice been governor of the state, the courtesy title lingered long after the office itself had been lost), "just how would you propose to adjust yourself to this rustic life? Wouldn't it be pretty quiet? What would you do?"

– 3 –

FIRST DATE AT #1: January 1, 1956
TOTAL WEEKS AT #1: 12

Andersonville
McKinley Kantor
WORLD PUBLISHING

Kantor's only trip to #1 was with his 31st book, a novel of life in and around the Andersonville prison during the Civil War, and the story of a native Georgian on whose land the prison was built. The book began a predictable decline after three months at #1, but then unexpectedly surged back to #2 for another two months. Kantor had been a reporter and a New York City policeman. A prolific writer, he lamented that "My stories have appeared in an appalling number of magazines; sublime, ridiculous, and penny-dreadful....I was well aware that the stuff I wrote had little value, except that in most cases it made entertaining narrative."

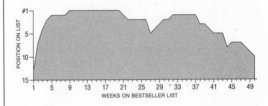

FIRST DATE AT #1: March 25, 1956
TOTAL WEEKS AT #1: 20

The Last Hurrah
Edwin O'Connor
LITTLE, BROWN

The big hit of 1956 was O'Connor's novel of Irish-American politics in an eastern city. The main character climbs high on the political ladder before facing defeat as his enemies conspire against him. (John F. Kennedy's first presidential campaign took place during the five months this book was in the #1 spot.) The author died in 1968.

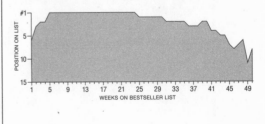

Vance Packard	5/22	Alexander P. de Seversky	6/7
Harry Emerson Fosdick	5/24	Barbara Bush	6/8
Priscilla Beaulieu Presley	5/24	Marcia Davenport	6/9
Robert Ludlum	5/25	Dean R. Koontz	6/9
Rachel Carson	5/27	Saul Bellow	6/10
John Cheever	5/27	Immanuel Velikovsky	6/10
Herman Wouk	5/27	Christina Crawford	6/11
Stephen Birmingham	5/28	William Styron	6/11
Bob Hope	5/29	Norman Dacey	6/13
John F. Kennedy	5/29	Whitley Strieber	6/13
Cornelia Otis Skinner	5/30	Erich Segal	6/16
Norman Vincent Peale	5/31	Harry Browne	6/17
Colleen McCullough	6/1	John Hersey	6/17
Peter Collier	6/2	W. L. White	6/17
Hedda Hopper	6/2	Laura Z. Hobson	6/18
Ken Follett	6/5	Sylvia Porter	6/18
Cornelius Ryan	6/5	Salman Rushdie	6/19

Morey Bernstein	6/21	Amy Wallace	7/3
Mary McCarthy	6/21	Nancy Reagan	7/6
François Sagan	6/21	David Eddings	7/7
Anne Morrow Lindbergh	6/22	Jean Kerr	7/10
Erich Maria Remarque	6/22	Bill Cosby	7/12
Richard Bach	6/23	Richard Simmons	7/12
Wil Huygen	6/23	Kenneth Clark	7/13
A. C. Kinsey	6/23	Irving Stone	7/14
Ravi Batra	6/27	A. J. Cronin	7/19
A. E. Hotchner	6/28	Ernest Hemingway	7/21
Gilda Radner	6/28	Francis Parkinson Keyes	7/21
Robert Traver	6/29	Rose Kennedy	7/22

continued on page 68

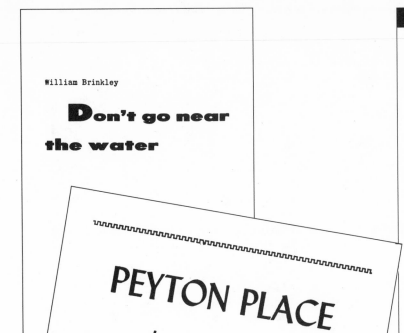

William Brinkley

Don't go near the water

PEYTON PLACE

by G—

derson. He could almost hear those same words coming from a contrite Betty on a summer night of long ago.

"I guess not," he said, and again he had the eerie feeling of having spoken those words before.

"Don't you be mad at me, doll," whispered Helen. "I'll be good to you. Just you take me back to the apartment, and I'll show you how good I can be. I'll be the best you ever had, baby, just you wait and see."

Playing at hard to get, in his turn, Rodney looked down at her and smiled. "How do I know?" he asked.

And then Helen did the most exciting thing that Rodney had ever seen in all of his twenty-one years. Right there in the car, with the lights of the drive-in shining all around them and people sitting in cars not six feet away from them on either side, Helen unbuttoned her blouse and showed him one perfect breast.

"Look at that," she said, cupping the breast with her hand, "no bra. I've got the hardest breasts you ever played with."

Rodney raced the car motor violently in his eagerness to be gone from the drive-in's parking lot. Helen did not rebutton her blouse, but leaned back in the seat, leaving her breast exposed. Every few seconds, she inhaled and sat up a little, running her hand sensuously over her bare skin, flicking her nipple with a snap of a fingernail. Rodney could not keep his eyes off her. She was like something that he had read about in what he termed "dirty books." He had never seen a woman so apparently enamored of her own body before, and to him there was something wicked, forbidden, exciting about it.

"Let me," he said, reaching for her as he sped along the highway toward Concord.

She snapped her head away from him quickly. "Look out!"

It was a scream of warning, uttered too late. When Rodney recovered himself enough to look up, the brightly lit trailer truck seemed to be right on top of him.

♦ 7 ♦

Each spring, it was the duty of Dexter Humphrey, as chairman of the Budget Committee, to act as moderator at town meeting. He took this responsibility seriously, reading each item of the

314

FIRST DATE AT #1: August 12, 1956
TOTAL WEEKS AT #1: 15

Don't Go Near the Water
William Brinkley
RANDOM HOUSE

One of the last World War Two books to reach #1, Brinkley's humorous third novel is about the Public Relations section of the navy, especially a unit based on a Pacific island called Tulara. It rose to #1 in its fourth week, where it sat for nearly four months. The author was a reporter and correspondent for *Life* magazine.

FIRST DATE AT #1: November 25, 1956
TOTAL WEEKS AT #1: 29

Peyton Place
Grace Metalious
MESSNER

If books had ratings like movies, Grace de Pepentigna Metalious's lurid story behind the seemingly placid lives in a small New England community would probably have been X-rated in its day, for its detailed accounts of adultery, incest, murder, and general nastiness. The public was clearly ready for this. The book had two long stays at #1, nearly four months apart, and was on the list for well over a year. Indeed, according to one report, this book outsold the total of all the books ever written by Fitzgerald, Hemingway, Melville, Dreiser, and James Joyce.

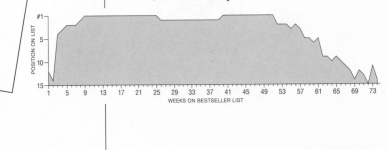

Dag Hammarskjold	7/29	Garrison Keillor	8/7
Edwin O'Connor	7/29	Adam Smith	8/10
David Reuben	7/29	Alex Haley	8/11
Robert Townsend	7/30	Danielle Steel	8/14
Milton Friedman	7/31	Bernard Baruch	8/17
James Baldwin	8/2	Vincent Bulgiosi	8/18
John Gunther	8/3	James Cozzens	8/19
P. D. James	8/3	Jacqueline Susann	8/20
Leon Uris	8/3	Robert John Donovan	8/21
Haim Ginott	8/5		

Frederick Forsyth	8/25	William Brinkley	9/10
Lloyd C. Douglas	8/27	Charles Kuralt	9/10
Nancy Friday	8/27	Franz Werfel	9/10
Michael Jackson	8/29	Jessica Mitford	9/11
Alan M. Dershowitz	9/1	Allan Bloom	9/14
Annemarie Selinko	9/1	Larry Collins	9/14
Timothy Zahn	9/1	Agatha Christie	9/15
Allen Drury	9/2	Lauren Bacall	9/16
Richard Wright	9/4	Laurence Peter	9/16
Hamilton Basso	9/5	Mary Stewart	9/17
Taylor Caldwell	9/7	Rachel Field	9/19
Elia Kazan	9/7	Mika Waltari	9/19
Henry Morton Robinson	9/7	Ladislas Farago	9/21
Grace Metalious	9/8	Stephen King	9/21
James Hilton	9/9	Rosamunde Pilcher	9/22

continued on page 72

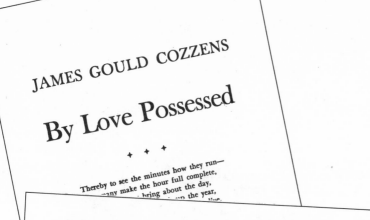

JAMES GOULD COZZENS

By Love Possessed

✦ ✦ ✦

Thereby to see the minutes how they run—
...any make the hour full complete,
...bring about the day,
...the year,

I was forced to put on his clothes. How he would laugh if he could see me now, a farcical figure with the pyjamas over my arm, hiding in a bathroom, with his wife in bed in the room next door. This was a situation that evoked screams of delight in the theatre, and I thought how very close to humour must disgust and horror always be. We laugh to stave off fear, or we are attracted because we are repulsed; in a bedroom farce it is disgust at what might happen—disgust mingled with a furtive excitement—that makes the audience scream. I wondered if Jean de Gué had foreseen this moment, or whether he had thought, as I had in the car driving to the château, that after an hour or two the game would be played out, the masquerade be over. It might be that never for an instant had he considered I would do what I had done. And yet, how definite our conversation of the preceding night, my wail at the emptiness of life, the lack of ties. What a chance for him to laugh and say, "Try mine!"

If he really intended to slip away himself and make me his scapegoat, then it clearly proved that he cared for no one at the château. The mother and the wife who loved him well counted for nothing. He did not mind what happened to them, or to any of the others: I could do with them as I pleased. Considered coldly, the masquerade was so cruel as to be inhuman. I turned off the dripping bath tap and went back to the dressing room. The elation and ease I had experienced when having dinner with the mother had changed to depression with her change of mood. Instead of dismissing the ravaged face as just another incident in a fantastic evening, I had wanted to placate her, to find the package quickly and hand it over to Charlotte. Now, with the realisation that the complaining Françoise was de Gué's wife, I wanted to placate her too: her tears distressed me. Downstairs in the salon they had been unreal to me, yet here, in the privacy of their rooms, these people were without defence, betraying me into emotion. The fact that they were unconscious victims of a practical joke was no longer funny. ...

BY THE SCAPEGOAT
DAPHNE
DU MAURIER

DOUBLEDAY & COMPANY, INC., GARDEN CITY, N.Y. 1957

FIRST DATE AT #1: March 24, 1957
TOTAL WEEKS AT #1: 14

The Scapegoat
Daphne du Maurier
DOUBLEDAY

Du Maurier was the first person to have five #1s with her story of an Englishman in France who meets a man who looks exactly like him, and is forced, against his will, to become that man and take over his roles in life. This, her 15th book, managed to interrupt a very lengthy stay at #1 by *Peyton Place* for a period of 14 weeks; then it fell swiftly while *Peyton Place* returned to the top. Du Maurier's own life took an interesting turn in the romance direction. A much older major in the Grenadier Guards piloted his motor launch past the du Maurier family home in hopes of getting a glimpse of the famous author. One thing led to another, and a few months later, du Maurier married the Major.

FIRST DATE AT #1: September 22, 1957
TOTAL WEEKS AT #1: 24

By Love Possessed
James Gould Cozzens
HARCOURT

Cozzens's only #1 book was a big one: a novel about 49 hours in the life of one man, the leading lawyer in a small town, and the many and varied kinds of love in his life. It rose to #1 in two weeks, and stayed there nearly half a year. Cozzens began the novel in 1949 with the intention of finishing it by 1952, but missed by half a decade.

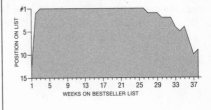

THE LIST OF LISTS

What's black and white and read and golden? *by L. J. Davis*

This is it. Playing the Palace. Numero uno, not only status-wise but historically—it was the *New York Times* that published the first weekly best-seller list, on Sunday, October 9, 1942. There are other lists: the one compiled by the *Los Angeles Times* is not sniffed at; an appearance there may ignite the attention of a dozing film magnate. And the list in *Publishers Weekly* gets read by the trade. But the *Times* . . . a mention even near the bottom of the list is regarded as a force equal to that of a full-page ad in the *Book Review*. It also provides a priceless opportunity to witness that most cherished (and lucrative) of publishing phenomena, the Self-Fulfilling Prophecy. An appearance on the list is likely to inspire one's publisher to recommend an infusion of money into one's book's ad budget, and to encourage booksellers to erect displays—actions taken, in other words, so best sellers might best sell.

It is a fact that people buy best-selling fiction because it happens to be best-selling. Once an author has nailed his flag to the top of the greasy pole, it is likely to spank smartly in the breeze for quite a little while. We are talking hard-bound novels here—paperbacks have their own list, and appearances by collections of short stories, while not unheard of (Welty, Bradbury, Cheever), are rare. It doesn't take much for a novel to make the list—maybe 30,000 copies during a slow summer. The top of the heap is another matter. By mid-January of this year, there were 885,000 copies of *The Talisman* in print, perhaps for use as doorstops.

Herewith, a noble attempt to identify a few books that are actually worth reading. Nobody knows if having one's book singled out as an "editors' choice" does any good beyond confirming what one already knew. But bear this in mind: it is not unheard of to discover no fewer than two books by *Times* staffers here. This week, of particular interest, find books by Alan Riding (the paper's bureau chief in Brazil) and Leonard Silk (its economics columnist).

Jan. 13, 1985

THE NEW YORK TIMES BOOK REVIEW

Best Sellers

Fiction

This Week		Last Week	Weeks On List
1	THE TALISMAN, by Stephen King and Peter Straub. (Viking, $18.95.) Two parallel worlds and a young boy who can travel between them.	1	12
2	THE SICILIAN, by Mario Puzo. (Linden Press/Simon & Schuster, $17.95.) A fictionalized life of Salvatore Giuliano, the Sicilian bandit-hero of the 1940's.	2	9
3	NUTCRACKER, by E. T. A. Hoffmann. (Crown, $19.95.) A new translation of the popular Christmas story, with 100 color illustrations by Maurice Sendak.	6	7
4	LOVE AND WAR, by John Jakes. (Harcourt Brace Jovanovich, $19.95.) The Civil War wages in this saga of a Pennsylvania family and a South Carolina family, begun in "North and South."	3	13
5	THE LIFE AND HARD TIMES OF HEIDI ABROMOWITZ, by Joan Rivers. (Delacorte, $8.95.) The comedienne tells the "true story" of her high school "friend," a notorious tramp.	4	
6	SO LONG, AND THANKS FOR ALL THE FISH, by Douglas Adams. (Harmony, $12.95.) Suddenly returned to Earth, the hero of the "Hitchhiker's Trilogy" science fantasy is confronted with new riddles to answer.	5	8
7	THE FOURTH PROTOCOL, by Frederick Forsyth. (Viking, $17.95.) A London jewel robbery leads to plots and counterplots behind the Iron Curtain.	7	22
8	JITTERBUG PERFUME, by Tom Robbins. (Bantam, $15.95.) Reflections on the olfactory senses and the tyranny of growing old, presented in an idiosyncratic fictional style.	13	
9	LINCOLN, by Gore Vidal. (Random House, $19.95.) Fictionalized account of the Civil War Presidency.	9	10
10	". . . AND LADIES OF THE CLUB," by Helen Hooven Santmyer. (Putnam, $19.95.) Life in an Ohio town, 1868 to 1932.	8	
11	GOD KNOWS, by Joseph Heller. (Knopf, $16.95.) King David describes his life in comic and anachronistic style.	10	14
12	ILLUSIONS OF LOVE, by Cynthia Freeman. (Putnam, $15.95.) A romantic triangle that spans a quarter of a century, from an Italian village to Manhattan to San Francisco.	14	7
13	STRONG MEDICINE, by Arthur Hailey. (Doubleday, $16.95.) A strong woman rises in the pharmaceutical industry.	11	16
14	LIFE ITS OWNSELF, by Dan Jenkins. (Simon & Schuster, $15.95.) The adventures of a Giants halfback turned television commentator.	12	12
15	THE BUTTER BATTLE BOOK, by Dr. Seuss. (Random House, $6.95.) A warning about the nuclear arms race in words and pictures.	15	20

And Bear in Mind

Editors' choices of other recent books of particular interest

AUGUST STRINDBERG, by Olof Lagercrantz. (Farrar, Straus & Giroux, $22.50.) Writing before Freud was published, Strindberg wanted to offer what Olof Lagercrantz's fascinating biography calls "the pure naked truth." Thus he, in his modernity, influenced many playwrights of our time, from O'Neill to Edward Albee.

COLLECTED POEMS 1947-1980, by Allen Ginsberg. (Harper & Row, $27.50.) The work of a poet who in his early years seemed a hipster, a poète maudit on his way to becoming a martyred legend but who, by confession, commitment and humor, survives impressively.

DISTANT NEIGHBORS: A Portrait of the Mexicans, by Alan Riding. (Knopf, $18.95.) Those who wish to understand the "many Mexicos" of wealth and poverty, of authoritarianism and democracy, of hideous TV serials and the art of Diego Rivera might well begin with this book by a correspondent for The Times.

ECONOMICS OF THE REAL WORLD, by Leonard Silk. (Simon & Schuster, $16.95.) The economics columnist for The Times is lively and informative on the interplay between politics and economics.

EQUAL DISTANCE, by Brad Leithauser. (Knopf, $17.95.) This first novel, by a young poet who lived in Japan for several years, concerns three Americans in Japan. It is filled with doubt, icy regret and a stubborn, almost illicit joy — all the right things.

HITLER AND THE FINAL SOLUTION, by Gerald Fleming. (University of California, $15.95.) A British scholar provides evidence to refute a theory advanced in recent years—that Hitler neither wished nor ordered the extermination of the Jews.

THOMAS MORE, by Richard Marius. (Knopf, $22.95.) Not an easy book to read but a very rewarding one about the British statesman who, in his conflict with Henry VIII, fought the divine right of kings—and in doing so, brought about his own beheading.

Nonfiction

This Week		Last Week	Weeks On List
1	IACOCCA: An Autobiography, by Lee Iacocca with William Novak. (Bantam, $17.95.) The rise of the automobile executive from immigrants' son to top jobs at Ford and Chrysler.	1	11
2	LOVING EACH OTHER, by Leo Buscaglia. (Slack/Holt, Rinehart & Winston, $12.95.) Suggestions for "setting our priorities right in order to enjoy life to the fullest."	3	20
3	PIECES OF MY MIND, by Andrew A. Rooney. (Atheneum, $12.95.) More essays by the journalist and television commentator.	2	13
4	"THE GOOD WAR," by Studs Terkel. (Pantheon, $18.95.) World War II as remembered by men and women who lived through it.	4	13
5	MOSES THE KITTEN, by James Herriot. (St. Martin's, $9.95.) A waif kitten is adopted by a pig; illustrated.	7	14
6	THE BRIDGE ACROSS FOREVER, by Richard Bach. (Morrow, $16.95.) The author of "Jonathan Livingston Seagull" recounts his search for a true love.	8	19
7*	DR. BURNS' PRESCRIPTION FOR HAPPINESS, by George Burns. (Putnam, $11.95.) The octogenarian comedian provides a regimen of laughs.	6	10
8	HEY, WAIT A MINUTE, I WROTE A BOOK! by John Madden with Dave Anderson. (Villard Books, $14.95.) An anecdotal autobiography of the popular television sports announcer.	5	17
9	THE BRAIN, by Richard M. Restak. (Bantam, $24.95.) A companion volume to the PBS television series.	12	13
10	HERITAGE, by Abba Eban. (Summit, $35.) An account of Jewish history by the Israeli diplomat who hosted the PBS show of the same name.	11	112
11	A LIGHT IN THE ATTIC, by Shel Silverstein. (Harper & Row, $12.95.) Light verse and drawings by the author.	9	
12	SON OF THE MORNING STAR, by Evan S. Connell. (North Point Press, $20.) A biography of George Armstrong Custer that is also a history of the Plains Indian wars.	13	5
13*	THE WEAKER VESSEL, by Antonia Fraser. (Knopf, $19.95.) Women's lot in 17th-century England.	14	13
14	ELVIS IS DEAD AND I DON'T FEEL SO GOOD MYSELF, by Lewis Grizzard. (Peachtree Publishers, $11.95.) Humorous observations on music, morals, food, fashion and other contemporary matters.	10	8
15	ONE WRITER'S BEGINNINGS, by Eudora Welty. (Harvard, $10.) The novelist recalls her childhood in Mississippi.	15	42

Advice, How-to and Miscellaneous

This Week		Last Week	Weeks On List
1	WHAT THEY DON'T TEACH YOU AT HARVARD BUSINESS SCHOOL, by Mark H. McCormack. (Bantam, $15.95.) Notes and tips of a "street-smart executive."	1	17
2	WOMEN COMING OF AGE, by Jane Fonda with Mignon McCarthy. (Simon & Schuster, $19.95.) Advice for middle-aged women on fitness, health and nutrition.		
3	CHEF PAUL PRUDHOMME'S LOUISIANA KITCHEN, by Paul Prudhomme. (Morrow, $19.95.) Recipes for Cajun and Creole cooking by a New Orleans chef.	5	13
4	EAT TO WIN, by Robert Haas. (Rawson, $14.95.) A regimen for participants in sports and fitness activities.		24
5	NOTHING DOWN, by Robert G. Allen. (Simon & Schuster, $16.95.) How to buy real estate with little or no money, revised edition of a 1980 book.		

The listings above are based on computer-processed sales figures from 2,000 bookstores in every region of the United States, statistically adjusted to represent sales in all bookstores. In Advice and How-to, five titles are listed because, beyond that point, sales in this category are not generally large enough to make a longer list statistically reliable.

*An asterisk before a book's title indicates that its sales are weighted to reflect the bookselling industry nationally, are barely distinguishable from those of the book above.

There were 1.1 million copies of Lee Iacocca's autobiography in print when this list appeared, which would seem to prove that if one wants to write a best seller, one should leave the writing to someone else. *Iacocca* isn't even a real ghosted autobiography; it is a series of occasionally entertaining, selectively sanitized anecdotes and after-dinner speeches in which, with astonishing vigor, the chairman of Chrysler does not run for president of the United States.

Once a best seller has been written—or, in the cases of Iacocca and John Madden, not written—how is it found, counted, *made*? This was long a source of mystery. Actually, compiling the list is simplicity itself: each week, some 2,000 bookstores, carefully selected in an effort to achieve balance in terms of location and size, receive three lists of hard-cover contenders: two of thirty-six each (fiction and nonfiction), one of twelve ("Advice, How-to and Miscellaneous"). Each bookseller is asked to arrange the week's picks in order of sales, adding any unlisted shooting stars that have appeared in his sales figures. At an appointed moment, the *Times* calls and asks for the tally. . .

. . . and then, it "statistically adjusts" its findings—a process that has reduced William Peter Blatty, for one, to a state bordering on incoherence. In August 1983, Blatty sued the *Times* when his novel *Legion* failed to make the list in sufficiently gratifying fashion—this despite its breathless prose and (more important) mega-big (he believed) sales. The *Book Review*'s adjustment, called weighting, works this way: if there are ten bookstores in a region, and the *Times* is in touch with three of them, each book sold by these stores is assigned a value of three and one third. Presumably, this gives a fairly reliable picture of national sales while winnowing out purely local phenomena. All this numbers-crunching is necessary because publishers gleefully release some sales figures while guarding others as though they were the Koh-i-noor. Which leads, quickly and neatly, to this question: If the publishers don't want to play, and there are authors who think the game is rigged, why not drop the whole thing?

FIRST DATE AT #1: March 9, 1958
TOTAL WEEKS AT #1: 29

Anatomy of a Murder
Robert Traver
St. Martin's

Michigan Supreme Court Justice John Donaldson Voelker adopted the name Robert Traver to write this procedural novel about a murder and the subsequent trial of the murderer, set in the upper peninsula of Michigan. The book was a huge success, rising to #1 in its second month on the list, and remaining there for more than half a year before beginning a slow decline. This was Voelker's fourth book. Later he would write a book on his hobby, *Anatomy of a Fisherman.*

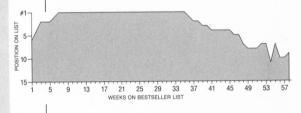

FIRST DATE AT #1: September 28, 1958
TOTAL WEEKS AT #1: 7

Lolita
Vladimir Nabokov
Putnam

Lolita, light of my life, fire of my loins, extremely controversial novel of Humbert Humbert's love affair with a 12-year-old nymphet. The book was rejected as obscene by four American publishers and was issued by Olympia in France, best known for its sexually explicit books. It was promptly banned in France, but when a copy was brought to America U.S. Customs agents unexpectedly found it unobjectionable. It was promptly brought out by the very respectable people of Putnam and soon rose to #1. Nabokov (pronounced na-BOAK-off), who once translated *Alice in Wonderland* from English into Russian, was as surprised as anyone.

LIBRA

Walter Lippmann	9/23	James Clavell	10/10
Louis Auchincloss	9/27	Eleanor Roosevelt	10/11
Catherine Marshall	9/27	Marion Hargrove	10/13
Truman Capote	9/30	Dwight D. Eisenhower	10/14
Fletcher Knebel	10/1	Bernie S. Siegel	10/14
Graham Greene	10/2	Sumner Welles	10/14
James Herriot	10/3	John Galbraith	10/15
Gore Vidal	10/3	Lee Iacocca	10/15
Anne Rice	10/4	Mario Puzo	10/15
Frederic Morton	10/5	Arthur Schlesinger	10/15
Thor Heyerdahl	10/6	Kathleen Winsor	10/16
Helen MacInnes	10/7	Robert C. Atkins	10/17
Michael Korda	10/8	John le Carré	10/19
Walter Lord	10/8		

SCORPIVS

Moss Hart	10/24	Carl Sagan	11/9
Harry Overstreet	10/25	John P. Marquand	11/10
Thomas Chastain	10/27	David Stockman	11/10
H. R. Haldeman	10/27	Howard Fast	11/11
Bill Mauldin	10/29	Van Wyck Mason	11/11
Robert H. Caro	10/30	Kurt Vonnegut	11/11
Roger Kahn	10/31	Alexander King	11/13
Dan Rather	10/31	P. J. O'Rourke	11/14
Scholem Asch	11/1	Harrison Salisbury	11/14
Martin Cruz Smith	11/3	Alistair Cooke	11/20
Tom Peters	11/7	Jim Bishop	11/21
Katherine Hepburn	11/8		

continued on page 74

THOR HEYERDAHL
Author of KON-TIKI

Aku-Aku

The Secret of Easter Island

with 62 photographs in full color

I HAD NO *aku-aku*.

Nor did I know what an *aku-aku* was, so I could hardly have used one if I had had it.

Every sensible person on Easter Island has an *aku-aku*. I too got one there, but at the moment I was organizing a voyage to that very place, so I did not possess one. Perhaps that was why arranging the journey was so difficult. Getting home again was much easier.

Easter Island is the loneliest inhabited place in the world. The nearest solid land the islanders can see is above, in the firmament, the moon and the planets. They have to travel farther than any other people to see that there really is land yet closer. Therefore, living nearest the stars, they know more names of stars than of towns and countries in our own world.

On this remote island, east of the sun and west of the moon, mankind once had one of its most curious ideas. No one knows who had it, and no one knows why. For it happened before Columbus led white

FIRST DATE AT #1: October 19, 1958
TOTAL WEEKS AT #1: 2

Aku-Aku
Thor Heyerdahl
RAND MCNALLY

This adventure of the Norwegian explorer was not nearly as popular as his first, *Kon-Tiki,* but it still was Rand McNally's second and last #1 bestseller. This account of an expedition to Easter Island, in attempt to unlock the secrets of the huge sculptures there did, however, remain afloat in the #2 spot for nearly four months before sinking rapidly. Heyerdahl's book about a third adventure, floating in a raft called Ra from Egypt to the Caribbean, was popular but never reached #1.

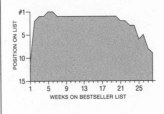

FIRST DATE AT #1: November 16, 1958
TOTAL WEEKS AT #1: 26

Doctor Zhivago
Boris Pasternak
PANTHEON

The second Russian-born #1 author in two months, Pasternak spent half a year atop the list with his only novel—the saga, set against the background of the Russian revolution, of a physician and poet who is married to one woman but loves another. A Russian publisher rejected the manuscript in 1956 with a 50-page letter of explanation detailing how the novel's spirit failed to accept the socialist revolution and thus served improper political aims. The manuscript was smuggled out, published first in Italy, and then in the U.S.

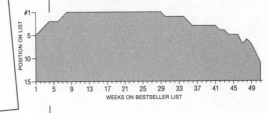

Charles Berlitz	11/22	Joe McGinnis	12/9
Dale Carnegie	11/24	Edward I. Koch	12/12
Helen Hooven Santmeyer	11/25	Ralph Martin	12/12
James Jones	11/26	Lillian Smith	12/12
Gail Sheehy	11/27	Betty Smith	12/15
Richard Tregaskis	11/28	William Bernard Ziff	12/20
Winston Churchill	11/30	Phil Donahue	12/21
Joseph Lash	12/2	Jane Fonda	12/21
Kenneth Roberts	12/8	Donald T. Regan	12/21

Robert Bly	12/23	Kathryn Hulme	1/6
Mary Higgins Clark	12/24	Peter Blatty	1/7
Frederic Wakeman	12/26	Victor Lasky	1/7
Louis Bromfield	12/27	Stephen Hawking	1/8
Sam Levenson	12/28	Alexandra Ripley	1/8
Robert Ruark	12/29	Judith Krantz	1/9
Catherine Drinker Bowen	1/1	Elmer Holmes Davis	1/13
J. Edgar Hoover	1/1	C. David Heymann	1/14
J. D. Salinger	1/1	Andrew A. Rooney	1/14
J. R. R. Tolkein	1/3	Maurice Herzog	1/15
Umberto Eco	1/5	J	1/15
E. L. Doctorow	1/6	Gwenthalyn Graham	1/18

continued on page 76

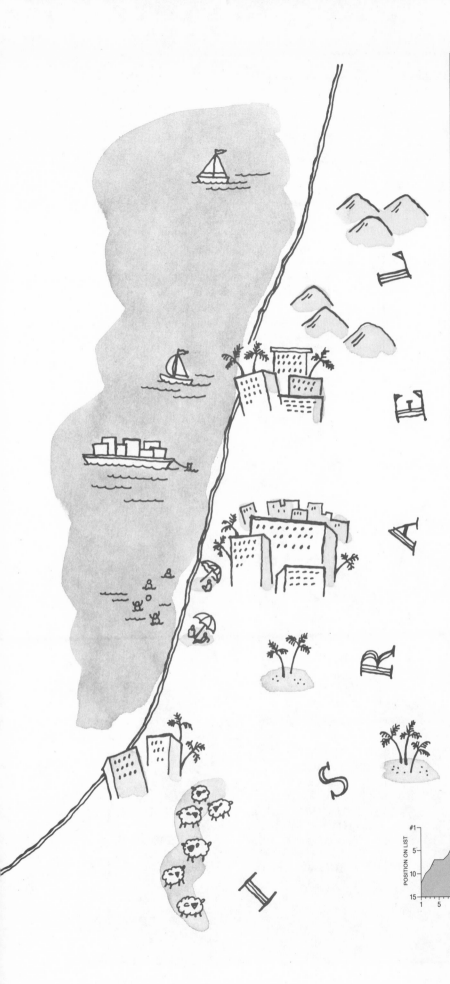

FIRST DATE AT #1: April 12, 1959
TOTAL WEEKS AT #1: 9

Mine Enemy Grows Older
Alexander King
SIMON & SCHUSTER

The first King to write #1 bestsellers tells of his life as a famous artist in the '20s, one of the first editors of *Life* magazine, and a victor over drug addiction. He was one of the first authors to promote himself and his book vigorously on television, both through regular appearances on the Jack Paar show and later with his own program, *Alex in Wonderland.*

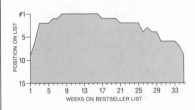

FIRST DATE AT #1: May 17, 1959
TOTAL WEEKS AT #1: 20

Exodus
Leon Uris
DOUBLEDAY

The first of Uris's three #1 bestsellers, *Exodus* tells the story of European Jews from the end of the nineteenth century to the establishment of the state of Israel. The central characters are a Palestinian agent of an illegal immigration organization and an American nurse. Uris reported that he read more than 300 books on Israel, traveled 12,000 miles in that country, and interviewed 1,200 people in the course of writing *Exodus.* The book reached #1 in its eighth month, but everyone was not thrilled. Critic Anthony Boucher wrote that Uris is "flagrantly unable to construct a plot, a character, a novel or a sentence in the English language."

Joy Adamson	1/20	Louis Nizer	2/6
George Burns	1/20	Sinclair Lewis	2/7
Fulton Oursler	1/22	Gay Talese	2/7
Desmond Morris	1/24	Alex Comfort	2/10
Somerset Maugham	1/25	Boris Pasternak	2/11
Douglas MacArthur	1/26	Sidney Sheldon	2/11
Robert Crichton	1/29	Elliot Paul	2/13
Germaine Greer	1/29	Chuck Yeager	2/13
Tallulah Bankhead	1/31	Carl Bernstein	2/14
Norman Mailer	1/31	Chaim Potok	2/17
John O'Hara	1/31	Margaret Truman	2/17
James Michener	2/3	Jean M. Auel	2/18
MacKinlay Kantor	2/4	Wendell L. Willkie	2/18
David Wallechinsky	2/5		

Erma Bombeck	2/21	Dr. Seuss	3/2
William Shirer	2/23	Tom Wolfe	3/2
Mark Lane	2/24	Ben Ames Williams	3/7
Irwin Shaw	2/27	Gene Fowler	3/8
John Steinbeck	2/27	Frank B. Gilbreth, Jr.	3/17
Dee Brown	2/28	Herman Tarnower	3/18
David Niven	3/1	John Updike	3/18
Judith Rossner	3/1	Philip Roth	3/19
John Irving	3/2	Irving Wallace	3/9

The town's lone Jew

WHEN he opens the store in the morning he may not know it, but the folks automatically identify him with Jeremiah, Isaiah, Amos, and the Second Coming, and all of this imposes a tremendous obligation on our "lone Jew" in a small Southern town.

When the Baptist Sunday School teacher is puzzled by some involved Biblical problem he immediately runs over to Goldstein's to get the information, right from the original source, as it were, and usually poor Goldstein hasn't the faintest idea what the fellow is talking about.

Recently I came into a small town to address a Lions Club, and as usual my gracious hosts remembered not to serve me the ham which was on the menu for the day. Instead they brought me a chicken platter, which in their extreme generosity, they had prepared in pure country butter.

During the dinner, my host, the leading citizen of the town, told me that he had been anxiously awaiting my coming: "I asked Mr. Goldstein, a f-i-n-e Jewish citizen in our town, what happened to the Ark of the Covenant, and he told me to ask you when you came here to speak."

As I discussed the Ark with my host, I thought of poor Gold-

For 2¢ Plain

by Harry Golden
Author of "Only In America"
FOREWORD BY CARL SANDBURG

FIRST DATE AT #1: June 14, 1959
TOTAL WEEKS AT #1: 17

The Status Seekers
Vance Packard
MCKAY

Packard's second #1 bestseller was his most popular, arriving at #1 two years after his first and a year before his last. A social science report summarizing studies on the class structure of American society, it emphasizes the importance of education in upward mobility. James Thurber's *The Years With Ross* was #2 for much of this period, but it never reached #1.

FIRST DATE AT #1: September 13, 1959
TOTAL WEEKS AT #1: 3

For 2¢ Plain
Harry Golden
WORLD

Golden's second #1 collection of folksy wisdom from his newspaper, reached #1 just a year after his first visit there, and at a time when *Only in America* was still on the list: the first time the same author had two #1 books on the list at the same time. His second book only lasted about 10% as long as the first in the top spot.

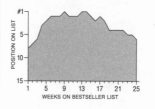

FIRST DATE AT #1: August 7, 1960
TOTAL WEEKS AT #1: 13

Born Free

Joy Adamson

PANTHEON

The story of a family in Kenya who raise an orphaned lion cub and, when it becomes necessary to free the fully grown lion, must attempt to teach it how to hunt and kill game. The Czech-born naturalist's first book was #1 throughout the entire Kennedy vs. Nixon presidential campaign and election. The two sequels, *Living Free* and *Forever Free*, made the list, but were never #1. In 1980, Adamson was murdered by a former employee.

FIRST DATE AT #1: November 6, 1960
TOTAL WEEKS AT #1: 4

The Waste Makers

Vance Packard

McKAY

Packard's third and last visit to #1 came with his look at a culture which had come to value consumption for consumption's sake and consider waste a virtue. After six months in the top three, it fell very quickly.

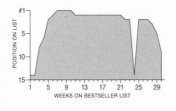

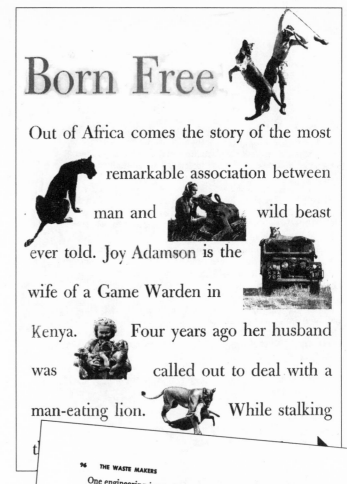

Born Free

Out of Africa comes the story of the most remarkable association between man and wild beast ever told. Joy Adamson is the wife of a Game Warden in Kenya. Four years ago her husband was called out to deal with a man-eating lion. While stalking t...

96   THE WASTE MAKERS

One engineering journal carried the charge in 1959 that engineers were falling down on the job because little was being achieved in prolonging the life of engines and improving their thermal efficiency. At least, however, the engineers were not charged with building engines for shorter life spans than formerly.

Laurence Crooks, the chief automotive expert at Consumers Union, has concluded that today's engines are "very good." However, his comments became scathing when he talked about the trend of automobile design as a whole. His auto-testing experience has convinced him that "the quality on the whole has been going downhill. . . . Stuff keeps falling off."

Mr. Crooks spoke nostalgically of the 1941 Chevrolet as a motorcar that really had built-in quality and sensible proportions. To cite another example, he said that few cars today were as solidly and sensibly built as the postwar Hudsons. And the 1952 Chevrolet is a car he remembered with fondness. He felt that the 1959 Chevrolet was no match for the 1956 model. Speaking of the quality of cars in general, he told me in 1959: "Cars were better built five years ago for the state of the technology existing at the time than they are today. The cars then were more honestly built."

The bodywork of motorcars and their structural rigidity were not as good as they had been a decade ago, he felt. And this widespread lack of structural rigidity had played a major role in promoting "creative obsolescence." Nothing makes a car seem old faster than rattles. And motorcars produced in recent years have tended to develop rattles faster than they did a decade earlier. Further, he said, "the rattling gets worse as the car grows older. With the vogue for hardtops—into which less structural stiffness can be built—this characteristic is getting worse." In 1959, *The Wall Street Journal* took note of all the complaints about late-model cars by conducting a survey. It quoted the owner of an automobile repair shop in Detroit as

FIRST DATE AT #1: October 4, 1959
TOTAL WEEKS AT #1: 30

Advise and Consent
Allen Drury
DOUBLEDAY

Had it not been for Michener's *Hawaii,* Drury's political novel might well have been the longest-running #1 fiction book ever. As it was, it spent more than seven months at #1, and a year at #2. It centers on the president's nominee for secretary of state, his appearance before a senate committee for confirmation, and the opposition he faces from one elderly senator. Drury wrote the first few chapters seven years earlier, and from time to time would take them out and say, "I really ought to do something with this.... I finally made up my mind that I certainly wasn't getting any younger, and that if I wanted ever to get this thing done, I was going to have to get busy and do it."

FIRST DATE AT #1: January 17, 1960
TOTAL WEEKS AT #1: 48

Hawaii
James Michener
RANDOM HOUSE

"I have only one bit of advice to the beginning writer," said the all-time king of #1 bestsellers: "Be sure your novel is read by Rodgers and Hammerstein." It was the royalties from the musical *South Pacific,* adapted from Michener's third book (the first two dealt with teaching social studies in the public schools) that enabled him, at the age of 40, to quit his job at Macmillan, and write the most successful of his nine #1 bestsellers. His huge historical novel followed the original settlers of Hawaii: people from Polynesia, the American missionaries, the Japanese, and the Chinese. The book had six different appearances at #1, ranging from one week to twelve, and, due to the upstart Mr. Schwarz-Bart, just missed out on being the only fiction book ever to spend a year at the top of the *Times* list.

WEEKS ON BESTSELLER LIST

FIRST DATE AT #1: December 4, 1960
TOTAL WEEKS AT #1: 39

The Rise and Fall of the Third Reich

William Shirer

SIMON & SCHUSTER

One of the few positive aspects of the McCarthy era blacklistings was that the blacklisted reporter, Shirer, had five years to do the research for this book. The blockbuster of 1961, it offered a detailed account of Hitler's rise to and fall from power. Following a fast climb to #1, it remained there for nine months, with only a one week hiatus for a new version of the Bible.

FIRST DATE AT #1: May 28, 1961
TOTAL WEEKS AT #1: 1

The New English Bible

OXFORD UNIVERSITY PRESS

Like the Revised Standard Version Bible a decade earlier, this edition of the New Testament in modern colloquial English only managed one week at #1, edging Adolph Hitler and colleagues briefly out of a long span at the top. A few disgruntled letter writers questioned the *Times's* decision to include the Bible on its nonfiction list.

THE FIRST PARAGRAPH OF THE OLD TESTAMENT:

{King James Version}

THE FIRST BOOK OF MOSES, CALLED

GENESIS

IN the beginning God created the heaven and the earth. And the earth was without form, and void; and darkness was upon the face of the deep. And the Spirit of God moved upon the face of the waters.

And God said, Let there by light; and there was light.

And God saw the light, that it was good; and God divided the light from the darkness.

And God called the light Day, and the darkness he called Night. And the evening and morning were the first day.

{New English Bible}

GENESIS

The creation of the world

IN THE BEGINNING OF CREATION, when God made heaven and earth, the earth was without form and void, with darkness over the face of the abyss, and a mighty wind that swept over the surface of the waters. God said, "Let there be light," and there was light; and God saw that the light was good, and he separated light from darkness. He called the light day, and the darkness night. So evening came, and morning came, the first day.

THE OPENING OF THE SERMON ON THE MOUNT:

{King James Version}

THE GOSPEL ACCORDING TO

SAINT MATTHEW

And seeing the multitudes, he went up into a mountain; and when he was set, his disciples came unto him;

And he opened his mouth, and taught them, saying,

Blessed are the poor in spirit; for theirs is the kingdom of heaven.

Blessed are they that mourn; for they shall be comforted.

{New English Bible}

MATTHEW

When he saw the crowds he went up the hill. There he took his seat and when his disciples had gathered round him he began to address them. And this is the teaching he gave:

"How blest are those who know their need of God; the kingdom of Heaven is theirs.

How blest are the sorrowful; they shall find consolation."

grandes novelistas

IRVING STONE

LA AGONÍA Y EL ÉXTASIS

EMECÉ

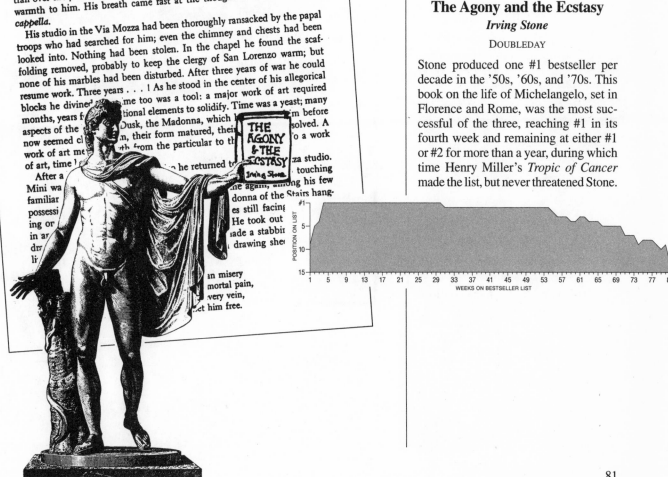

558   THE WAR

On a mid-November day he heard some[...]
clear. Gazing downward from the bell tower,
in a huge fur coat, hands cupped to his mo[...]
"Michelangelo, come down!"
He took the circular wooden stairs thre[...]
saw Spina's long narrow eyes gleaming.
"The Pope has pardoned you. He sent word through Prior Figiovanni
that if you were found you were to be treated kindly, your pension restored,
and the house by San Lorenzo . . ."
" . . . why?"
"The Holy Father wants you to return to work in the sacristy."
While Michelangelo gathered his things Spina surveyed the tower.
"It's freezing up here. What did you use to keep warm?"
"Indignation," said Michelangelo. "Best fuel I know. Never burns out."
As he walked through the streets in the late autumn sun he let his fingers
trail over the *pietra serena* blocks of the houses; slowly they imparted their
warmth to him. His breath came fast at the thought of returning to the
cappella.
His studio in the Via Mozza had been thoroughly ransacked by the papal
troops who had searched for him; even the chimney and chests had been
looked into. Nothing had been stolen. In the chapel he found the scaf-
folding removed, probably to keep the clergy of San Lorenzo warm; but
none of his marbles had been disturbed. After three years of war he could
resume work. Three years . . . ! As he stood in the center of his allegorical
blocks he divine[...] me too was a tool: a major work of art required
months, years f[...] tional elements to solidify. Time was a yeast; many
aspects of the [...] Dusk, the Madonna, which [...] m before
now seemed cl[...] n, their form matured, their [...] solved. A
work of art me[...] th from the particular to t[...] o a work
of art, time [...] za studio.
After a [...] he returned to [...] touching
Mini wa[...] [...]e again, [...]ong his few
familiar[...] donna of the Stairs hang-
possessi[...] es still facing
ing or[...] He took out
in ar[...] [...]ade a stabbin[...]
dr[...] drawing she[...]
li[...]
[...]an misery
[...]mortal pain,
[...] very vein,
[...]t him free.

FIRST DATE AT #1: March 26, 1961
TOTAL WEEKS AT #1: 4

The Last of the Just
André Schwarz-Bart
ATHENEUM

The only hyphenated author ever to
make #1, Schwarz-Bart quit his French
factory job in order to write this book.
The story follows 36 generations of the
Levy family, Jews who suffered a po-
grom in England in 1185, and the gas
chambers of Auschwitz 760 years later.
The book reached #1 for four weeks in
the middle of Michener's run, just long
enough to keep *Hawaii* from being the
only fiction book at #1 for a year.

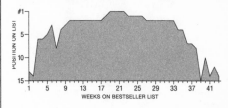

FIRST DATE AT #1: April 23, 1961
TOTAL WEEKS AT #1: 27

The Agony and the Ecstasy
Irving Stone
DOUBLEDAY

Stone produced one #1 bestseller per
decade in the '50s, '60s, and '70s. This
book on the life of Michelangelo, set in
Florence and Rome, was the most successful of the three, reaching #1 in its
fourth week and remaining at either #1
or #2 for more than a year, during which
time Henry Miller's *Tropic of Cancer*
made the list, but never threatened Stone.

FIRST DATE AT #1: September 10, 1961
TOTAL WEEKS AT #1: 20

The Making of the President—1960

Theodore H. White

ATHENEUM

The country was fascinated by its new young president, and by the process that elected him. White's day-by-day account of the Kennedy-Nixon campaign appeared less than six months after the Kennedy inaugural, and was the #1 bestseller for nearly five months. It was also the first of nine #1 bestsellers by or about members of the Kennedy family.

FIRST DATE AT #1: January 21, 1962
TOTAL WEEKS AT #1: 9

My Life in Court

Louis B. Nizer

DOUBLEDAY

The famous trial lawyer's retelling of some of his most famous cases became the first #1 nonfiction book whose time on the list was interrupted by a newspaper strike—although its #1 status was almost certainly not affected.

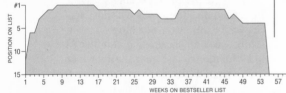

FIRST DATE AT #1: March 25, 1962
TOTAL WEEKS AT #1: 13

Calories Don't Count

Herman Taller

SIMON & SCHUSTER

The first diet book ever to make #1 on the *Times* list, Dr. Taller's much criticized, highly controversial book spent the entire spring of 1962 at the top of the list, following a four-month ascent.

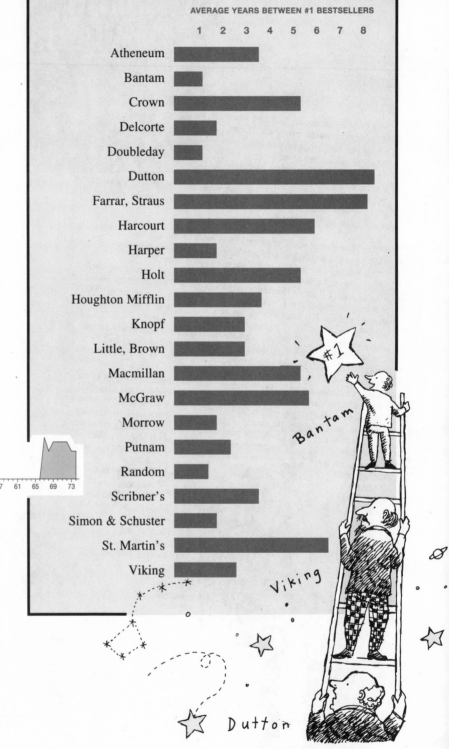

Average Number of Years Between #1 Bestsellers

Bantam, Random House, and Doubleday each averaged less than one year between bestsellers. Dutton had five #1 books in 38 years, and averages more than seven years.

AVERAGE YEARS BETWEEN #1 BESTSELLERS

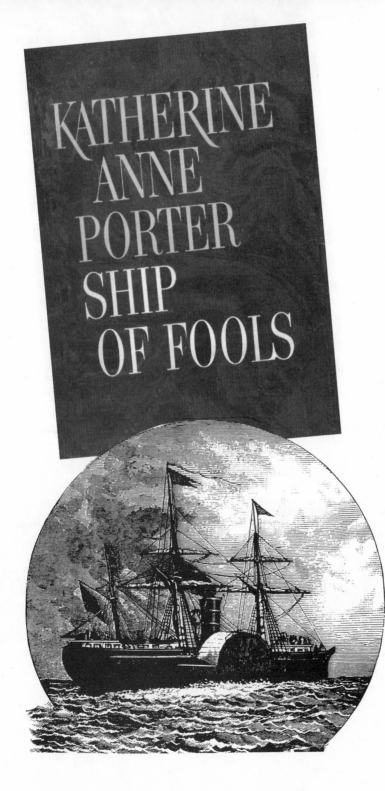

FIRST DATE AT #1: October 29, 1961
TOTAL WEEKS AT #1: 25

Franny and Zooey

J. D. Salinger

LITTLE, BROWN

Catcher in the Rye came close, but never made #1. Salinger's third book, short stories and vignettes of life in the Glass family didn't have James Jones and Herman Wouk to contend with, and so spent nearly half a year as the #1 bestseller. The now reclusive Salinger once worked as an entertainer on a Caribbean cruise ship.

FIRST DATE AT #1: April 29, 1962
TOTAL WEEKS AT #1: 26

Ship of Fools

Katherine Anne Porter

LITTLE, BROWN

Porter's 15th book justified its advance publicity by rising to #1 in its third week and remaining there for half a year. It is the story of a German passenger freighter on a four-week journey from Mexico to Germany in 1931, and the interplay among the disparate passengers. Porter told the *Paris Review,* "I practiced writing in every possible way that I could. . . . This has been the intact line of my life which directs my actions, determines my point of view, profoundly affects my character and personality, my social beliefs and economic status and the kind of friendships I form. . . . I made no attempt to publish anything until I was thirty, but I have written and destroyed manuscripts quite literally by the trunkful. . . . Yet for this vocation I was and am willing to live and die, and I consider very few other things of the slightest importance." *Ship of Fools* came 41 years after Porter's first published book.

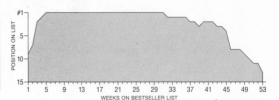

FIRST DATE AT #1: June 24, 1962
TOTAL WEEKS AT #1: 16

The Rothschilds

Frederic Morton

ATHENEUM

Morton focused more on the people and their personal lives than on the details of how the great family fortune was won and employed. It was the hot "summer read" of 1962. The Austrian-born author said that he is "amazed when I see another book come out," because he belongs to the "Teutonic school of peripatetic procrastination." When the weather is nice he goes for walks; when it rains, he stays home and does acrobatics. Morton earned a degree in chemistry with the intention of running a bakery, but when he won a college writing prize, he changed his goals.

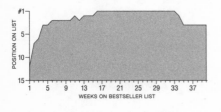

FIRST DATE AT #1: October 21, 1962
TOTAL WEEKS AT #1: 26*

Travels with Charley

John Steinbeck

VIKING

Steinbeck had recently won the Nobel Prize, and his account of a long drive around America with his faithful dog Charley caught the public's fancy. Since the book was #1 both before and after the 12-week strike, it seems reasonable to assume that it was #1 continuously, but the 26 weeks get an asterisk all the same. Around this time *Oh Ye Jigs and Juleps,* a recently discovered book by a Victorian 9-year-old, became very popular and actually rose as high as #2. Robert Frost also made the list for the first and only time, but never challenged for the #1 position.

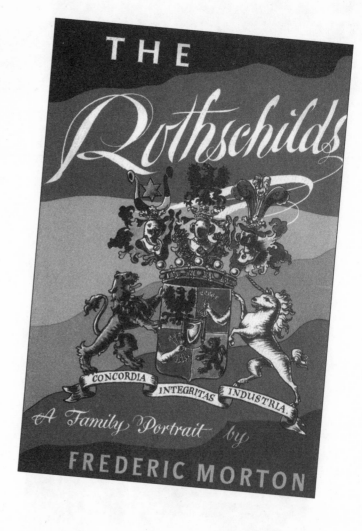

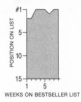

ALLEN DRURY
A SHADE
OF DIFFERENCE

I

In the great pearl-gray slab of a room that is the North Delegates' Lounge of the United Nations in New York the late-September sun slanted down through the massive east windows and fell across the green carpets, the crowded chairs and sofas, the little knots of delegates standing or sitting or milling about in the midmorning hours before the General Assembly's seven committees began. Riding over their noisy hubbub came the heavy voices of the young ladies at the telephone desk, relaying via the public-address system their bored yet insistent summonses to the myriad sons of man:

"Mr. Sadu-Nalim of the delegation of Iran, please call the Delegates' Lounge! . . . Senator Fry of the United States, please! . . . Ambassador Labaiya-Sofra of the delegation of Panama, please call the Delegates' Lounge! . . . His Royal Highness the M'Bulu of Mbuele, please . . . Secretary Knox of the United States . . ."

Surveying the immense and noisy chamber from his vantage point near the door, Senator Harold Fry of West Virginia, one of the two Senate members and acting head of the United States delegation, wondered with some impatience where Orrin Knox was now. The Secretary of State had been in town two days and Hal Fry had hardly seen him for ten minutes at a time, so busy had the Secretary been with conferences, diplomatic receptions, U.S. delegation business, and what Senator Fry termed with some disparagement "giving beads to the natives." Not that he was above giving a few himself, he thought wryly as he waved with vigorous cordiality to a passing Nigerian and bestowed a glowing smile upon the delegate from Gabon; but at least he could take it or leave it. Secretary Knox seemed to be going about it with a determination that bordered on the grim; Orrin acted at moments as though the fate of the world depended upon it. Which, of course, Senator Fry conceded abruptly with a loud "Hello!" to the delegate of Nepal, it quite possibly did.

A momentary look of concentration and unease touched his face at the thought, an expression of sudden melancholy that went almost as soon as it appeared. The Ambassador of India materialized at his elbow and seized upon it with unfailing accuracy.

"My dear Hal," Krishna Khaleel said with his air of half-jocular concern, "first you are being so jolly with everybody and then suddenly you look so sad. What is the matter with the Great Republic of the West this morning? Or is it only the distinguished delegate who feels something unsettling in his tummy, perhaps?"

"My tummy's all right, K.K.," Senator Fry said. "In fact, I was at the Guinean reception last night and ate like a horse. I'm just wondering where Orrin is."

"Ah, yes," said Krishna Khaleel with a little agreeing hiss. "Orrin is so

FIRST DATE AT #1: October 28, 1962
TOTAL WEEKS AT #1: 4

A Shade of Difference

Allen Drury

DOUBLEDAY

It seems safe to say that Drury was the first real victim of a *Times* strike. The sequel to his hugely successful *Advise and Consent* had recently reached #1 when the *Times* disappeared, and when the newspaper reappeared more than three months later, it was off the list entirely. The book continues the story of *Advise and Consent*, dealing with the interplay between whites and African blacks as they meet in the forum of the United Nations General Assembly.

FIRST DATE AT #1: November 18, 1962
TOTAL WEEKS AT #1: 17*

Seven Days in May

Fletcher Knebel

HARPER

At a time when presidential prestige is very low, the Joint Chiefs of Staff and other officers attempt a military takeover of the United States government. Since the reporter and columnist's second book was #1 for one week before and after the second long *Times* strike, it seems reasonable to give it the benefit of the doubt, and assume it would have been #1 during the strike, as its main challenger, Salinger's Glass family, was still working its way up the slope. In later years, Knebel said "the interesting thing for me is exploring new things. Books are no longer a big part of my life." Knebel's interests turned to the human potential movement, and from political concerns to environmental ones.

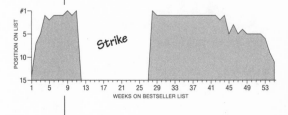

FIRST DATE AT #1: October 28, 1962
TOTAL WEEKS AT #1: 5*

Silent Spring
Rachel Carson

HOUGHTON MIFFLIN

Carson's second #1 bestseller was not nearly as successful as her first, *The Sea Around Us,* although its indictment of the effects of poisonous chemicals by the agriculture industry would prove to be more enduring and more influential. Still, we will probably never know if it might have shooed Charley out of the #1 spot for some portion of the strike. *The Saturday Review* called it "a devastating, heavily documented, relentless attack upon human carelessness, greed and irresponsibility.... If her present book does not possess the beauty of *The Sea Around Us,* it is because she has courageously chosen, at the height of her powers, to educate us upon a sad, an unpleasant, an unbeautiful topic...." Carson was dying of cancer at the time her book was on the *Times* list.

FIRST DATE AT #1: May 19, 1963
TOTAL WEEKS AT #1: 7

The Whole Truth and Nothing But
Hedda Hopper

DOUBLEDAY

The former actress and syndicated gossip columnist reminisces about life in Hollywood. She changed her name from Elda Furry when her husband, De Wolf Hopper, regularly confused her with his first four wives, Ella, Ida, Edna, and Nellie. A numerologist chose the name 'Hedda' for her. She died in 1966.

The author of THE SEA AROUND US and THE EDGE OF THE SEA questions our attempt to control the natural world about us

SILENT SPRING
Rachel Carson

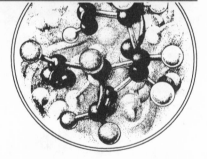

3. Elixirs of Death

FOR THE FIRST TIME in the history of the world, every human being is now subjected to contact with dangerous chemicals, from the moment of conception until death. In the less than two decades of their use, the synthetic pesticides have been so thoroughly distributed throughout the animate and inanimate world that they occur virtually everywhere. They have been recovered from most of the major river systems and even from streams of groundwater flowing unseen through the earth. Residues of these chemicals linger in soil to which they may have been applied a dozen years before. They have entered and lodged in the bodies of fish, birds, reptiles, and domestic and

J. D. Salinger Wins Landmark Suit; His Letters Cannot be Published

NEW YORK, January 30. The U.S. Court of Appeals yesterday handed reclusive author J. D. Salinger, author of two #1 *New York Times* bestselling books, a major victory in his effort to keep Random House from publishing a biography in which some of his unpublished correspondence was quoted and paraphrased.

Current copyright law permits authors to quote limited portions of published works, but this so-called "fair use" provision typically does not apply to unpublished materials.

The broughaha began when London *Times* literary critic Ian Hamilton submitted a manuscript entitled *In Search of J. D. Salinger* to Random House. In the course of his three-year research project, Hamilton discovered that letters from Salinger to friends and others had been deposited in three university libraries: Harvard, Princeton and Texas.

When Salinger learned of the intended use of his letters, he sued for copyright infringement. Random House argued that unauthorized use of the letters was acceptable under the well-established doctrine of fair use.

In its sweeping decision, the U.S. Court of Appeals for the Second Circuit ruled that not only could Hamilton not publish excerpts from the letters, he could not even *describe* the letters; that he had "no inherent right to copy the accuracy or the vividness of the letter writer's expression."

The U. S. Supreme Court declined to review this decision.

As a result of this case, some publishing houses now refuse to accept manuscripts that quote or even describe unpublished materials. Many authors and historians are alarmed at this situation. Senator Patrick Leahy has co-sponsored legislation that would extend the "fair use" doctrine to unpublished materials as well. As Leahy wrote in a *New York Times* article, "unpublished materials...constitute the soul of probing, illuminating history."

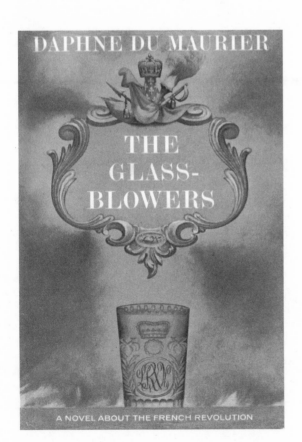

DAPHNE DU MAURIER

THE GLASS-BLOWERS

A NOVEL ABOUT THE FRENCH REVOLUTION

FIRST DATE AT #1: March 10, 1963
TOTAL WEEKS AT #1: 11

Raise High the Roof Beam, Carpenters

J. D. Salinger

LITTLE, BROWN

Salinger's last published work reached (or returned to; we'll never know) #1 the week after the strike, and remained at or near the top for half a year before disappearing virtually overnight.

FIRST DATE AT #1: May 19, 1963
TOTAL WEEKS AT #1: 6

The Glass Blowers
Daphne du Maurier

DOUBLEDAY

Du Maurier became the first person with six #1 bestsellers in this, her last appearance at the top of the list, sixteen years after her first. This book tells the story of the author's ancestor, Robert du Maurier, a glass blower who fled France to London at the start of the French Revolution. Based on letters written by Robert's sister, the book tells the story of the family from 1747 until Robert's death in 1811. Du Maurier was to write three further books, but none reached #1. She died in 1989.

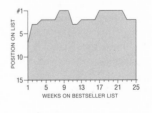

FIRST DATE AT #1: July 7, 1963
TOTAL WEEKS AT #1: 12

The Fire Next Time
James Baldwin
DIAL PRESS

"I am the grandson of a slave, and I am a writer," Baldwin wrote. "I must deal with both." A collection of essays on various themes relating to black Americans and issues of race in America, this book had an unusual pattern of a rise (to #3), decline, then starting the process all over, this time with a three-month stay at #1.

FIRST DATE AT #1: July 21, 1963
TOTAL WEEKS AT #1: 1

I Owe Russia $1200
Bob Hope
DOUBLEDAY

The comedian's second #1 bestseller rose quickly to #2 for a long stay there, with only one week at #1.

FIRST DATE AT #1: October 6, 1963
TOTAL WEEKS AT #1: 9

JFK: The Man and the Myth
Victor Lasky
MACMILLAN

By chance, the first highly unflattering book about John Kennedy was atop the list on the day of his assassination. It began as a short campaign "hatchet job" that took three weeks to write; after the Kennedy-Nixon election, it was expanded to more than double its original size. Its disappearance from the list one week reflected either a brief sharp decline in sales, or was done as a sign of respect for the slain president. While it never regained #1, *JFK* was on the list for another three months.

#1 Author's First Names

SHORTEST FIRST NAMES

The pseudonymous author "J" presumably has no first name, since "J" is generally listed as her last name. The only author with an authentic two-letter first name (unless we declare Dr. Seuss's first name to be "Dr.") is Cy Janos, coauthor of Yeager. There are 18 three-letter first names:

Amy	Bel	Ben	Bob
Dag	Dan	Dee	Gay
Jim	Joe	Joy	Ken
Lee	Leo	Ric	Sam
	Tom	Wil	

LONGEST FIRST NAMES

The longest is the 10-letter Jacqueline (Susann). There are fifteen 9-letter first names.

Alexander	Alexandra	Annemarie
Catherine	Christina	Cornelius
Dominique	Elizabeth	Ernestine
Françoise	Gwethalyn	Katherine
Priscilla	Rosamunde	Whittacker

Only two of the nineteen shortest names belong to women. Only three of the sixteen longest names belong to men.

The
Shoes of the
Fisherman

A NOVEL BY

MORRIS L.
WEST

I

THE POPE was dead. The Camerlengo had announced it. The Master of Ceremonies, the notaries, the doctors, had consigned him under signature into eternity. His ring was defaced and his seals were broken. The bells had been rung throughout the city. The pontifical body had been handed to the embalmers so that it might be a seemly object for the veneration of the faithful. Now it lay, between white candles, in the Sistine Chapel, with the Noble Guard keeping a deathwatch under Michelangelo's frescoes of the *Last Judgment*.

The Pope was dead. Tomorrow the clergy of the Basilica would claim him and expose him to the public in the Chapel of the Most Holy Sacrament. On the third day they would bury him, clothed in full pontificals, with a mitre on his head, a purple veil on his face, and a red ermine blanket to warm him in the crypt. The medals he had struck and coinage he had minted would be buried with him to identify him to any who might dig him up a thousand years later. They would seal him in three coffins —one of cypress; one of lead to keep him from the damp and to carry his coat of arms, and the certificate of his

---

FIRST DATE AT #1: June 30, 1963
TOTAL WEEKS AT #1: 14

The Shoes of the Fisherman
Morris West
MORROW

The Australian-born West came close a few other times with some of his 10 earlier books, but his only #1 bestseller was this tale of a newly elected Pope— a man who had spent 17 years in Russian prisons—and the various people's lives in which he becomes involved. It reached #1 in its fourth week and remained at #1 or #2 for half a year.

FIRST DATE AT #1: October 6, 1963
TOTAL WEEKS AT #1: 20

The Group
Mary McCarthy
HARCOURT

The story of eight Vassar girls, class of '33, who live together during their senior year at the college, and their lives after leaving Poughkeepsie. McCarthy told an interviewer, "What I really do is take real plums and put them in an imaginary cake. If you're interested in the cake, you get rather annoyed with people saying what species the real plum was. I do try…to be as exact as possible about the essence of a person, to find the key that works the person both in real life and in the fiction." The book spent nearly five months at #1, and a full year on the list.

FIRST DATE AT #1: December 8, 1963
TOTAL WEEKS AT #1: 3

The American Way of Death

Jessica Mitford

SIMON & SCHUSTER

Mitford's muckraking exposé of the American funeral and undertaking industry reached #1 just after the assassination. Mitford reported later that "The best thing that happened was that a Middle Western [coffin] manufacturer wrote to me [about] a very cheap coffin he was proposing to market as the Jessica Mitford Casket, so you can say, 'I'm going to be buried in a Mitford.'"

FIRST DATE AT #1: December 29, 1963
TOTAL WEEKS AT #1: 12

Profiles in Courage

John F. Kennedy

HARPER

Senator Kennedy's book of inspirational stories about politicians who displayed courage in the performance of their duties had been a publishing phenomenon in the mid-1950s: on the *New York Times* list for more than two years, but never reaching #1. After President Kennedy's assassination, a special memorial edition was rushed out, and in three weeks it rose to an extended period at #1.

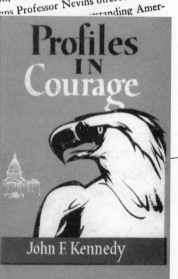

‖‖‖ PREFACE ‖‖‖

Since first reading—long before I entered the Senate—an account of John Quincy Adams and his struggle with the Federalist party, I have been interested in the problems of political courage in the face of constituent pressures, and the light shed on those problems by the lives of past statesmen. A long period of hospitalization and convalescence following a spinal operation in October, 1954, gave me my first opportunity to do the reading and research necessary for this project.

I am not a professional historian; and, although all errors of fact and judgment are exclusively my own, I should like to acknowledge with sincere gratitude those who assisted me in the preparation of this volume.

I am deeply grateful to Professor Allan Nevins of Columbia University, one of the foremost political historians and biographers of our times, for kindly consenting to contribute the Foreword. In addition, the entire manuscript was greatly improved by the criticisms Professor Nevins offered.

I owe a special debt ____standing American institution—the ____ many months of my ____ lative Reference and ____ all of my requests fo____ cheerful courtesy. ____ the Prints and Pho____

I

BRIAN'S JOURNAL

SEPTEMBER 10, 1939. I have always wanted to keep a journal, but whenever I am about to start one, I am dissuaded by the idea that it is too late. I lose heart when I think of all the fascinating things I could have described had I only begun earlier. Not that my life has been an exciting one. On the contrary, it has been very dull. But a dull life in itself may be an argument for a journal. The best way for the passive man to overtake his more active brothers is to write them up. Isn't the Sun King himself just another character in Saint-Simon's chronicle?

In Europe a world war has started while in this country Brian Aspinwall is about to go to work ~~~~~~~ t job. Surely if I am ever to keep a journa~~~~~~~~~~~~~~~ first job at twenty-seven. ~~~~~~~~~~~~~~ t Justin Martyr, an ~~~~~~~~~~~~~~~~~ es west of Boston. ~~~~~~~~~~~~~~~~ yesterday. One of ~~~~~~~~~~~~~~~ the RCAF which ~~~~~~~~~~~~~~~ ws. It makes me ~~~~~~~~~~~~~ rmy before I left ~~~~~~~~~~~~~ n about an un-~~~~~~~~~~~~ Perhaps had I ~~~~~~~~~~~ ne, they might ~~~~~~~~~~~ ay I can feel

BY AND ABOUT #**1** AUTHORS:

"[Louis Achincloss] is a second-rate Stephen Birmingham. And Steven Birmingham is third rate."

—**Truman Capote**

FIRST DATE AT #1: February 23, 1964
TOTAL WEEKS AT #1: 34

The Spy Who Came in from the Cold
John le Carré
COWARD-MCCANN

Alec Leamas is 50 years old and longing to quit the spy business, but he takes on one last assignment before his hoped-for retirement. The first of seven #1 bestsellers by former Eton tutor and British foreign service officer David Cornwell, writing as John le Carré, was by far his biggest, remaining at #1 for nearly three-quarters of 1963. Cornwell maintains that he has forgotten where the name "le Carré" came from.

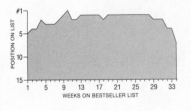

FIRST DATE AT #1: October 4, 1964
TOTAL WEEKS AT #1: 1

The Rector of Justin
Louis Auchincloss
HOUGHTON MIFFLIN

The 88-year-old rector of a New England Episcopal private school is seen through the eyes of both admirers and detractors in attorney Auchincloss's only #1 bestseller, the ninth of his 23 novels. A *Times* reviewer suggested that Auchincloss "is far from the swarming hot center of American literary intellectualisms; he's a museum of all that American writing valued before its World War I baptism of despair. . . ."

FIRST DATE AT #1: March 22, 1964
TOTAL WEEKS AT #1: 12

Four Days
UPI/American Heritage
AMERICAN HERITAGE

A scrapbook of newspaper articles and photos from the Kennedy assassination and subsequent events was rushed into print, made the *Times* list 10 weeks after the shooting in Dallas, and spent three months in the #1 position. Other than the Bible, it was the first #1 bestseller without an author, and only one of two such, the other being *A Day in the Life of America*.

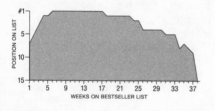

FIRST DATE AT #1: June 14, 1964
TOTAL WEEKS AT #1: 19

A Moveable Feast
Ernest Hemingway
SCRIBNER'S

Hemingway had not done much new writing in recent years, but this collection of sketches from his life in Paris in the 1920s became his second #1 bestseller. With this book, Hemingway became the second of five writers to have both a nonfiction and a fiction #1 bestseller (Steinbeck was the first). Many reviewers commented on, and even looked for meaning in, Hemingway's use of the older and less common spelling of "movable."

Authors Who Reached #1 on Both the Fiction and Nonfiction Lists

Only five authors achieved #1 on both the fiction and the nonfiction lists. For four of these authors (all but William Styron), those two appearances were the *only* two times they made #1.

Ernest Hemingway — *Across the River and into the Trees* (F)
A Moveable Feast (NF)

Dr. Seuss — *Oh, the Places You'll Go* (F)
You're Only Old Once! (NF)

John Steinbeck — *East of Eden* (F)
Travels with Charley (NF)

William Styron — *The Confessions of Nat Turner* (F)
Sophie's Choice (F)
Darkness Visible (NF)

Irving Wallace — *The Word* (F)
The Book of Lists (coauthor, NF)

FIRST DATE AT #1: October 25, 1964
TOTAL WEEKS AT #1: 29

Herzog
Saul Bellow
VIKING

Bellow's only #1 bestseller tells the story of a man whose beliefs in humanity and in himself, and his experiences in life, seem to be at odds with each other. *Herzog* reached #1 in its third week on the list and stayed there nearly seven months, the longest such reign from any winner of the Nobel Prize in literature. Bellow told an interviewer that his work is improving as he ages: "Yeah, I think I'm getting better. I can think of any number of writers who got better as they got older. Thomas Hardy got very good....The painter Titian got really hot when he was in his 80s. Sophocles also wrote some of his very best things in his 80s. A writer in his 60s and 70s always has subjects laid aside. Will they be ripe when I'm 90? It's a good reason to hang in there." Regarding his critics, Bellow wrote, "In the sea of literature there are more ichthyologists than fish."

Sept. 7

Dear Ellen,

I had begun a letter to you this morning but was interrupted, and now I can't find it in the flood of papers in which I am drowning.

Perhaps it's just as well; I couldn't possibly succeed in describing this place to you: the homeroom, the Assembly, the chaos of clerical work, the kids—whom I had come to guide and "gladly teche."

I've been here less than a day, and already I'm in hot water. A boy had "incurred a fall" in class, and I failed to report it on the proper form. Another left the room without a pass and is suspected of stealing a wallet from a locker which wasn't locked because I had neglected to inspect it. This was Joe Ferone, *the* problem-boy of Calvin Coolidge, who earlier, in homeroom, had been flagrantly rude to me, and insolent, and contemptuous.

While I was writing you the other letter (Where can it be? Among the Circulars? Directives? Faculty Mimeos? Department Notices? In the right-hand desk drawer? Left-hand? In my wastebasket, perhaps?), during what was presumably my lunch period, Admiral Ass (a Mr. McHabe, who signs himself Adm. Asst.) appeared in my room with Joe Ferone.

43

FIRST DATE AT #1: May 16, 1965
TOTAL WEEKS AT #1: 8*

Up the Down Staircase
Bel Kaufman
PRENTICE HALL

The granddaughter of playwright and humorist Sholom Aleichem taught in New York City schools for more than 20 years. Her first novel is about a young teacher's struggles during her first year at a New York high school, told through a series of letters, memos, student compositions, and other documents. The title comes from a memo written by a real administrator: "Please admit bearer to class. Detained by me for going up the Down staircase and subsequent insolence."

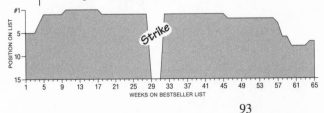

FIRST DATE AT #1: October 25, 1964
TOTAL WEEKS AT #1: 10

Reminiscences
Douglas MacArthur
McGraw

Before the old soldier faded away for good, he left us with this volume of memoirs of his life, particularly his 50-year military career, serving in eight presidential administrations. (He also left us with the longest one-word title of any #1 bestseller.) MacArthur died in the spring of 1964, a few months before his book appeared on the *Times* list. Jean-Paul Sartre was on the list at this time, for *The Words,* but never challenged for the #1 spot.

FIRST DATE AT #1: December 20, 1964
TOTAL WEEKS AT #1: 31

Markings
Dag Hammarskjold
Knopf

After the United Nations secretary general's death in a mysterious African plane crash in 1961, his private diary, including memoirs and poetry, was translated from the Swedish by W. H. Auden and Leif Sjoeberg. The public was fascinated by this glimpse into the very private life of the public figure, and the book remained the #1 bestseller for more than half of 1964. Dr. Hammarskjold (he had a Ph.D. from the University of Stockholm as well as a law degree) wrote candidly of his homosexuality.

Why Bestsellers Sell Best and Other Publishing Secrets
by Sandra Salmans
New York Times Book Review

...In the publishing industry, the common wisdom is that, while good books may languish and die without the necessary investment, money alone cannot buy success. If it ever had been possible to spend one's way to the bestseller list, "the days when we could do it all with mirrors is over," said Paul Fedorko, the marketing director of Bantam Books. "Money is very important [says Howard Kaminsky, editor-in-chief of Random House], "But there's no guarantee of money making something happen. You need a book with intrinsic value, even if it's frivolous intrinsic value." Michael Korda, editor-in-chief of Simon & Schuster agreed: "What you can't do is build bricks without straw."

Still, after the selection of the book itself, the amount of money spent and the way it is spent are pivotal concerns for any publisher. While there are some authors—Danielle Steel and Sidney Sheldon are frequently cited—who will reach the bestseller list almost regardless of how they are marketed, there are a much larger number, particularly in the nonfiction category, whose sales may rise or fall as a result of promotion.... Accordingly, publishers are continually tinkering with the most cost-effective formula for marketing books: a blend of advertising, authors tours and talks shows, and promotion to and through booksellers. The mix varies with the kind of book, the personality of the author, the predisposition of booksellers, and, above all, the number of copies the publisher projects it will sell.

The economics of book publishing prohibits the massive promotional campaigns used by packaged good manufacturers whose products may sell in vast quantities for years. The guideline for the promotion of hard-cover books is "a buck a book," or $1 spent for every copy printed. For the average bestseller, that means an outlay of about $40,000 to $80,000—a minuscule sum compared with the promotion budget of a packaged good—and even for the blockbuster book, an expenditure of $200,000 is extraordinary. "If you spend more than a buck a book, you might as well close the shop," Mr. Korda said....

A publisher may actually wait for a book to reach the bestseller list before promoting it heavily. "Really successful books tend to be successful before the advertising," Mr. Korda said. "With the big bestsellers, we won't start advertising until it's on the list, the stores are committed, there are 100,000 copies out there. Then we advertise that it's on the list."

But if a book is a flop, publishers say, not even a fortune can turn it into a bestseller. The favorite example of many publishers is *A Remarkable Medicine Has Been Overlooked* by Jack Dreyfus, a wealthy businessman, that was published by Simon & Schuster in 1982. Mr. Dreyfus spent about $2 million of his own money promoting the book with full-page ads in newspapers and magazines; nonetheless it was a conspicuous failure. Last year almost $1 million was spent— with similar results—to advertise *The Trinitab Factor*....

It might be argued that neither of those books was particularly salable. But more than $100,000 worth of advertising was wasted last September in promoting *Treasure* [which] employed the find-the-clue device that had been used successfully in *Who Killed the Robins Family?* Warner Books offered a prize of $500,000 and a gold trinket, printed more than 100,000 copies, and waited for the orders to pour in. They never did. "Advertising doesn't get people out to buy a book," [said Kaminsky]. "A lot of advertisements are for the author, his mother, and his agent."

In fact, publishers like to rattle off lists of bestsellers—*In Search of Excellence, Watership Down*—that received little or no advertising when they were launched. The real key to selling books is word of mouth, and, Mr. Kaminsky said, "no matter how much you spend, you can't buy that." But that doesn't stop publishers... from trying. When Warner Books published John Naisbitt's *Megatrends,* for example, it sent copies to the chief executives of the nation's 500 largest companies. "We created a groundswell of acknowledgment for an unknown book," Mr. Kaminsky said....

Publishers often favor promotional devices that may

continued on page 96

"[Jacqueline Susann] looks like a
truck driver in drag."

—Truman Capote

FIRST DATE AT #1: July 11, 1965
TOTAL WEEKS AT #1: 36

The Source
James Michener
RANDOM HOUSE

Michener's second huge #1 success came more than five years after his first, *Hawaii. The Source* covers twelve thousand years of history, woven around a fictional archaeological site in Israel called Makor, ending with the establishment of the modern state of Israel. It became #1 in its sixth week on the list, remaining there for 36 uninterrupted weeks, then spending nearly six additional months in the top five. Michener "is the Will Durant of novelists," writes *Time* critic Lance Morrow. He is "less an artist than a kind of historical compacter." Michener, an orphan, has no idea when or where he was born.

FIRST DATE AT #1: May 8, 1966
TOTAL WEEKS AT #1: 28

Valley of the Dolls
Jacqueline Susann
GEIS

The first of Susann's three #1 bestsellers was one of the first fiction books to be tirelessly promoted by the author, through television appearances, and other publicity. It was the big book of 1966 and remained in the top five for more than a year. The story tells of three glamorous women—a model, a singer, and an actress—and how they cope with success and failure. Of this book, Nora Ephron wrote, "*Valley*...described the standard female fantasy—of going off to the big city, striking it rich, meeting fabulous men—and went on to show every reader that she was far better off than the heroines in the book—who took pills, killed themselves, and made general messes of their lives. It was, essentially, a morality tale."

FIRST DATE AT #1: August 1, 1965
TOTAL WEEKS AT #1: 13*

The Making of the President—1964

Theodore H. White

ATHENEUM

White's day-by-day account of the Johnson-Goldwater presidential campaign didn't do as well as the 1960 version, but fared better than the 1968 and 1972 versions (which didn't make #1). It is reasonable to assume it would have been at #1 during the *Times*'s third strike.

FIRST DATE AT #1: October 31, 1965
TOTAL WEEKS AT #1: 10

Kennedy

Theodore Sorensen

HARPER

John Kennedy's close friend and special counsel was first out of the gate with a book of reminiscences of JFK's life and times. It rose quickly to #1, and remained there until replaced by the next JFK book to reach #1 ten weeks later. Some critics accused Sorensen of being too discrete, causing Alistair Cooke to write that "If discretion is a fault, it is a very welcome one."

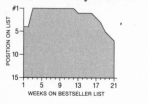

FIRST DATE AT #1: January 9, 1966
TOTAL WEEKS AT #1: 4

A Thousand Days

Arthur Schlesinger

HOUGHTON MIFFLIN

Schlesinger had taken careful notes in order to assist Kennedy with his own memoirs one day. After the assassination, Schlesinger incorporated those notes into his own book about the Kennedy years.

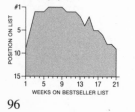

from page 95

be less costly but more effective than a major advertising campaign. Because of rising travel costs, the author's tour is no longer the bargain it was, but at its best—appearances on television's *Tonight Show* and morning news shows—it is a superb investment. Admittedly, tours are most appropriate for authors of nonfiction books, and only if they are personable, or "tourable" as publishers say. Novelists must be so well established—Stephen King, say, or Jackie Collins—that they have a built-in audience. Otherwise, Mr. Korda asks rhetorically, "What can they say? 'I prefer an Olympia typewriter?'" But even novelists can travel the rubber-chicken circuit and give newspaper interviews. "You can sell an awful lot of copies by doing book-and-author luncheons," said Mr. Korda, a best-selling author himself. "It's not the 100 copies they ask you to sign, but the fact that local stores react to your presence...."

If a key bookseller such as B. Dalton or Waldenbooks sees that a publisher believes in a book—measured by its advertising budget, plans for an author tour or other commitments—it is more likely to order many copies and display them prominently.

"The first printing is a good barometer to us," said Jim Adamson, the president of B. Dalton. "We know by the kind of book what percent [of total sales] Dalton represents." In other words, if a publisher prints 100,000 copies of a popular author's book, B. Dalton may estimate that it will sell 12,000 and orders accordingly. The publishing company's commitment is not everything, he cautioned; a publisher might tout a book and guarantee a big promotional budget, and even so B. Dalton might hold back. B. Dalton's buyers read manuscripts and use "gut and instinct" to evaluate their sales potential, Mr. Adamson said. So they ignore the size of the publisher's promotional budget? On the contrary, he said, "they always ask." ■

FIRST DATE AT #1: November 20, 1966
TOTAL WEEKS AT #1: 18

The Secret of Santa Vittoria
Robert Crichton
SIMON & SCHUSTER

Crichton reached #1 for the only time with the story of Santa Vittoria, a small Italian hill town whose inhabitants managed to outwit the invading Nazis and protect the source of their wealth, one million bottles of wine. Crichton told *Contemporary Authors* that "telling a story to convey feeling and experience is, despite all efforts to disown it, as natural to man and as vital to man, and as intuitive and ageless, as is the urge to laugh or cry, to embrace when in love, and to flee when in fear."

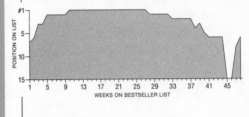

FIRST DATE AT #1: March 26, 1967
TOTAL WEEKS AT #1: 23

The Arrangement
Elia Kazan
STEIN & DAY

The famous film director, who began life in Turkey as Elia Kazanjoglous, took some writing lessons from a prominent coach, and then created this very popular novel about a successful advertising man whose attempts to escape from his orderly life eventually lead him to attempted suicide and mental breakdown. None of his five subsequent novels had anywhere near the success of this one.

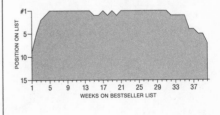

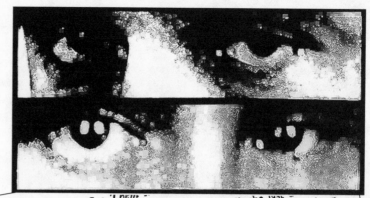

FIRST DATE AT #1: February 6, 1966
TOTAL WEEKS AT #1: 10

In Cold Blood
Truman Capote
RANDOM HOUSE

Truman Streckfus Persons set aside *Answered Prayers*, which he was to work on for 25 years, to explore "a theme not likely to darken and yellow with time: [to bring] the art of the novelist together with the technique of journalism to produce a new genre, the nonfiction novel." The book is an extremely detailed accounting of the events surrounding the mass murder of a Kansas farm family. Capote's friend Harper Lee (*To Kill a Mockingbird*) assisted him in his Kansas research.

FIRST DATE AT #1: May 8, 1966
TOTAL WEEKS AT #1: 9

The Last Battle
Cornelius Ryan
SIMON & SCHUSTER

The Irish-born Ryan spent $60,000 on research while writing of the last three weeks of the war against Germany in World War Two, and the fall of Berlin to Soviet forces.

The Last To See Them —

slept in. So we walked to the end of the hall, the last of there, on her bed, that's where we found Mrs. Clutter. She'd been tied, too. But differently—with her hands in front of her, so that she looked as though she were praying—and in one hand she was holding, *gripping*, a handkerchief. Or was it Kleenex? The cord around her wrists ran down to her ankles, which were bound together, and then ran on down to the bottom of the bed, where it was tied to the footboard—a very complicated, artful piece of work. Think how long it took to do! And her lying there, scared out of her wits. Well, she was wearing some jewelry, two rings—which is one of the reasons why I've always discounted robbery as a motive—and a robe, and a white nightgown, and white socks. Her mouth had been taped with adhesive, but she'd been shot point-blank in the side of the head, and the blast—the impact—had ripped the tape loose. Her eyes were open. Wide open. As though she were still looking at the killer. Because she must have had to watch him do it—aim the gun. Nobody said anything. We were too stunned. I remember the sheriff searched around to see if he could find the discharged cartridge. But whoever had done it was much too smart and cool to have left behind any clues like that.

"Naturally, we were wondering where was Mr. Clutter? And Kenyon? Sheriff said, 'Let's try downstairs.' The first place we tried was the master bedroom—the room where Mr. Clutter slept. The bedcovers were drawn back, and lying there, toward the foot of the bed, was a billfold with a mess of cards spilling out of it, like somebody had shuffled through them hunting something particular—a note, an I.O.U., who knows? The fact that there wasn't any money in it didn't signify one way or the other. It was Mr. Clutter's billfold, and he never did carry cash. Even I knew that, and I'd only been in Holcomb a little more than two months. Another thing I knew was that neither Mr. Clutter nor Kenyon could see a darn without his glasses. And there were Mr. Clutter's glasses sitting on a bureau. So I figured, wherever they were, they weren't there of their own accord. We looked all over, and nothing disturbed. Except the office, where the telephone was off the hook, thing was just as it should be—no sign of a struggle, nothing dis-

'I'll give TRUMAN CAPOTE if you can produce a writer who can honestly say he was ever helped by the prissy carpings and condescentions of reviewers.'

'[Truman Capote] would be all right if he took his finger out of his mouth.'
HAROLD ROBBINS

'[Truman Capote is] a Republican housewife from Kansas with all the prejudices.'
GORE VIDAL

'Truman [Capote] is canny as hell, but he's not the brightest guy in the world.'
NORMAN MAILER

'[Truman Capote] was a full-fledged master of the language before he was old enough to vote.'
WILLIAM STYRON

JAMES MICHENER
'Like Toulouse-Lautrec [Truman Capote] will come to represent his period, and he will be treasured for the masterly way he epitomized it.'

FIRST DATE AT #1: June 4, 1967
TOTAL WEEKS AT #1: 4

The Eighth Day
Thornton Wilder
HARPER

Wilder once told the *Paris Review,* "I'm the kind of man whom timid old ladies stop on the street to ask about the nearest subway station. News vendors in university towns call me 'professor,' and hotel clerks, 'doctor.'" He has said that his fiction ideas often come to him in the shower. A graduate of Yale and Princeton, he taught at the Universities of Chicago and Hawaii, and was Professor of Poetry at Harvard. Although best known as a playwright, Wilder reached #1 twice, 19 years earlier with *The Ides of March,* and then with this saga of two families in Coaltown, Illinois in the early twentieth century, whose lives became interestingly intertwined.

FIRST DATE AT #1: October 1, 1967
TOTAL WEEKS AT #1: 4

The Chosen
Chaim Potok
SIMON & SCHUSTER

The conservative Rabbi's first published novel revolves around two teenage Jewish boys growing up in Brooklyn in the 1940s. It reached #1 in its fifth month on the list, remaining a short time before starting a slow decline. Potok says "It generally takes me anywhere from one to three full books, without exaggeration, before I finally hit upon the voice of the individual that I'm writing about— or, to put it more accurately, through whom I end up seeing the world. It isn't unusual for me to write one, two, or three novels that I throw out before I actually get the sounds right."

99

FIRST DATE AT #1: July 17, 1966
TOTAL WEEKS AT #1: 17

How to Avoid Probate

Norman Dacey

CROWN

One of only three "how to" books ever to make #1, Dacey spent four months atop the list with advice on avoiding probate by setting up a living trust, thereby avoiding payments to lawyers and the government. This may be the only originally self-published book (it was later taken on by Crown) to reach #1. It has appeared on the list at various other times, but never close to #1. While the book was at #1, the New York County Lawyers' Association sued Dacey for practicing law without a license (for the legal advice in the book). The New York Supreme Court ruled in favor of the lawyers, and ordered the book taken off the market, but in late 1967 the U.S. Court of Appeals reversed this decision, and ruled in favor of Dacey.

FIRST DATE AT #1: November 13, 1966
TOTAL WEEKS AT #1: 8

Rush to Judgment

Mark Lane

HOLT

Attorney Lane's exposé of the Warren Commission report on Kennedy's assassination was the only one of many assassination books to reach the list at all, much less #1. Lane remained an assassination investigator, and 24 years later, in 1992, a new summary of his findings also reached the *Times* list. *Rush* was the second-to-last #1 *John* Kennedy book, although Rose and Jackie are still waiting in the wings.

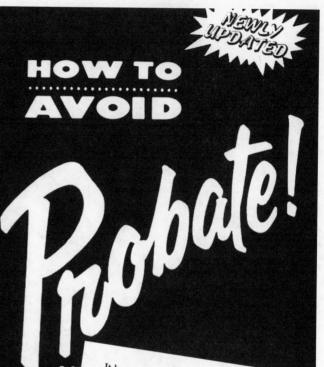

It began on an evening in 1964.

During thirty-five years of professional estate planning I had become acutely aware of the abuses of the probate system—and of a little-known method of avoiding them—and I had begun telling people how to use that method.

On the evening in question, I arrived home, picked up the newspaper, and was confronted by a headline that read: "Dacey Enjoined from Practice of Law." Without giving me any notice or opportunity to be heard, the Connecticut Bar Association had arranged for a judge who was one of its members to issue an injunction requiring me to stop telling people how to avoid probate. My lengthy subsequent efforts to have the injunction lifted proved fruitless, and I puzzled over how the court's gag order might be circumvented. Finally I concluded that if I could not *tell* people the formula for probate avoidance, the answer was simply to write a book that they could read and thus gain the knowledge that the legal establishment was so determined to keep from them.

The result, in 1966, was *How to Avoid Probate!*, a large paperback book that not only explained what probate was and spelled out the ways in which it was victimizing the country's widows and orphans, but provided a do-it-yourself guide to probate avoidance. Within thirteen weeks the book had become the Number 1 best seller. The Masters and Johnson book, *Human Sexual Response*, was Number 2 on the list. I don't claim, of course, that I made probate more interesting than sex—it was just that millions of American families had had painful contact with the probate system at one time or another. They knew that they had been "taken," but they did not understand the mechanics of how it had been accomplished. All they knew was that family money, which should have come to them, had gone instead to strangers. *How to Avoid Probate!* told them exactly how it had been done. It explained how greedy lawyers and politicians had preyed upon rich and poor alike for generations.

One and a half million copies of the book were sold—and the cries of public outrage rattled the windows in the Chicago headquarters of the American Bar Association.

Vernon Demerest, still in the aisle of the tourist cabin where he had held himself by instinctively seizing a seatback, roared, "Get on oxygen!" He grabbed a mask himself.

Through knowledge and training, Demerest realized what most others did not: The air inside the cabin was now as rarefied as that outside, and insufficient to support life. Only fifteen seconds of full consciousness remained to everyone, unless oxygen was used at once from the aircraft's emergency system.

Even in five seconds, without the aid of oxygen, a degree of lessened judgment would occur.

In another five seconds a state of euphoria would make many decide not to bother with oxygen at all. They would lapse into unconsciousness, not caring.

Airlines had long been urged, by those who understood the hazards of decompression, to make pre-flight announcements about oxygen equipment more definite than they were. Passengers should be told, it was argued: *The instant an oxygen mask appears in front of you, grab it, stick your face into it, and ask questions after. If there is a real decompression, you haven't a single second to spare. If it's a false alarm, you can always take the mask off later; meanwhile it will do no harm.*

Pilots who took decompression tests were given a simple demonstration of the effect of oxygen lack at high altitudes. In a decompression tank, with an oxygen mask on, they were told to begin writing their signatures, and part way through the exercise their masks were removed. The signatures tailed off into a scrawl, or nothingness. Before unconsciousness occurred, the masks were put back on.

The pilots found it hard to believe what they saw on the page before them.

Yet airline managements, theorizing that more definite oxygen advice might create alarm among passengers, persisted in the use of innocuous flight announcements only. Smiling stewardesses, seeming either bored or amused, casually demonstrated the equipment while an unseen voice—hurrying to get finished before takeoff—parroted phrases like: *In the unlikely event . . .* and *. . . Government regulations require that we inform you.* No mention was ever made of urgency, should the equipment be required for use.

As a result, passengers became as indifferent to emergency oxygen

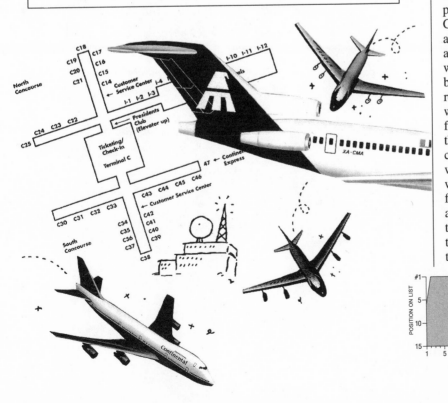

FIRST DATE AT #1: November 5, 1967
TOTAL WEEKS AT #1: 21

The Confessions of Nat Turner
William Styron
RANDOM HOUSE

Styron is one of five authors to have both a fiction and a nonfiction #1 bestseller. The first and most successful of his three books to make #1 is tour de force describing an 1831 slave uprising in Southampton, Virginia through the eyes of its instigator. It rose to #1 in its third week, and remained there for an uninterrupted span of five months. Styron explained in a letter to the *Nation* that an exact transcription of historical events was not his intent. "Had perfect accuracy been my aim, I would have written a book of history rather than a novel."

FIRST DATE AT #1: April 7, 1968
TOTAL WEEKS AT #1: 30

Airport
Arthur Hailey
DOUBLEDAY

The Canadian businessman became a professional author when, on a trans-Canada flight in 1955, he began to think about what would happen if the pilot and co-pilot both became disabled. Two weeks later, he completed what would become a popular television play. He returned to the aviation disaster mode with his sixth novel which became the first of his four #1 bestsellers, and was in the #1 spot longer than the other three combined. It reached #1 in its second week on the list and stayed there for 30 weeks, with but a one week incursion from John Updike. The novel tells how an airport manager and others cope with troubles and disasters in the middle of a terrible snowstorm at Lincoln International Airport.

FIRST DATE AT #1: January 8, 1967
TOTAL WEEKS AT #1: 13

Everything But Money
Sam Levenson
SIMON & SCHUSTER

Levenson, a former high school Spanish teacher, checks in with *his* account of growing up poor but happy in a New York Jewish family. Using the forum of his sizable national radio and television audiences, Levenson was not shy in talking about his book. Perhaps as a direct result, *Everything But Money* was in the top five for 10 months, and on the list for over a year.

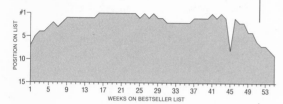

FIRST DATE AT #1: March 12, 1967
TOTAL WEEKS AT #1: 4

Madame Sarah
Cornelia Otis Skinner
HOUGHTON MIFFLIN

Miss Skinner's second #1 bestseller came 24 years after her first, *Our Hearts Were Young and Gay:* a record for the time span between appearances. *Madame Sarah* is a biography of the actress Sarah Bernhardt, one that some critics felt was less than objective. Critic C. H. Simonds wrote that the book "relies heavily on the actress' heavily romanticized memoirs and on adulatory volumes by her friends and relations. But should a dry-as-dust revisionist someday attempt to demolish the Bernhardt legend, he'll doubtless be dismissed as a surly spoilsport."

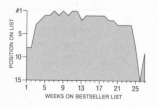

The National Book Award and *The Times* List

There are some who feel the National Book Award may be a bit more oriented to the mass market. In any event, none of the five #1 bestselling books that won Pulitzers also won a National Book. And none of the seven National Book winners that were #1 bestsellers also won a Pulitzer. The National Book winners that also were #1 bestsellers are:

From Here to Eternity (Jones)

Herzog (Bellow)

The Eighth Day (Wilder)

Sophie's Choice (Styron)

The Sea Around Us (Carson)

A Thousand Days (Schlesinger)

Eleanor and Franklin (Lash)

Twelve National Book Awards went to #1 best-selling authors, but *not* for the book that made them #1:

Catherine Bowen for *The Lion and the Throne*

Saul Bellow for *Mr. Sammler's Planet* and *The Adventures of Augie March*

John Cheever for *The Wapshot Chronicle*

E. L. Doctorow for *World's Fair*

Norman Mailer for *The Armies of the Night*

John O'Hara for *Ten North Frederick*

Katherine Ann Porter for *Collected Stories*

Philip Roth for *Goodbye Columbus*

John Updike for *The Centaur* and *Rabbit Is Rich*

Tom Wolfe for *The Right Stuff*

Thin Ice : 189

"And it was splendid."

"Not bad."

"You each had seven orgasms and read Henry Miller to each other between times."

"You see it very clearly."

"Working from your many vivid descriptions."

"Piet. Stop being a bastard. I'm tired of being a bitch. Come see me. Just for coffee."

"Just for coffee is as bad as for screwing if we're caught."

"I miss you."

"Here I am."

"You have somebody else, that's it, isn't it?"

"Dollink," he said, "you know me better than that."

"I can't believe it's that Whitman girl. She's just too stiff and pretty-pretty for you. She's not your type."

"You're righ[t] [abou]t her. It's Julia little-Smith."

"Foxy's too [   ] [   ] make yourself ridiculous."

"Not only [   ] [   ] [   ] [   ] [h]igh-class chick like you ever [   ]

Georgene [   ]
high-bridge[d] [   ]
slope of sur[   ]
Lattices. C[   ]
wonder. I'[   ]
lust swept [   ]
gether. T'[   ]

A fina[l] [   ]
winners, [   ]
and Pie[t] [   ]
flattene[d] [   ]
nants. [   ]
ward [   ]
no wi[   ]
shoul[d] [   ]
whe[   ]
thei[r] [   ]
Ta[   ]

FIRST DATE AT #1: June 30, 1968
TOTAL WEEKS AT #1: 1

Couples
John Updike
KNOPF

Updike's lone visit to the #1 spot came with the story of 10 middle-class couples in a Boston suburb who are obsessed with sex, and among whom infidelity is common. Updike told *Life* magazine "There's a 'yes-but' quality about my writing that evades entirely pleasing anybody. It seems to me that critics get increasingly querulous and impatient for madder music and stronger wine, when what we need is a greater respect for reality, its secrecy, its music."

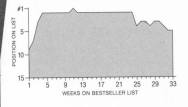

FIRST DATE AT #1: November 10, 1968
TOTAL WEEKS AT #1: 18

The Salzburg Connection
Helen MacInnes
HARCOURT

A chest buried in a lake in the Austrian Alps contains a list of men who secretly aided Hitler's cause, and who could be blackmailed into doing so again. Many people, including the CIA and the Russians, desperately want this chest, for a variety of reasons. MacInnes's 15th book is her only one to reach #1, but it also holds the record for the longest stay at #1 for a pure mystery novel. The Scottish-born author says that in her novels, "suspense is not achieved by hiding things from the reader. . . . A reader may know everything, but still be scared stiff by the situation."

BY AND ABOUT #1 AUTHORS:

"I cannot greatly care what the critics say of my work; if it is good, it will come to the surface in a generation or two and float, and if not, it will sink, having the meantime provided me with a living, the opportunities of leisure, and a craftsman's intimate satisfactions."

—John Updike

FIRST DATE AT #1: April 23, 1967

TOTAL WEEKS AT #1: 12

The Death of a President

William Manchester

HARPER COLLINS

As a close family friend, and working with the full cooperation of the Kennedy family, Manchester was expected to write the definitive account of the Kennedy years. The public was clearly eager to see what he had to say, but after 12 weeks at #1 or #2, the book slid very rapidly from the list.

FIRST DATE AT #1: July 23, 1967

TOTAL WEEKS AT #1: 7

The New Industrial State

John K. Galbraith

HOUGHTON MIFFLIN

The prominent Harvard professor of economics examines the roles of industry, the state, and the individual in the new industrial state that he believes will emerge in the post-Vietnam era. It is impossible to find such data on most people, but it may well be that at 6′ 8″, Galbraith is the tallest of all the #1 authors. And, he says, that is not irrelevant. "The superior confidence which people repose in the tall man is well merited. Being tall, he is more visible than other men and being more visible he is much more closely watched. In consequence, his behavior is far better than that of smaller man." Galbraith has said that the dry wit for which his books are known is added in the fifth draft of his manuscripts.

THE DEATH OF A PRESIDENT

NOVEMBER 20—NOVEMBER 25

1963

Glossary

The following are key U.S. Secret Service (SS)–White House Communications Agency (WHCA) code terms which were in use in November 1963:

The First Family

Lancer	The President
Lace	The First Lady
Lyric	Caroline Kennedy
Lark	John F. Kennedy, Jr.

Vice Presidential Group

Volunteer	The Vice President
Victoria	Mrs. Johnson
Velvet	Lynda Bird Johnson
Venus	Lucy Baines Johnson
Vigilant	Walter Jenkins

Places

Castle	The White House—Executive Mansion plus the two office wings (WHCA)
Crown	The Executive Mansion (WHCA)
Angel	Aircraft 26000 (Air Force One)
Charcoal	Temporary Residence of President (sometimes "Base")
SS 100 X	Presidential automobile
Halfback	Presidential follow-up car (SS)
Varsity	Vice Presidential follow-up car (SS)
Cabin	Hyannis Port, Massachusetts
Hamlet	Auchincloss home on O Street

Château	Glen Ora, Presidential retreat
Crossroads	Middleburg, Virginia
Acrobat	Andrews Field
Calico	Pentagon
Carpet	White House garage
Cork	FBI headquarters, Washington
Central	Executive Office Building (EOB)
Volcano	LBJ Ranch, Texas

Official Family

Wand	Kenneth O'Donnell
Willow	Evelyn Lincoln
Wayside	Pierre Salinger
Market	Dr. George Burkley
Watchman	General Chester Clifton
Warrior	Malcolm Kilduff
Wing	General Godfrey McHugh
Witness	Captain Tazewell Shepard
Tiger	Colonel James Swindal
Freedom	Secretary Dean Rusk

Secret Service Agents

Domino	James Rowley
Duplex	Gerald Behn
Deacon	Floyd Boring
Dazzle	Clint Hill
Dandy	Lem Johns
Digest	Roy Kellerman
Daylight	Jerry Kivett
Debut	Paul Landis
Dusty	Emory Roberts

xv

Size of Stable

Publishing houses talk about their "stable" of authors which, in fact, can be their main assets, whether or not they show up on the books in that manner. For instance, Delacorte has had thirteen #1 bestsellers, and nine of them are by Danielle Steel. So another way of comparing publishers, besides number of #1 books and total #1 weeks on the list, is to look at the size of their stable.

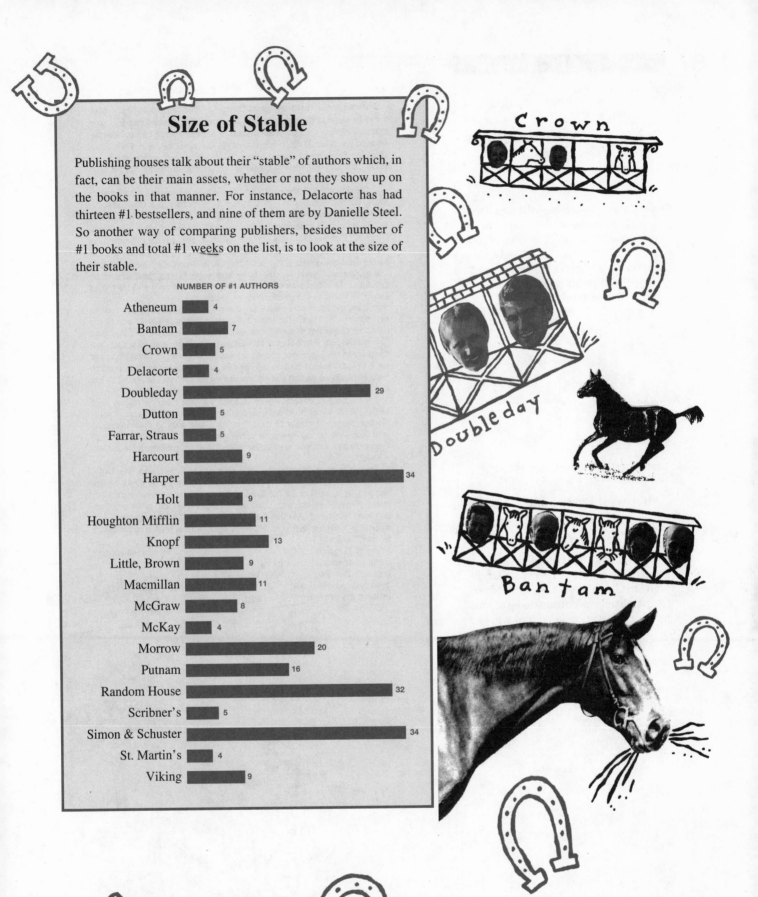

NUMBER OF #1 AUTHORS

Atheneum	4
Bantam	7
Crown	5
Delacorte	4
Doubleday	29
Dutton	5
Farrar, Straus	5
Harcourt	9
Harper	34
Holt	9
Houghton Mifflin	11
Knopf	13
Little, Brown	9
Macmillan	11
McGraw	8
McKay	4
Morrow	20
Putnam	16
Random House	32
Scribner's	5
Simon & Schuster	34
St. Martin's	4
Viking	9

Crown

Doubleday

Bantam

FIRST DATE AT #1: September 10, 1967
TOTAL WEEKS AT #1: 24

Our Crowd: The Great Jewish Families of New York

Stephen Birmingham

HARPER

This history of some of the wealthier families, from the middle of the nineteenth century onward, got off to a shaky start, falling from the list entirely after one week, but then lasted nearly half a year in the #1 position. Birmingham has said, "I think rich people are more interesting than poor people."

FIRST DATE AT #1: February 25, 1968
TOTAL WEEKS AT #1: 8

Between Parent and Child

Haim Ginott

MACMILLAN

Dr. Spock's all-time bestseller came too soon for the *New York Times* list. Israeli-born Dr. Ginott's common sense advice for establishing and maintaining normal parent-adolescent relationships was one of the most popular books of 1968. While only at #1 for eight weeks, it was in the top five for nearly a year.

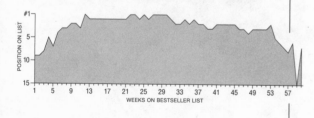

Jeff had some charming social theories. Once, in a newspaper interview, he came out strongly against the practice of shaking hands, saying that this custom sped the transmission of germs. Instead of handshaking, he recommended kissing. He also suggested that the New York Street Cleaning Department should not sprinkle streets their entire length, but leave little dry gaps every block or so, so that old ladies could cross without getting their feet wet.

Jeff Seligman had the health and welfare of the whole human race at heart. He had been made a partner in J. & W. Seligman & Company, but he was never really interested in banking, and there is no evidence that he did any work, executed a single order, or participated in a single decision. But instead, as Geoffrey Hellman has written, "Somewhere along the line he got off on a novel tack. He began to establish himself as the fruit-and-ginger Seligman." He had a theory that plenty of fruit and ginger was good for the body and good for the brains, and he arrived at the office each morning with his basket of fruit and his box of ginger. Starting in the partners' room, where the brains of the company were supposedly concentrated, he distributed his goods to his cousins and uncles. "On even the busiest days, the partners would accept the fruit and ginger Jeff offered," a former Seligman employee told Hellman. "He would then distribute the remainder to the lower echelons. One day, when I was talking to one of the partners in the partners' room, Jeff gave me a banana. I went back to my desk in another room, and a little while later Jeff showed up and started to hand me an orange. He peered at me, and withdrew the orange. 'You've already had your fruit,' he said."

J & W. Seligman eventually established a dining room on the top floor of their Wall Street building, and, having checked to make sure that the kitchen contained plenty of fresh fruit, Jeff was able to discontinue his fruit line, but he continued to serve ginger. Jeff Seligman was Peggy Guggenheim's favorite uncle. She called him "a gentleman of the old school."

Peggy's mother, Florette, was not without her little quirks. She had a strange nervous habit of repeating phrases three times. Once, when stopped by a policeman for driving the wrong way down a one-way street, Florette replied, with some logic, "But I was only going one way, one way, one way." Another family story insists that Florette once told a clerk in a department store, "I want a hat with a feather, a feather, a feather," and was _____ feathers.

Peggy Guggen_____ _____ _____grandmother's circle of friends _____ _____ geoisie." But Pe_____ beholder. Certai____ in their uptown _____

New #1 Books per Year

There has been a highly significant increase in the number of new fiction books that reach #1 each year, between 1960 and now. The number of new books has risen from three or four to nine or ten. In nonfiction, the increase began in 1985, but the climb has been steeper: from four or five a year to 13 in 1991.

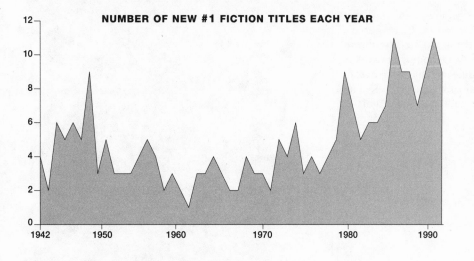

NUMBER OF NEW #1 FICTION TITLES EACH YEAR

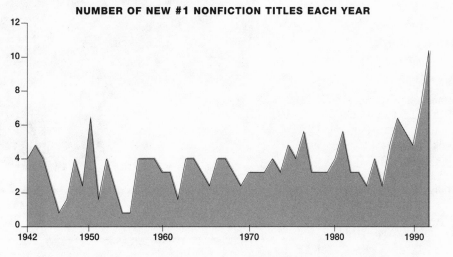

NUMBER OF NEW #1 NONFICTION TITLES EACH YEAR

NUMBER OF NEW #1 NONFICTION AND FICTION TITLES EACH YEAR

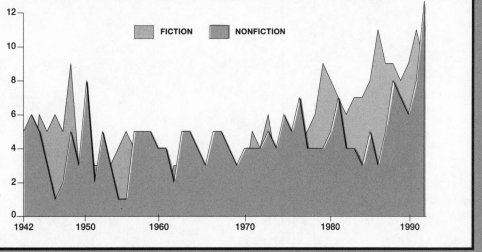

FICTION   NONFICTION

FIRST DATE AT #1: March 3, 1968
TOTAL WEEKS AT #1: 11

The Naked Ape
Desmond Morris
MCGRAW

The Naked Ape addresses in words the same sort of thing that Clare Barne's 1949 #1 hit, *White Collar Zoo* did in photographs. Anthropologist Morris draws on animal behavior studies to show how humans (naked apes) and other animals have much behavior in common.

FIRST DATE AT #1: July 7, 1968
TOTAL WEEKS AT #1: 42

The Money Game
Adam Smith
RANDOM HOUSE

This is a rare instance in which the *New York Times* acknowledged an author's pseudonym by putting "Adam Smith" in quotes every week. Economist George G. Goodman's book about Wall Street, how the money game is played there, and how the players *really* behave, reached #1 in its third week and remained there for 42 consecutive weeks, one of the longest unbroken spans at #1 for any book.

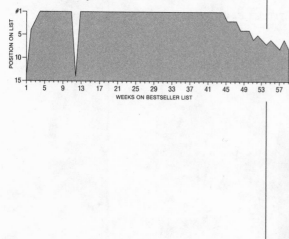

#1 Love and Money Titles

LOVE

Love Is Eternal
The Love Machine
Love Story   MONEY
Men in Love
Love, Medicine and Miracles   *The Moneyman*
                                Everything But Money
*Loves Music, Loves to   *The Money Game*
Dance*   *The Moneychangers*
*By Love   *Sylvia Porter's
Possessed*   Money Book*

PORTNOY'S COMPLAINT

33

"Hamburgers," she says bitterly, just as she might say *Hitler,* "where they can put anything in the world in that they want—and *he* eats them. Jack, make him promise, before he gives himself a terrible *tsura,* and it's too late."

"I *promise!*" I scream. "I *promise!*" and race from the kitchen—to where? Where else.

I tear off my pants, furiously I grab that battered battering ram to freedom, my adolescent cock, even as my mother begins to call from the other side of the bathroom door. "Now this time don't flush. Do you hear me, Alex? I have to see what's in that bowl!"

Doctor, do you understand what I was up against? My wang was all I really had that I could call my own. You should have watched her at work during polio season! She should have gotten medals from the March of Dimes! Open your mouth. Why is your throat red? Do you have a headache you're not telling me about? You're not going to any baseball game, Alex, until I see you move your neck. Is your neck stiff? Then why are you moving it that way? You ate like you were nauseous, are you nauseous? Well, you ate like you were nauseous. I don't want you drinking from the drinking fountain in that playground. If you're thirsty wait until you're home. Your throat is sore, isn't it? I can tell how you're swallowing. I think maybe what you are going to do, Mr. Joe Di Maggio, is put that glove away and lie down. I am not going to allow you to go outside in this heat and run around, not with that sore throat, I'm not. I want to take your temperature. ... To be very frank, I

PI

FIRST DATE AT #1: March 16, 1969
TOTAL WEEKS AT #1: 14

Portnoy's Complaint
Philip Roth
RANDOM HOUSE

Alexander Portnoy, a brilliant Jewish lawyer, fumbles with the meaning of life, his infatuation with gentile girls, and his continuing battles with his mother, as he pours out his life story to his analyst. Roth was writer in residence at the University of Pennsylvania when he wrote this, his fifth novel, and the only one to reach #1.

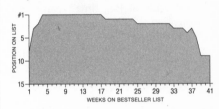

FIRST DATE AT #1: June 22, 1969
TOTAL WEEKS AT #1: 13

The Love Machine
Jacqueline Susann
SIMON & SCHUSTER

Three years after the huge success of *Valley of the Dolls,* Susann returns to #1 with the tale of the rise and fall of Robin Stone, a television network giant called "the love machine" because of his extensive sexual activities, described as vividly as the laws of the 1960s would allow. While a huge financial success, it was not a critical triumph. The *Times* reviewer said "I doubt if I've ever read a novel that made less of an impression. It goes down quickly and easily. It is the kernel of an idea, the seed of an inspiration exploded into bite-sized nothingness."

FIRST DATE AT #1: May 4, 1969
TOTAL WEEKS AT #1: 2

The 900 Days
Harrison Salisbury
HARPER

A *New York Times* journalist's account of the three-year Nazi siege of what was then known as Leningrad during World War Two. The author told *Contemporary Authors* he "first saw Leningrad four or five days after the siege was lifted. I spent about ten days there, became acquainted with the people.... I got the story in crude outline, as much as one could at that time." But much information was unavailable because of censorship imposed by Stalin. After Stalin's death in 1954 Salisbury returned to Russia and began to collect the added information needed for this book.

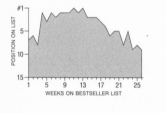

FIRST DATE AT #1: May 11, 1969
TOTAL WEEKS AT #1: 9

Jennie
Ralph Martin
SIGNET

Martin's 12th book and only #1 bestseller is a portrait of Winston Churchill's American-born mother, Lady Randolph Churchill, and her life during the years 1854 to 1895.

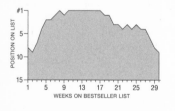

The Best-Selling Book of the Year... But It Never Made #1

Making #1 on the *Times* list requires a large volume of sales in a short period of time. It is possible for a book to be the #1 selling book for an entire *year* without ever having been the #1 bestseller during any single *week*. Indeed, if it happens to be the sort of book the *Times* does not choose to include in its figures, a book can be the #1 seller for the year without appearing on the *Times* list at all.

For whatever the reason, there have, over the last fifty years, been twelve nonfiction books and one fiction book which, according to *Publishers Weekly,* sold more than any other for that year, but which did not make the *Times* list.

FICTION

1947 . . . . *The Miracle of the Bells,* Russell Janey

NONFICTION

1950 . . . . *Betty Crocker Picture Cookbook*
1958 . . . . *Kids Say the Darndest Things,* Art Linkletter
1959 . . . . *Twixt Twelve & Twenty,* Pat Boone
1960 . . . . *Folk Medicine,* William Jarvis
1963 . . . . *Happiness Is a Warm Puppy,* Charles Schultz
1965 . . . . *How to Be a Jewish Mother,* Dan Greenburg
1968 . . . . *Better Homes and Gardens New Cookbook*

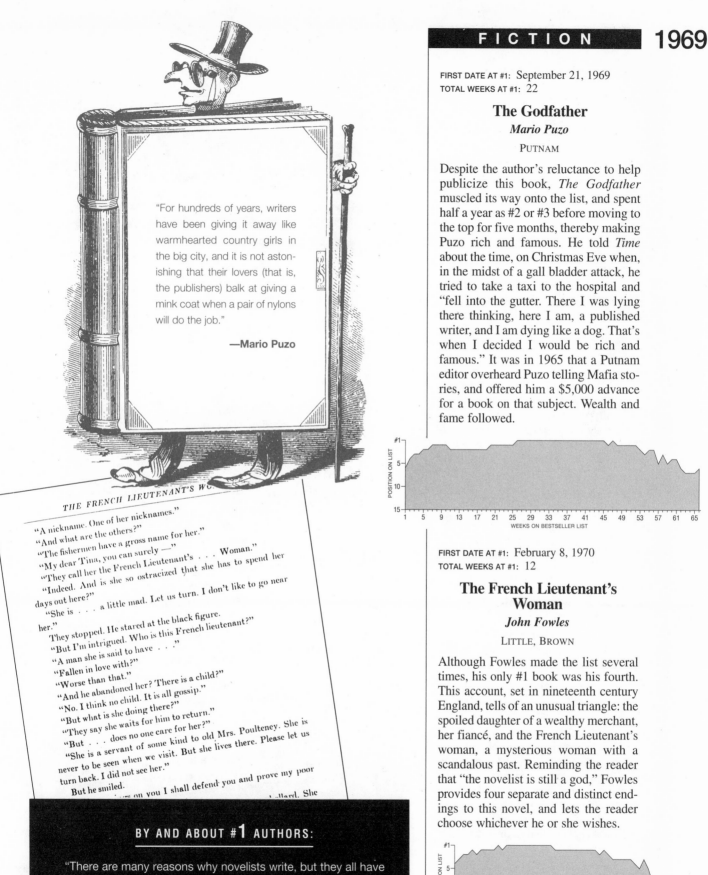

"For hundreds of years, writers have been giving it away like warmhearted country girls in the big city, and it is not astonishing that their lovers (that is, the publishers) balk at giving a mink coat when a pair of nylons will do the job."

—Mario Puzo

THE FRENCH LIEUTENANT'S WO...

"A nickname. One of her nicknames."

"And what are the others?"

"The fishermen have a gross name for her."

"My dear Tina, you can surely —"

"They call her the French Lieutenant's . . . Woman."

"Indeed. And is she so ostracized that she has to spend her days out here?"

"She is . . . a little mad. Let us turn. I don't like to go near her."

They stopped. He stared at the black figure.

"But I'm intrigued. Who is this French lieutenant?"

"A man she is said to have . . ."

"Fallen in love with?"

"Worse than that."

"And he abandoned her? There is a child?"

"No. I think no child. It is all gossip."

"But what is she doing there?"

"They say she waits for him to return."

"But . . . does no one care for her?"

"She is a servant of some kind to old Mrs. Poulteney. She is never to be seen when we visit. But she lives there. Please let us turn back. I did not see her."

But he smiled.

". . . . . on you I shall defend you and prove my poor

. . . . llard. She

BY AND ABOUT #1 AUTHORS:

"There are many reasons why novelists write, but they all have one thing in common: a need to create an alternative world."

—John Fowles

FIRST DATE AT #1: September 21, 1969
TOTAL WEEKS AT #1: 22

The Godfather
Mario Puzo
PUTNAM

Despite the author's reluctance to help publicize this book, *The Godfather* muscled its way onto the list, and spent half a year as #2 or #3 before moving to the top for five months, thereby making Puzo rich and famous. He told *Time* about the time, on Christmas Eve when, in the midst of a gall bladder attack, he tried to take a taxi to the hospital and "fell into the gutter. There I was lying there thinking, here I am, a published writer, and I am dying like a dog. That's when I decided I would be rich and famous." It was in 1965 that a Putnam editor overheard Puzo telling Mafia stories, and offered him a $5,000 advance for a book on that subject. Wealth and fame followed.

FIRST DATE AT #1: February 8, 1970
TOTAL WEEKS AT #1: 12

The French Lieutenant's Woman
John Fowles
LITTLE, BROWN

Although Fowles made the list several times, his only #1 book was his fourth. This account, set in nineteenth century England, tells of an unusual triangle: the spoiled daughter of a wealthy merchant, her fiancé, and the French Lieutenant's woman, a mysterious woman with a scandalous past. Reminding the reader that "the novelist is still a god," Fowles provides four separate and distinct endings to this novel, and lets the reader choose whichever he or she wishes.

FIRST DATE AT #1: July 20, 1969
TOTAL WEEKS AT #1: 22

The Peter Principle

*Laurence Peter and
Raymond Hull*

MORROW

Like *Parkinson's Law* years earlier, *The Peter Principle* became an extremely popular #1 bestseller because of one simple, comprehensible, and brilliant "law," in this instance the contention that people are promoted in an organization until they are no longer able to do the job; they then remain at their level of incompetency forever. Dr. Peter's second book (and the British-born Hull's fourth) was the first of a long series of business-related books that would regularly appear at #1 over the next two decades. Peter once explained that "it was never my intention to decry the sins, mistakes, vanities and incompetencies of my fellow human beings. I am at least as guilty as they." He went on to describe an unsuccessful fundraising effort he organized, at the end of which he followed his own advice: "Quit while you're behind."

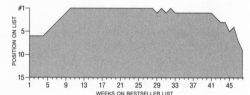

FIRST DATE AT #1: November 30, 1969
TOTAL WEEKS AT #1: 11

The Selling of the President—1968

Joe McGinnis

TRIDENT

Theodore White's third *Making of the President* book didn't make #1, but a young Philadelphia lawyer's account of the inside workings of the Nixon campaign did reach the top. McGinnis informally joined the Nixon forces early in the presidential campaign. His book describes the methods used by advertising and television professionals to make Nixon acceptable to the American voter.

112

The Principle in Action 29

The Case of the Conformist

An incompetent teacher is ineligible for promotion. Dorothea D. Ditto, for example, had been an extremely conforming student in college. Her assignments were either plagiarisms from textbooks and journals, or transcriptions of the professors' lectures. She always did exactly as she was told, no more, no less. *She was considered to be a competent student.* She graduated with honors from the Excelsior Teachers' College.

When she became a teacher, she taught exactly as she herself had been taught. She followed precisely the textbook, the curriculum guide and the bell schedule.

Her work goes fairly well, except when no rule or precedent is available. For example, when a water pipe burst and flooded the classroom floor, Miss Ditto kept on teaching until the principal rushed in and rescued the class.

"Miss Ditto!" he cried. "In the Name of the Superintendent! There are three inches of water on this floor. Why is your class still here?"

She replied, "I didn't hear the emergency bell signal. I pay attention to those things. You know I do. I'm certain you didn't sound the bell." Flummoxed before the power of her awesome *non sequitur*, the principal invoked a provision of the school code giving him emergency powers in an extraordinary circumstance and led her sopping class from the building.

So, although she never breaks a rule or disobeys an order, she is often in trouble, and will never gain promotion. Competent as a student, *she has reached her level of incompetence as a classroom teacher, and will therefore remain in that position throughout her teaching career.*

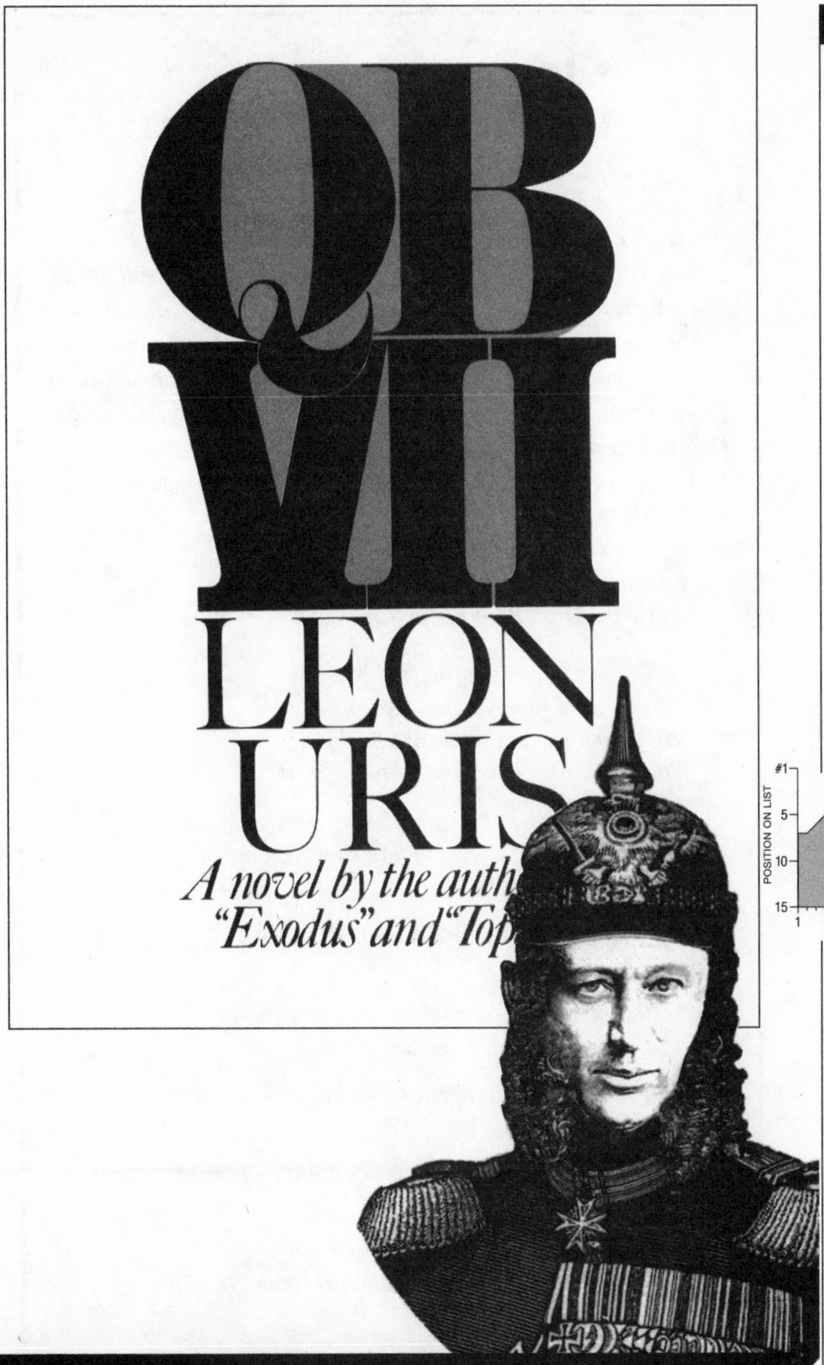

QB VII
LEON URIS

A novel by the auth
"Exodus" and "Top

FIRST DATE AT #1: May 10, 1970
TOTAL WEEKS AT #1: 41

Love Story
Erich Segal

HARPER

What can you say about a beautiful
young girl who spent 10 months as the
#1 bestseller? Yale professor Segal's
heartrending tale of a beautiful, talented,
and happy young woman who slowly
dies captured the hearts of the book-
buying public. It was originally written
as a screenplay (Segal coauthored the
script for *Yellow Submarine*), but when
no one would produce it, he turned it
into a book. When it was informally
nominated for a National Book Award,
the five-judge panel all threatened to
resign, and the trial balloon was de-
flated. This is the last book to have 40
or more weeks in the #1 position.

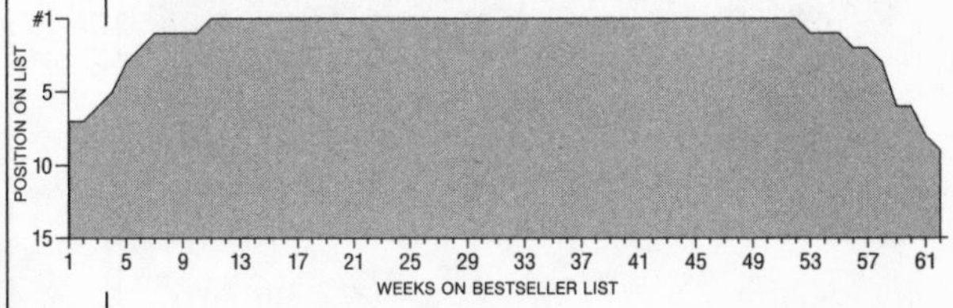

FIRST DATE AT #1: February 21, 1971
TOTAL WEEKS AT #1: 9

QB VII
Leon Uris

DOUBLEDAY

Uris returns to #1 for the first time since
Exodus 12 years earlier with the only
"Q" title ever to make #1. *QB VII* refers
to the courtroom named Queen's Bench
Seven, where an American novelist is
on trial for saying, in a book, that a
brilliant surgeon performed experimental surgery on unwilling Jewish inmates
of a Nazi concentration camp.

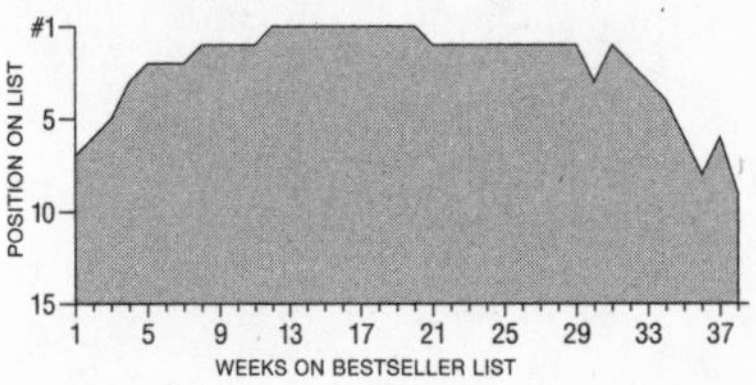

FIRST DATE AT #1: March 1, 1970
TOTAL WEEKS AT #1: 25

Everything You Always Wanted to Know About Sex (But Were Afraid to Ask)

David Reuben

McKay

The book with the longest title of any #1 bestseller also had one of the longer successes on the list: six months at #1 and six more months in the top five. The book consists of Dr. Reuben's light-hearted yet helpful responses to questions about sex. Gore Vidal wrote that Reuben "is a moralist, expressing the hang-ups of today's middle-aged, middle-class urban American Jews."

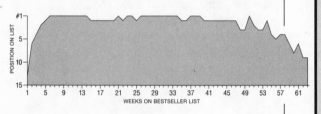

FIRST DATE AT #1: May 3, 1970
TOTAL WEEKS AT #1: 8

Up the Organization

Robert Townsend

Knopf

Extremely practical yet lighthearted advice on succeeding in or running a large organization, from the man who was then the innovative head of Avis car rental. Townsend later said that "I really mean every word I say. I've tested it all in practice. It works. The main point: to get you and the people you work with fired up to achieve whatever goals you select. And always remember: getting there isn't half the fun—it's all the fun."

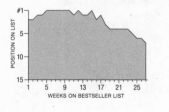

THE LONGEST TITLES

The issue here is how to deal with colons. Many titles, long and short, have a colon, as in *Our Crowd: The Great Jewish Families of New York*. The *Times* is not consistent with regard to including that which follows the colon as part of the title. It seems to be a literary decision: do the words on the right of the colon seem an essential part of the title (as in *Motherhood: The Second Oldest Profession*), or do they merely elaborate it (as in *The Great Depression of 1990: Why It's Got to Happen—How to Protect Yourself*). In most cases, we follow the *Times* usage (when it seems right).

30 LETTERS

Raise the High Roof Beam, Carpenters

31 LETTERS

How to Stop Worrying and Start Living
The Complete Scarsdale Medical Diet
You Can Profit from a Monetary Crisis

33 LETTERS

You'll Never Eat Lunch in this Town Again

34 LETTERS

The Holy Bible: Revised Standard Version

35 LETTERS

Motherhood: The Second Oldest Profession

41 LETTERS

All I Really Need to Know I Learned in Kindergarten

44 LETTERS

If Life Is a Bowl of Cherries, What Am I Doing in the Pits?

47 LETTERS

When You Look Like Your Passport Photo, It's Time to Go Home

57 LETTERS

Everything You Always Wanted to Know About Sex (But Were Afraid to Ask)

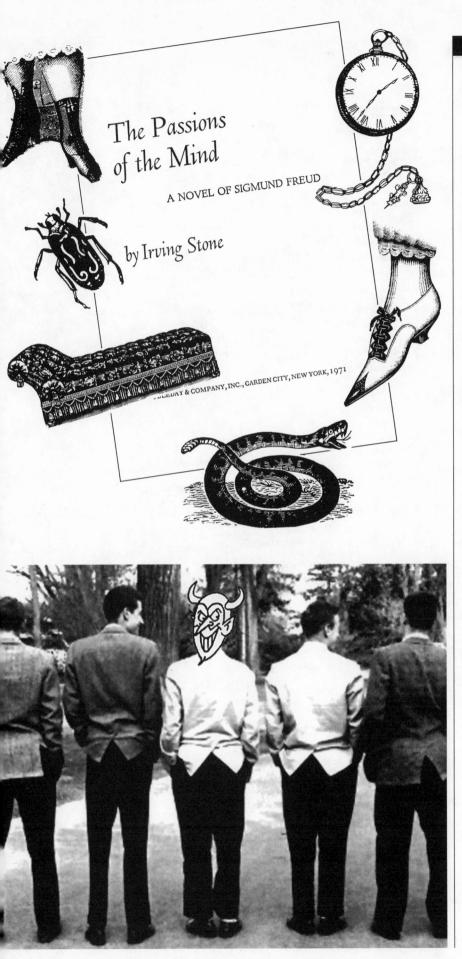

The Passions
of the Mind

A NOVEL OF SIGMUND FREUD

by Irving Stone

DOUBLEDAY & COMPANY, INC., GARDEN CITY, NEW YORK, 1971

FIRST DATE AT #1: April 25, 1971
TOTAL WEEKS AT #1: 13

The Passions of the Mind
Irving Stone
DOUBLEDAY

Lincoln in the '50s, Michelangelo in the '60s, and now Stone returns to #1 for the third and last time with Sigmund Freud in the '70s. His biographical novel was the "summer read" for 1971, at least until Freud was displaced by a demon.

FIRST DATE AT #1: July 25, 1971
TOTAL WEEKS AT #1: 12

The Exorcist
William Peter Blatty
HARPER

The first out-and-out horror story to reach #1, Blatty's book deals with a young girl who is possessed by the devil, and the attempts made to remove same. The author, a former vacuum cleaner salesman and beer truck driver said, "I knew it was going to be a success. I couldn't wait to finish it and become famous." The reviewer for *Time* also predicted success: "Pretentious, tasteless, abominably written, redundant pastiche of superficial theology, comic book psychology, Grade C movie dialogue and Grade Z scatology. In short, [it] will be a best seller..."

FIRST DATE AT #1: September 20, 1970
TOTAL WEEKS AT #1: 8

The Sensuous Woman
"J"

LYLE STUART/CARROLL PUBLISHING

The first #1 bestseller by an obviously pseudonymous author (unless "Adam Smith" in quotes can be considered obvious). The author was later revealed to be Joan Terry Garrity, a staff member at Lyle Stuart who had previously written a book on shopping in New York, and who was at the time writing a book on golf resorts in Florida. *The Sensuous Man*, a few years later, reached the list but never came close to #1—just the reverse of the Kinsey report, where the male made it but the female didn't.

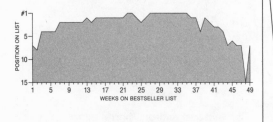

FIRST DATE AT #1: December 27, 1970
TOTAL WEEKS AT #1: 20

The Greening of America
Charles Reich

RANDOM HOUSE

Subtitled "How the youth rebellion is trying to make America livable," this attorney's book about the revolution against many of the values technology has thrust upon us, asks whether America can develop a new consciousness. While the public loved it, not all the critics agreed. The *Atlantic Monthly* reviewer suggested that "his book is such a tissue of imprecisions, contradictions, and generalizations, not to mention unsubstantiated predictions and prophecies of the most apocalyptic kind, it is difficult indeed to associate it with an outstanding legal mind."

THE SENSUOUS WOMAN

I've never met a woman yet who didn't occasionally fake it.

And if you feel very Bernhardtish and want to throw in a few extra wriggles and a yelp or two along the way, to match his passion, go ahead. But be careful not to ham it up too much. Then he really will suspect you're acting and feel very disillusioned and inadequate, which is, of course, the opposite of the response you are lovingly trying to create.

Women have been faking since time began. Some of the biggest fakes have been women famous for their sexual prowess—courtesans, mistresses, love goddesses. When in some instances their lives or reputations depended upon their being a hot and erotic playmate, those ladies weren't about to let a little lack of true passion interfere with their lovemaking. They a____d their beautiful little heads and bodies off ____ ____gets up on the wrong side ____ ____make love, ____ stays ____ head ____ the ____

I ____ wo____ ev____

ORGASM—YOURS, NOT HIS

learning to be an expert fake yourself. There are three good reasons for it:

1. You make him happy.
2. A happy lover comes back again, and the next time you will probably be wild with passion and can hardly wait to make love.
3. Sometimes, if you are a really proficient actress, you fake yourself right into a *real* orgasm.

To become a fabulous fake, study again every contortion, muscle spasm and body response that lead to and make up the orgasm and rehearse the process privately until you can duplicate it.

But, keep very clearly in mind that, no matter how furious you become at him, no matter how much you may at some moment want to hurt him, no matter how much you may want to temporarily destroy him, you must *never, never* reveal to him that you have acted sometimes in bed.

You will betray a trust shared by every other female in the world if you do.

There are some secrets each sex should never reveal to the other. This is one of them.

And, on the practical side again, if you do squeal and later patch up the disagreement,

181

Anatomy of a Plot

The Englishman nodded, satisfied.

"All right. I think I had better take the gun and the ammunition now. I shall contact you again on Tuesday or Wednesday next week."

The Belgian was about to protest when the customer forestalled him.

"I believe I still owe you some seven hundred pounds. Here"—he dropped another few bundles of notes onto the blotter—" is a further five hundred. The outstanding two hundred pounds you will receive when I get the rest of the equipment."

"*Merci, monsieur,*" said the armourer, scooping the five bundles of twenty five-pound notes into his pocket. Piece by piece he disassembled the rifle, placing each component carefully into its green baize-lined compartment in the carrying case. The single explosive bullet the assassin had asked for was wrapped in a separate piece of tissue paper and slotted into the case beside the cleaning rags and brushes. When the case was closed, he proffered it and the box of shells to the Englishman, who pocketed the shells and kept the neat attaché case in his hand.

M. Goossens showed him politely out.

The Jackal arrived back at his hotel in time for a late lunch. First he placed the case containing the gun carefully in the bottom of the wardrobe, locked it, and pocketed the key.

In the afternoon he strolled unhurriedly into the main post office and asked for a call to a number in Zurich, Switzerland. It took half an hour for the call to be put through and another five minutes until Herr Meier came on the line. The Englishman introduced himself by quoting a number and then giving his name.

Herr Meier excused himself and came back two minutes later. His tone had lost the cautious reserve it had prev̶i̶o̶u̶s̶ ̶had. Customers whose accounts in dollars ̶a̶n̶d̶ ̶ ̶ ̶ ̶ ̶ eadily merited ̶ ̶ourteous t̶ ̶ ̶ question, and ̶ ̶ ̶ ̶ e back on the ̶ ̶ ̶e customer's ̶ ̶ ̶ ̶ying it. ̶ ̶ ̶ ̶hone booth. ̶ ̶ ̶ inform you

/ 113

The Day of the JACKAL

Frederick Forsyth

New York / THE VIKING PRESS

FIRST DATE AT #1: October 17, 1971
TOTAL WEEKS AT #1: 7

The Day of the Jackal
Frederick Forsyth
VIKING

Forsyth makes the first of his three appearances at #1 with this novel about an Englishman known as "The Jackal" who takes on an assignment from a secret French army organization to murder Charles DeGaulle, and must evade the French security forces unleashed against him. The *Washington Post* reported that Forsyth's plot was so plausible, French newspapers launched their own investigation to see if parts of the book might be true. The author paid close attention to background details and said he consulted with a professional assassin, a passport forger, and a manufacturer of illegal weapons in the course of researching this book.

FIRST DATE AT #1: November 7, 1971
TOTAL WEEKS AT #1: 7

Wheels
Arthur Hailey
DOUBLEDAY

The second of Hailey's four #1 bestsellers, this extremely detailed account of how the automobile manufacturing world works is woven into a fictionalized account of some of its players. Hailey has told interviewers that he spends about a year researching his subject, six months reviewing notes and planning, and 18 months writing. When he interviews people, he neither tapes them, nor takes notes, in an effort to keep them relaxed and talkative. As soon as possible, he dictates his findings into a tape recorder.

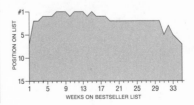

FIRST DATE AT #1: January 10, 1971

TOTAL WEEKS AT #1: 1

Civilisation

Kenneth Clark

HARPER

The first public television #1 bestseller, the book is a compilation of 13 lectures originally presented by Dr. Clark (Ph.D., Oxford) in a BBC series. The result is a history of western Europe from the fall of Rome to the present, constructed from the evidence of its visible artifacts. To critics who suggested that he claimed to be an expert on almost everything, Clark said, "I've never tried to be an expert on all of those things. If you like to say I'm a popularizer, I have no objection. My main aim has been to make things understandable to people."

FIRST DATE AT #1: May 30, 1971

TOTAL WEEKS AT #1: 25

Bury My Heart at Wounded Knee

Dee Brown

HOLT

The settlement of the West as the Indian saw it; the 19th book and only #1 by a man who had been an agricultural librarian for more than 30 years. Brown said he kept his perspective by saying, every night, "I am a very very old Indian and I am remembering the past and I am looking toward the Atlantic Ocean."

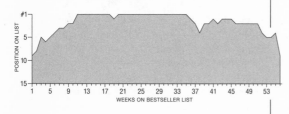

Total Time on the List for #1 Books

This is a list of *total* time on the *New York Times* list for books that spent at least one week in #1. There are a few books that spent a year or more on the list without ever reaching the top. Indeed, *Games People Play* was on the list about two years without ever reaching #1.

4 YEARS OR MORE

A Light in the Attic	Shel Silverstein

3 TO 4 YEARS

Peace of Mind	Joshua Liebman
The Power of Positive Thinking	Norman Vincent Peale
The Robe	Lloyd Douglas

2 TO 3 YEARS

Advise and Consent	Allen Drury
Auntie Mame	Patrick Dennis
A Brief History of Time	Stephen Hawking
The Caine Mutiny	Herman Wouk
A Man Called Peter	Catherine Marshall
Oh, the Places You'll Go	Dr. Seuss

1½ TO 2 YEARS

The Agony and the Ecstasy	Irvine Stone
All I Really Need to Know I Learned in Kindergarten	Robert Fulghum
The Complete Book of Running	James Fixx
The Egg and I	Betty MacDonald
Exodus	Leon Uris
Jane Fonda's Workout Book	Jane Fonda
Forever Amber	Kathleen Winsor
Hawaii	James Michener
Iacocca	Lee Iacocca
Not as a Stranger	Morton Thompson
The Sea Around Us	Rachel Carson

1 TO 1½ YEARS

Airport	Arthur Hailey
Anatomy of a Murder	Robert Traver
Between Parent and Child	Haim Ginott
The Bible, Revised Standard Version	
The Big Fisherman	Lloyd Douglas
Bonfire of the Vanities	Tom Wolfe
Brave Men	Ernie Pyle
Bury My Heart at Wounded Knee	Dee Brown
Centennial	James Michener
Cosmos	Carl Sagan
Désireé	Annemarie Selinko

FIRST DATE AT #1: January 23, 1972
TOTAL WEEKS AT #1: 21

The Winds of War
Herman Wouk

LITTLE, BROWN

Twenty years after *The Caine Mutiny*, Wouk (his name is pronounced 'Woke') returns to World War Two with this story of the remarkable Commander Henry, whose position in 1939 puts him in contact with Roosevelt, Hitler, Stalin, and Churchill, while his sons go off to war, his daughter is embroiled in a sordid love affair, and his wife contemplates divorce.

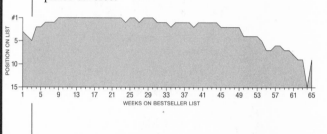

FIRST DATE AT #1: May 14, 1972
TOTAL WEEKS AT #1: 2

The Word
Irving Wallace

SIMON & SCHUSTER

Wallace is one of five authors to have both a fiction and a nonfiction #1. The 15th of his 32 books (all but one starting with "The"), *The Word* is the story of a public relations man hired to help promote a radical new translation of the Bible that includes sections allegedly written by James, the brother of Jesus. As he investigates the work, his belief in its authenticity falters. Wallace reports he received "endless letters...asking me if the Gospel According to James, which I had invented, really had been dug up by archeologists...." Wallace died in 1990.

FIRST DATE AT #1: July 25, 1971
TOTAL WEEKS AT #1: 1

The Female Eunuch

Germaine Greer

MCGRAW

An English teacher at Warwick University reviews reasons for female discontent, considers women's cultural history and relationships to men, and proposes social reforms to help liberate women.

FIRST DATE AT #1: November 28, 1971
TOTAL WEEKS AT #1: 1

Honor Thy Father

Gay Talese

WORLD

A history of the Mafia, beginning with its origins in Sicily, through its growth, prosperity, and (the author says) decline in America, focusing on members of the Bonano family. The author survived to produce another #1 bestseller nine years later.

FIRST DATE AT #1: December 5, 1971
TOTAL WEEKS AT #1: 15

Eleanor and Franklin

Joseph Lash

NORTON

Based on the private papers of Eleanor Roosevelt, this biography focusing on her unusual relationship with her husband, the president. The author met the first lady in 1939 en route to defend himself before the House Unamerican Activities Committee; a 20-year friendship ensued.

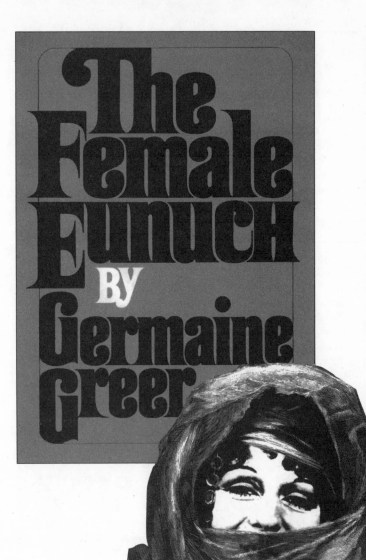

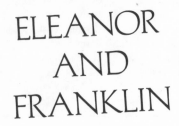

JOSEPH P. LASH

Foreword by Arthur M. Schlesinger, Jr.

Introduction by Franklin D. Roosevelt, Jr.

ELEANOR
AND
FRANKLIN

*The story of their relationship, based on
Eleanor Roosevelt's private papers*

They came in the evening, then, and found Jonathan gliding peaceful and alone through his beloved sky. The two gulls that appeared at his wings were pure as starlight, and the glow from them was gentle and friendly in the high night air. But most lovely of all was the skill with which they flew, their wingtips moving a precise and constant inch from his own.

Without a word, Jonathan put them to his test, a test that no gull had ever passed. He twisted his wings, slowed to a single mile per hour above stall. The two radiant birds slowed with him, smoothly, locked in position. They knew about slow flying.

He folded his wings, rolled, and dropped in a dive to a hundred ninety miles per hour. They dropped with him, streaking down in flawless formation.

At last he turned that speed straight up into a long vertical slow-roll. They rolled with him, smiling.

He recovered to level flight and was quiet for a time before he spoke. "Very well," he said, "who are you?"

"We're from your Flock, Jonathan. We are your brothers." The words were strong and calm. "We've come to take you higher, to take you home."

"Home I have none. Flock I have none. I am Outcast. And we fly now at the peak of the Great Mountain Wind. Beyond a few hundred feet, I can lift this old body no higher."

46

FIRST DATE AT #1: July 2, 1972
TOTAL WEEKS AT #1: 38

Jonathan Livingston Seagull
Richard Bach
MACMILLAN

Bach's fourth book is a parable about a seagull who loves to fly. After being banished from his flock, he practices the art of flying until he is transported to a higher world for gulls who, like him, seek perfection. The book was rejected by many publishers, but Macmillan brought out a small first printing. The author told a reporter that "Something invisible guides any ideal into communication. Jonathan came in the '70s, when people needed to hear what he is saying to them. If I had finished the manuscript in the late '50s when I started it, the book probably would not have been accepted."

FIRST DATE AT #1: March 25, 1973
TOTAL WEEKS AT #1: 1

The Odessa File
Frederick Forsyth
VIKING

ODESSA is an acronym for an organization established to shield Nazi SS officers living under new names. When a young German reporter attempts to penetrate the organization, they must do everything in their power to stop him in this, the second of Forsyth's three #1s. Regarding his literary skills, he once told *Contemporary Authors,* "I'm a writer with the intent of selling lots of copies and making money. I don't think my work will ever be regarded as great literature or classics. I'm just a commercial writer and I have no illusions about it."

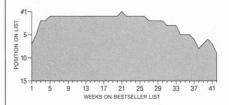

121

FIRST DATE AT #1: March 19, 1972
TOTAL WEEKS AT #1: 10

The Game of the Foxes
Ladislas Farago
MCKAY

In the U.S. National Archives, the author discovered a metal box full of microfilm about the German intelligence service. After analyzing those materials, his 15th book told "the untold story of German espionage in the U.S. and Britain during World War Two."

FIRST DATE AT #1: May 28, 1972
TOTAL WEEKS AT #1: 6

The Boys of Summer
Roger Kahn
HARPER

In the summer of '72, the big hit was a nostalgic look at the summers of the late 1940s, and the great Brooklyn Dodgers baseball teams of that period. Another baseball book (*The Summer Game*) by another Roger (Angell) was popular around the same time.

THE GAME OF THE FOXES

The Untold Story of German Espionage in the United States and Great Britain During World War II

Ladislas Farago
Author of PATTON

Prologue

Him

HE BURST upon the theatrical scene in 1945. He was Mike Wayne—a born winner. He had been known as the best crap shooter in the Air Force, and the thirteen thousand dollars in cash, strapped around his waist, proved the legend to be fact.

When he was in his late teens he had already figured the stock market and show business to be the two biggest crap games in the world. He was twenty-seven when he got out of the Air Force and crazy about girls, so he picked show business. He parlayed his thirteen thousand into sixty with five hot days at Aqueduct.

By investing it in a Broadway show he became co-producer. The show was a hit and he married Vicki Hill, the most beautiful girl in the chorus.

Vicki wanted to be a star, and he gave her the chance. In 1948 he produced his first big lavish musical on his own and starred his wife. It was a hit, in spite of her. The critics praised his theatrical know-how in surrounding her with talented performers, a foolproof book, and a hit score. But they all agreed that Vicki was less than adequate.

When the show ended its run, he "retired" her. ("Baby, you gotta know how to walk away from the table when the dice are cold. I gave you your shot. Now you give me a son.")

On New Year's Day, 1950, she presented him with a baby girl. He [...] and when the nurse put the ba[...] world[...]

Wh[...]
wife.[...]

Jacqueline Susann

Once Is Not Enough

FIRST DATE AT #1: May 6, 1973
TOTAL WEEKS AT #1: 8

Once Is Not Enough
Jacqueline Susann
MORROW

The last of her three #1s, and her shortest time at the top. A woman who grows up worshipping her producer father and wishing only to take her place by his side becomes disillusioned at the age of 20 and must search desperately for her own fulfillment. About her writing, Susann once said, "The day is over when the point of writing is just to turn a phrase that critics will quote, like Henry James. I'm not interested in turning a phrase; what matters to me is telling a story that involves people. The hell with what critics say. I've made characters live, so that people talk about them at cocktail parties, and that, to me, is what counts. You have to have a divine conceit in your judgment. I have it." Susann died in 1974.

FIRST DATE AT #1: July 1, 1973
TOTAL WEEKS AT #1: 10

Breakfast of Champions
Kurt Vonnegut
DELACORTE

Probably the only #1 bestseller in which the leading characters are a Pontiac dealer, a science fiction writer (Philboyd Sludge, apparently modeled after the author), and an artist. Also one of the few #1 books also illustrated by the author or, as he described his doodles, "trying to clear my head of all the junk in there." The themes include racial tensions, sexual fantasies, and pollution. The first of Vonnegut's two #1s.

FIRST DATE AT #1: June 25, 1972
TOTAL WEEKS AT #1: 23

I'm OK, You're OK
Thomas Harris
HARPER

Harris describes a method of psychiatric group treatment called transactional analysis, and shows how it applies to problems relating to marriage, child-rearing, violence, and war. It spent a year in the top five, nearly half of that at #1. The title refers to the proper attitude for a mature adult who is at peace with himself or herself and with the world. Another transactional analyst, Eric Berne, had been on the list for more than two years with his book *Games People Play,* but it never reached #1.

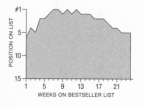

FIRST DATE AT #1: July 23, 1972
TOTAL WEEKS AT #1: 4

O Jerusalem!
Larry Collins and Dominique LaPierre
SIMON & SCHUSTER

The authors describe people and events in the 1948 battle between Arabs and Jews for control of the city of Jerusalem. The two men had a unique style of collaboration. "We do a very detailed outline.... Then Dominique may take the first section and write it in French. I'll take the second and write it in English. Then we read them to each other. I'll translate his French into English while he's doing the reverse to my draft.... The process yields two final manuscripts, one in French, and one in English." This book was the first on the subject published in Hebrew and Arabic. "We were attacked by the extremists on both sides, so we knew we had to be doing something right."

THOMAS A. HARRIS, M.D.

I'M OK—
YOU'RE OK

A
PRACTICAL GUIDE
TO TRANSACTIONAL
ANALYSIS

The Subject Matter of #1 Fiction Bestsellers

Putting the subject matter of a book into categories is a very subjective sort of thing. But the following categories seemed to make good sense for the kinds of books that appear at #1 on the *New York Times* list. The charts show the number of books in each category during the 1940s through the 1980s (which includes the beginning of the 1990s). Clearly Thrillers are the growth industry.

THRILLERS	'40s	'50s	'60s	'70s	'80s+
Horror	0	0	0	2	13
Spy	0	0	1	1	12
Mystery/Crime	0	1	1	6	15
High-Tech Saga	0	0	2	2	6
The Sum of all Thrillers	**0**	**1**	**4**	**11**	**46**

PEOPLE	'40s	'50s	'60s	'70s	'80s+
One person's upbeat story	3	5	1	0	3
One person's ordeal story	6	3	3	7	12
"Life review"	4	3	1	0	0
Family story	9	3	5	0	10
Total for People	**22**	**14**	**10**	**7**	**25**

SAGAS	'40s	'50s	'60s	'70s	'80s+
Romance	4	6	3	2	2
Historical	8	3	3	6	11
Political	1	3	1	4	1
Total for Sagas	**13**	**12**	**7**	**12**	**14**

MISCELLANEOUS	'40s	'50s	'60s	'70s	'80s+
War	0	0	0	2	2
Fantasy	0	0	0	1	3
Stort Stories	0	0	0	0	3

FIRST DATE AT #1: September 9, 1973
TOTAL WEEKS AT #1: 11

The Hollow Hills
Mary Stewart
MORROW

A rare instance in which a sequel (to *The Crystal Cave*, which never made #1) does better than the original. In Stewart's second book about the wizard Merlin, Arthur is born and sent into hiding. Merlin does not see Arthur again until he is nearly a man. A successful author of Gothic thrillers Stewart told *Contemporary Authors* that she "always planned [to] write a historical novel, and I intended to use Roman Britain as the setting. But then, quite by chance, I came upon a [book describing] Merlin, the Arthurian 'enchanter.' Here was a new story, offering a new approach to a dark and difficult period.... It has been a tough job and a rewarding one. I have learned a lot, not least that the powerful themes of the Arthurian ... are as cogent and real today as they were fourteen centuries ago. And Merlin's story has allowed me to return to my first avocation of all, that of poet."

FIRST DATE AT #1: January 14, 1973
TOTAL WEEKS AT #1: 3

Harry S. Truman
Margaret Truman
MORROW

The late president's daughter writes about her father, from his early days as a haberdasher to his retirement years. With *Mommie Dearest,* this is one of only two #1 books by a child about a parent. Miss Truman went on to write a popular series of murder mysteries, even though "I am always glad when a book is finished. I promise myself never to write another one, but I shall probably do one."

FIRST DATE AT #1: January 21, 1973
TOTAL WEEKS AT #1: 2

The Best and the Brightest
David Halberstam
RANDOM HOUSE

Pulitzer Prize-winning reporter Halberstam described the decision-making process that got us into the Vietnam war and kept us there, particularly the men who made those critical decisions. Regarding the years of research that went into this book, Halberstam told *Maclean's,* "What I like to think about myself is that I work harder than people who are smarter and that I'm smarter than people who work harder...I talk to everybody. I just don't see the generals—what I call four-star interviews where everything is all set up for you. I start with the privates so when I get to the top I know what I'm talking about." Thirteen years later, Halberstam returned to the #1 spot with a baseball book.

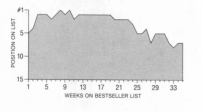

Harry S. Truman

BY Margaret Truman

f becoming a one-... *imes* gave Dewey ...ried a picture of ...e next President ... Francisco Bay." ...sist that there was no

That afternoon my father pulled his neatest trick of the campaign. He went to lunch at the Rockwood Country Club, where he was the guest of honor at a party given by the mayor of Independence, Roger Sermon. There were about thirty old friends at this hoedown, and they gleefully connived in his plan. While the hapless reporters lurked outside, Dad excused himself, supposedly to go to the men's room. Then, with three Secret Service men in tow, he went out the back door and drove to the Elms Hotel at Excelsior Springs, about twenty-five miles from Independence. There he had a Turkish bath, ate a ham sandwich, drank a glass of milk, and proceeded to do exactly what he had predicted he was going to do that morning—go to bed.

This was very shrewd from his point of view, but it left Mother and me alone to cope with squadrons of frantic reporters. I am not using that word "frantic" loosely either. It became more and more apropos as the votes began to come in. At first everyone was told that there would be a Dewey victory message at nine P.M. But Harry Truman seemed to be winning at nine P.M.—as a matter of fact, Dad never was behind—and this historic Republican event was postponed. By midnight we were 1,200,000 votes ahead. But commentator H. V. Kaltenborn kept insisting that there was nothing to worry about, the Democratic candidate was a sure loser. At the Elms Hotel, Dad woke up and heard this prediction, couched in Mr. Kaltenborn's slightly Germanic tones. The candidate chuckled and went back to sleep.

On Delaware Street, meanwhile, reporters were practically storming the house. Again and again I was forced to go out on the porch in my best black dress and ballet slippers (great for weary feet) to assure them that my father was not in the house. When they finally believed me, they began trying to wheedle out of me exactly where he was. That was one night when I was grateful for my native Missouri stubbornness. I sometimes wonder if I

[40]

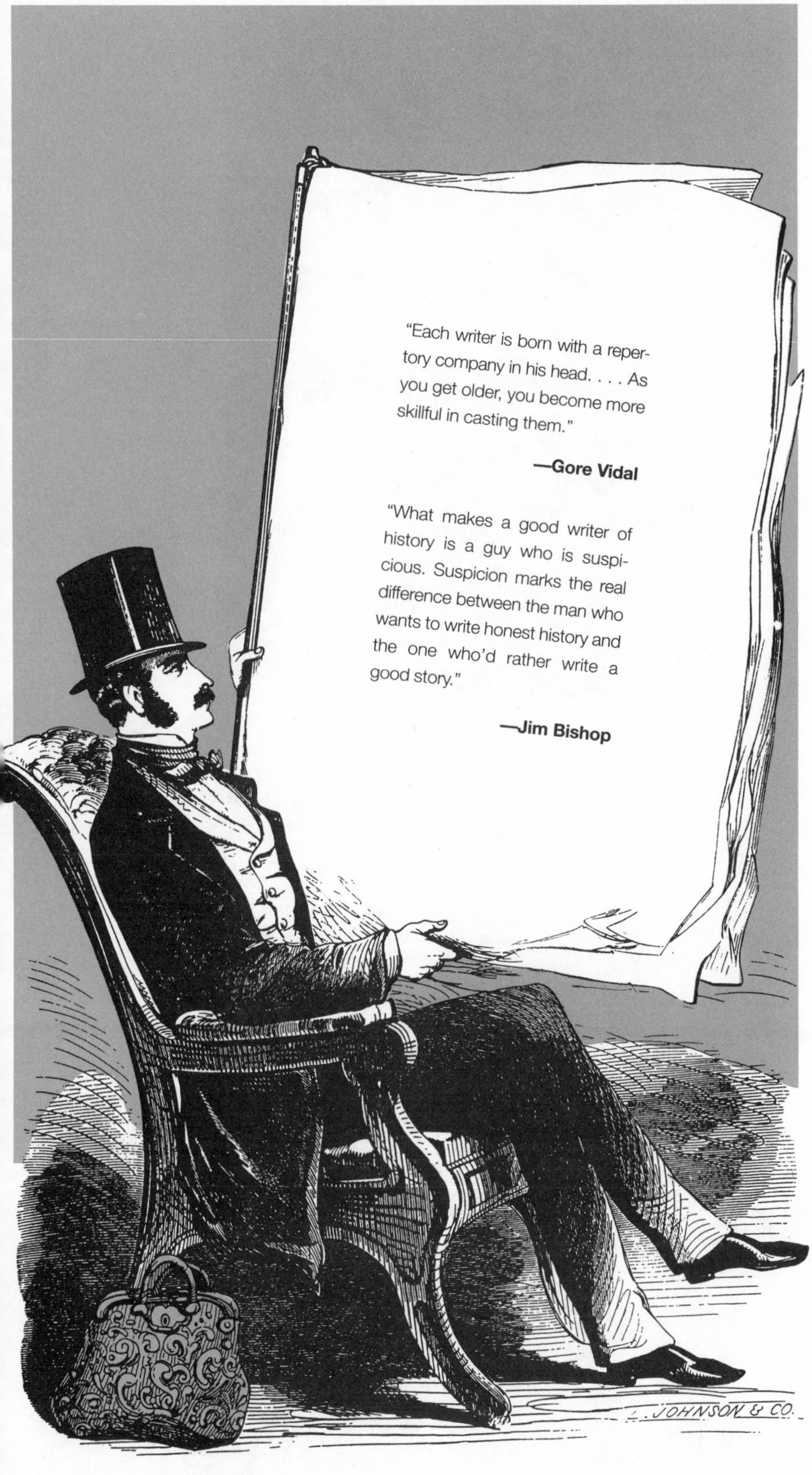

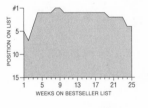

"Each writer is born with a repertory company in his head. . . . As you get older, you become more skillful in casting them."
—Gore Vidal
"What makes a good writer of history is a guy who is suspicious. Suspicion marks the real difference between the man who wants to write honest history and the one who'd rather write a good story."
—Jim Bishop
L. JOHNSON & CO.

FIRST DATE AT #1: November 25, 1973
TOTAL WEEKS AT #1: 2

The Honorary Consul

Graham Greene

SIMON & SCHUSTER

Greene published at least 50 books before this, his only #1 bestseller. This tale of men who make great sacrifices in order to try to live in conscience and help the poor in a tyrannical world centers on the politically motivated kidnapping of a British functionary near Argentina's Paraguayan border. Greene has said that the writers who most affected him were Ford Madox Ford, Joseph Conrad, and his idol, Henry James. But to say James influenced him is "a bit absurd, like saying a mountain influenced a mouse."

#1
5
10
15
POSITION ON LIST
1 5 9 13 17 21 25
WEEKS ON BESTSELLER LIST

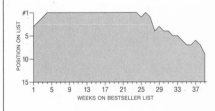

FIRST DATE AT #1: December 9, 1973
TOTAL WEEKS AT #1: 22

Burr

Gore Vidal

RANDOM HOUSE

Vidal takes a witty look at the early days of American history, and manages to transform Aaron Burr, a textbook villain, into a cynical observer of his contemporaries, the country's founding fathers.

#1
5
10
15
POSITION ON LIST
1 5 9 13 17 21 25 29 33 37
WEEKS ON BESTSELLER LIST

FIRST DATE AT #1: February 18, 1973
TOTAL WEEKS AT #1: 28

Dr. Atkins' Diet Revolution
Robert C. Atkins

MCKAY

The New York internist's "high calorie way to stay thin forever" took nearly three months to rise to #1, but once there, it remained for more than half a year, before food gave way to sex.

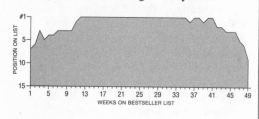

FIRST DATE AT #1: August 5, 1973
TOTAL WEEKS AT #1: 11

The Joy of Sex
Alex Comfort

CROWN

Dr. Comfort's how-to guide to improving sexual techniques suffered from *primus interruptus* on six occasions, but managed to stay up in the top five for 70 consecutive weeks, 11 of them at #1. The author, a medical doctor who also has a Ph.D., is the author of eight novels, nine books of poetry, two plays, and a dozen textbooks. He has told interviewers that he divides his time between medicine, science, and politico-social agitation. Seventeen years later, a revised and reillustrated (somewhat more graphic) version was popular, but never came near the #1 spot.

WHAT THIS BOOK WILL REVEAL TO YOU · 3

THIS IS A NO-HUNGER DIET. One of the happy side effects of this deliberately unbalanced therapeutic diet is the fantastic change that it brings about in your hunger pattern.

My patients lose whether they eat more or less on this no-hunger diet. Most people eat less, but it's only because what they get on this diet so completely satisfies their hunger. They find they just can't eat as much as they used to.

But some have lost thirty, forty, one hundred, or more pounds, while consuming two to three thousand calories or more a day, enough to make the point that if you want to eat that much, you *still* can lose.

They've lost weight on bacon and eggs for breakfast, on heavy cream in their coffee, on mayonnaise in their salads, butter sauce on their lobster; on spareribs, roast duck, pastrami; on my special cheesecake for dessert. (See recipe, page 246.) And on this diet, cholesterol levels usually go down, and even more important, triglyceride levels (you'll learn about this in the recipe chapter) almost always go down. My patients have shed years along with the pounds. They have gained energy, cheerfulness, self-confidence. They're new people. And they no longer count calories.

This is because I don't believe that losing weight is a simple matter of counting calories and of just operating the body on a calorie deficit.

THE CALORIE-COUNTING APPROACH HAS FAILED. Orthodox medicine's conspicuous lack of success in treating overweight hasn't caused the profession to search widely for alternatives to calorie-counting approaches.

Instead, other events have taken place. A gigantic low-calorie food and drink industry has exploded into being. The drug industry has produced a multicolored Niagara of diet pills. Have all these appetite suppressants and all these low-calorie victuals and drinks turned us from a fat nation into a trim nation? You know the answer! Every year more of us worry about overweight, and rightly so, for every year in our increasingly sedentary society, more of us age and die

Places in #1 Titles that Cannot Be Found on a Map

CENTENNIAL (Colorado)

Raintree County

Santa Vittoria (Italy)

KELL

Lake Wobegon (MINNESOTA)

Watership Down

Peyton Place

FIRST DATE AT #1: May 5, 1974
TOTAL WEEKS AT #1: 11

Watership Down
Richard Adams
MACMILLAN

The only #1 bestseller in which all the leading characters are rabbits. This is the saga of a heroic band of bunnies searching for a new home. Adams, then a British civil servant, told the story to his daughters, then wrote it down. After it was rejected at least seven times, he approached Rex Collings, who had just reissued an animal fantasy book. Collings brought out a limited edition of 2,000. Penguin reprinted it as a juvenile book in England, but Macmillan brought it out as an adult book in America. Not everyone loved it. The *National Review* critic wrote, "Athos, Porthos and D'Artagnan on a diet of grass. *Watership Down* is pleasant enough, but it has about the same intellectual firepower as *Dumbo*."

FIRST DATE AT #1: August 4, 1974
TOTAL WEEKS AT #1: 10

Tinker, Tailor, Soldier, Spy
John le Carré
KNOPF

In le Carré's second of seven #1s, secret agent Smiley is lured out of retirement in a desperate effort to locate a Soviet double agent, the spymaster Karla. The success of le Carré's spy novels enabled him to quit the British Foreign Office. He told the *Times* of London, "I had said to my accountant, if my assets reach £20,000, would you let me know?... When he told me I had reached that amount... it was a great relief. I gave in my resignation."

FIRST DATE AT #1: October 14, 1973
TOTAL WEEKS AT #1: 5

How to Be Your Own Best Friend

Mildred Newman, Bernard Berkowitz and Jean Owen

RANDOM HOUSE

The third and last "How to" book to reach #1, and one of only four books in 50 years with three authors, takes the form of a conversation with two psychoanalysts. The authors believe we can help ourselves only when we take the responsibility for our own choices. The book was on the list for nearly a year, and rose to #1 four times over a five-month period.

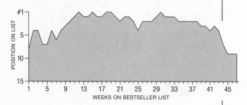

FIRST DATE AT #1: December 9, 1973
TOTAL WEEKS AT #1: 9

Alistair Cooke's America

Alistair Cooke

KNOPF

Clark's success with *Civilisation* was followed by another book by an Englishman (though actually Cooke has been an American citizen since 1941). Cooke expanded his popular 13-week television series into a personal history of the United States. Alfred Alistair Cooke first came to America in 1932 to study at Yale. His "Letters from America" broadcasts are popular on the BBC, but the *Times* of London found this book to be "grandiose in interest but deficient in substance."

Words with which Titles Begin

Common belief has it that a title should begin with a real attention-getter. "How to" and "You" are often given as examples. Yet among the nearly 500 #1 titles, there are only three "How tos" (*Avoid Probate, Be Your Own Best Friend,* and *Stop Worrying and Start Living*). "You" and "Your" appear only once each, although each with just the sort of title that 'common belief' might expect: *You Can Profit from a Monetary Crisis* and *Your Erroneous Zones.* The only two #1s starting with "I" are from the pen of Bob Hope. The most common first word, not surprisingly, is "The" (152, or nearly a third of all titles), followed distantly by "A" (16 cases). The only nouns that appear more than once are "Love" (3 times), "East" (3), "Doctor" (2), "Everything" (2), "Men" (2), "Andy Rooney," and "Trump" (2).

#1 Authors Who Put Themselves in the Title

Doctor Atkins['s Diet Revolution]

[See Here,] Private Hargrove

Alistair Cooke['s America]

[A Few Minutes with] Andy Rooney

[And More by] Andy Rooney

Baruch[: My Own Story]

Donahue

[Aunt] Erma['s Cope Book]

Iacocca

Jane Fonda['s Workout Book]

Lauren Bacall[: By Myself]

[The] Peter [Principle]

Shelley [Also Known as Shirley]

Sylvia Porter['s Money Book]

Trump[: The Art of the Deal]

Trump[: Staying at the Top]

Yeager

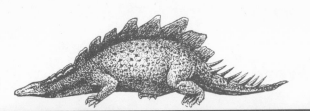

FIRST DATE AT #1: October 13, 1974
TOTAL WEEKS AT #1: 29

Centennial
James Michener
RANDOM HOUSE

Michener's third #1 wasn't quite as successful as his first and second (but outperformed the next six). It follows the town of Centennial, Colorado, and the history of the western United States over a period of 136 million years. It didn't hurt that the book emerged as bicentennial fever was beginning to strike the American public. *Time* reviewer Lance Morrow laments that "practically entire forests have been felled to produce [Michener's] trunk-sized novels.... [*Centennial*] begins with the first faint primordial stirrings on the face of the deep and slogs onward through the ages until he hits the day before yesterday."

FIRST DATE AT #1: May 4, 1975
TOTAL WEEKS AT #1: 14

The Moneychangers
Arthur Hailey
DOUBLEDAY

In the third of his four #1s, Hailey applies his trademark combination of incredible detail, inside information, and page-turning plots to the banking industry and the intrigue and power struggles in a major financial institution. Hailey writes as few as 600 words a day, but since he rewrites and revises as he goes along, sometimes redoing a paragraph 20 times, those 600 words are ready for publication.

BY AND ABOUT #1 AUTHORS:

"Unless you think you can do better than Tolstoy, we don't need you."

—James Michener

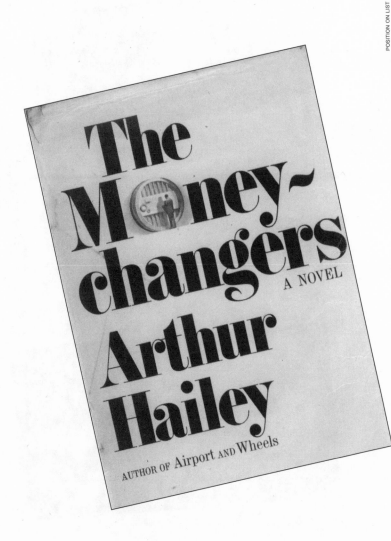

131

FIRST DATE AT #1: February 24, 1974

TOTAL WEEKS AT #1: 11

Plain Speaking

Merle Miller

PUTNAM

Miller compiled, as much as wrote, his 14th book, this oral biography of Harry S. Truman, largely taken from Truman's own words, and those of his friends and colleagues. In the years immediately after Truman's death in 1972, his popularity ratings were higher than during his life, as reflected in two very popular and very favorable #1 books about him: his daughter's and his friend's. Miller's sequel on Lyndon Johnson was not nearly as popular.

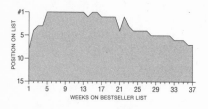

FIRST DATE AT #1: April 28, 1974

TOTAL WEEKS AT #1: 1

You Can Profit from a Monetary Crisis

Harry Browne

MACMILLAN

One of very few #1 books, over 50 years, to offer advice on surviving and making money during hard times, Browne's investment strategies kept his book in the top five for nearly eight months, although he only managed to dislodge Truman from #1 for one week. Browne, a former area manager for the John Birch Society, had previously written *How You Can Profit from the Coming Devaluation*. He listed his interests as "opera, classical music, travel, love, playing with speculative investments, making money, reading, and lying on the couch, not necessarily in that order."

34

ON J. EDGAR HOOVER

MR. PRESIDENT, what did you think of J. Edgar Hoover?
"To tell you the truth, I never gave him all that much thought. He was, still is inclined to take on, to try to take on more than his job was, and he made quite a few too many speeches to my mind, and he very often spoke of things that, strictly speaking, weren't any of his business, but then a lot of people do that, especially in Washington. As long as he did his job, I didn't pay too much attention to him.

"One time they brought me a lot of stuff about his personal life, and I told them I didn't give a damn about that. That wasn't my business. It was what he did *while* he was at work that was my business."

Plain Speaking
an oral biography of
Harry S. Truman
by
Merle Miller

FIRST DATE AT #1: August 3, 1975
TOTAL WEEKS AT #1: 3

Looking for Mr. Goodbar

Judith Rossner

SIMON & SCHUSTER

This psychological thriller about the seduction and murder of a Manhattan singles bar habitué had a somewhat unusual pattern, in that it rose quickly to #1, dropped back, then reached the top again briefly three months later. The author was working as a secretary when this, her third novel, was published. She had hoped it might earn her $40,000, enabling her to take one year off work.

FIRST DATE AT #1: August 25, 1975
TOTAL WEEKS AT #1: 13

Ragtime

E. L. Doctorow

RANDOM HOUSE

If the *Times* had a "part fiction, part nonfiction" list, *Ragtime* would be a prime candidate. It blends real people (notably J. P. Morgan, Harry Houdini, Henry Ford, and Emma Goldman) and events with fictitious ones (a rich family, a poor family, and a black ragtime musician), in a sometimes serious, sometimes comic novel of turn-of-the-century America. Edgar Laurence Doctorow had been a reader for Columbia pictures, where he "had to suffer one lousy western after another." He decided he could do better himself, and wrote one western and one science fiction novel before *Ragtime*.

"Good writing is supposed to evoke sensation in the reader—not the fact that it's raining, but the feeling of being rained upon."

—E. L. Doctorow

FIRST DATE AT #1: May 10, 1974

TOTAL WEEKS AT #1: 6

Times to Remember
Rose Kennedy
DOUBLEDAY

The 84-year-old matriarch of the Kennedy clan became the first parent to reach #1 by writing about her or his children, with these reminiscences of her life and her well-known offspring. The two surprises about this book were that Mrs. Kennedy apparently wrote it all by herself, and that it was very well reviewed. The *New York Times* said "As a political document...it is the most revealing tract on the Kennedys in all the shelves of Kennedy literature," and "It is prose with all the proprietary tenderness and determination only an Irish mother can give."

FIRST DATE AT #1: June 30, 1974

TOTAL WEEKS AT #1: 20

All the President's Men
Carl Bernstein and Bob Woodward
SIMON & SCHUSTER

The two *Washington Post* reporters responsible for unraveling the Watergate cover-up describe their investigation in this book which reached #1 five weeks before Nixon's resignation and remained there for 15 weeks after. Woodward, who wrote quickly and comprehensively, would do the first drafts, while the slower and more methodical Bernstein did the rewrites. They reportedly would argue at length over a single sentence, perhaps one reason all but one of Woodward's subsequent #1 books were written without Bernstein.

Some Well-Known Authors Who Never Had a #1 Bestseller

Peter Benchley
Robert Benchley
John Mason Brown
Pearl Buck
James Branch Cabell
Erskine Caldwell
Albert Camus
Willa Cather
John Dos Passos
Theodore Dreiser
Albert Einstein

Paul Erdman
James T. Farrell
William Faulkner
Edna Ferber
C. S. Forester
Dick Francis
Anne Frank
Paul Gallico
Erle Stanley Gardner
Andre Gide
Rumer Godden
Billy Graham
Robert Graves
Lewis Grizzard
Herman Hesse
Eric Hoffer
L. Ron Hubbard
Aldous Huxley
Robinson Jeffers
Arthur Koestler
Harper Lee
Elmore Leonard
Shirley MacLaine
Bernard Malamud
Thomas Mann
Phyllis McGinley
Iris Murdoch

Gunnar Myrdal
Sean O'Casey
Flannery O'Connor
George Orwell
Ayn Rand
Harold Robbins
Tom Robbins
Damon Runyon
Carl Sandburg
William Saroyan
Albert Schweitzer
George Bernard Shaw
Nevil Shute
Upton Sinclair
H. Allen Smith
C. P. Snow
Alexander Solzhenitsyn
George Rippey Stewart
I. F. Stone
Booth Tarkington
James Thurber
Alvin Toffler
Mary Jane Ward
Alice Walker
Joseph Wambaugh
Robert Penn Warren
Evelyn Waugh
E. B. White
T. H. White
Frank Yerby

The Bestselling Books of All Time

Every ten years, for forty years, Alice Hackett analyzed sales figures as reported in *Publishers Weekly* and from other sources, and calculated the total number of books sold in all editions, hardcover, paperback, book clubs, etc. The emphasis must be on the word *selling* since books that are given away by the carload, notably the Bible, and the works of Chairman Mao and V. I. Lenin, are not included. Here are the top thirty from her list. Books that also appeared as #1 *New York Times* bestsellers are in **boldface**.

Pocket Book of Baby and Child Care	Benjamin Spock	23,285,000
Better Homes & Gardens Cookbook		18,685,000
Webster's New World Dictionary		18,500,000
The Guiness Book of World Records	Norris and Ross	16,4557,000
Betty Crocker's Cookbook		13,000,000
The Godfather	Mario Puzo	12,140,000
The Exorcist	William Blatty	11,700,000
To Kill a Mockingbird	Harper Lee	11,120,000
Peyton Place	Grace Metalious	10,670,000
English-Spanish Dictionary	Carlos Castillo	10,190,000
Love Story	Erich Segal	9,905,000
Valley of the Dolls	Jacqueline Susann	9,500,000
Jaws	Peter Benchley	9,475,000
Jonathan Livingston Seagull	Richard Bach	9,055,000
The Joy of Cooking	Rombauer & Becker	8,990,000
The Sensuous Woman	J	8,815,000
Gone With the Wind	Margaret Mitchell	8,630,000
New American Roget's Thesaurus		8,442,000
The Dell Crossword Dictionary	Kathleen Rafferty	8,290,000
God's Little Acre	Erskine Caldwell	8,260,000
1984	George Orwell	8,150,000
Everything You Always Wanted to Know About Sex	David Reuben	8,000,000
In His Steps	Charles M. Sheldon	8,000,000
The American Heritage Dictionary		7,485,000
Larousse French-English Dictionary		7,350,000
Mythology	Edith Hamilton	7,275,000
The Carpetbaggers	Harold Robbins	7,170,000
The Happy Hooker	Xaviera Hollander	7,140,000
Animal Farm	George Orwell	7,070,000
Roget's Pocket Thesaurus		7,020,000

FIRST DATE AT #1: November 30, 1975
TOTAL WEEKS AT #1: 19

Curtain
Agatha Christie
DODD, MEAD

In Christie's last year of life, it was revealed that in 1946 she had written two books, which would be the final cases for her two great detectives, Miss Marple and Hercules Poirot. Dodd, Mead had their first two #1 bestsellers in decades with *Curtain,* in which a dramatic surprise ending unfolds after Poirot's death. The 85-year-old Christie had originally intended *Curtain* to be published posthumously, but decided she wanted to be around to enjoy the experience. (She died six weeks after the book reached #1.) This was the first of her more than 70 books ("Oh, I'm an incredible sausage machine," she once said) to reach #1. The other "vault book" followed close behind.

THE MOST-TRANSLATED AUTHORS

Of the 20 authors most translated into other languages, according to the UNESCO Statistical Yearbook, only one has also been a #1 *New York Times* bestselling author: Agatha Christie, who comes in third place, right after V. I. Lenin and Walt Disney.

FIRST DATE AT #1: November 17, 1974
TOTAL WEEKS AT #1: 11

All Things Bright and Beautiful

James Herriot

ST. MARTIN'S

James Alfred Wight, writing as James Herriot, had the first of his three #1 bestsellers with these tales of the animals and the humans that he dealt with as he made his Yorkshire rounds. Since veterinarians are not permitted to advertise in Britain, Wight, who had been in practice since 1940, felt it was necessary to cloak himself in secrecy, although letters addressed to Dr. Herriot in the fictitious town of Darrowby (thousands of them) were all promptly delivered to Dr. Wight.

FIRST DATE AT #1: February 2, 1975
TOTAL WEEKS AT #1: 18

The Bermuda Triangle

Charles Berlitz

DOUBLEDAY

Charles L. Frambach, the scion of the language school family, adopted his grandfather's surname and had a huge success with his uncritical collection of theories that explain the allegedly mysterious disappearances of ships and planes in a certain patch of the Atlantic ocean. There were those who felt this book belonged on the fiction side of the list; *Time* magazine called it a "hodgepodge of half truths, unsubstantiated reports, and unsubstantial science." Berlitz defended his work, writing that "some of the theories I mentioned . . . are pretty far out but that doesn't mean they couldn't happen."

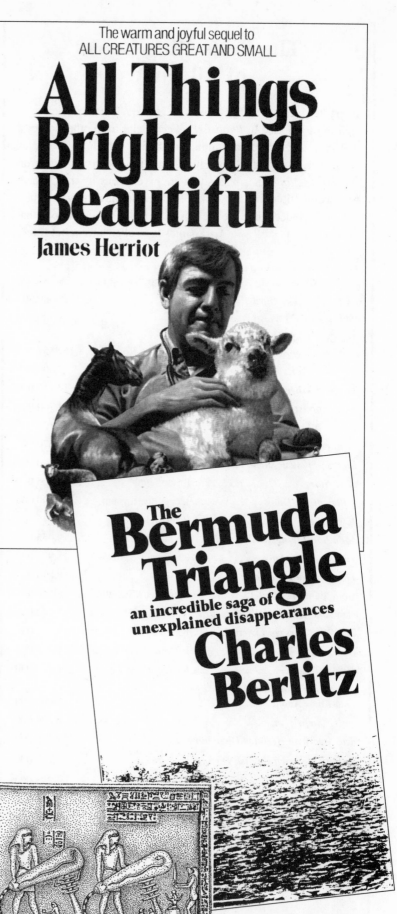

The warm and joyful sequel to
ALL CREATURES GREAT AND SMALL

All Things Bright and Beautiful

James Herriot

The Bermuda Triangle

an incredible saga of unexplained disappearances

Charles Berlitz

Berlitz suggests that these may be ancient Egyptian lightbulbs.—J.B.

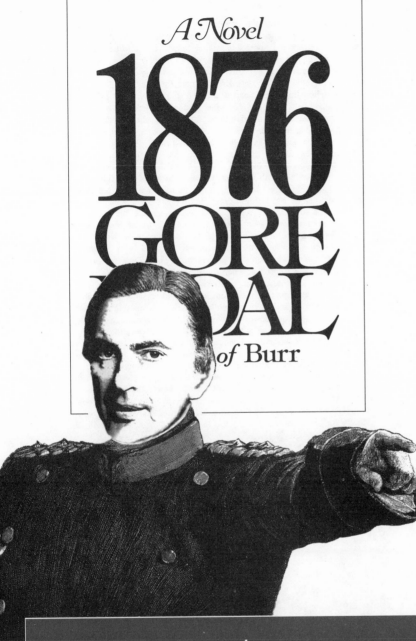

FIRST DATE AT #1: April 11, 1976
TOTAL WEEKS AT #1: 10

1876
Gore Vidal
RANDOM HOUSE

"The only thing I've ever really wanted in my life was to be president," the author once told *Time* magazine. Three years after *Burr* spent 22 weeks at #1, Vidal returns to the top with the sequel, focusing on America at age 100 in the midst of a hotly disputed presidential election. 1876 had interesting parallels to 1976: Grant and Nixon, the Whiskey Ring scandal and Watergate. There was some dispute over how to deal alphabetically with the only #1 to have a purely numeric title—put it before all the lettered titles, after them, under "e" for "eighteen" or even, in a few cases, under "o" for "one eight seven six."

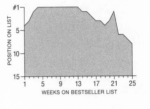

FIRST DATE AT #1: June 13, 1976
TOTAL WEEKS AT #1: 36

Trinity
Leon Uris
DOUBLEDAY

Uris's last #1 bestseller was also his biggest by far. A century of Ireland's troubled modern history is illustrated in the lives of one Irish family. It reached #1 following nearly three months at #2, and remained there for the better part of a year, with only a short drop to #2 behind Miss Marple. During this period, books by Harold Robbins, Helen MacInnes, Robert Ludlum, Irving Wallace, and Spiro T. Agnew all challenged for #1, but none displaced *Trinity*.

BY AND ABOUT #1 AUTHORS:

"You can lie to your wife or your boss, but you cannot lie to your typewriter. Sooner or later you must reveal your true self in your pages."

—Leon Uris

FIRST DATE AT #1: February 19, 1975
TOTAL WEEKS AT #1: 1

The Palace Guard
Dan Rather and Gary Paul Gates
HARPER

Being watched by millions of television viewers does not guarantee millions of book sales. The first book by a news anchor to reach #1 lasted only a week before being displaced by yet another book about the Nixon White House and the events leading up to the Watergate scandals. At the time, Rather was one of the reporters on *60 Minutes*.

FIRST DATE AT #1: June 15, 1975
TOTAL WEEKS AT #1: 12

Breach of Faith
Theodore H. White
ATHENEUM

White returned to #1 for the third time with this account of the un-making of a president: the story of Nixon's downfall in 1973–1974. At this time, a book about a nastier villain was in the #2 position: *Helter Skelter*, the story of Charles Manson.

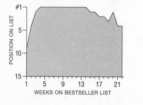

FIRST DATE AT #1: September 7, 1975
TOTAL WEEKS AT #1: 12

Sylvia Porter's Money Book
Sylvia Porter
DOUBLEDAY

The popular syndicated financial columnist tells us what to do with our money. While the book was extremely popular, more than one reviewer felt the book's advice was marred by the author's prejudices in matters of women, class, and the American economic system.

Chapter 13   Breach of Faith   333

Unless one is satisfied that Nixon is a total hypocrite, a man of unrelieved brutishness, one must ask how he could stomach what he authorized and learned about his administration and its underground. And the answer can come only by imagining that here was a man who could not, in his waking moments, acknowledge the man he recognized in his own nightmares—the outsider, the loner, the loser.

Throughout his career, except for a few brief years in 1971 and 1972, that had been his inner role—the outsider, the loser. "They" were against him, always, from the rich boys of Whittier College to the hostile establishment that sneered at his Presidency. His authority as President was being challenged by the news system, the rioters, the Congress, the intellectuals. The culture, the manners, the credos of his lonely life of striving were being wiped out by the fashions of the new culture. Nixon could deal masterfully with Russians, Chinese, Arabs of the Middle East by the old set rules of power. But at home the rules were being changed against him, and he was losing. Losers play dirty; he, too, would change the rules. His ruthlessness, vengefulness, nastiness were the characteristics of a man who has seen himself as underdog for so long that he cannot distinguish between real and fancied enemies, a man who does not really care whom he slashes or hurts when pressed, who cannot accept or understand when or what he has won. Thus, then, the portrait of a man who saw himself at Thermopylae or Masada.

Over and over again, as one reads the transcripts of his inner thoughts from the tape recordings, one sees he did consider such matters as honor and faith, and even thought of himself as honorable and faithful. But then he came down, knowingly, against honor, against faith. Cornered by history, he seemed to be defending all at once the authority of the Presidency, his cultural values, his confederates—and his own skin.

And always, in the crisis, he reacted as the cornered loser. He could not shake that characteristic—which made of the election of 1972 not only a political paradox but a personal paradox: the loser had won —and won by such a margin as to unsettle even more stable personalities. He had won so largely that he could misread his victory. It was a victory for his ideas and politics. But ...

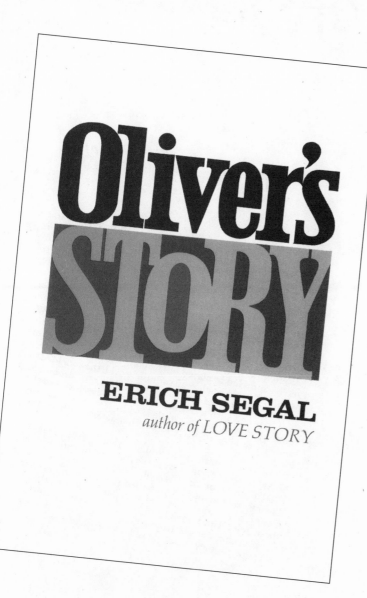

Oliver's STORY

ERICH SEGAL

author of LOVE STORY

FIRST DATE AT #1: November 7, 1976
TOTAL WEEKS AT #1: 7

Sleeping Murder
Agatha Christie
DODD, MEAD

Soon after Dame Agatha's own demise under non-mysterious circumstances, her publisher unveiled the last Miss Marple book, which she had written in 1946 and stored in a vault. It promptly rose to #1, only eight months after the final Poirot book did likewise. This book was published 53 years after Christie's first, *The Mysterious Affair at Styles,* a book which sold 2,000 copies and earned her $70. In her long career, the author never wrote anything but mysteries.

FIRST DATE AT #1: April 10, 1977
TOTAL WEEKS AT #1: 7

Oliver's Story
Erich Segal
HARPER

What can you say about a six-year-old bestseller that died? Six years after Professor Segal's mega-bestseller *Love Story* finally left the list after 41 weeks at #1, the sequel picks up the story of the young husband alone and grieving. Segal, at the time an Associate Professor of Classics and Contemporary Literature at Yale said, "I read classics, I write ephemera." Living in London, he noted that "John le Carré lives right down the block. I see him driving his oldish station wagon and I want to go say hello, but I'm too shy."

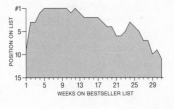

FIRST DATE AT #1: November 23, 1975
TOTAL WEEKS AT #1: 1

Power!

Michael Korda

RANDOM HOUSE

Subtitled "How to get it; How to use it," this is the first #1 book by a top executive of a publishing house (Simon & Schuster). *Power!* offers the corporate climber advice on manipulating the corporate system to gain corporate power. This is only the second #1 title with an exclamation point, but each of Korda's first three books used one *(Success!* and *Male Chauvinism!* were his other titles). In England, *Power!* was called *Power in the Office*, no exclamation point. Korda apparently published his book through one of his competitors to avoid accusations of an inside job.

FIRST DATE AT #1: November 30, 1975
TOTAL WEEKS AT #1: 12

Bring On the Empty Horses

David Niven

PUTNAM

With his anecdotes and reminiscences of vintage Hollywood and its characters, Niven becomes the first famous actor to write a #1 bestseller (unless, of course, one considers Bob Hope a famous actor). Although Niven's previous book, *The Moon's a Balloon* made the list, it never reached #1. Niven apologized for writing about his fellow celebrities so much. "People in my profession who, like myself, have the good fortune to parlay a minimal talent into a long career, find all sorts of doors opened that would otherwise have remained closed. Once behind those doors, it makes little sense to write about the butler when Chairman Mao is sitting down to dinner."

4

Hedda and Louella

HOLLYWOOD invented a macabre party game called Airplane. This concerned a sizable transport which, owing to some mechanical defect, was destined to take off and never again to land, its crew and passengers doomed to fly around and around forever. The game consisted of providing tickets for those the players felt they could well do without. Hedda Hopper and Louella Parsons, unassailably the two most powerful gossip columnists in the world, had no difficulty whatever in finding space and, a refinement of torture, were usually allotted seats next to each other.

Compared to Lucretia Borgia, Lady Macbeth and others, Louella and Hedda played only among the reserves, but with their 75,000,000 readers all over the world, they wielded and frequently misused enormous power. Only Hollywood could have spawned such a couple, and only Hollywood, headline-hunting, self-inflating, riddled with fear and insecurity, could have allowed itself to be dominated by them for so long.

The reader must try to visualize that at every Hollywood breakfast table or office desk the day started with an avid perusal of the columns of Louella Parsons and Hedda Hopper. The fact that many had paid their press agents large sums of money to make up lies and exaggerations and then plant these items with Louella and Hedda detracted nothing from the pleasure they got from seeing this nonsense in the morning papers—they even believed it when they saw it.

81

FIRST DATE AT #1: May 22, 1977
TOTAL WEEKS AT #1: 3

Falconer
John Cheever
KNOPF

In Cheever's only #1 book, the protagonist is a well-bred but drug-addicted college professor convicted of murdering his brother. Sent to Falconer Prison, he overcomes his addiction but finds himself embroiled in the desperation of prison life. Cheever himself taught writing at Sing Sing prison, wrote television scripts for *Life with Father*, and had dozens of his more-than-200 short stories published in the *New Yorker*. He died in 1982.

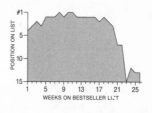

FIRST DATE AT #1: June 19, 1977
TOTAL WEEKS AT #1: 15

The Thorn Birds
Colleen McCullough
HARPER

"The great Australian novel" is an epic saga of an Australian family, and the love of a young woman for a Roman Catholic Cardinal. McCullough, who had been a bus driver in the Outback and a neurology researcher at Yale, took inspiration from Segal's *Love Story*: "I thought it was bloody awful," she said, but she noted that it made people cry "buckets of tears" and that's why they liked it. Believing no one would publish a first novel as long as *The Thorn Birds,* she set it aside and wrote *Tim,* to establish her reputation. *The Thorn Birds* was written in three months, 15,000 words a day, while McCullough worked full time at Yale.

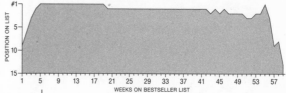

FIRST DATE AT #1: December 21, 1975
TOTAL WEEKS AT #1: 1

The Relaxation Response
Herbert Benson
MORROW

Benson, a Harvard M.D., teaches readers simple techniques for relieving hypertension through meditation. The book was at #1 only during Christmas week of 1975. Some people achieve relaxation through meditation, others seem to prefer Doris Day anecdotes.

POSITION ON LIST
WEEKS ON BESTSELLER LIST

FIRST DATE AT #1: March 14, 1976
TOTAL WEEKS AT #1: 5

Doris Day: Her Own Story
A. E. Hotchner
MORROW

The actress and singer's good friend (and vice president of Paul Newman's food company) offers Miss Day's candid reminiscences of her not always meditative or tranquil life.

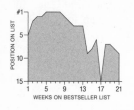

POSITION ON LIST
WEEKS ON BESTSELLER LIST

Books that Many People Assume Must Have Been #1 (But Weren't)

Catch 22

Jaws

Battle Cry

Catcher in the Rye

Dune

The Third Wave

To Kill a Mockingbird

Giant

The Ugly American

Prologue

DORIS DAY and I first met in the luncheon garden of the Beverly Hills Hotel in the summer of 1973. Doris's son, Terry Melcher, had picked me up at my hotel and we sat at a shaded table drinking Heineken beer while we waited for her.

"You'll like my mother," Terry said.

"I'm sure I will."

"She has a lot going for her."

I had met Terry the evening before. He is a low-key, thoughtful, attractive young man, drooped hair, drooped moustache, by trade a producer of records and albums. He knew that I had come to Beverly Hills at the instigation of the William Morrow & Company publishers, who were urging me to do a book with and about Doris. I had told Terry (and the publisher) that I had my doubts that a woman who was so apple-pie buoyantly happy and *healthy* (an appraisal exclusively based on observing her on the silver screen) would be a compelling subject for the kind of book that would interest me; but after some Morrow prodding I consented to fly out from New York and have this lunch before definitely making up my mind. I also felt that Doris Day, who, I had learned, had always been rather circumspect about writers, should have a good look at me.

"I'm surprised your mother wants me to do this book with her."

"She admired your book on Papa Hemingway."

"But that was a very frank book that pretty much told everything there was to tell."

"Maybe that's what Doris wants."

"But is there much to tell? I mean, does she have things in her life that are unexpected and that she's never told?"

Terry looked at me soberly, smoothing down his moustache with thumb and forefinger. "Yes . . . yes . . . quite a lot."

9

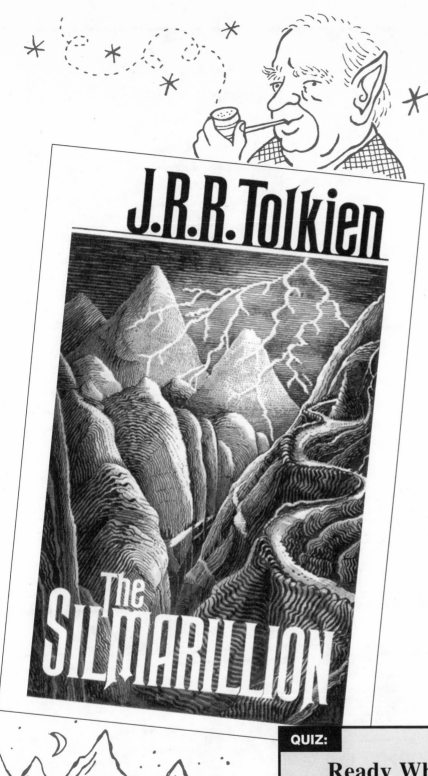

FIRST DATE AT #1: October 2, 1977
TOTAL WEEKS AT #1: 23

The Silmarillion
J. R. R. Tolkein
HOUGHTON MIFFLIN

The Hobbit never made it. *The Lord of the Rings* trilogy never made it. But Tolkein's complex, murky tale of life in Middle Earth before the hobbits entered the list at #2, rose to #1 the following week, and remained there for over five months. Assembled from bits and pieces left behind at his death in 1973, it was to have been followed by a final book, *Akallabeth*, about the downfall of Numenor, that was never written. Tolkein typed laboriously with two fingers. When asked what the *Ring* cycle was about, he said, "It's not about anything but itself." When asked if he wrote for children, the author said, "If you're a youngish man and don't want to be made fun of, you *say* you do...."

QUIZ:

Ready When You Are, J.D.

Eight #1 authors have chosen to be known by their initials rather than their names; seven with two initials and one with three. The modest challenge here is to identify the author, and triple marks if you can supply the full names. (Answers on the next page.)

A. E.   A. J.   E. L   H. R.
J. D.   J. R. R.   P. D.   P. J.

FIRST DATE AT #1: April 25, 1976
TOTAL WEEKS AT #1: 20

The Final Days
Bob Woodward and Carl Bernstein
SIMON & SCHUSTER

The first book ever to join the list at the #1 position, this account of the decline and fall of the Nixon administration was originally planned as a view of Nixon's impeachment as seen through the eyes of six Senators. The book was begun one week after the resignation; Woodward wrote the first half, Bernstein the second. It spent nearly five months at #1, another at #2, then declined rapidly, falling off the list around the time of the Carter-Ford election.

FIRST DATE AT #1: August 29, 1976
TOTAL WEEKS AT #1: 14

Passages
Gail Sheehy
DUTTON

Subtitled "The Predictable Crises of Adult Life," this academically oriented study of the phases of ones life spent three months at #1 before becoming a long-term #2 to Alex Haley. After more than a year, its passage from the list was very abrupt. A U.C.L.A. psychiatrist filed a large plagiarism suit against the author, claiming that he was to have been a collaborator. The case was settled for a small cash sum and a percentage of the royalties.

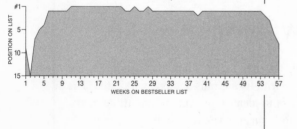

Ready When You Are, Jerome David
(answers from the previous page)

Alfred Edward Hotchner

Archibald Joseph Cronin

Edgar Laurence Doctorow

Harry Robbins Haldeman

Jerome David Salinger

John Ronald Reuel Tolkein

Phyllis Dorothy James

It's P. J. O'Rourke, but the full names appear nowhere in any biodata available in print.

New #1 Fiction and Nonfiction Bestsellers on the Same Day

Considering that there have been more than 2,500 Sundays in the 50 years of the *New York Times* list, it is unexpected that only 24 times were there a new fiction and nonfiction bestseller on the same day.

AUGUST 16, 1942

The Song of Bernadette (Werfel)
Victory Through Air Power (de Seversky)

DECEMBER 17, 1944

The Green Years (Cronin)
Brave Men (Pyle)

DECEMBER 19, 1948

The Big Fisherman (Douglas)
Roosevelt and Hopkins (Sherwood)

DECEMBER 25, 1949

The Egyptian (Waltari)
This I Remember (E. Roosevelt)

OCTOBER 15, 1950

Across the River and into the Trees (Hemingway)
Look Younger, Live Longer (Hauser)

SEPTEMBER 22, 1957

By Love Possessed (Cozzens)
Baruch: My Own Story (Baruch)

OCTOBER 28, 1962

A Shade of Difference (Drury)
Silent Spring (Carson)

OCTOBER 6, 1963

The Group (McCarthy)
JFK: The Man and the Myth (Lasky)

OCTOBER 25, 1964

Herzog (Bellow)
Reminiscences (MacArthur)

MAY 8, 1966

Valley of the Dolls (Susann)
The Last Battle (Ryan)

JULY 25, 1971

The Exorcist (Blatty)
The Female Eunuch (Greer)

DECEMBER 9, 1973

Burr (Vidal)
Alistair Cooke's America (Cooke)

NOVEMBER 30, 1975

Curtain (Christie)
Bring on the Empty Horses (Niven)

OCTOBER 28, 1979

The Establishment (Fast)
Aunt Erma's Cope Book (Bombeck)

MARCH 23, 1980

The Bourne Identity (Ludlum)
Donahue (Donahue)

SEPTEMBER 16, 1984

The Fourth Protocol (Forsyth)
Loving Each Other (Buscaglia)

FEBRUARY 1, 1987

The Eyes of the Dragon (King)
A Season on the Brink (Fennstein)

JUNE 7, 1987

Misery (King)
The Closing of the American Mind (Bloom)

MAY 15, 1988

Zoya (Steel)
Moonwalk (Jackson)

JULY 3, 1988

Alaska (Michener)
Talking Straight (Iacocca)

NOVEMBER 20, 1988

The Sands of Time (Sheldon)
The Last Lion (Manchester)

FEBRUARY 4, 1990

The Bad Place (Koontz)
Megatrends 2000 (Naisbitt)

SEPTEMBER 16, 1990

Four Past Midnight (King)
Darkness Visible (Styron)

AUGUST 25, 1991

The Sum of All Fears (Clancy)
Parliament of Whores (O'Rourke)

FIRST DATE AT #1: November 21, 1976

TOTAL WEEKS AT #1: 22

Roots

Alex Haley

DOUBLEDAY

The history of one man's family begins when Kunta Kinte is brought from Gambia to America as a slave, and continues through dozens of generations, to the author himself. When Haley retired from a long career in the Coast Guard in 1959, he headed for Greenwich Village, determined to become a successful writer. He was down to his last 18 cents (and two cans of sardines) when a check arrived for an article he had written, and he decided to struggle on. Haley described *Roots* as "faction"—somewhere between fact and fiction. The *Times* decided to put him on their nonfiction list.

FIRST DATE AT #1: May 8, 1977

TOTAL WEEKS AT #1: 14

Your Erroneous Zones

Wayne Dyer

FUNK & WAGNALLS

When Dyer became convinced that he needed to take control of his own life he stopped worrying about being bald, stopped feeling guilty about his divorce, and decided to write a bestseller. After two years of reflection, he wrote this book in 13 days. Then he quit his job as a guidance counselor, bought a new car, filled it with copies of the book, and set out on a 48-state tour of the country. He did more than 600 interviews and stopped at every bookstore to sell books in what *People* magazine called "a self-marketing tour de force." Dr. Dyer's self-help pep talk stayed in the top five for nearly nine months before it finally rose to #1. The book is subtitled "Bold but simple techniques for eliminating unhealthy behavior patterns."

Narcissism: The Proof Is in the Card File

by Jack C. Horn
Psychology Today, June 1985

Narcissism received its official seal of disapproval in 1980 when it appeared for the first time in the third edition of the American Psychiatric Association's *Diagnostic and Statistical Manual of Mental Disorders.* Now the idea that me-firstism has increased sharply in recent decades has received further support from another objective standard: the Dewey Decimal Classification System (DDCS).

Psychologist Richard E. Kopelman and librarian Lyn S. Mullins combined talents to analyze the subjects covered by the best-selling nonfiction books of the 1950s, 1960s, and 1970s. Kopelman and Mullins first identified 10 categories of the DDCS that focussed on narcissistic topics such as the self, consciousness, and personality; individual psychology, personality, personal development, self-realization; physical fitness, exercise; and diet therapy.

The researchers then used two sources to create a list of nonfiction bestsellers for each year from 1950 to 1979: the Bowker Company's annual compilation, and two similar lists made up of titles that appeared in the *New York Times Book Review* each year on the first Sunday in July after July 4 and the second Sunday in January.

The final step was to see what percentage of the bestsellers for each decade fell into the narcissistic DDCS categories. [The results show] a steady growth in narcissism through the years. Combining the three listings, the percentage increased from 5% to 8% to 16% in the three decades.

The Bowker listings are consistently higher in narcissism than the *New York Times* listings. Since the Bowker figures "reflect bestsellers for an entire year," while the *New York Times* listings "are for one-week periods," Mullins and Kopelman suggest that "the Bowker listings...are a more comprehensive (and probably more accurate) measure of popular taste." ∎

Note: In response to this study, Dr. M. C. Bear points out that narcissism is not the same thing as "interest in oneself," which may be what this study is really about.

Authors with Three or More #1 Titles

Of the 18 on the top two shelves, only six are still writing. Of the "Big 9" on the lower six shelves, all but one are still writing.

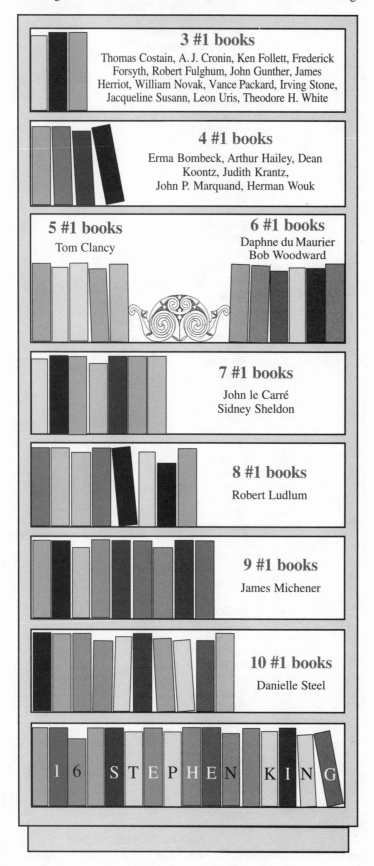

3 #1 books

Thomas Costain, A. J. Cronin, Ken Follett, Frederick Forsyth, Robert Fulghum, John Gunther, James Herriot, William Novak, Vance Packard, Irving Stone, Jacqueline Susann, Leon Uris, Theodore H. White

4 #1 books

Erma Bombeck, Arthur Hailey, Dean Koontz, Judith Krantz, John P. Marquand, Herman Wouk

5 #1 books
Tom Clancy

6 #1 books
Daphne du Maurier
Bob Woodward

7 #1 books

John le Carré
Sidney Sheldon

8 #1 books

Robert Ludlum

9 #1 books

James Michener

10 #1 books

Danielle Steel

1 6 S T E P H E N K I N G

FIRST DATE AT #1: March 12, 1978
TOTAL WEEKS AT #1: 13*

Bloodline
Sidney Sheldon
MORROW

At the age of 50, the highly successful television and film producer had no intention of writing books. But then he "got an idea that was so introspective I could see no way to do it as a television series, movie, or Broadway play, because you had to get inside the character's mind. With much trepidation, I decided I'd try a novel." That first book, *The Naked Face,* sold only 17,000 copies, but Sheldon's second sold millions and his new career was born. As with le Carré, Michener, Wouk, and other multiple #1 authors, Sheldon's first #1 book was his most successful. This tale of love and high financial intrigue on three continents remained at #1 for three months and might have returned there had it not been for yet another long *Times* strike.

FIRST DATE AT #1: June 18, 1978
TOTAL WEEKS AT #1: 4*

Scruples
Judith Krantz
CROWN

Krantz got a "B" in a fiction writing class at Wellesley and gave up on the field for 30 years. At the age of 50, she worked 32 hours a week for nine months writing *Scruples,* a racy (for 1978) story of a woman's rise in the world of fashion. It might have had a few more weeks at #1 during the time of the strike, but we'll never know. Each of Krantz's first four novels reached #1, an unmatched record.

NONFICTION

FIRST DATE AT #1: July 24, 1977
TOTAL WEEKS AT #1: 3

The Book of Lists

David Wallechinsky, Irving Wallace and Amy Wallace

MORROW

The only #1 bestseller written (or compiled) by a father and his two children (David goes by his grandfather's name), *The Book of Lists* presents all manner of facts and opinions in list form. While lasting only three weeks at #1, it remained in the top three for more than eight months. This team produced seven other books, including three *People's Almanacs,* but none ever reached #1.

FIRST DATE AT #1: August 21, 1977
TOTAL WEEKS AT #1: 1

Looking Out for Number One

Robert J. Ringer

FUNK & WAGNALLS

Ringer, a master of self-promotion, helped propel his book onto the list with both traditional (talk shows and interviews) and nontraditional (full page newspaper ads) methods. The individualist's guide to success in business and life only spent a week at #1, but then remained on the list for nearly nine months more. Ringer told *Contemporary Authors* that he wrote only to make money. "This is the kind of honesty that has given me ten million readers for my first two books."

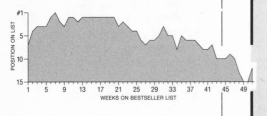

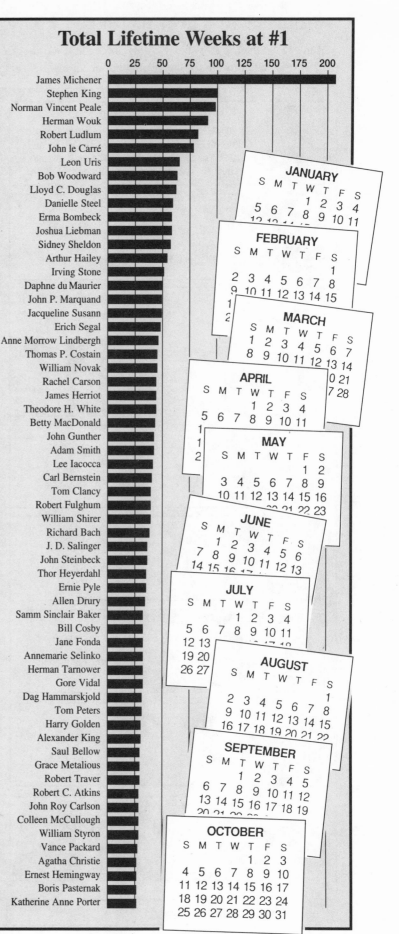

Total Lifetime Weeks at #1

CHESAPEAKE

James A. Michener

Random House   New York

Voyage One: 1583

FOR SOME TIME NOW THEY HAD BEEN SUSPICIOUS of him. Spies had monitored his movements, reporting to the priests, and in the tribal councils his advice against going to war with those beyond the bend had been ignored. Even more predictive, the family of the girl he had chosen to replace his dead wife had refused to accept the three lengths of roanoke he had offered as her purchase price.

Reluctantly he was coming to the conclusion that he must leave this tribe which had done everything but outlaw him publicly. As a child he had watched what happened to men declared outcasts, and he had no desire to experience what they had suffered: the isolation, the scorn, the bitter loneliness.

So now, as he fished along the great river or hunted in the meadows or merely sat in contemplation, always alone, he felt he must go. But how? And where?

The trouble had started that day when he voiced his apprehension over a raid proposed by the high chief. For more than a year now relations with tribes beyond the northern bend had been amicable, and during this interval the river had known prosperity, with more than normal trade passing north and south. But the Susquehannocks of the middle section had never in Pentaquod's life been easy in times of peace; they felt intuitively that they should be on the warpath, proving their manhood. So it was within tradition for the high chief to devise justifications for sending his warriors forth: if they triumphed, their victory would redound on him; and if they lost, he would claim that he was merely protecting the boundaries of the tribe.

Pentaquod had argued, 'Those of the northern bend have respected their promises. They have not stolen our beaver nor trespassed on our

---

FIRST DATE AT #1: July 9, 1978
TOTAL WEEKS AT #1: 1*

The Holcroft Covenant
Robert Ludlum
PUTNAM

Ludlum was a popular Broadway and television actor ("I usually played a lawyer or a homicidal maniac") and producer who, at the age of 44, "got bored to death with the theater and was looking for a new career." He dug out an old story idea and turned it into *The Scarlatti Inheritance*. After five more "The" books, he reached #1 for the first of eight times with this thriller about a secret Nazi plan to found a Fourth Reich. This book, up against Michener, Hailey, Wouk, and a long newspaper strike, was at #1 for only a week. His next seven #1 bestsellers all did better.

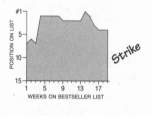

FIRST DATE AT #1: July 23, 1978
TOTAL WEEKS AT #1: 24*

Chesapeake
James Michener
RANDOM HOUSE

Michener's third appearance was also the first fiction book ever to reach the chart as number one. (Since Michener's weighty historical saga of life in Maryland was #1 before and after the strike, it seems safe to assume it would have been #1 throughout the strike as well.) The appearance of Wouk and Hailey at the same time caused an unusual amount of shuffling among the top three spots. *Chesapeake* covers four centuries of life along Maryland's eastern shore, from a time when Indians and crabs were dominant to the present-day developers and polluters.

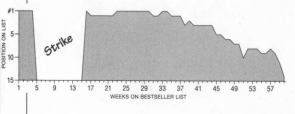

FIRST DATE AT #1: September 11, 1977
TOTAL WEEKS AT #1: 24

All Things Wise and Wonderful

James Herriot

ST. MARTIN'S

The third in the series, and the second to reach #1, these are the further adventures in the everyday life of the beloved Yorkshire veterinarian.

FIRST DATE AT #1: February 26, 1978
TOTAL WEEKS AT #1: 11

The Complete Book of Running

James Fixx

RANDOM HOUSE

The author's death at an early age while out running in Hardwick, Vermont, seems to have done little to dampen the sales of this enduring book, which may well have returned to #1 during an extended newspaper strike. As it was, it spent nearly two years on the list, including at least two and a half months at the top. The author (and his estate) earned more than $2 million in royalties alone. Around this time another athlete, Arnold Schwarzenegger, reached the list with his book *Arnold,* but never threatened Fixx at #1.

FIRST DATE AT #1: November 12, 1978
TOTAL WEEKS AT #1: 9

War and Remembrance
Herman Wouk

LITTLE, BROWN

Wouk's fourth and last appearance at #1, 27 years after his first, was his poorest showing, but that still meant two months at #1 and more than a year on the list. The sequel to *The Winds of War* follows the ubiquitous Henry family throughout World War Two. It was said that Wouk received higher than 100% royalties for his later books; the publisher paid him more than the book sold for, in the expectation of making money on paperback, movie, and television sales.

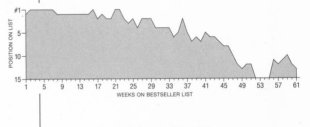

FIRST DATE AT #1: February 25, 1979
TOTAL WEEKS AT #1: 2

Overload
Arthur Hailey

DOUBLEDAY

Like Wouk, Hailey made his fourth and last appearance at #1, and it, too, was his weakest showing. Perhaps people were tiring of his procedural dramas, or perhaps a detailed look at the public utility industry did not catch the public's imagination, but this book had just two weeks at #1, and one of the shorter total weeks on the list for any book.

FIRST DATE AT #1: March 26, 1978
TOTAL WEEKS AT #1: 2*

The Ends of Power
H. R. Haldeman and Joseph DiMona

TIMES

Haldeman's account/explanation of what happened at Watergate rose to #1 in its second week and was gone from the list entirely eight weeks later. It was while sitting in prison watching David Frost interview Richard Nixon that Harry Robbins Haldeman vowed to write a "stinging exposé" of what really happened. The reviews were mostly poor. *Time* found it to be "badly flawed, frustratingly vague and curiously defensive." Coauthor DiMona had previously collaborated with stripper Ann Corio on a history of burlesque.

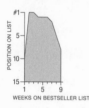

FIRST DATE AT #1: May 28, 1978
TOTAL WEEKS AT #1: 26*

If Life Is a Bowl of Cherries, What Am I Doing in the Pits?
Erma Bombeck

McGRAW-HILL

Twelve years and three children after leaving her feature-writing job for the *Dayton Journal-Herald*, Bombeck determined that "I do not feel fulfilled cleaning chrome faucets with a toothbrush. It's my turn." She began writing for the weekly *Kettering-Oakwood Times* at $3 per column. The Dayton paper soon offered her $5 per column. Books derived from her columns followed, and her fifth, with the second-longest title of any #1 book, quickly reached the top of the list, and stayed there half a year (assuming it would have stayed in that position throughout the *Times*'s fourth and last strike).

The Big Nine

Nine authors have accounted for 73 #1 bestsellers. In other words, or numbers, just over 2% of all #1 authors have accounted for more than 14% of all #1 bestsellers. Eight of the nine (all but du Maurier) are alive and well and still writing, so we may expect the number to increase. However, while the number of titles are increasing, the number of weeks in the #1 position are generally declining. The books of the Big Nine are listed below in chronological order. If James Michener were a stock, it would be time to think about selling short.

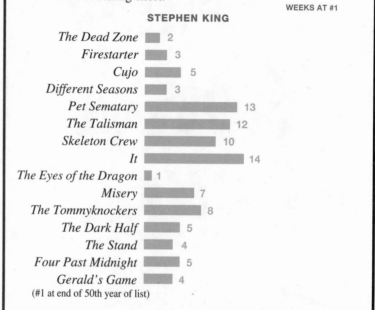

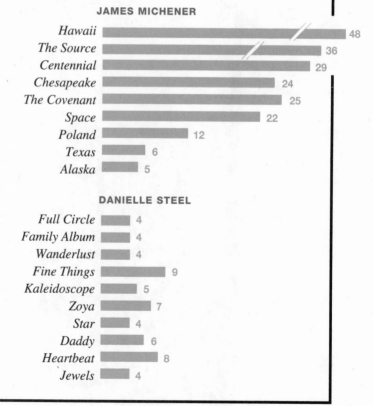

Chart (left panel)

WEEKS AT #1

ROBERT LUDLUM

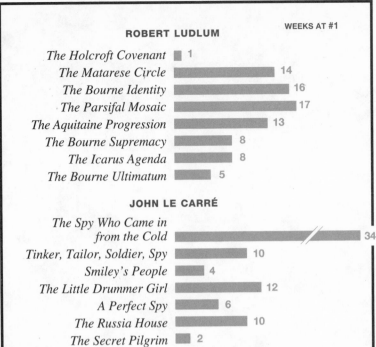

Title	Weeks
The Holcroft Covenant	1
The Matarese Circle	14
The Bourne Identity	16
The Parsifal Mosaic	17
The Aquitaine Progression	13
The Bourne Supremacy	8
The Icarus Agenda	8
The Bourne Ultimatum	5

JOHN LE CARRÉ

Title	Weeks
The Spy Who Came in from the Cold	34
Tinker, Tailor, Soldier, Spy	10
Smiley's People	4
The Little Drummer Girl	12
A Perfect Spy	6
The Russia House	10
The Secret Pilgrim	2

SIDNEY SHELDON

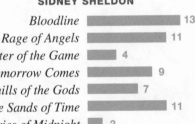

Title	Weeks
Bloodline	13
Rage of Angels	11
Master of the Game	4
If Tomorrow Comes	9
Windmills of the Gods	7
The Sands of Time	11
Memories of Midnight	2

BOB WOODWARD

Title	Weeks
All the President's Men	20
The Final Days	20
The Brethren	9
Wired	4
Veil	4
The Commanders	5

DAPHNE DU MAURIER

Title	Weeks
The King's General	6
The Parasites	5
My Cousil Rachel	8
Mary Anne	11
The Scapegoat	14
The Glass Blowers	6

TOM CLANCY

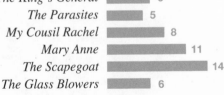

Title	Weeks
Red Storm Rising	6
Patriot Games	5
The Cardinal of the Kremlin	12
Clear and Present Danger	9
The Sum of All Fears	7

Right panel

FIRST DATE AT #1: April 8, 1979
TOTAL WEEKS AT #1: 14

The Matarese Circle
Robert Ludlum

RICHARD MAREK

Ludlum's eighth book and the second of his eight #1 books was one of the most popular, with more than three months at #1. The plot concerns American and Soviet agents who manage to save western civilization.

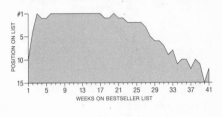

FIRST DATE AT #1: April 22, 1979
TOTAL WEEKS AT #1: 2

Good as Gold
Joseph Heller

SIMON & SCHUSTER

Catch-22 never reached #1, but Heller's next book, published more than a decade later, rose quickly to #1 where it remained only two weeks, dropped to spend eight weeks at #2, then declined rapidly. It uses the story of an author named Gold who has received a big advance for a book on the Jewish experience in America to examine the ambitions and agonies of American Jews. Some reviewers found the book (Heller's, not Gold's) offensive to Jews. The *Village Voice* review said "If Heller believes (and I'm willing to think he thinks he does) that everything is rotten to the core, this goes double for the Jews.... The Jews in *Good as Gold* are portrayed as snivelling, deceitful, self-aggrandizing, and ambitious beyond their worth...."

FIRST DATE AT #1: November 26, 1978
TOTAL WEEKS AT #1: 10

Mommie Dearest
Christina Crawford

MORROW

Joan Crawford's daughter reveals how very difficult it was to live with her film star and soft drink executive mommie.

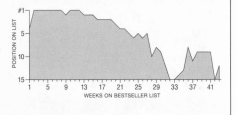

FIRST DATE AT #1: January 14, 1979
TOTAL WEEKS AT #1: 1*

Gnomes
Wil Huygen and Rien Poortvliet

ABRAMS

This droll and witty picture book by a Dutch medical doctor and his artist friend holds the record for the slowest-rising #1, not reaching that level until it had been on the list well over a year. Huygen recalled that "Four times we stopped because we were certain that it was going to be a flop. The ridiculous success of the book... I can only explain by guessing that [it] fills in something which mankind thought was lost...." Why is this book classified as nonfiction? As Ian Ballantine tells the story, when *Gnomes* made the list, the *Times* called him up to ask if it was fiction or nonfiction. He thought they were putting him on, so he said, "If it's all true, then of course it's nonfiction. And if it isn't true, then it's satire, which is also nonfiction." The *Times* agreed, and *Gnomes* is officially nonfiction.

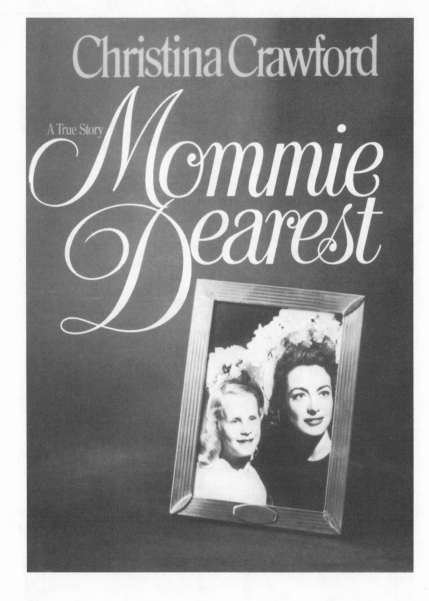

Sophie's Choice

Sophie's Choice

One

In those days cheap apartments were almost impossible to find in Manhattan, so I had to move to Brooklyn. This was in 1947, and one of the pleasant features of that summer which I so vividly remember was the weather, which was sunny and mild, flower-fragrant, almost as if the days had been arrested in a seemingly perpetual springtime. I was grateful for that if for nothing else, since my youth, I felt, was at its lowest ebb. At twenty-two, struggling to become some kind of writer, I found that the creative heat which at eighteen had nearly consumed me with its gorgeous, relentless flame had flickered out to a dim pilot light registering little more than a token glow in my breast, or wherever my hungriest aspirations once resided. It was not that I no longer wanted to write, I still yearned passionately to produce the novel which had been for so long captive in my brain. It was only that, having written down the first few fine para~~graphs~~, I could not produce any others, or—to approxim~~ate~~ ~~Ge~~rude Stein's remark about a lesser writer of the ~~Lost G~~eneration—I had the syrup but it ~~wouldn't~~ po~~ur~~. ~~To~~ make matters worse, I was out of a job a~~nd~~ ~~had litt~~le money and was self-exiled to Flatbus~~h—~~ ~~like another~~ country-men, another lean and ~~hungry~~ ~~young S~~outherner wan-dering amid the Kingdom ~~of the Jews.~~

Call me Stingo, which wa~~s the nickname I was known~~ by in those days, if I wa~~s called anything at all. The name~~ derives ~~somehow~~ ~~from my prep-school days back in the state~~ of V~~irginia.~~ ~~This school was~~ ~~...~~ I wa~~s...~~

> "A great book should leave you with many experiences, and slightly exhausted at the end."
>
> **—William Styron**

> "When I used to teach creative writing, I would tell the students to make their characters want something right away—even if it's only a glass of water. Characters paralyzed by the meaning-lessness of modern life still have to drink water from time to time."
>
> **—Kurt Vonnegut**

FIRST DATE AT #1: July 22, 1979

TOTAL WEEKS AT #1: 6

Sophie's Choice
William Styron
RANDOM HOUSE

Twelve years after *Nat Turner*, Styron returns to #1 with a dark tale that explores the nature of evil through the lives of two doomed lovers: Sophie, a beautiful Polish gentile and Nathan, a mad, brilliant Jew. Eleven years later, Styron reached #1 on the nonfiction list with an account of the dark times in his own life. *Sophie* came to the list at #2, and remained at or near the top for three months, then spent another seven months moving back and forth in the lower regions of the list.

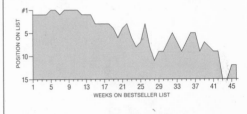

FIRST DATE AT #1: September 9, 1979

TOTAL WEEKS AT #1: 4

The Last Enchantment
Mary Stewart
MORROW

The further adventures of Merlin, King Arthur, and their colleagues are described in Stewart's second and last appearance at #1. Stewart says that "I believe that it is not enough to produce what one sees as 'plain reality,' to hold up a mirror to the ordinary and nothing else. If the writers of an age settle for the mediocre, or even the plain nasty as the norm of an age, then imperceptibly but definitely that does become the norm of the age...." After three months in the top three spots, the book cycled rhythmically up and down for a while between #6 and #4.

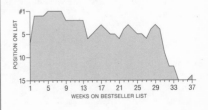

FIRST DATE AT #1: February 11, 1979
TOTAL WEEKS AT #1: 7

Lauren Bacall by Myself

Lauren Bacall

KNOPF

In the footsteps of *Tallulah* and laying the groundwork for Hepburn, Bacall shares her memoirs of life before, during, and after Bogart. The book was written without outside help, in long-hand on yellow legal paper. The reviews were generally favorable. As reviewer Nan Robertson wrote, it is "notable for generosity to others, honesty about herself and restraint—three qualities that are seldom present in show business memoirs."

FIRST DATE AT #1: April 1, 1979
TOTAL WEEKS AT #1: 32

The Complete Scarsdale Medical Diet

Herman Tarnower and Samm Sinclair Baker

RAWSON WADE

Dr. Tarnower told his readers that they could lose up to 20 pounds in 14 days by following his plan. The book that topped the list for nearly eight months began as mimeographed handouts that the Scarsdale internist and cardiologist used to give to his patients. Samm Baker has written and co-written many self-help books and says that he always "makes sure by intensive research and checking that the diet...works. That's why the books work. It's simple to write a best seller...isn't it?" This is probably the only #1 bestseller in which the author thanks someone who was later to murder him.

THE COMPLETE SCARSDALE MEDICAL DIET

PLUS

DR. TARNOWER'S LIFETIME KEEP-SLIM PROGRAM

ACKNOWLEDGEMENTS

WE ARE GRATEFUL *to Jean Harris for her splendid assistance in the research and writing of this book . . .*

Natalie Baker organized the excellent tables, created many of the recipes, and in her quiet, intelligent way provided a great many fine suggestions . . .

Suzanne van der Vreken, an imaginative nutritionist and artist, created many of the Gourmet and International recipes . . .

We wish, especially, to thank Lynne Tryforos, Phylis Rogers, Grace Clayton, Lydia Eichhammer, and Jeevan Procter, for their assistance with the diets, writing, and manuscript preparation . . .

Also, our thanks to all the staff at the Scarsdale Medical Center for their help and patience with diet inquiries: Barbara Strauss, Linda Francis, Maria Kenny, Ruth Aroldi, Terri Alesandro, Elizabeth Bennett, Phyllis Berger, Barbara Cavallo, Sandra Engstrom, Mary Fujimoto, Elaine Gracey, Margaret Gutierrez, Beth Hollender, Jean Lukaczyn, Dita Malter, Kathleen Monahan, Joan Mosca, Majda Remec, Frances Rose, Anita Schwartz, June Spinner, Victoria Spinner, Joan Tubel, William Twasutyn, Sharon Wallberg, and Florence Weitzner.

And . . . our special thanks to a brilliant gentleman and friend, Oscar Dystel, who suggested and made this book possible.

Also, high compliments to Eleanor and Kennett Rawson for their excellent editing and stewardship.

vii

And I lifted my old hands from the folded bedding and I clapped three times.

Another fighter plane leaped up from the tip of a nearby runway, tore the sky to shreds. I thought this: "At least I don't smoke anymore." It was true. I, who used to smoke four packages of unfiltered Pall Malls a day, was no longer a slave to King Nicotine. I would soon be reminded of how much I used to smoke, for the gray, pinstripe, three-piece Brooks Brothers suit awaiting me over in the supply room would be riddled with cigarette burns. There was a hole the size of a dime in the crotch, I remembered. A newspaper photograph was taken of me as I sat in the back of the federal marshal's green sedan, right after I was sentenced to prison. It was widely interpreted as showing how ashamed I was, haggard, horrified, unable to look anyone in the eye. It was in fact a photograph of a man who had just set his pants on fire.

I thought now about Sacco and Vanzetti. When I was young, I believed that the story of their martyrdom would cause an irresistible mania for justice to the common people to spread throughout the world. Does anybody know or care who they were anymore?

No.

I thought about the Cuyahoga Massacre, which was the bloodiest single encounter between strikers and an employer in the history of American labor. It happened i_____ in front of the main ga____ _____ Christmas morning in _____ That was long before I w_____ dren in the Russian Emp_____ who sent me to Harvar_____ watched it from the factor_____ father and his older broth_____

BY AND ABOUT #1 AUTHORS:

"You can survive as a writer on hustle: you get paid very little for each piece, but you write a lot of pieces. Christ, I did book reviews, I did anything. It was $85 here, $110 there—I was like Molly Bloom: Yes I will, yes I will, yes.' Whatever anybody wanted done, I did it."

—Kurt Vonnegut

FIRST DATE AT #1: October 7, 1979
TOTAL WEEKS AT #1: 5

Jailbird
Kurt Vonnegut
DELACORTE

Vonnegut's second and last #1 book describes one man's fumbling career from World War Two to Watergate. In *The New Fiction*, Vonnegut explained why his books are as short as they are. "I do not furnish transportation for my characters; I do not move them from one room to another; I do not send them up the stairs; they do not get dressed in the mornings; they do not put the ignition key in the lock and turn on the engine and let it warm up and look at all the gauges, and put the car in reverse, and back out, and drive to the filling station, and ask the guy there about the weather. You can fill up a good-sized book with this connective tissue. . . ."

FIRST DATE AT #1: October 14, 1979
TOTAL WEEKS AT #1: 2

The Dead Zone
Stephen King
VIKING

People magazine chose King as one of 20 people who defined the 1980s. The all-time leader in number of #1 bestsellers made his debut at the top of the list with his fifth novel, perhaps the least violent of his 16 #1 hits. It is the story of a man who comes out of a coma with the ability to foretell the future. He doesn't like what he sees, and sets about to change it. (King's first four non-#1 novels are *Carrie, Salem's Lot, The Shining,* and the first incarnation of *The Stand.*)

FIRST DATE AT #1: October 28, 1979
TOTAL WEEKS AT #1: 10

Aunt Erma's Cope Book
Erma Bombeck
MCGRAW-HILL

Aunt Erma's second #1 bestseller, and the one with the shortest title, offers more humorous advice and observations on getting through the week. The subtitle is "How to get from Monday to Friday in 12 days." *Contemporary Authors* asked Bombeck how she managed to write so much with the children at home. "It could be from early reporting days when there would be 75 people milling around the newsroom and you'd have to shut them out and think only of what was in your typewriter....I always worked at home in the middle of some traffic pattern....I always had people around me. I...just pull myself over to the side and think of anything else, and I won't even know there's anyone here."

FIRST DATE AT #1: December 30, 1979
TOTAL WEEKS AT #1: 9

The Brethren
Bob Woodward and Scott Armstrong
SIMON & SCHUSTER

Bob Woodward returns to #1 for the third of his six appearances, this time with coauthor Armstrong, for an inside and in-depth look at the Supreme Court of the United States and profiles of the nine justices.

fallen. Edith Marishna and her energy. As I sat in my lotus position, I was struck by a brutal truth. It would take an Act of God to get me to my feet.

It was discouraging. Just as soon as I got my head together, my body went. It wasn't fair. All my life I had dieted. I was bored talking about it . . . bored thinking about it—and tired of planning my next meal.

As I sat there sucking in my stomach and seeing nothing move, the twelfth major religion of the world began to form in my mind.

A religion founded in the twentieth century based on the four ignoble truths:

BLOUSES WORN OUTSIDE THE SLACKS FOOL NO ONE.
ONE-SIZE-FITS-ALL IS AN INCOMPLETE SENTENCE.
IF THERE'S LIFE AFTER WHIPPED CREAM, IT'S IN THIGH CITY.
STARCHING A CAFTAN NEVER SOLVES ANYTHING.

I would call my new religion FATSU. The disciples would be every woman who has ever gone to bed hungry and who sought a destiny of pantyhose that bagged at the knee.

The day of worship would be Monday, what else?
And the daily chant would be MaryTylerMoore . . . MaryTylerMoore . . . MaryTylerMoore . . .

in your own home for fun and profit **69**

The Bestseller Book Scandal Cover-Up

by Franky Schaeffer
Saturday Evening Post, **January 1983**

...The secular world increasingly applies a double standard to art produced by Christians. The myth of neutrality holds sway in the arts, as it does in politics and the law. This must be attacked and exposed for the bigotry and provincial narrow-mindedness that it is if art made by Christians is to play its important role in redemption.

To cite an example of anti-Christian bigotry in this area, think of the books, both nonfiction and fiction, that appear on the bestseller lists. The *New York Times'* bestseller list...contributes without a doubt to the sale and popularity of the works on these lists; when a title appears, it immediately enjoys a boost in sales and comes to the attention of an enormous public that otherwise might not hear of it....

Books by Christians published by Christian book companies, however, both nonfiction and fiction titles, almost never appear on these lists, even though many Christian books in any given year sell far in excess of the number of copies which qualify a book to appear....

The reason that books by Christians rarely appear on the bestseller lists, even though they outsell their contemporary secular counterparts, often by a ratio of 3 to 1, is simple: The secular world is provincial, narrow-minded, and bigoted....

Those works that appear on the bestseller lists generally espouse secular humanism, and so they are 'neutral.' It's the same old story...If the bestseller lists were really what they claim to be, books by Christians would show up with startling frequency; their sales figures would put them at the top of these lists regularly. And this would impress the general public that Christians might actually have something to say and would make it necessary for those in the media to take Christianity seriously.

This, however, is what an organization such as the *New York Times*...want to avoid like the plague. They deliberately promote the idea of a despiritualized, secular world, while at the same time continuing to claim the bestseller lists are completely accurate. ∎

FIRST DATE AT #1: October 28, 1979
TOTAL WEEKS AT #1: 6

The Establishment
Howard Fast
HOUGHTON MIFFLIN

In his only #1 appearance, Fast continues the story of the Lavette family, begun in *The Immigrants* and *Second Generation;* a family that survives and prospers in post-World War Two America. This is Fast's 67th book, including 14 written as E.V. Cunningham. When the author was blacklisted for his political views, he started his own publishing company, Blue Heron Press, whose first book was Fast's *Spartacus.* About his writing future at age 75, Fast said, "One of those I've loved most in my life was Louis Untermeyer, who continued to write and work until he was ninety-two. His mind was clear as a bell. But that's a very rare thing. Here I am at age 75 and I say, Well today is all right, but I don't know about tomorrow! But I'm pretty much with it, and have high hopes for other books."

FIRST DATE AT #1: December 9, 1979
TOTAL WEEKS AT #1: 2

Triple
Ken Follett
ARBOR HOUSE

Follett had just turned 30 when the first of his three #1 books reached the top. All three would have comparable patterns, spending two weeks each at the top of the list. Follett was a London newspaper reporter who began writing fiction in his spare time when he needed money for car repairs. He told the *Chicago Tribune,* "It was a hobby for me.... Some men go home and grow vegetables. I used to go home and write novels....I sold them for far more than you could sell vegetables for."

FIRST DATE AT #1: March 23, 1980

TOTAL WEEKS AT #1: 2

Donahue
Phil Donahue
SIMON & SCHUSTER

The talk show host's life through 1979 was many years in the making because of the author's busy schedule. The book includes a chapter written by members of his staff, in which they tell anecdotes and explain the nature of their jobs. Books by other talk show hosts, including Johnny Carson, Geraldo Rivera, Joan Rivers, and Jack Paar have made the list, but only Donahue reached #1.

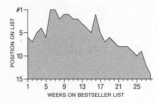

FIRST DATE AT #1: April 6, 1980

TOTAL WEEKS AT #1: 6

Free to Choose
Milton and Rose Friedman
HARCOURT

The Nobel laureate economist and his wife discuss the relationship between government and the economy in a book based on their public television series. This is the only #1 book to date by a husband and wife team who not only have the same last name but bill themselves with an "and" in this fashion. It is Dr. Milton Friedman's 27th book, the third written with Rose Director Friedman, and the first #1 for either.

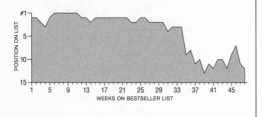

Just Find a Million Readers and Success Will Surely Follow
by Mordecai Richler
New York Times Book Review

. . . On book-tour flights to Washington, Miami, Seattle, and San Francisco, I devoured those recent bestsellers most likely to pollute this summer's beaches, shamelessly searching for hints on how to do it. I studied books by Danielle Steel, Tom Clancy, Robert Ludlum, Janet Dailey, Harvey Machay, Stephen King, and Barbara De Angelis, Ph.D., among others . . .

Danielle Steel has already had over 125 million satisfied customers and Tom Clancy, a maven of 'knife edge suspense' is also unequaled at illuminating character through dialogue. Take, for instance, this telling exchange from his latest blockbuster, *Clear and Present Danger:*

"Two-Six Alpha, this is Eight-Three Quebec, do you read, over?

Eight Three Quebec, this is Two Six Alpha. I read you five by five, over . . .

We have a target on profile, bearing one-nine-six range two-one-zero, Speed two six five, Over . . .

Roger, copy. Out . . ."

Although many an impecunious literary man thinks that if only he held his nose long enough he could turn his hand to churning out a blockbuster beach book, the truth is—as Tug McGraw once observed in a different context—you gotta believe. And none, it strikes me, is more sincere than sudsy Danielle Steel. One of her recent novels, *Daddy,* is truly yummy, heartwarming, beyond compare, and thus has sold in the millions. It tells the story of the admirable Oliver Watson, a 44-year-old successful advertising executive, ostensibly the happily married father of three who is shocked to discover that Sarah, his wife for 18 years, has decided to abandon him and her comfy suburban home to go back to Harvard for a master's degree and just possibly to write a novel.

"You need a good shrink, that's what you need," Oliver says. "You're acting like a bored neurotic housewife." To which Sarah replies, "You don't know anything about me . . . You don't know what it's like giving up everything you've ever dreamed of. You've got it all, a career, a family, a wife, waiting for you at home like a faithful little dog, waiting to bring you the newspaper and fetch your slippers. Well what about me, God damn it! When do I get mine? When do I get to do what I want to do? When you're dead, when the kids are gone, when I'm ninety? Well I'm not going to wait that long. I want it now, before I'm too old to do anything worthwhile, before I'm too old to give a damn anymore, or enjoy it. . . . "

Ms. Steel's prose is penny plain, functional, its vocabulary limited, not given to surprising metaphors or stylistic flourishes.

But when she's overcome by emotion, her sentences, like those in an old Walter Winchell column, tend to suffer from highly charged ellipses, as in "until finally he slept in her arms . . . Oliver . . . the boy she had loved long since . . . the man he had become . . . the love that had begun and now might end at Harvard."

Bouncing high in the skies on a flight from Washington to Seattle . . . I had to admit that I was incapable of composing such dulcet concoctions as *Daddy* . . . clearly aimed at daydreaming women. But, mining my rich experience as a high school air cadet, possibly I could enhance the sales allure of my fiction by gilding it with military detail, like the superstar Tom Clancy, whom I took to be a man's man. On the evidence, however, Tom Clancy's macho novels are not meant so much for men as overgrown boys. The sexiest items in his novels are the pieces of military hardware, which are unfailingly described in loving, sensuous detail.

Reading a writer for the first time, searching for ideas I can steal for profit, I like to sniff out the early influences. The author's debt to, say, Henry James, Conrad, Joyce, Hemingway, or whomever. In the case of Mr. Clancy's latest, *Clear and Present Danger,* the formative influences are obvious: *Popular Mechanics, Jane's Fighting Ships,* John Wayne movies, and Action Comics. His machines are three-dimensional, but his characters are so wooden they could be used as kindling. Their dialogue, such as it is, would be more appropriate rising out of comic strip-type balloons than enclosed by quotation marks. To be fair, however, he can spin a yarn, as they say, and he flatters sedentary civilians with Inside Military Dope, or IMD as he would surely have it. . . .

I finally turned to Stephen King, the prolific author of perennial bestsellers, who can really write very well indeed. In *Misery,* his extremely clever and witty 1987 novel, the protagonist is Paul Sheldon, an author of romance novels whom I take to be Mr. King's alter ego. At one point Sheldon muses, "There are lots of guys out there who write a better prose line than I do and who have a better understanding of what people are really like and what humanity is supposed to mean—hell, I know that . . . There's a million things in this world I can't do. Couldn't hit a curve ball, even back in high school. Can't fix a leaky faucet. Can't roller skate or make an F-chord on the guitar. . . . But if you want me to take you away to scare you or involve you or make you cry or grin, yeah, I can. I can bring it to you and keep bringing it until you holler uncle. I am able. I CAN. . . ."

Misery, like all good novels, has a subtext. Obviously Annie Wilkes . . . [the] enormous, goofy former nurse, equally proficient with the reward of pain-killing drugs or the punishing blow of an ax . . . is an astute take on the relentless muse that continues to inspire Danielle Steel, Janet Dailey, and many another indispensable novelist. Or, *pace* Harvey Mackay, she is the carrot, always slightly out of reach, that prods best-selling authors to scale the literary heights. Roger, copy, out, as Tom Clancy would say. ∎

FIRST DATE AT #1: January 20, 1980
TOTAL WEEKS AT #1: 4

Smiley's People
John le Carré
KNOPF

All right, just this once. George Smiley, the great British spy, delays his retirement one last time for a final confrontation with Karla, his Russian counterpart, whom he tries to get to defect to the West. Le Carré's third #1 book reached the top 16 years after the first. The hero is short, fat, and his clothes "hang about his squat frame like skin on a shrunken toad."

FIRST DATE AT #1: February 17, 1980
TOTAL WEEKS AT #1: 5

Princess Daisy
Judith Krantz
CROWN

The second of Krantz's four #1 bestsellers tells of a woman's fight for survival in a world of glitter, from the Czar's St. Petersburg to Manhattan's SoHo district. It reached #1 in its third week, and after a month there spent nearly four months at #2. The sale of paperback rights to *Princess Daisy* for a very large sum brought criticism in the *Times* of "the growing practice of investing in 'blockbuster' properties to the possible detriment of less commercial authors." It was suggested that the amount paid for *Daisy* could have bought the rights to 60 non-blockbuster books. Publishers responded that this was an accountant's, not an editor's way of thinking; that Krantz's books bring people into bookstores where they buy other books too, and that the $3 million she was paid was a capital investment that would not otherwise have gone to non-blockbuster authors.

FIRST DATE AT #1: May 18, 1980
TOTAL WEEKS AT #1: 1

Men in Love
Nancy Friday
DELACORTE

The author reaches #1 for the only time with her book about men's fantasies about women and sex—as the author described it, the "very powerful, primitive feelings which arouse deep anxiety. The way I see it, the fantasies and feelings don't need an intellectual response; they need a gut level deeply felt reaction, and that's how I read them." *Newsweek*'s male reviewer felt that "Her thesis, that men's love of women is filled with rage, is pretty enough, but entirely unsupported by any of the... stupefying quantity of testimony...she has assembled."

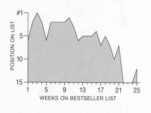

FIRST DATE AT #1: May 25, 1980
TOTAL WEEKS AT #1: 10

Thy Neighbor's Wife
Gay Talese
DOUBLEDAY

Nine years after his exposé of the Mafia, Talese returns to #1 for the second and last time with this analysis of how American sexuality has changed in recent years. The author disdained the use of fictitious or composite characters, and used people's real names. He said that is the main reason the book took eight years to write: developing relationships with his interviewees, persuading them to let him tell their stories, and getting the necessary releases.

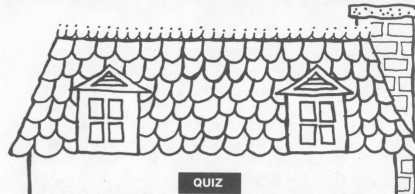

Twenty #1 Authors Whose Names Are Not Household Words

Being the author of a #1 *New York Times* bestseller is not necessarily a ticket to fame. Here, for example, are the names of twenty authors (or pairs of authors) who have had a #1 bestseller, *just in the last ten years.* Actually only sixteen of the following twenty authors (or pairs of authors) have had a #1 bestseller. Your challenge is to find the four fictitious authors (or pairs of authors), and then, for triple marks, supply the #1 titles for the sixteen real ones. The year of reaching #1 is provided for the 16 real ones (and a fake year for the fake ones). Answers on page 165.

Peter Cartwright (1991)

Timothy Zahn (1991)

David Eddings (1991)

Bruce Henderson (1991)

Ken Burns (1990)

Charles Leerhsen (1990)

Janet Carpenter (1990)

Bryan Burrough and John Helyar (1990)

Sonny Kleinfeld (1988)

Tony Schwartz (1988)

John Fennstein (1987)

Bruce Douglas and Christopher Green (1986)

Sandra Harmon (1985)

Cy Janos (1985)

Peter Collier and David Horowitz ((1984)

Bill Adler and Thomas Chastain (1984)

W. William Raven (1984)

C. Charles Crow (1984)

Robert Waterman (1983)

Joan D. Vinge (1983)

1

The trawler plunged into the angry swells of the dark, furious sea like an awkward animal trying desperately to break out of an impenetrable swamp. The waves rose to goliathan heights, crashing into the hull with the power of raw tonnage; the white sprays caught in the night sky cascaded downward over the deck under the force of the night wind. Everywhere there were the sounds of inanimate pain, wood straining against wood, ropes twisting, stretched to the breaking point. The animal was dying.

Two abrupt explosions pierced the sounds of the sea and the wind and the vessel's pain. They came from the dimly lit cabin that rose and fell with its host body. A man lunged out of the door grasping the railing with one hand, holding his stomach with the other.

A second man followed, the pursuit cautious, his intent violent. He stood bracing himself in the cabin door; he raised a gun and fired again. And again.

The man at the railing whipped both his hands up to his head, arching backward under the impact of the fourth bullet. The trawler's bow dipped suddenly into the valley of two giant waves, lifting the wounded man off his feet; he twisted to his left unable to take his hands away from his head. The boat surged upward, bow and midships more out of the water than in it, sweeping the figure in the doorway back into the cabin, a fifth gunshot fired wildly. The wounded man screamed, his hands now lashing out at anything he could grasp, his eyes blinded by blood and the unceasing spray of the sea. There was nothing he could grab, so he grabbed at nothing; his legs buckled as his body lurched forward. The boat rolled violently

FIRST DATE AT #1: March 23, 1980
TOTAL WEEKS AT #1: 16

The Bourne Identity
Robert Ludlum

RICHARD MAREK

The first of the Bourne trilogy and Ludlum's third #1 book, relates the melodramatic adventures of an amnesiac trying to find out who he really is. Ludlum told an interviewer that he begins his writing day at 4:15 a.m. and writes for five to six hours, taking about 18 months to complete a book. His word processor is a Ticonderoga #2 pencil. "I'll go to that great bookstore in the sky with one of those in my hands."

FIRST DATE AT #1: July 13, 1980
TOTAL WEEKS AT #1: 11

Rage of Angels
Sidney Sheldon

MORROW

In the second of Sheldon's seven #1 bestsellers, an idealistic young female lawyer eventually triumphs over two vengeful men. Sheldon told the *Los Angeles Times* that he writes visually: "It's my training from movies and TV. I have this goal. And it's for a reader to not be able to go to sleep at night. I want him to keep reading another four pages, then one more page. The following morning, or night, he's anxious to get back to the book."

FIRST DATE AT #1: August 3, 1980

TOTAL WEEKS AT #1: 6

Shelley: Also Known as Shirley

Shelley Winters

MORROW

Shirley Schrift writes of her progress from a little girl from a Brooklyn ghetto to two Oscars, three homes, four hit plays, five Impressionist paintings, six mink coats, and 99 films. The reading public was also titillated by her accounts of affairs with the likes of Marlon Brando, Errol Flynn, Burt Lancaster, William Holden, and Adlai Stevenson. Tell-all books by Ingrid Bergman and Gloria Swanson also made the *Times* list around this time.

FIRST DATE AT #1: September 21, 1980

TOTAL WEEKS AT #1: 10

Crisis Investing

Douglas R. Casey

HARPER

With mortgage interest rates around 20%, and both inflation and unemployment at an alarmingly high rate, Casey offers what he calls "opportunities and profits in the coming Great Depression."

CHAPTER 1

Who is Shirley Schrift? What happened to her, and what metamorphosis took place that changed her into Shelley Winters, movie star?

Adolescence is the time when most children struggle with their identity. I have come to feel that when adolescents are forced by circumstances to change their name, for whatever reason, they somehow bury part of that identity and for much of their adult life are compelled to try to reclaim and rejoin it into a unified feeling of a complete self.

So it was with me. At about fifteen, I was in the office of the Group Theatre in New York to read for an understudy in a play called *Retreat to Pleasure* by Irwin Shaw. I didn't have a clue what kind of part it was. I only knew I had to have it. The secretary asked me my name.

"Shirley Schrift."

She wrote it down on a little card, then asked me if I was registered with Equity.

I quickly replied, "I don't want to rush things."

"Shirley Schrift isn't a very good name for an actress," she told me. "Let's see if we can figure out another one. . . . What's your mother's maiden name?"

"Winter," I told her.

She wrote it down. "Do you like 'Shirley'?" she asked.

"God, no, there's millions of Shirleys all over Brooklyn, all named after Shirley Temple."

"Well, wouldn't you like a name that sounds like Shirley in case someone calls you?"

I thought for a moment. "Shelley is my favorite poet, but that's a last name, isn't it?"

She wrote it on the card in front of "Winter." She looked at it. "Not anymore it isn't. Shelley Winter. That's your name."

She handed m̶e̶ ̶c̶a̶r̶d̶ and I looked at it. It felt like me. Half poetic and ̶.̶.̶.̶ ̶"̶S̶h̶a̶w̶,̶"̶ I told her. "Send it in."

Years later, i̶n̶ S to "Winter" a̶

Answers to the "Household Words" Quiz

(from page 162)

Timothy Zahn (1991)
Heir to the Empire

David Eddings (1991)
The Seeress of Kell

Bruce Henderson (1991)
And the Sea Will Tell (coauthor)

Ken Burns (1990)
The Civil War (coauthor)

Charles Leerhsen (1990)
Trump: Staying at the Top (coauthor)

Bryan Burrough and John Helyar (1990)
Barbarians at the Gate

Sonny Kleinfeld (1988)
Talking Straight (coauthor)

Tony Schwartz (1988)
Trump: The Art of the Deal (coauthor)

John Fennstein (1987)
A Season on the Brink

Sandra Harmon (1985)
Elvis and Me (coauthor)

Cy Janos (1985)
Yeager (coauthor)

Peter Collier and David Horowitz (1984)
The Kennedys: An American Drama

Bill Adler and Thomas Chastain (1984)
Who Killed the Robbins Family?

W. William Raven (1984)
Mayor (coauthor)

Robert Waterman (1983)
In Search of Excellence (coauthor)

Joan D. Vinge (1983)
The Return of the Jedi

FIRST DATE AT #1: September 28, 1980
TOTAL WEEKS AT #1: 3

Firestarter
Stephen King

VIKING

The second of King's 16 #1 books is about an eight-year-old girl who can set things on fire just by looking at them. After college, King wrote what he called a "parable of women's consciousness," and then threw it away. His wife retrieved it from the trash and suggested that he expand it into a novel which became *Carrie*. As *Contemporary Authors* puts it, "the novel was marketed as horror fiction and the genre had found its juggernaut."

FIRST DATE AT #1: October 19, 1980
TOTAL WEEKS AT #1: 2

The Key to Rebecca
Ken Follett

MORROW

Follett returned to the top less than a year after his first #1 book with this tale of German espionage in Egypt during the desert campaigns of 1942. In 1974, Follett left his job as a reporter and joined the staff of a large publishing house, Everest Books. Later, he told the *Chicago Tribune* "A good deal of it was curiosity to know what made books sell. Some books sell and others don't. All the books I had written up to that point fell into the category of those that did not."

FIRST DATE AT #1: November 9, 1980
TOTAL WEEKS AT #1: 16

Cosmos
Carl Sagan

RANDOM HOUSE

The well-known astronomer and space scientist explains billions and billions of years (13 billion, actually) of cosmic evolution in this book tie-in with his extremely popular public television series. Sagan reports that when he was a boy, he told his grandfather he wanted to be an astronomer. His grandfather replied, "Yes, but how will you make your living?" It was not until sometime later that he learned astronomers are actually paid for what they do. One of the universe's unsolved mysteries is why this book plunged to #7, then fell from the list entirely, in the midst of its #1 stay. (For what it's worth, the plunge began the week Reagan was inaugurated and the Iranian hostages were freed.)

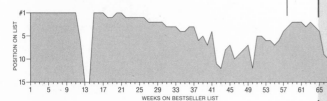

FIRST DATE AT #1: March 8, 1981
TOTAL WEEKS AT #1: 11

Never Say Diet
Richard Simmons

WARNER

Bolstered by heavy television promotion, this exercise, diet, and lifestyle regimen devised by the Hollywood television personality, spent nearly a year in the top three, including two pairs of #1 appearances more than half a year apart. At one point in Simmons's reign, there were seven money and business books on the list at once (*Nothing Down, Money Dynamics, You Can Negotiate Anything, Paper Money,* etc.), but none ever reached #1.

Life on the List, or My Struggle with 'Moses the Kitten'
by Andrew A. Rooney
New York Times Book Review, **March 17, 1985**

A lot of bad things that have nothing to do with writing start happening to an author once a book is published. The pinnacle of good times for the writer is the instant the book is completed. It's all downhill from there no matter what honors the book gets or how much money it brings in. Nothing makes an author feel as good as he felt when he finished the book.

It would seem, for example, as though a writer whose book appears on the *New York Times* Bestseller List would be pleased and proud, but there are so many negative aspects to the experience that the pain often exceeds the pleasure.

First, it soon becomes obvious to the writer that most of the people who read The List don't read books. A great many more people congratulate the writer for making The List than for writing the book. The author infers that either they have read it and didn't like it or they considered it a book not worth reading. "Congratulations," they say, "I see you're No. 2."

These people have not bought or read the book and have no intention of doing either. They're Bestseller List fans who are interested in seeing what people are reading even though they haven't read a book themselves since *The Old Man and the Sea.* If there are nonbooks there are also nonreaders.

All these things mitigate, for the author, the joy of having his book listed. . . .

For many people, part of the pleasure of reading The Bestseller List comes from how easy it is to feel superior to both The List and the authors on it. I have been superior hundreds of times in the last four years when a book of mine was on The List.

"Congratulations," an ill-meaning acquaintance will say. "I see you beat out *Moses the Kitten* this week."

Or, "*A Light in the Attic* sure hangs in there doesn't it," someone else will say.

Or, "I'm surprised an as-told-to book like *Iacocca* is doing so well."

Two years ago they never failed to bring up Jane Fonda's exercise book which, for all but a few weeks, was ahead of mine.

"Are you on top or underneath Jane Fonda this week?" they'd say and then laugh so I'd know it was a dirty joke.

The thoughts of many literature-lovers who read The Bestseller List immediately turn to money when they see a friend's name on it. Most people I talk to who have seen *Pieces of My Mind* listed are not prompted to consider the possibility that I might have written a good book. They think about how much money I've made from it. . . .

No one is more disdainful of The Bestseller List than acquaintances who have written books themselves that didn't appear on it. This category also includes people who have been meaning to write a book that has not, of course, appeared on The List either. (Almost everyone who reads the *New York Times Book Review* has been meaning to write a book.)

The *Book Review* editors want to make it clear that they concur with their readers in their disdain for The List. Its editors chose the 15 best books of 1984 in December. None of their selections had ever appeared on The Bestseller List.

continued on page 168

FIRST DATE AT #1: November 2, 1980
TOTAL WEEKS AT #1: 25

The Covenant
James Michener
RANDOM HOUSE

In his fifth #1 book, Michener covers fifteen thousand years of South African history. Michener told an interviewer, "I don't think the way I write books is the best or even the second best. The really great writers are people like Emily Brontë who sit in a room and write out of their limited experience and unlimited imagination. But people in my position also do some very good work. I'm not a stylist like Updike or Bellow, and don't aspire to be. I'm not interested in plot or pyrotechnics, but I sure work to get a steady flow.... The way the words flow, trying to maintain a point of view and a certain persuasiveness—that I can do."

FIRST DATE AT #1: April 26, 1981
TOTAL WEEKS AT #1: 2

Gorky Park
Martin Cruz Smith
RANDOM HOUSE

The first of Smith's two #1 murder mysteries set in Russia, *Gorky Park* begins with a crime committed in a Moscow park, and leads to a chase across two continents in pursuit of a murderer. Smith sold the idea to Putnam for $15,000. After years of work and some disharmony, he bought the rights back. He said "I have never been so excited in my life, except for the birth of children, as when I wrote the last line. Because I knew it was just right. I had this marvelous book and I was damned if I was going to sell it for anything less than a marvelous price. The words 'one million' seemed to come to mind." And that was the price for which he resold it to Random House.

1

ALL NIGHTS should be so dark, all winters so warm, all headlights so dazzling.

The van jacked, stalled and quit on a drift, and the homicide team got out, militia officers cut from a pattern of short arms and low brows, wrapped in sheepskin greatcoats. The one not in uniform was a lean, pale man, the chief investigator. He listened sympathetically to the tale of the officer who had found the bodies in the snow: the man had only strayed so far from the park footpath in the middle of the night to relieve himself, then he saw them, himself half undone, as it were, and just about froze, too. The team followed the beam of the van's spotlight.

The investigator suspected the poor dead bastards were just a vodka troika that had cheerily frozen to death. Vodka was liquid taxation, and the price was always rising. It was accepted that three was the lucky number on a bottle in terms of economic prudence and desired effect. It was a perfect example of primitive communism.

Lights appeared from the opposite side of the clearing, shadow trees sweeping the snow until two black Volgas appeared. A squad of KGB agents in plainclothes were led from the cars by a squat, vigorous major called Pribluda. Together, militia and KGB stamped their feet for warmth, exhaling drafts of steam. Ice crystals sparkled on caps and collars.

The militia—the police arm of the MVD—directed traffic, chased drunks and picked up everyday corpses. The Committee for State Security—the KGB—was charged with grander, subtler responsibilities, combating foreign and domestic intriguers, smugglers, malcontents, and while the agents had uniforms, they preferred anonymous plainclothes. Major Pribluda was full of rough early-morning humor, pleased to reduce the professional animosity that strained cordial rela-

FIRST DATE AT #1: May 17, 1981
TOTAL WEEKS AT #1: 9

The Lord God Made Them All

James Herriot

ST. MARTIN'S

The popular Yorkshire vet returns with his fourth book and third #1 bestseller, this time with stories from home and travels in Russia. While this book was #1, another animal book of sorts, *Miss Piggy's Guide to Life* rose as high as #4, as did Frank Herbert's *God Emperor of Dune,* the second-highest level attained by any *Dune* book. Stephen King made the nonfiction list for the only time with *Danse Macabre,* but it never challenged for #1.

FIRST DATE AT #1: July 12, 1981
TOTAL WEEKS AT #1: 9

The Beverly Hills Diet

Judy Mazel

MACMILLAN

If they can lose weight in Scarsdale, they can lose weight in Beverly Hills. The "pineapple diet" espoused by a southern California nutrition guru was roundly attacked by dieticians, but gobbled up by the public, who kept it at #1 for two months.

from page 166

Friends, editors and *Book Review* readers are not the only ones who look down on The Bestseller List. The writer himself may have a long history of sneering Sunday mornings over coffee at the books and authors on it. Inevitably, however, he gains new respect for the wisdom of a mass audience when his book appears there. My own confidence in the standard of public taste fluctuates as my book moves up and down The List.

After the first few glorious weeks, the writer begins to scan The List more critically. He looks, sometimes desperately, for books that will lend class to it. He wants good neighbors.

Two years ago, *And More by Andy Rooney,* a title I detested, appeared on The List. The competition at that time, which friends never let me forget, was not *Moses the Kitten* but *Garfield the Cat, Jane Fonda's Workout Book,* and Leo Buscaglia's *Living, Loving & Learning.*

Every week I looked for more substance. When Russell Baker's fine Pulizer Prize winner, *Growing Up,* made The List, I was cheering for it. . . .

When the first of [my] three recent books made The List in 1981, the capsule comment after the title read, "By Andrew A. Rooney, the television personality." I cannot, offhand, think of anything more insulting to be called than "a television personality." While I understood perfectly well that it's bad form to write an angry letter to a book reviewer or especially a *Book Review* editor, I wrote one to the editor at *The Times.* I never heard back, but the following week I was designated "the journalist and television commentator." It was the nicest thing an editor has ever done for me.

Another unpleasant by-product of an appearance on The Bestseller List is the manuscripts it brings in for the author to read. People assume that, because the writer has a successful book, he or she knows how to do it and can explain how with a few penciled comments in the margins of the manuscript. It's as insulting as the dinner guests who ask for the recipe of a dish, as though they could make it themselves if you named the ingredients. . . .

This week for the first time in 27 weeks, my book *Pieces of My Mind* has dropped off The Bestseller List. It's been a constant source of worry. I knew there was nothing but heartbreak ahead. An author with a book on The Bestseller List is like a hypochondriac who loves life so much that he spends his whole life worrying about dying. ■

NOBLE HOUSE 21

John Chen's stomach twisted uneasily. He hated the interminable quarreling, his father apoplectic with rage, his wife in tears, his children petrified, his stepmother and brothers and cousins all gloating, wanting him gone, all of his sisters, most of his uncles, all their wives. Envy, greed. The hell with it and them, he thought. But Father's right about Bartlett, though not the way he thinks. No. This one is for me. This deal. Just this one then I'll be free forever.

They were almost through the long, brightly lit Customs Hall now.

"You going racing Saturday?" John Chen asked.

"Who isn't!" The week before, to the ecstasy of all, the immensely powerful Turf Club with its exclusive monopoly on horse racing—the only legal form of gambling allowed in the Colony—had put out a special bulletin: "Though our formal season does not start this year until October 5, with the kind permission of our illustrious Governor, Sir Geoffrey Allison, the Stewards have decided to declare Saturday, August 24 a Very Special Race Day for the enjoyment of all and as a salute to our hardworking population who are bearing the heavy weight of the second worst drought in our history with fortitude. . . ."

"I hear you've got Golden Lady running in the fifth," Armstrong said.

"The trainer says she's got a chance. Please come by Father's box and have a drink with us. I could use some of your tips. You're a great punter."

"Just lucky. But my ten dollars each way hardly compares with your ten thousand."

"But that's only when we've one of our horses running. Last season was a disaster. . . . I could use a winner."

"So could I." Oh Christ how I need a winner, Armstrong thought. But you, Johnny Chen, it doesn't matter a twopenny tick in hell if you win or lose ten thousand or a hundred thousand. He tried to curb his soaring jealousy. Calm down, he told himsel̲ ̲ ̲ ̲-̲ ̲ ̲ ̲re a fact and it's your job to catch them if you can—however ric̲h̲ ̲ ̲ ̲ ̲ ̲ ̲ ̲ ̲ ̲ ̲-̲ be content with your rotten pay when every s̲ ̲ ̲ ̲ ̲ ̲ ̲ ̲ ̲ ̲. Why envy this bastard—he's for th̲ ̲ ̲ ̲ ̲ ̲ ̲ ̲ ̲. the way, I sent a constable to you̲ ̲ ̲ ̲ ̲ ̲ ̲ ̲ waiting at the gangway for you a̲ ̲ ̲ ̲.

"Oh, that's great, thanks. Sorr̲ ̲ ̲ ̲

"No trouble. It's a matter of ̲ ̲ ̲ ̲ special for you to come yourself.̲'̲

"As I said, nothing's too much ̲ ̲ ̲

John Chen kept his̲ ̲ ̲ ̲ite smil̲ ̲ ̲ because of ̲ ̲ ̲ ̲ ̲ ̲ ̲ ̲ a ver̲ ̲ ̲ debt.

FIRST DATE AT #1: May 10, 1981
TOTAL WEEKS AT #1: 15

Noble House
James Clavell
DELACORTE

The first of Clavell's two #1 novels, describes the struggle between British and Chinese businessmen for control of a Hong Kong trading house. The Australian-born author was a Hollywood screenwriter (he wrote *The Fly*) until a strike forced him to consider other directions, and he began writing novels. *Noble House* is his fourth. "I'm not a novelist, I'm a storyteller," he told *National Review*. "I work very hard and try to do the best I can and I try and write for myself, thinking that what I like, other people may like. My attitude is perhaps more romantic than psychiatric. I've never been trained as a writer, either. I stumbled into it in a funny way. I do not know how it works; and I'm petrified that it will vanish as easily as it came!"

FIRST DATE AT #1: August 23, 1981
TOTAL WEEKS AT #1: 5

Cujo
Stephen King
VIKING

Less than a year after *Firestarter,* King reached #1 for the third time with a dog story, the account of a New York family seeking peace in a rural Maine town only to be tormented by a rabid dog. Of his critics, King told an interviewer, "People like me really do irritate people like them, you know. In effect, they're saying 'What right do you have to entertain people. This is a serious world with a lot of serious problems. Let's sit around and pick scabs; *that's* art.'"

FIRST DATE AT #1: November 29, 1981
TOTAL WEEKS AT #1: 14

A Light in the Attic

Shel Silverstein

HARPER

The poet, song writer, and *Playboy* editor's collection of humorous poems and drawings is the all-time champion for *New York Times* bestseller list longevity—over 180 weeks at last count. It tends to reappear toward the bottom of the list, hang on for a few weeks, and then go away for a while. The complete performance chart would require a fold-out page, so only the first third is shown here. Silverstein rarely appears in public, saying "I won't go on television because who am I talking to? Johnny Carson? The camera? Twenty million people I can't see. Uh uh." And yet, "I have an ego. I have ideas. I want to be articulate....People who say they create only for themselves and don't care if they're published...I hate to hear talk like that. If it's good, it's too good not to share. That's the way I feel about my work. So I'll keep on communicating, but only my way."

His Mother Called Him William, His Sister Called Him Bill

One might have predicted that the dignified business of book publishing would dictate use of one's first name. William, not Bill for instance. In the majority of cases, this is in fact the case, but for almost every proper name used (Joseph Heller), there is at least one case of the nickname appearing on the cover (Joe McGinnis). There are two mixed messages. One comes from Mr. Rooney, whose two #1 books are entitled *A Few Minutes with Andy Rooney* and *And More from Andy Rooney,* with the author author of each listed as Andrew A. Rooney. The other is from Mr. Peters, who called himself Thomas in his first #1 book and Tom in his second. Here are the rest of the nickname data:

Andrew	1	Judith	2
Andy	0	Judy	1
William	6	Kenneth	2
Bill	2	Ken	1
Charles	3	Robert	12
Chuck	1	Bob	2
James	10	Samuel	1
Jim	1	Sam	1
John	16	Stephen/Steven	3
Jack	1	Steve	0
Joseph	2	Thomas	4
Joe	1	Tom	2

FIRST DATE AT #1: March 7, 1982
TOTAL WEEKS AT #1: 1

A Few Minutes with Andy Rooney

Andrew A. Rooney

ATHENEUM

Reflections on contemporary life by the *60 Minutes* television commentator whom the *Los Angeles Times* called "the most-listened-to curmudgeon in recent times." Rooney once wrote jokes and stories for Arthur Godfrey, Sam Levenson, and Victor Borge. His first book, *Air Gunner,* was published 38 years earlier.

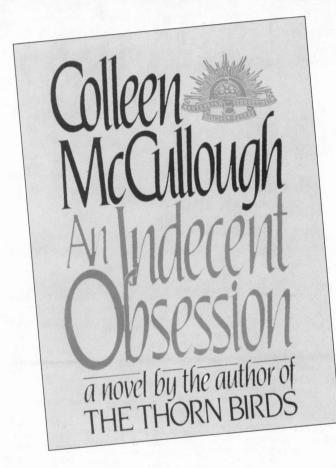

Colleen McCullough
An Indecent Obsession
a novel by the author of
THE THORN BIRDS

FIRST DATE AT #1: September 27, 1981
TOTAL WEEKS AT #1: 9

The Hotel New Hampshire
John Irving
DUTTON

The World According to Garp never reached #1, but Irving was there twice, first with this novel about an eccentric family that moves from America to Europe and back, staying in and running equally eccentric hotels.

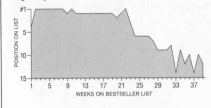

FIRST DATE AT #1: November 15, 1981
TOTAL WEEKS AT #1: 13

An Indecent Obsession
Colleen McCullough
HARPER

Four years after *The Thorn Birds*, McCullough returns to #1 for the second and last time with this novel about a World War Two nurse engaged to one patient but attracted to another.

FIRST DATE AT #1: February 28, 1982
TOTAL WEEKS AT #1: 3

North and South
John Jakes
HARCOURT

Jakes's 39th book and only #1 bestseller is about two wealthy families, one in Pennsylvania, the other in the Carolinas, whose friendship is severely strained by the Civil War. Jakes feels a sense of responsibility to his readers as "the only source of history that some of these people had ever had. Maybe they'll never read a Barbara Tuchman . . . but down at the K Mart, they'll pick up one of mine."

171

FIRST DATE AT #1: March 14, 1982
TOTAL WEEKS AT #1: 32

Jane Fonda's Workout Book

Jane Fonda

SIMON & SCHUSTER

The queen of the exercise videos also became, for nearly two years, queen of the bestseller list. The book version of her famous workout rose quickly to #1 for more than half a year, and spent a total of 16 months in the top five. During Fonda's time at the top, one other fitness book (*Working Out*) and three diet books (*Mary Ellen's, Dr. Abravenel's,* and *The F-Plan Diet*) were all high on the list.

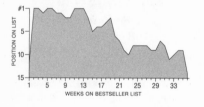

POSITION ON LIST

#1
5
10
15

1 5 9 13 17 21 25 29 33 37 41 45 49 53 57 61 65 69 73 77 81 85 89 93

WEEKS ON BESTSELLER LIST

FIRST DATE AT #1: August 8, 1982
TOTAL WEEKS AT #1: 7

Life Extension

Durk Pearson and Sandy Shaw

WARNER

Their ideas were challenged by experts but the public loved this simply written medical science book. Offering approaches that could add years to your life and life to your years, this was the first #1 book to sell for more than $20.

POSITION ON LIST

#1
5
10
15

1 5 9 13 17 21 25 29 33

WEEKS ON BESTSELLER LIST

Afterword
The Laugh That Lasts—For the Life Extenders

No great discovery is ever made without a bold guess.

—Newton

The existence and potential of life extension research is just beginning to become familiar to the public. Articles have been appearing in many magazines, newspapers, and even on television about this fascinating subject. On the other hand, practical applications of life extension technology have not been receiving as much publicity for several reasons.

• Most people are afraid to be among the early users of new technologies, they prefer to "wait and see."

• Government policies, as we have shown, greatly discourage applications of medical research findings. Manufacturers of vitamins, nutrients, and prescription drugs cannot legally make life extension claims, even if well supported by the scientific literature.

• Many people are hoping for eventual development of a definitive anti-aging pill which not only will eliminate aging entirely but also will be approved by medical authorities and the government. They will do nothing until that day arrives. We think that may be a very long time indeed.

• People are not used to acting on their own judgment in health matters.

• Most popular writers about life extension research are doing little or nothing about their own aging. They write about life extension research, but they don't apply the findings to themselves. It makes you wonder if they themselves really believe what they say!

We're laughing because the hard job of presenting our ideas to you is nearly over. We can sit back, relax, and dream about new research projects made possible by this book. With the proceeds from this book, we plan to buy more scientific

526

THE PRODIGAL DAUGHTER

wording was correct. Pierre Levale then spoke to Bishop O'Reilly and explained how he should administer the oath.

In the living room of her Cape Cod home, Florentyna Kane stood beside her family, with Colonel Max Perkins and Edward Winchester acting as witnesses. She took the Bible in her right hand and repeated the words after Bishop O'Reilly.

"I, Florentyna Kane, do solemnly swear that I will faithfully execute the office of President of the United States and will to the best of my ability preserve, protect and defend the Constitution of the United States."

Thus Florentyna Kane became the forty-third President of the United States.

William was the first to congratulate his mother and then they all tried to join in at once.

"I think we should leave for Washington, Madam President," the colonel suggested a few minutes later.

"Of course." Florentyna turned to the old family priest. "Thank you, Your Excellency," she said. But the bishop did not reply; for the first time in his life, the little Irishman was lost for words. "I shall need you to perform another ceremony for me in the near future."

"And what might that be, my dear?"

"As soon as we have a free weekend Edward and I are going to be married." Edward looked even more surprised and delighted than he had at the moment he heard Florentyna had become President.

"I remembered a little too late," she continued, "that if you fail to complete a hole in match-play competition, it is automatically awarded to your opponent."

Edward took her in his arms as Florentyna said, "My darling, I will need your wisdom and your strength, but most of all your love."

"You've already had them for nearly forty years, V.P. I mean . . ." Everyone laughed.

"I think we should leave now, Madam President," the colonel prompted. Florentyna nodded in agreement as the phone rang. Edward walked over to the desk and picked it up. "It's Brooks. Says he needs to speak to you urgently."

FIRST DATE AT #1: March 21, 1982
TOTAL WEEKS AT #1: 17

The Parsifal Mosaic

Robert Ludlum

RANDOM HOUSE

The fourth of Ludlum's eight #1 books spent the longest time at #1: four months, having entered the list in the top position. Secret agent Michael Havelock has many adventures and narrow escapes while managing to save the world from nuclear destruction.

FIRST DATE AT #1: July 4, 1982
TOTAL WEEKS AT #1: 5

The Prodigal Daughter

Jeffrey Archer

LINDEN PRESS

The first of Archer's two appearances at #1 was with this sequel to his popular *Kane and Abel,* in which the children of those antagonists marry each other. To write his novels, the former conservative member of Britain's Parliament moves his household—cook, typist, and researcher—to a Caribbean island hideaway for two months of uninterrupted work.

FIRST DATE AT #1: November 21, 1982
TOTAL WEEKS AT #1: 9

And More by Andy Rooney
Andrew A. Rooney
ATHENEUM

Less than a month after Rooney's first collection of essays dropped from the list, his second arrived and also rose quickly to the #1 spot. Jimmy Carter's *Keep the Faith* was at #3, the highest performance for presidential memoirs.

FIRST DATE AT #1: February 27, 1983
TOTAL WEEKS AT #1: 8

Megatrends
John Naisbitt
WARNER

Naisbitt tells us what to expect in politics, economics, and social developments over the next 10 years, based on an analysis of conditions at the time of writing.

FIRST DATE AT #1: April 24, 1983
TOTAL WEEKS AT #1: 30

In Search of Excellence
Thomas J. Peters and Robert H. Waterman, Jr.
HARPER

Lessons to be learned from well-run American corporations.

Words in #1 Titles that Are Not in the Dictionary

There are only six, other than fictitious people, things, and places.

FIVE ARE 'ALMOST' WORDS:

Megatrends (what John Naisbitt observes)

Moonwalk (what Michael Jackson does)

Seeress (the female seer of Kell)

Sematary (how Stephen King's characters misspelled the burial ground)

Spycatcher (what Peter Wright did)

ONE IS J. R. R. TOLKEIN'S NAME FOR A BODY OF KNOWLEDGE:

Silmarillion

---

40   **Toward New Theory**

ANALYTIC IVORY TOWERS

The reason behind the absence of focus on product or people in so many American companies, it would seem, is the simple presence of a focus on something else. That something else is overreliance on analysis from corporate ivory towers and overreliance on financial sleight of hand, the tools that would appear to eliminate risk but also, unfortunately, eliminate action.

"A lot of companies overdo it," says Ed Wrapp. "They find planning more interesting than getting out a salable product. . . . Planning is a welcome respite from operating problems. It is intellectually more rewarding, and does not carry the pressures that operations entail. . . . Formal long-range planning almost always leads to overemphasis of technique." Fletcher Byrom of Koppers offers a suggestion. "As a regimen," he says, "as a discipline for a group of people, planning is very valuable. My position is, go ahead and plan, but once you've done your planning, put it on the shelf. Don't be bound by it. Don't use it as a m̶ to the decision-making process. Use it mainly to recogni̶ ̶ ̶ ̶lace." In a similar vein, *Business Week* rece̶ ther Johnson & Johnson, nor T̶ ward thinking—has anyone on '̶

David Ogilvy, founder of (̶ "The majority of businessmen̶ cause they are unable to esca̶ vard's renowned marketing ̶ "Modelers build intricate d̶ is exceeded only by the aw̶ the technocrats who const̶ count of a Standard Bra̶ ject failure. The reason,̶ was that Standard Bra̶ gave them something a̶

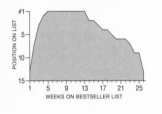

In Search of
EXCELLENCE
Lessons from America's Best-Run Companies

Thomas J. Peters and Robert H. Waterman Jr.

QUIZ:

Pen Names

This category includes only those authors who chose to write a book under a name quite different from their own, and neither a modification of their name (*Janet Miriam* Taylor Caldwell, *Phyllis Dorothy James* White, etc.), nor a name changed permanently for reasons other than publishing a book (Edna Furry to Hedda Hopper, Robert Conrad to Moss Hart, etc.). Here are the eight *real* names of #1 authors. Your task is to supply the pen names. Added points for supplying at least one #1 title for each author. (Three of the eight have more than one title.) Answers page 205.

Françoise Quoirez
Edward Everett Tanner
John Donaldson Voelker
David Cornwell
George G. Goodman
Joan Terry Garrity
Theodore S. Geisel
James Alfred Wight

FIRST DATE AT #1: August 15, 1982
TOTAL WEEKS AT #1: 3

Different Seasons
Stephen King
VIKING

The first collection of shorter works, in this instance four novellas, to make #1, this essentially non-horror book marks King's fourth #1 appearance in three years.

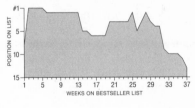

FIRST DATE AT #1: September 12, 1982
TOTAL WEEKS AT #1: 4

Master of the Game
Sidney Sheldon
MORROW

The third of Sheldon's seven #1 novels centers on the hidden truth behind a female business tycoon's rise to power. Sheldon told an interviewer that he writes about women "because women are more sensitive than men and more complex [and] more vulnerable."

FIRST DATE AT #1: October 10, 1982
TOTAL WEEKS AT #1: 22

Space
James Michener
RANDOM HOUSE

A fictionalized history of America's space program, this was Michener's fifth #1 book, all of which lasted at least five months in the top position.

FIRST DATE AT #1: October 23, 1983
TOTAL WEEKS AT #1: 21

Motherhood: The Second Oldest Profession

Erma Bombeck

McGRAW-HILL

Her seventh book and third #1 is a humorous look at the most important on-the-job training program ever. Speaking once to a group of students, Bombeck said that "writer's block was like North Dakota: it did not exist.... Write humor on demand? Of course you can. I hear these literary people all the time say you can't force anything. Of course you can. I do it three times a week, twenty years now."

FIRST DATE AT #1: February 26, 1984
TOTAL WEEKS AT #1: 8

Mayor

Edward Koch and W. William Raven

SIMON & SCHUSTER

The mayor of New York City offered opinions on his job, his city, and the world. Koch says that most of his friends and political advisors urged him not to write this book while still in office or planning to run for reelection or higher office. He overruled them because "I believe that no matter how interesting books on public life are, if they are published long after the events occurred when the individual...is no longer in office and gone from the scene, those books are purchased and placed on coffee tables and read by very few and have no major impact. I want this book to be read."

THE 1977 CAMPAIGN

I have said: "I hold Mario Cuomo responsible for what happened." I also hold him responsible for the same thing happening in 1982, but we'll get to that later.

Cuomo's response was that I should apologize to him because my campaign made attacks on him to the effect that he was part of the Mafia. He alleged that his son had said he'd heard a truck with a loudspeaker say, "A vote for Cuomo is a vote for the Mafia." I don't believe that ever happened. And if it did happen —which I don't believe—it was an isolated incident (someone obviously doing it on his own and whose name I never heard), as opposed to a campaign with photocopied posters;* with Cuomo campaign people engaging in attacks and hiring detectives; with Cuomo himself raising the homosexuality issue on television and radio programs.

In the midst of all this, we were informed by a couple of reporters that Cuomo's people were hiring a renegade cop to perjure himself. He was apparently either someone who was on the force and no good, or someone who had been thrown off the force. Anyway, he was going to swear to having arrested me as a result of an alleged fight in my apartment. He was also going to swear to having arrested me for soliciting male prostitutes on the street. He was going to perjure himself. The allegations were inherently unbelievable; but, of course, when that sort of story gets out on the weekend of an election, what can you do? By the time you catch up to this guy the election is over. The story got so far as to be "on hold" on the AP wire, which means that it had been written and was in the AP's computer, waiting to be transmitted.

David Garth was very good about this. Before the story got on the AP wire, Samuel DeMilia, the president of the Patrolmen's Benevolent Association, had come up to Garth's office. Now, according to Garth, who told me later what took place, DeMilia had said he had an affidavit from this cop who swore he had arrested me on two occasions: once after a fight in my apartment and once with a male prostitute. DeMilia said it would be terrible to have a Mayor who was subject to blackmail and that the story had to come out before the election.

* Someone who had an interest in Mario Cuomo's victory put up flyers around the city that read, "VOTE FOR CUOMO, NOT THE HOMO." We never knew who it was, but there were a lot of those flyers up during that campaign.

35

FIRST DATE AT #1: February 22, 1983

TOTAL WEEKS AT #1: 1

Mistral's Daughter

Judith Krantz

BANTAM

The third of Krantz's four #1 books, *Mistral's Daughter* follows several generations of powerful women, from the art world of the 1920s to the fashion industry of the 1980s. *The Mists of Avalon* was moving rapidly up the list at this time but it never reached #1.

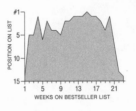

FIRST DATE AT #1: March 20, 1983

TOTAL WEEKS AT #1: 12

The Little Drummer Girl

John le Carré

KNOPF

This was going to be another Smiley book, but the author couldn't find a place for him in this account of an English girl caught between Israeli intelligence agents and Palestinian terrorists. It is the first le Carré book to join the list in the #1 position.

192

A few weeks after the Germans came to Avignon a black Citroën stopped before the gates to Mistral's *mas*. A German officer in his green uniform got out, followed by two soldiers with cocked machine guns. Rigid and pale, Marte Pollison made haste to open the gates so that they could drive in.

"Is this the home of Julien Mistral?" the officer asked in passable French.

"Yes, sir."

"Go and get him."

No Frenchman answered the summons of a German officer without fear, even Mistral, who had no hidden radio tuned to the BBC wavelength, who had taken no part in any Resistance effort, who was perfectly *en règle* with the Vichy authorities.

The captain introduced himself with a flourish. "Kapitän Schmitt." He extended his hand and Mistral shook it. The German waved his arm at the soldiers and they lowered their guns.

"It is a great honor to meet you, Monsieur Mistral," Schmitt said. "For years I have admired your work. In fact I am a bit of a painter myself—only an amateur, of course, but nevertheless I have a great love of all art."

"Thank you," Mistral replied. The man sounded like one of the dozens of daubers he had taken pains to avoid in the past. His uniform seemed totally at odds with his friendly words.

"I was stationed in Paris until recently and I had the pleasure of visiting Picasso in his studio. I had hoped that if it wasn't inconvenient you might allow me to see your own studio—I have read so much about it."

"Certainly," Mistral answered. He led the way to the studio wing of the *mas*. Schmitt looked carefully at the canvases Mistral had piled against the walls. His exclamations of pleasure were perceptive and intelligent and showed a thorough knowledge of the body of Mistral's work. Before the war, he explained, growing more talkative, he had visited Paris every year in the autumn to see the new exhibitions and tour the museums. At his home outside Frankfurt he had his own little studio, and even now, in Avignon, whenever he had the time, he worked at his portable easel. "I can't resist painting, it's my weakness. I painted in Paris every weekend for two years, you understand how it is."

"Perfectly."

The captain gave his soldiers an order and one of them ran out to the black car and returned a minute later with a bottle of cognac.

#1 in the U.S. vs. #1 in England

The two countries may not even have a language in common, as Churchill suggested, but there is considerable overlap in #1 bestsellers, although not always at the same time. Some books that are big in the U.S. become big in England a year, even two years later, and vice versa. Over a 10-year period (1976 to 1985), out of 120 top bestsellers in England, only 23 were also #1 *New York Times* bestsellers in the U.S.

1976

Agatha Christie's *Curtain,* Doctorow's *Ragtime,* a James Heriot book, and *Alistair Cooke's America* were among the top books in England, but the year's bestsellers were Mary Stewart's *Touch Not the Cat* (fiction) and Jacob Bronowski's *The Ascent of Man* (nonfiction).

1977

Oliver's Story was #1 in England. Tolkein's *Silmarillion* was the only other English book that was also a U.S. #1. It was Queen Elizabeth's Silver Jubilee year, and books about her and the royals dominated the nonfiction list.

1978

The Silmarillion was the top fiction book of the year in the U.K. but otherwise there was no overlap between England and the U.S.

1979

The two-country overlap included Heller's *Good as Gold,* Mary Stewart's *The Last Enchantment,* Herman Wouk's *War and Remembrance,* and *Lauren Bacall: By Myself.* But the #1 fiction in England was Wilbur Smith's *Wild Justice,* and in nonfiction it was Edith Holden's *Country Diary of an Edwardian Lady.*

1980

John le Carré's *Smiley's People* was the only overlapping book. The big fiction in England was Frederick Forsyth's *The Devil's Alternative,* and in nonfiction it was James Heriot's *Yorkshire,* and, most unusually, two versions of David Attenborough's *Life on Earth,* from two different publishers, one version larger than the other.

1981

James Clavell's *Noble House* was #1 in fiction in both places, as was Carl Sagan's *Cosmos* and James Heriot's *The Lord God Made Them All.* With Charles and Di tying the knot, the *Debrett Book of the Royal Wedding* was big in the U.K.

1982

In fiction, Archer's *The Prodigal Daughter* and Ludlum's *The Parsifal Mosaic* were #1 in both countries. But while Jane Fonda reigned supreme in the U.S., the big nonfiction books in England were *Roget's Thesaurus, The Concise Oxford Dictionary,* and *The Michelin Guide to France.*

1983

John le Carré's *The Little Drummer Girl* was #1 in both places, and Jane Fonda became big in England, too, although the #1 nonfiction books there were *The Official Sloane Ranger Handbook, Madhur Jaffrey's Indian Cookery,* and *Delia Smith's Complete Cookery Course.*

1984

Jeffrey Archer was #1 in both lands again with *First Among Equals.* Eco's *The Name of the Rose* and Ludlum's *The Aquitaine Progression* were also #1 in both. There was no overlap in the nonfiction ranks. The three biggest in England were David Attenborough's *The Living Planet,* Stephen Knight's *The Brotherhood,* and, once again, *The Country Diary of an Edwardian Lady.*

1985

In England, the top fiction books included *The Growing Pains of Adrian Mole* and *The Secret Diary of Adrian Mole, Aged 13 3/4,* both by Sue Townsend. Wilbur Smith had his fourth British #1 in eight years, *The Burning Shore.* But the only two overlapping books were Sidney Sheldon's *If Tomorrow Comes* and Barbara Bradford's *Hold the Dream.* There was no nonfiction overlap. The big ones in Britain were Lloyd, Fluck & Law's *Spitting Image, The Guinness Book of World Records* (which probably would have made the *New York Times* list if such books were included), and *The Vegetable Expert* by Dr. D. G. Hessayon.

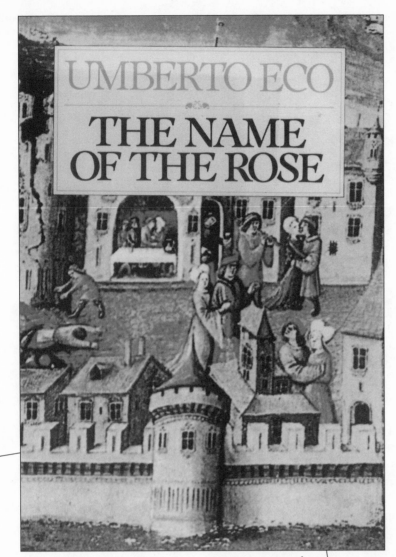

UMBERTO ECO

THE NAME OF THE ROSE

*I*n the beginning was the Word and the Word was with God, and the Word was God. This was beginning with God and the duty of every faithful monk would be to repeat every day with chanting humility the one never-changing event whose incontrovertible truth can be asserted. But we see now through a glass darkly, and the truth, before it is revealed to all, face to face, we see in fragments (alas, how illegible) in the error of the world, so we must spell out its faithful signals even when they seem obscure to us and as if amalgamated with a will wholly bent on evil.

Having reached the end of my poor sinner's life, my hair now white, I grow old as the world does, waiting to be lost in the bottomless pit of silent and deserted divinity, sharing in the light of angelic intelligences; confined now with my heavy, ailing body in this cell in the dear monastery of Melk, I prepare to leave on this parchment my testimony as to the wondrous and terrible events that I happened to observe in my youth, now repeating verbatim all I saw and heard, without venturing to seek a design, as if to leave to those who will come after (if the Antichrist has not come first) signs of signs, so that the prayer of deciphering may be exercised on them.

May the Lord grant me the grace to be the transparent witness of the happenings that took place in the abbey whose name it is only right and pious now to omit, toward the end of the year of our Lord

FIRST DATE AT #1: June 12, 1983
TOTAL WEEKS AT #1: 9

The Return of the Jedi
Joan D. Vinge
RANDOM HOUSE

The very popular movie came first, then the copiously illustrated tie-in storybook created by science fiction writer Vinge (pronounced VIN-jee). Until almost the last minute, the title was *The Revenge of the Jedi.* In 1982, the storybook version of *ET: The Extraterrestrial* had been called the bestselling book of the year, but sales were so spread out that it never made #1.

FIRST DATE AT #1: August 7, 1983
TOTAL WEEKS AT #1: 7

The Name of the Rose
Umberto Eco
HARCOURT

Just when critics are ready to dismiss the book-buying public as a cretinous mob with a two-digit IQ, along comes an unexpected success like *The Name of the Rose* to shake everything up. A complex historical novel and murder mystery set in a fourteenth-century Italian monastery, the Italian author's only #1 book remained in the top five for eight months. Dr. Eco is professor of semiotics at the University of Bologna. This is his 19th book, and the second to be translated into English (by William Weaver). For one week, it was tied for #1 with *The Jedi,* the only such tie in the list's history.

FIRST DATE AT #1: June 24, 1984
TOTAL WEEKS AT #1: 4

Wired
Bob Woodward
SIMON & SCHUSTER

Woodward's fourth #1 book, and his first without a coauthor, is an account of the troubled life and premature death of actor John Belushi.

FIRST DATE AT #1: July 22, 1984
TOTAL WEEKS AT #1: 7

The Kennedys: An American Drama
Peter Collier and David Horowitz
SUMMIT

Four generations of the glamorous and the dark side of the prominent family. Two assassination books were also on the list around this time. A long-time #2, David Yallop's *In the Name of God,* was about the alleged murder of Pope John Paul I. Gore Vidal's *Lincoln* also made the list, although never at #1. (This is not the David Horowitz of *Fight Back* but one of three others, all about the same age, who have published books.)

• 404 •

Gigi said that the paramedics and Briskin were both on their way.

Briskin ran down to his Mercedes 450 SL convertible, got in and raced the two miles up Sunset to bungalow 3. He walked through the open door and to the back bedroom. Wallace was leaning over doing mouth-to-mouth.

"Get out of here!" Wallace screamed. The next words almost flaked off his mouth incomprehensibly: *"John's dead!"*

Briskin began crying.

"If you can't take this . . . you'd better get out," Wallace said.

Briskin ran back to the living room and outside. He spotted the ambulance and started screaming for it. Just then Susan Morton returned. She saw the ambulance and suspected, almost knew, why it was there. She broke into hysterical tears.

At twelve thirty-six two paramedics came in and went to the back bedroom with Wallace. Briskin was pounding the walls in the living room and crying.

"Let's get him on the floor," one said.

They lifted John's naked body and rested it on the floor to examine it. Wallace urged them to try defibrillation to see if they could start his heart.

It was useless, they said. At twelve forty-five John was formally pronounced dead. One of the paramedics took a sheet from the bed and covered his body.

"Is that all you're going to do?" Wallace said.

John had been dead perhaps two, three or four hours. There was nothing they could do, one said.

"Is that all the fuck you're going to do?" Wallace asked, a high-pitched, accusatory strain in his voice.

"Okay, everyone out," one of the paramedics said.

"You'll play hell trying," Wallace said. "You touch me, I'll kill you. . . . I'm staying with John."

The paramedics stepped back.

"John, you dumb son of a bitch! You dumb son of a bitch!" Wallace screamed. A few minutes later he addressed the corpse. "John, the fucking game's over. Get up and let's go to the meeting."

Wallace was sure he had seen at least two needle marks on John's arms.

Brillstein and Gigi drove over to Cedars-Sinai hospital, just south of the Chateau on Beverly Boulevard. Whatever the problem, the paramedics would bring John there. While they waited, there was a call for

Nature's Favourite Resonance

by John Sutherland

The Nation, May 2, 1981 (from his book
Bestsellers: Popular Fiction of the 1970s)

In 1976 a comprehensive guide to British and American Contemporary Novelists was prepared by St. James Press, London, and St. Martin's Press, New York. It is a massive volume, more like a building block than a book. Some 1,650 pages long, it represents the efforts of two editors, twenty-nine advertisers (all distinguished academics or otherwise literary dignitaries) and 194 contributors. This critical regiment has produced entries on nearly 700 novelists, arranged alphabetically, Abbas to Sol Yurick. The comprehensiveness of the work is astonishing; everyone will find authors whom he has never heard of but whose contribution to contemporary fiction is clearly substantial. And equally astonishing is the encyclopedia's omission of novelists one cannot but have heard of but whom the advertisers regard as beneath notice. Even a reference work of this extensiveness can find no room for Harold Robbins (with an estimated 200 million sales), Alistair MacLean (with an estimated 150 million sales), Frederick Forsyth (with an estimated 50 million sales), Mickey Spillane (with an estimated 150 million sales), Barbara Cartland (with an estimated 100 million sales), Jacqueline Susann (whose best-selling novel has sold more than 6 million in the United States), or Peter Benchley (whose best-selling novel has sold more than 10 million in the United States).

There are good reasons for this quite typical neglect. Academic and higher-education journalism approaches habitually establish a critic/subject to literary object relationship, which the bestseller slips out of. The bestseller is never static or sufficiently complete in itself for criticism either to get to work on it or to make the work worthwhile. We have no critical vocabulary for applauding the ingenious, polymorphic tie-ins of an otherwise poor novel (its media adaptability), or for congratulating a novelist who writes indifferently—or even appallingly—but promotes his or her book with genius (Jacqueline Susann was a prime example). Above all, criticism has great difficulty in coming to terms with the ephemeral product; there is no good criticism of the bestseller for the same reason that there is no good criticism of television: the thing is never around long enough to be engaged. Denied his customary durable object, the reviewer/critic falls back on a kind of Podsnappery ("Not literature!") and saves his time for more worthwhile activities.

continued page 182

FIRST DATE AT #1: September 11, 1983
TOTAL WEEKS AT #1: 12

Poland
James Michener
RANDOM HOUSE

For Michener, a mere three months at #1 is almost a failure. None of his previous six #1 books had lasted less than 22 weeks, but none of his future ones stayed longer. *Poland* offers us seven centuries of Polish history interweaving fictional characters with real events. The *Times Book Review* section summarizes Michener thus: He "has found a formula. It delivers everywhere—Hawaii, Africa, Afghanistan, America, Israel, even outer space. The formula calls for experts, vast research, travel...and it calls for good guys and bad guys (both real and imagined) to hold the whole works together. It's a formula millions love. Mr. Michener gratifies their curiosity and is a pleasure to read."

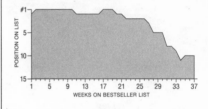

FIRST DATE AT #1: November 13, 1983
TOTAL WEEKS AT #1: 13

Pet Sematary
Stephen King
DOUBLEDAY

King's fifth and, to date, longest-running #1 bestseller is the gruesome story of a new family in town discovering the horrors that lie in a neighboring cemetery.

from page 181

Yet for some purposes, the utility of bestsellers lies in the very fact that they often have no literary merit to distract us. We are not therefore detained by any respect for their sanctity as "texts." Nor are we automatically led to think of them as finished products in their own right; instead, we can view them as integrated and dependent parts of a frankly commercial machinery, itself the product of a particular society at a particular period of history. Seen in this way, the best-selling novel may be reckoned as subordinate to other parts of the manufacturing and consuming system—such as the publicity which helps sell it, the author's "image" or the public's "needs. . ."

There is a hand-in-glove relationship between the bestseller, its time and its productive apparatus. Withdrawn from this relationship, Pop lit perplexes us: why, one wonders, should close to 2 million otherwise sensible Americans in 1972 have wanted to buy *Jonathan Livingston Seagull?* Answers can only be found by looking at the historical and book trade circumstances in which Richard Bach's book "made it."

. . . A whole range of sustaining and (largely) amiable Anglo-Saxon stupidity is openly displayed in its best-selling fiction. We are daily bombarded with gloomy news, and most of the population live lives of quiet desperation. Nevertheless, bestsellers invariably have upliftingly happy or providential endings. The enemy may be at the gate, but in our novels the shark is killed, the hijack foiled, the plague narrowly averted, the demon exorcised, civilization as we know it saved from innumerable close-run things. There are 2 million unemployed in Britain, but novels like Arthur Hailey's resolutely continue to celebrate the noble fulfillments and unbounded opportunities of the "little man."

. . . Even where they touch on "real" social problems in an "enlightened" frame of mind, the tendency is for bestsellers to be safely behind the times. The muck they rake is never fresh, the causes they espouse never genuinely new. Thus a work like Marilyn French's *The Women's Room* comes in, fists flailing, when the fight for female emancipation has moved to other arenas. Novels such as hers and Erica Jong's do not, as advertisements impudently claim, "change lives." Insofar as they have a useful function it is in serving to domesticate alien, life-changing social ideas for the mass population. . . . Essentially these works have much the same appeal as the pure romance which they affect to oppose (bodice rippers and Westerns, for instance). They are anodynes. They soothe. No one could guide his life by the codes, awareness and information which bestsellers furnish. But they clearly make life more livable for millions of British and American consumers. . . . ∎

The blow came suddenly, without warning, the impact such that Joel doubled over, his breath knocked out of him, and gripped his stomach. In front of him the surly bull of a captain was shaking his right hand, the grimace on his face indicating sharp pain. The German's fist had crashed into the gun lodged in Converse's belt. Joel staggered back into the bulkhead, leaned against it, and lowered himself to the floor as he reached under his jacket and took out the weapon. On his haunches, his legs bracing him against the wall, he aimed the automatic at the captain's huge chest.

"That was a rotten thing to do," said Converse, breathing hard, still holding his stomach. "Now, you bastard, *your* jacket!"

"*Was. . . ?*"

"You heard me! Take it off, hold it upside down, and shake the god-damned thing!"

The German slowly, reluctantly, slid off his waist-length coat, twice darting his eyes to the left of Joel, toward the wheelhouse door. "I look only for drugs."

"I'm not carrying any, and if I were, I suspect whoever sold them to me would have a better way to get across the river than with you. Turn it upside down! *Shake* it!"

The captain held his coat by the bottom edge and let it fall away. A short, ugly revolver plummeted to the floor, clacking on the wood, followed by the lighter sound of a long knife encased in a flat bone handle, flared at the end. As it struck the deck the blade shot out.

"This is the river," said the German without elaboration.

"And I just want to cross it without any trouble—and trouble to someone as nervous as I am is anyone walking through that door." Converse angled his head, gesturing at the wheelhouse entrance on his left. "In my state of mind, I'd fire this gun. I'd probably kill you and whoever else came in here. I'm not as strong as you, Captain, but I'm afraid, and that makes me much more dangerous. Can you understand that?"

"*Ja.* I not hurt you. I look only for drugs."

"You hurt me plenty," corrected Joel. "And that frightens me."

"*Nein. Bitte . . .* please."

"When do you take the boat out?"

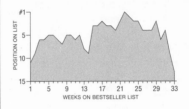

FIRST DATE AT #1: January 29, 1984
TOTAL WEEKS AT #1: 1

Who Killed the Robins Family?

*Bill Adler and
Thomas Chastain*

MORROW

The only #1 book to credit a creator (Adler) and an author (Chastain), it is also the first interactive "gimmick" book to reach #1: Readers were invited to solve the murder mystery, with a large cash prize for the best solution. (*Masquerade*, a real treasure hunt in book form, nearly made #1 a few years earlier.)

FIRST DATE AT #1: March 11, 1984
TOTAL WEEKS AT #1: 13

The Aquitaine Progression

Robert Ludlum

RANDOM HOUSE

Ludlum's fifth #1, and second in a row to debut in the #1 position (a first), concerns a lawyer who finds himself caught up in a conspiracy to take over the world. Dr. Seuss's *Butter Battle Book* took over #2 from *Pet Sematary,* but never reached #1.

FIRST DATE AT #1: September 16, 1984
TOTAL WEEKS AT #1: 7

Loving Each Other
Leo Buscaglia
HOLT

Dr. Felice Leonardo Buscaglia, popular psychologist sometimes known as "Dr. Hug," makes his first of two #1s with a collection of suggestions for "setting our priorities right to enjoy life to the fullest." One reviewer has called him "the Pavarotti of positive thinking." Buscaglia (pronounced boos-KAL-yuh) suggests that "people are estranged from love, afraid to reach out and touch one another. We're afraid to appear sentimental or speak in platitudes because people will say 'What a jerk!' It takes courage in our culture to be a lover." At this time, Andy Rooney's third book rose to #2, but unlike his two earlier ones, it did not make #1.

FIRST DATE AT #1: November 4, 1984
TOTAL WEEKS AT #1: 39

Iacocca
Lee Iacocca and William Novak
BANTAM

Iacocca was reluctant to do a book at all, and Novak had never written a book, but something clicked and the story of Lido Anthony Iacocca's rise from immigrant's son to top executive at Ford and Chrysler, became the most successful #1 business book ever, returning to #1 for a second brief stay six months after the first time. Novak has become the most successful "as told to" author ever, returning later to #1 with Nancy Reagan and Oliver North.

What Publishers Will Do for a Place on the Right List
by Roger Cohen
New York Times, August 12, 1990

When they talk about what it takes to break the sales barrier and get a book onto that self-perpetuating marketing machine called the best-seller list, publishers often sound more like auto executives than purveyors of literature. They discuss a book's "velocity." They talk of "revving up the sales force." They wonder how best to "put an author on the road." And they mumble arcane technical terms like "the Oprah factor," which, they claim, may be the key to sending a book racing off the grid.

No matter that only perhaps 0.008 percent of the 800,000 books in print are on a major best-seller list at any time. Because of the high stakes imposed by six-figure advance payments to authors, pushing more books onto the lists has become increasingly important, and many publishers increasingly inventive in trying to engineer a presence there.

Their efforts amount to an assault on the traditional "Mysterious Alchemy" school of publishing, which holds that a book's success depends on factors that are thankfully too shadowy to comprehend or manipulate. The modern "Build a Best Seller" school holds that books, like any product, respond to aggressive marketing.

"Sure, you can make a best seller," said Brenda Marsh, senior vice president of sales and marketing at HarperCollins, formerly Harper & Row. "The big factor is the author's energy and personality and empathy with the audience for the book. If the author is not shy, you have a real leg up on the situation."

Not all authors are thrilled at the notion that, like Lee Iacocca, they should personally peddle their wares.

Mordecai Richler, the Canadian writer, was recently dispatched by his publisher, Alfred A. Knopf, on a tour of New York bookstores to promote his latest novel, "Solomon Gursky Was Here." He said he ran into about 30 other writers "doing the mik run that day." Not a very edifying sight, Mr. Richler said. "The only interesting thing about a writer is his work. Sending him to market can be very embarrassing."

To publishers, however, such efforts are increasingly important. For the amount of money they now often pay, they feel they are due some leg work as well as some writing.

Publishers say that getting onto a best-seller list—particularly that of the closely watched New York Times Book Review—guarantees an author prominent

continued on page 186

"The end of an era: we lose the last of our charter members . . ."

During the early months of 1930 and afterward, Rausch Cordage Company fought to keep the mill running. Ludwig called the hands together one noon and explained the situation. The factory must either close down for a while or run part time, with reduced pay for everyone, from top executive down to unskilled laborers. He intended to keep the mill operating if at all possible, but orders were very hard to get. If worst came to worst, they would do what his grandfather had once done, in equally hard times: make any kind of hemp produce, down to oakum, and store it until the depression was over. The company could help make up for the lower wages; although the plant no longer operated on steam power, except for the whistle, it could buy coal by the carload and sell it to the hands at carload rates. He asked the men to choose a representative who would come to him in his office and tell him what the workman were willing to do. The verdict was what he expected: they would work on reduced pay and hours. They knew very well that men were being laid off everywhere, and that there would be little chance, particularly for the unskilled, and for the comparatively well-paid rope-makers, to find jobs anywhere else. Ludwig asked the hands' spokesman to thank the men for their loyalty. He said, "No one knows how long this depression will last, but I promise you that the mill will run as long as our capital reserves hold out; until then no one will be fired except for cause."

Ludwig's decision was hard for Gib to accept; he was as fretful about it as an old man. In fact, Ludwig thought sadly, at sixty his father was an old man, broken by his anxiety for his children a dozen years ago. His son tried to buoy him up. "One good thing: the price of hemp—manila and sisal both—is dropping fast, and will drop lower: we can stock up—fill a warehouse, maybe. We haven't a great supply on hand; haven't had since we got rid of the war surplus in the good years. We haven't a big inventory, either: for some time we have made no more than enough to fill orders.

1141

FIRST DATE AT #1: June 3, 1984
TOTAL WEEKS AT #1: 4

Full Circle
Danielle Steel
DELACORTE

Danielle Steel makes her #1 debut with this novel examining how a mother and daughter's relationship changes with the changing values of the past 40 years. Steel had previously published 17 books, many of them in the romance genre (*Passion's Promise, Season of Passion*, etc.). She began writing bigger books "because I wanted to appeal to men and I wanted the hardcover market, too."

FIRST DATE AT #1: July 8, 1984
TOTAL WEEKS AT #1: 7

"...and Ladies of the Club."
Helen Hooven Santmeyer
PUTNAM

The oldest woman ever to reach #1, the 87-year-old Santmeyer is also the only author to put her title in quotation marks, or to begin the title with an ellipsis. Her first novel was published in 1925, her second in 1929; this is her third, 55 years later: the story of life in an small Ohio town between 1868 and 1932. Santmeyer worked on the book off and on for more than 10 years following her retirement as an English professor. The Ohio State University Press published it in a first edition of 1,500 copies and sold 200, mostly to libraries. Three years later, a woman in Cleveland overheard another library patron raving about this book. She sent a copy to her son, a Hollywood producer who gave it to an agent who sold it to Putnam. Santmeyer's response to her huge success: "Isn't that nice. I just can't believe it." She kept her fame in perspective, acknowledging that "Part of the interest is because I'm an old lady." Santmeyer died in 1986.

FIRST DATE AT #1: June 9, 1985
TOTAL WEEKS AT #1: 1

A Passion for Excellence

Tom Peters and Nancy Austin

RANDOM HOUSE

Expanding on the message of Peters's first #1 book, *In Search of Excellence,* two years earlier, Peters and Austin report on effective management techniques and offer hints for applying them to any business. With this book, Peters becomes the first and only #1 author to bill himself differently on different works: "Thomas J." for his first and "Tom" for his second.

FIRST DATE AT #1: July 21, 1985
TOTAL WEEKS AT #1: 18

Yeager

Chuck Yeager, Cy Janos and Leo Janos

BANTAM

The autobiography of a West Virginia hillbilly who became a World War Two fighter pilot, the first man to fly faster than the speed of sound, and ultimately a role model for a great many Americans who kept his book on the list for a full year. The Janoses did the actual writing, based on more than 100 hours of taped interviews with Yeager. Leo Janos, a former Peace Corps executive and speechwriter for President Johnson, told *Contemporary Authors* that "As for specialization, I believe a writer is a writer is a writer. He or she should be able, with hard work and deft research, to operate successfully on a broad range of issues and projects."

continued from page 184

display, big stacks and steep discounts at the Waldenbooks, B. Dalton and Crown chain stores, which dominate the retail book business. So if a book is listed, its sales tend to be self-generating, and the big advance may indeed prove to have been justified.

Best-seller lists were not always the hinge on which the business turned. The first list "in the order of demand" appeared in 1895 in a monthly New York magazine called *The Bookman.* But for several decades after that, said the publishing historian John Tebbel, such popularity was considered "a sign of mediocrity," and the press paid little attention.

But today the best-seller list has become a preoccupation for both publishers and the media. When Barry Lippman, president of Macmillan's general book publishing division, recently ordered a study of what factors, if any, the company's last 10 best sellers shared, he found they had all been featured on national television shows. And indeed getting an author onto the "Today" show or "Good Morning America" or "Donahue" or "Geraldo" is now a coveted publishing prize. Best of all is "Oprah Winfrey," whose mid-afternoon shows can create an instant best seller.

Harville Hendrix, an author whose *Getting the Love You Want* was published in 1988 by Henry Holt & Co., said his book made little impact until he appeared on "Oprah" in August of that year. It then made the best-seller list for one week. When he reappeared on the show in February 1989, it came back for another seven weeks. "It's everybody's dream to go on TV," he said.

When Villard Books published Ellen Kreidman's *Light His Fire: How to Keep Your Man Passionately and Hopelessly in Love with You* last year, the book did nothing until the author expounded her theories on "Oprah." It then zoomed up the best-seller list. "Oprah" also launched Robert Fulghum, whose books of homespun wisdom have now been on best-seller lists for a couple of years.

Publishers have various ways of enticing producers of shows with their latest books. The most common is the "debate bait." So, if you are publishing on Erica Jong novel, persuade a television producer that it would boost ratings to have a panel of media stars (suggested names available on request) discussing female sexuality. If it's Jay McInerney, the glitter set could discuss their nights on the town. Publishing Kafka, today's houses might have found a panel to discuss depression. And so on.

Of course, many authors are shy, private people who hate the thought of appearing on television. Sue Miller, author of *The Good Mother,* said she "gets nervous before breakfast." So when her novel, *Family Pictures,* came out this year, she was reluctant to go on the air for her publisher, HarperCollins.

In the end, however, she agreed to appear before a smaller but very important audience: the publisher's sales force. At a sales meeting in Arizona, she read a passage from the novel that was so moving, said Ms. Marsh of HarperCollins, that "in the end there was not a dry eye in the place." That is called "revving up the sales force."

It worked. *Family Pictures* made the best-seller list. Of course it also helped that her previous novel was a best seller. Publishers also resort to traditional advertising in newspapers and magazines. But Peter Gethers, the editorial director of Villard, said it can be more cost-effective to "put an author on the road." That costs about $1,000 per city. So an author can do a dozen or so cities for the price that many publications charge for a single advertisement. With advertising budgets for even big books seldom exceeding $50,000, he believes the peripatetic author, oozing charm, is the answer.

Others remain skeptical. Jason Epstein, the editorial director of Random House, said: "Nothing you can do can make a book happen if it's not going to happen. And when it does happen, the best thing is to get out of the way." Many publishers live for the constant surprises, like Kevin Phillips' *The Politics of Rich and Poor,* a dissection of the legacy of Reaganomics that was published with 7,500 copies. Now more than 100,000 are in print.

In the long term, many books actually outsell best sellers, but because they don't achieve a high "velocity of sales," selling thousands of copies in a single week, they never leap onto the lists. Even as gauges of short-lived popularity, the lists are unreliable because the number of sales needed to get on them can vary significantly according to the season. Moreover, the lists are increasingly clogged with brand-name authors like Stephen King, Danielle Steel and Tom Clancy, so other authors have an ever slimmer chance of getting there.

"The reading public is being directed down the best-seller road," lamented Joseph Gable, the president of the independent Borders book store in Ann Arbor, Mich. "When considering a gift, they don't think in terms of what is right for a person, but what is big. Personally, I'd be happy to see the best-seller list abolished." ∎

FIRST DATE AT #1: August 26, 1984
TOTAL WEEKS AT #1: 2

First Among Equals
Jeffrey Archer
LINDEN PRESS

Archer returns to #1 with a political novel about three young men competing to be chosen Prime Minister of Great Britain. Archer once told an interviewer, "I don't pretend to be a great writer, but I am a good storyteller. . . . I just give 'em a good yarn, m'dear."

FIRST DATE AT #1: September 16, 1984
TOTAL WEEKS AT #1: 6

The Fourth Protocol
Frederick Forsyth
VIKING

In Forsyth's third and last #1, an ordinary-seeming London jewel robbery leads to elaborate plots and counterplots behind the Iron Curtain. New books by Joseph Heller, Arthur Hailey, and John Jakes all rose to #2 around this time, then fell back.

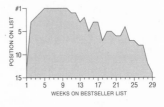

FIRST DATE AT #1: October 28, 1984
TOTAL WEEKS AT #1: 12

The Talisman
Stephen King and Peter Straub
VIKING

Two well-known fantasy-horror authors connected their word processors by telephone modem. The end result is King's sixth #1 book and Straub's first, a fantasy novel about two parallel worlds and a young boy who travels between them in search of a magic object that will cure his dying mother.

FIRST DATE AT #1: September 29, 1985
TOTAL WEEKS AT #1: 9

Elvis and Me

Priscilla Beaulieu Presley with Sandra Harmon

PUTNAM

Seven years after his death, Elvis Presley's widow remembers the King as friend, lover, mentor, husband, and father.

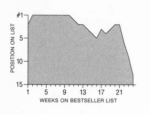

FIRST DATE AT #1: February 23, 1986
TOTAL WEEKS AT #1: 4

Bus 9 to Paradise

Leo Buscaglia

MORROW

The ebullient advocate of hugging returns to #1 for the second and last time with directions for another journey to happiness. *Contemporary Authors* asked Dr. Hug how he found time for himself on his busy schedule. He replied that he has "a private time every day, and that I insist upon. There's a private time here in my office when I simply tell my secretary that for all intents and purposes I've disappeared, and I take a half-hour or an hour and read something very calmly, or I close my eyes and rest, or I meditate. I do that all the time."

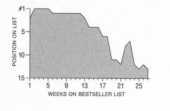

FIRST DATE AT #1: January 20, 1985
TOTAL WEEKS AT #1: 2

The Sicilian

Mario Puzo

SIMON & SCHUSTER

Sixteen years after *The Godfather,* Puzo returns with his second #1 book, the fictionalized life story of Salvatore Giuliano, a Sicilian bandit-hero.

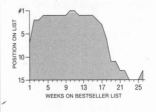

FIRST DATE AT #1: February 3, 1985
TOTAL WEEKS AT #1: 9

If Tomorrow Comes

Sidney Sheldon

MORROW

The fourth of Sheldon's seven #1 books is about a young woman serving an undeserved prison term and her plans for destroying the crime lords who framed her.

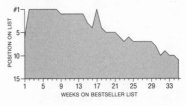

FIRST DATE AT #1: March 31, 1985
TOTAL WEEKS AT #1: 4

Family Album

Danielle Steel

DELACORTE

Steel returns to the top with the story of a married couple and their five children coping with life in contemporary America. Steel herself is a mother of eight, and a pillar of San Francisco society. She "just wrote what was in my head. I don't think anybody sets out deliberately to do a certain kind of writing—unless they do porno. I think most people just do what's in them and are sometimes startled to realize what's there."

FIRST DATE AT #1: March 30, 1986
TOTAL WEEKS AT #1: 7

You're Only Old Once

Dr. Seuss

RANDOM HOUSE

The *Times* described this book by Theodore Seuss Geisel, better known as Dr. Seuss, as "a checkup at the golden years clinic, done in pictures and rhyme." It rose quickly to #1, then spent half a year at #2 behind Bill Cosby. After 13 years as an advertising artist for Standard Oil, mostly creating creatures for the "Quick, Henry, the Flit" insecticide campaign, Seuss began writing while on a ship from Europe in 1936. Bored, he wrote a poem to the rhythm of the ship's engine, illustrated it, and later published it as *And to Think That I Saw It on Mulberry Street. You're Only Old Once* is his 60th book, including 13 done under the name Theo LeSieg.

FIRST DATE AT #1: May 11, 1986
TOTAL WEEKS AT #1: 2

The Triumph of Politics

David Stockman

HARPER

People were curious to know what the head of Reagan's Office of Management and Budget had to say and his "insider" book, subtitled "Why the Reagan revolution failed" came on the list at #1. When Stockman resigned, he had said that he knew that "my original ideological errors had given rise to a fiscal calamity and a political disorder probably beyond correction." As people learned that Stockman didn't have much to say about how our country's budget got so far out of control, his book plummeted from the list.

Is this a children's book? Well...not immediately. You buy a copy for your child now and you give it to him on his 70th birthday.

Prologue

The President's eyes were moist. It was unmistakable—they glistened. But while he made no effort to hide it, I had barely even noticed. My own eyes had hardly wavered from the center of my plate, from the olive atop the scoop of tuna salad. I had been trying to explain my involvement in the article in *The Atlantic Monthly,* and had rambled on nonstop for fifteen minutes. It seemed like forever.

The press had made it into a roaring overnight scandal. The story line made for a red-hot melodrama: The President had been cynically betrayed. I was the Judas who had disavowed the President's economic program and undercut his presidency. . . . His mettle was being tested. . . . I was hanging by a thread. . . . He was angry. That's what the newshounds in the White House press room were braying. And they were building it up by the hour.

The reality inside the Oval Office was quite different. We were sitting at a small luncheon table in front of a crackling fire. Aside from the popping sound of the wood sap, it was quiet and serene. It was the only time I had ever been alone with him.

After the White House stewards had served soup and tuna salad, the President turned to the business at hand. "Dave, how do you explain this?" he said softly. "You have hurt me. Why?"

My explanation soon meandered off into a total digression. It amounted to a capsule of my life story. . . .

I had grown up in a small midwestern town as he had. My grandfather had taught me the truths of Christianity and Republicanism. I'd been thrilled by Ronald Reagan's clarion call to conservatives at the 1964 Republican Convention.

But then I had gone off to college and fallen into the clutches of

1

Characters

THE MATRIARCH

EMMA HARTE LOWTHER AINSLEY, known as Emma Harte

HER CHILDREN

EDWINA, THE DOWAGER COUNTESS OF DUNVALE, her illegitimate daughter by Edwin Fairley

CHRISTOPHER "KIT" LOWTHER, her son by her first husband, Joe Lowther

ROBIN AINSLEY, her son by her second husband, Arthur Ainsley

ELIZABETH DE RAVELLO, Robin's twin, her daughter by Arthur Ainsley

DAISY MCGILL AMORY, her illegitimate daughter by Paul McGill

HER GRANDCHILDREN

PAULA MCGILL AMORY FAIRLEY, daughter of Daisy, granddaughter of Paul McGill

PHILIP MCGILL AMORY, son of Daisy, grandson of Paul McGill

EMILY BARKSTONE, daughter of Elizabeth, granddaughter of Arthur Ainsley

ALEXANDER BARKSTONE, son of Elizabeth, grandson of Arthur Ainsley

SARAH LOWTHER, daughter of Kit, granddaughter of Joe Lowther

JONATHAN AINSLEY, son of Robin, grandson of Arthur Ainsley

ANTHONY STANDISH, the Earl of Dunvale, son of Edwina, grandson of Edwin Fairley

AMANDA LINDE, daughter of Elizabeth, granddaughter of Arthur Ainsley

FRANCESCA LINDE, Amanda's twin, daughter of Elizabeth, granddaughter of Arthur Ainsley

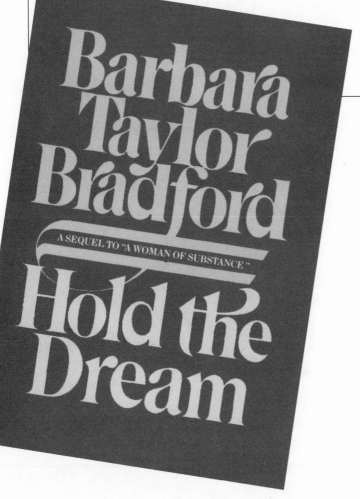

FIRST DATE AT #1: April 28, 1985
TOTAL WEEKS AT #1: 4

Thinner

Richard Bachman (Stephen King)

NAL BOOKS

Anyone who doubts the value of a proven author's name need only examine the case of *Thinner,* a very modest success at best, until it was revealed that Bachman was actually Stephen King and it became a #1 bestseller. It is the story of a young lawyer who is cursed by a gypsy and finds that his body is wasting mysteriously away. King began writing stories as Bachman while in college, but did not consider publishing them until he was already a well established author. His publisher feared the market was already saturated with King books. Four weeks after *Thinner* fell from the #1 spot, the next Stephen King book reached #1.

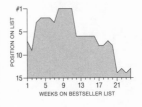

FIRST DATE AT #1: June 9, 1985
TOTAL WEEKS AT #1: 1

Hold the Dream

Barbara Taylor Bradford

DOUBLEDAY

The family saga, *A Woman of Substance,* was very popular but never reached #1. Its sequel, *Hold the Dream,* rose quickly to #1, but remained there only a week. Bradford's previous 13 books covered such diverse topics as the Bible, dressing to please your husband, and decorating an apartment. When asked if she enjoyed being a popular author, the British-born author replied "Do you think I'd rather be an unpopular author?" "If I didn't write fiction," she says, "they'd take me away in a strait-jacket, because I have all this *stuff* going on in my head. I have to get it out." Her writing days begin at six in the morning and often last ten to twelve hours.

The Top Five Fiction and Nonfiction Books of the 1980s

Not all publishers report the numerical sales of specific titles they have published, although these numbers are often supplied to *Publishers Weekly* in confidence for the purpose of making rankings. As it happened, the publishers of the top five fiction and nonfiction books of the 1980s were all among those who do supply exact numbers, thus making the following charts possible. (The numbers are books, not dollars.)

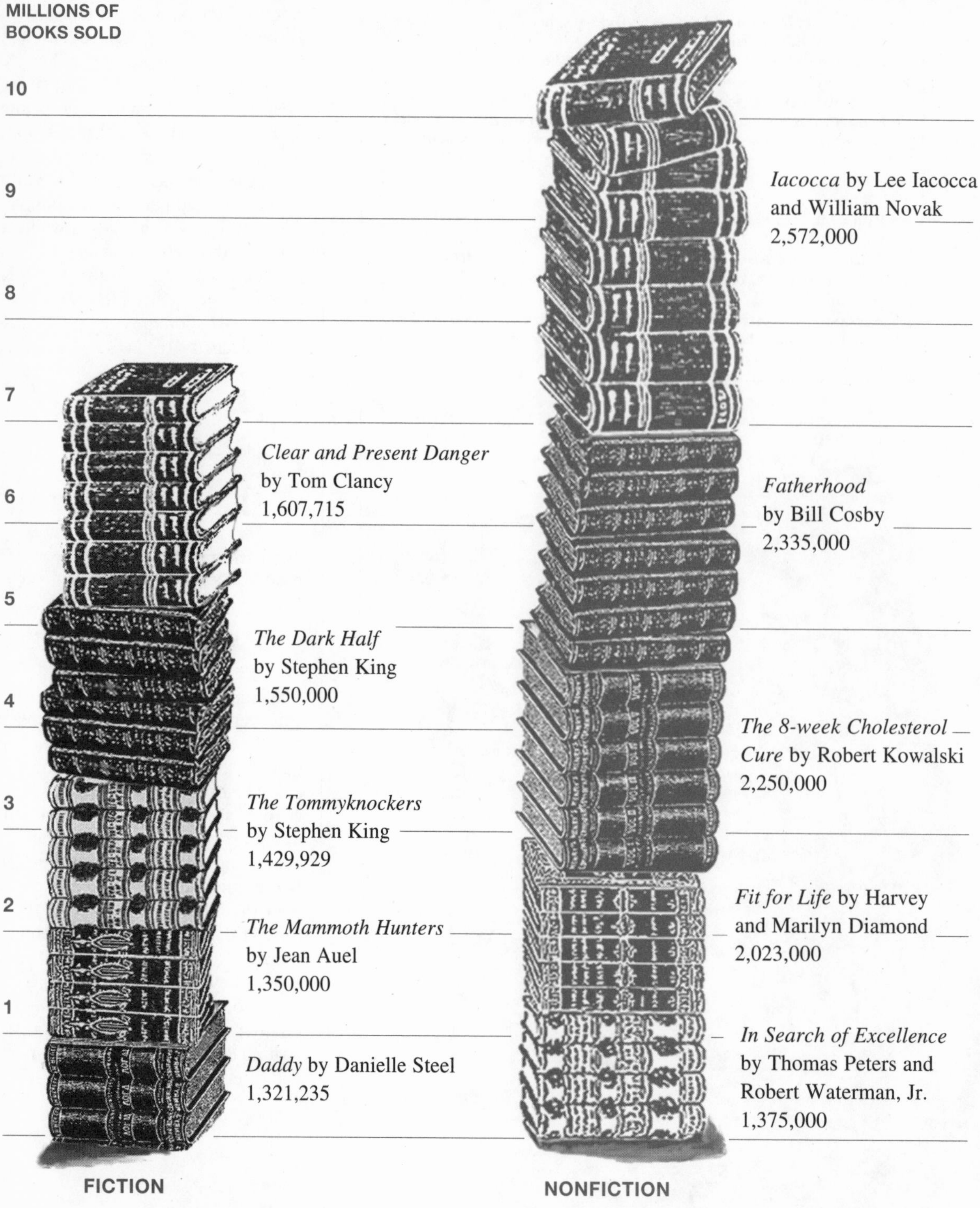

MILLIONS OF BOOKS SOLD

10

9 — *Iacocca* by Lee Iacocca and William Novak 2,572,000

8

7 — *Clear and Present Danger* by Tom Clancy 1,607,715

6 — *Fatherhood* by Bill Cosby 2,335,000

5 — *The Dark Half* by Stephen King 1,550,000

4 — *The 8-week Cholesterol Cure* by Robert Kowalski 2,250,000

3 — *The Tommyknockers* by Stephen King 1,429,929

2 — *The Mammoth Hunters* by Jean Auel 1,350,000 — *Fit for Life* by Harvey and Marilyn Diamond 2,023,000

1 — *Daddy* by Danielle Steel 1,321,235 — *In Search of Excellence* by Thomas Peters and Robert Waterman, Jr. 1,375,000

FICTION

NONFICTION

The Shortest #1 Titles

2 LETTERS

It   *Me*

4 LETTERS (OR NUMBERS)

1876   *Burr*

Cujo   *Star*

Uh-Oh   *Veil*

Zoya

5 LETTERS

Daddy   *Lucky*

Mayor   *Power!*

QB VII   *Roots*

Space   *Texas*

Wired

6 LETTERS

Act One   *Aku-Aku*

Alaska   *Cosmos*

Exodus   *Gnomes*

Gracie   *Hawaii*

Herzog   *His Way*

Jennie   *Lolita*

Misery   *My Turn*

Poland   *Triple*

Wheels   *Yeager*

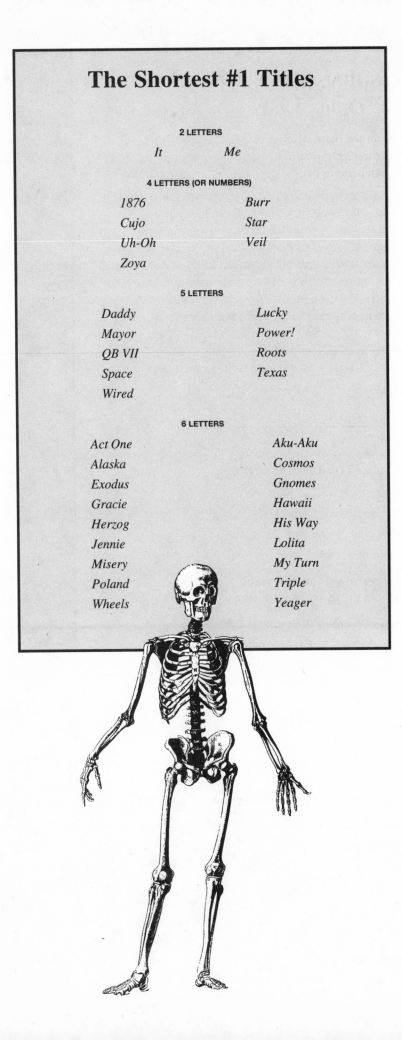

FIRST DATE AT #1: June 16, 1985
TOTAL WEEKS AT #1: 1

Cider House Rules
John Irving
MORROW

Irving's second and last #1 bestseller describes life in an orphanage in Maine during the early years of this century.

FIRST DATE AT #1: June 23, 1985
TOTAL WEEKS AT #1: 10

Skeleton Crew
Stephen King
PUTNAM

This collection is the only book of short stories that has made #1. King writes every day of the year except the Fourth of July, Christmas, and his birthday. According to *Contemporary Authors,* "He likes to work on two things simultaneously, beginning his day early with a two or three mile walk. . . . He devotes his afternoon hours to rewriting. . . . While he is not particular about working conditions, he is about his output. Despite chronic headaches, occasional insomnia, and even a fear of writer's block, he produces six pages daily. 'And that's like engraved in stone,' he says."

FIRST DATE AT #1: September 1, 1985
TOTAL WEEKS AT #1: 2

Lucky
Jackie Collins
SIMON & SCHUSTER

In Jackie Collins's only #1 bestseller, the heiress to a crime lord takes on the heiress to a shipping tycoon in fashionable spots all over the world.

Recent Megasellers that Did Not Reach #1 on the *Times* List

Publishers Weekly calls the "new breed" of super bestsellers "megasellers" to distinguish them from mere bestsellers. *Publishers Weekly* looks at total numerical sales for a year (or a decade), while the *Times* looks at the numbers week by week. A book that sold 100,000 copies in one week would surely make the *Times* list for that week, even if not another copy was ever sold. However, if a book sold 20,000 copies a week for an entire year, it would never show up as a #1 *Times* bestseller, even though it might be the best-selling book of the entire year.

In their list of the 25 best-selling fiction and nonfiction books of the 1980s, there are, in fact, two fiction books and eight nonfiction books that were never #1 *Times* bestsellers. It is reasonable that nonfiction books tend to have a much longer shelf life. Once a fiction book has started to decline in popularity, the bookstores begin sending them back for refunds, while cook books, diet books, business books, and the like may be kept around, in the belief and expectation they will eventually sell.

According to *Publishers Weekly,* the bestselling fiction book of the '80s was Tom Clancy's *Clear and Present Danger* (1,607,715 copies), and the best-selling nonfiction was *Iacocca: An Autobiography* (2,572,000 copies).

TOP FICTION BOOKS OF THE '80S THAT NEVER MADE #1 ON THE *TIMES* LIST

#18: *Leaving Home* (Garrison Keillor)

#23: *Caribbean* (James Michener)

TOP NONFICTION BOOKS OF THE '80S THAT NEVER MADE #1 ON THE *TIMES* LIST

#3: *The 8-Week Cholesterol Cure* (Robert Kowalski)

#4: *Fit for Life* (Harvey and Marilyn Diamond)

#8: *The Frugal Gourmet* (Jeff Smith)

#11: *Nothing Down* (Robert Allen)

#15: *The Frugal Gourmet Cooks with Wine* (Jeff Smith)

#16: *The Rotation Diet* (Martin Katahn)

#23: *The One Minute Manager* (Spencer Johnson with Kenneth Blanchard)

SPRING

The Sons of Knute Ice Melt contest starts on Groundhog Day, when they tow Mr. Berge's maroon 1949 Ford onto the lake, park it forty yards offshore with a long chain around the rear axle, and wait for spring. It's the car Mr. Berge was driving one warm March day when he hung a right at the dam and headed out to his fish house to check the dropline, forgetting he had hauled in the house three weeks before because the ice was melting. Now, the ice was even thinner, though covered with fresh snow. The car slowed down suddenly a hundred yards out, and when he gunned it she stopped dead and dropped a foot as if all four tires went flat. He couldn't open the door so he cranked down the window and climbed out and crawled up on the roof. His cries for help brought out the Volunteer Fire Department, which sent him one end of a rope tied to his dog Mike and dragged both of them through the slush back to shore. The car sank a few days later in six feet of water. They got a chain on her that summer, though, and winched her out. Mr. Berge, who had made some extravagant promises to God while lying on the roof, donated the car to the lodge, and so

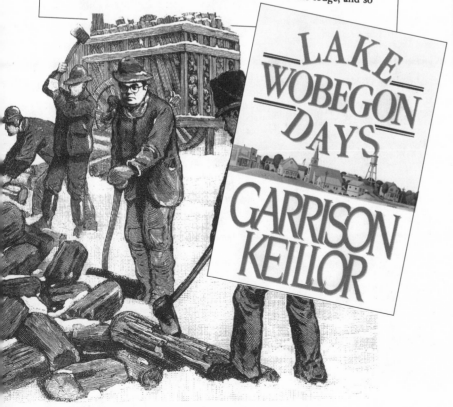

FIRST DATE AT #1: September 15, 1985
TOTAL WEEKS AT #1: 6

Lake Wobegon Days
Garrison Keillor
VIKING

National Public Radio brought us news about Lake Wobegon, Minnesota, where all the women are strong, all the men are good-looking, and all the children are above average. Keillor predicted to *Publishers Weekly* that "a minimum of 15 reviews of this book will refer to me as 'a modern day Mark Twain.' Anyone who comes from anywhere west of Eighth Avenue is another Mark Twain." At this time, Shirley MacLaine's *Dancing in the Light* entered the list at #2 but never made it to #1.

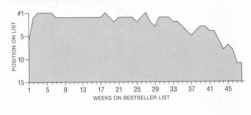

FIRST DATE AT #1: October 13, 1985
TOTAL WEEKS AT #1: 6

Texas
James Michener
RANDOM HOUSE

Texas started out with a bang, but followed with the weakest performance of Michener's eight #1s. It covers four hundred and fifty years of Texas history, from Spanish settlers to the modern day, blending fictional stories with actual facts and events. Although many critics are fast to attack Michener, Jonathan Yardley wrote in the *New York Times Book Review* that he "deserves more respect than he usually gets. Granted that he is not a stylist and that he smothers his stories under layers of historical and ecological trivia, nonetheless he has earned his enormous popularity honorably. Unlike many other authors whose books automatically rise to the upper reaches of the bestseller lists, he does not get there by exploiting the lives of the famous or the notorious; he does not treat sex cynically or pruriently; he does not write trash."

FIRST DATE AT #1: May 25, 1986
TOTAL WEEKS AT #1: 26

Fatherhood
Bill Cosby
DOUBLEDAY

The big book of 1986 was Dr. Cosby's ruminations and anecdotes covering just about every aspect of fatherhood. The television star and holder of an earned doctorate is the father of five, but the invitation to write this book was based on his role as a perfect father on the popular television sitcom, *The Cosby Show*. He did much of the writing in shorthand and with a dictating machine in and among his show business commitments.

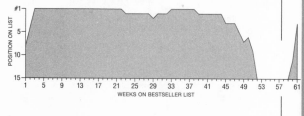

FIRST DATE AT #1: October 12, 1986
TOTAL WEEKS AT #1: 7

His Way
Kitty Kelley
BANTAM

Kelley's two famous unauthorized biographies had almost identical histories: a huge amount of prepublication publicity inducing legal action by the subject, a debut on the *Times* list at #1, and a fairly rapid decline and disappearance from the list. This book about Frank Sinatra followed this pattern, and it would be that way five years later with her book about Nancy Reagan. When Sinatra sued to prevent publication, a large coalition of writers rose to Kelley's defense. "Sinatra's suit is a chilling example of how a powerful figure using money and influence can orchestrate what the public shall know about him. . . . Sinatra . . . has now concluded that it is within his exclusive power to let the public know what he wants it to know about his life." Eventually, Sinatra reluctantly dropped his suit.

Wheeler-Dealer

Buying a stereo is merely a father's practice for the Big Buy: a car. When his child requests a car, a father will wish that he were a member of some sect that hasn't gone beyond the horse.

"Dad, all my friends say I should have my own car," the boy says earnestly one day.

"Wonderful. When are they going to buy it?"

"No, Dad. They think that you and Mom should buy me the car."

"Is there any particular reason why we should?"

"Well, that's what parents *do*."

"Not *all* parents. Did Adam and Eve get Abel a car? And he was the *good* one. Tell me this: why do you *need* a car?"

"To go places by myself."

"Well, you'd be surprised how many people manage to do that on public transportation. Elderly *ladies* do it every day. It's called a bus and I'd be happy to buy you a token. I won't even wait for your birthday."

"Dad, *you* know a bus isn't cool. My friends say I shouldn't have to ride on a bus now that I'm sixteen."

"They say that? Well, they couldn't be *good* friends

1

The night of December 22, 1938, two constables from Hackensack, New Jersey, headed for the Rustic Cabin in Englewood Cliffs to arrest Frank Sinatra.

Armed with a warrant charging adultery, the two officers walked into the dim little roadhouse looking for the skinny singer who waited tables and sang with Harold Arden's band over the radio line to WNEW in New York.

They waited until Frank finished his midnight broadcast and then sent word that they wanted to give him a Christmas present from one of his admirers. Falling for the ruse, Sinatra walked over to their table, where the criminal court officers arrested him and took him off to the courthouse. After posting bail for five hundred dollars, he was released on his own recognizance.

The next day a Hoboken newspaper carried a story headlined: SONGBIRD HELD IN MORALS CHARGE, but no one in Hoboken paid much attention. They were accustomed to seeing the Sinatra name in print for getting into trouble with the law. Frank's uncle Dominick, a boxer known as Champ Sieger, had been charged with malicious mischief; his uncle Gus had been arrested several times for running numbers; his other uncle, Babe, had been charged with participating in a murder and had been sent to prison. His father, Marty, was once charged with receiving stolen goods, and his mother, Dolly, was regularly in and out of courthouses for performing illegal abortions. And Frank himself had been arrested just a month before on a seduction charge.

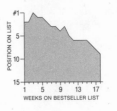

10

There was a lull in the activities of the Lion Camp in the early afternoon. Though their largest meal of the day was usually around noon, most people skipped the midday meal, or picked at leftovers from the morning, in anticipation of a feast that promised to be delicious for all that it was unplanned. People were relaxing; some were napping, others checked on food now and then, a few were talking quietly, but there was a feeling of excitement in the air and everyone was looking forward to a special evening.

Inside the earthlodge, Ayla and Tronie were listening to Deegie, who was telling them the details of her visit to Branag's Camp, and the arrangements for their joining. Ayla listened with interest at first, but when the two young Mamutoi women began speaking about this relative or that friend, none of whom she knew, she got up, with a comment about checking the ptarmigan, and went out. Deegie's talk of Branag and her coming Matrimonial made Ayla think of her relationship with Jondalar. He had said he loved her, but he had never proposed a joining to her, or spoken of Matrimonials, and she wondered about it.

She went to the pit where her birds were cooking, checked to make sure she could feel heat, then noticed Jondalar with Wymez and Danug off to the side, where they usually worked, away from the paths people normally used. She knew what they were talking about, and even if she hadn't, she could have guessed. The area was littered with broken hunks and sharp chips of flint, and several large nodules of the workable stone were lying on the ground near the three toolmakers. She often wondered how they could spend so much time talking about flint. Certainly they must have said everything there was to say by now.

While she was not an expert, until Jondalar came Ayla had made her own stone tools, which adequately served her needs. When she was young, she had often watched Droog, the clan toolmaker, and learned by copying his techniques. But Ayla had known the first time she watched Jondalar that his skill far surpassed hers, and while there was a similarity in feeling toward the craft, and perhaps even in rela-

FIRST DATE AT #1: November 24, 1985
TOTAL WEEKS AT #1: 11

The Mammoth Hunters
Jean M. Auel
CROWN

The Clan of the Cave Bear never reached #1, but two of its sequels did. The continuing prehistoric adventures of Ayla had a strong following that brought it to the list as #1 and kept it in the top five for half a year, then in the lower realms of the chart for another five months. After earning her MBA, Auel had an idea for a short story, that ended up a six-part 2,000-page opus. But when she read it, "I realized I had to learn something about writing. All of the wonderful passion that I felt was not on the page." Eschewing a local class, she taught herself the craft from several library books, notably *Techniques of Fiction Writing* by Leon Surmelian.

FIRST DATE AT #1: February 16, 1986
TOTAL WEEKS AT #1: 2

Lie Down with Lions
Ken Follett
MORROW

Follett's third and last #1 bestseller deals with the conflict between love and loyalty. An Englishwoman is in wartorn Afghanistan caught between the American CIA and the Russian KGB.

Making the List

by James Atlas

Atlantic Monthly

In August, William Peter Blatty, a screen writer and author of *The Exorcist,* filed a $6 million suit against the *New York Times,* charging that the paper had damaged sales of *Legion,* his latest novel, by failing to include it on the bestseller list despite clear evidence that it was selling enough copies to qualify. "It doesn't matter if you're on any other national list," Blatty told a reporter from the *Washington Post.* "The only one that influences the bookstores is the *New York Times.* If you're not on that one, you need a microscope and Sherlock Holmes to find your book." His novel, which showed up on other lists, eventually appeared on the *Times*'s list, in the last spot, for a week in September; but that was too late to satisfy Blatty, who claimed intentional negligence on the newspaper's part. "I want to know how they compile that list," he said. "What is so scientific about the way they put their numbers together?"

Since Blatty's suit, the *Times* has been wary of discussing its exact procedure but, according to Adam Clymer, who supervises the *Times*'s list, it's as close to a science as it can get. Like *Publishers Weekly* and *Time,* which publish their own bestseller lists, the *Times* has devised an elaborate system of keeping score that reflects sales across the country. The bestseller list is based on a sample; obviously, not every bookstore in the country can be polled. The system's intent is to estimate sales figures throughout the country based on data from the stores polled. Every week, a battery of *Times* staffers canvasses some 500 independent bookstores—"a lot of people make a lot of phone calls," says Clymer—and collates the results with sales reported by about 1,400 stores that are affiliates of local chains and by the two major national chains, Walden and B. Dalton. The figures reported by independent stores and local chains represent only a sample of sales by such stores, whereas the figures from the national chains reflect their total volume of business. To make sure that the bestseller list is not too heavily biased in favor of the national chains, the *Times* uses a weighting system that assigns a predetermined value to each outlet, based on its size and volume of business. Clymer explains, by way of analogy: "In a public-opinion poll you tend to reach fewer blacks, and fewer still black men. It's easy to reach well-educated whites. So the numbers you get are multiplied by slightly less or more than one for balance. We do something comparable with independent bookstores...."

PW [*Publishers Weekly*] determines its list [by] polling close to 2,000 outlets every week, 1,500 of which are members of local chains. "I don't want a book selling at Dalton to be worth more than a book selling in some local store," said Daisy Mayles, the senior editor in charge of *PW*'s bestseller list....

The *Times* and... *PW* generally have in common four out of the top five titles (though often in different order) on the hardcover fiction and nonfiction lists....

To the author of a book that's selling well but hasn't shown up on the list, this general correlation isn't much comfort. You're either on the list or off the list. Appearance on the *Times* or *PW*'s list can influence the sale of movie rights and the floor price of paperback editions, and its known in the trade that books move out of the stores just because they're on the list. ...

How many copies does a book have to sell to get on a list? The estimate that I heard most often was 40,000 to 50,000.... But these numbers are highly speculative, and the reality depends on the season and other variables. Thomas Stewart [editor in chief of Atheneum] recalls a novel—Robertson Davies's *Fifth Business*—that was on, briefly, when fewer than 15,000 copies had been shipped. Nearly everyone I talked to cited books that felt should have been on but weren't. "We must have sold 175,000 copies of the *Foxfire Book*," Loretta Barrett [executive director at Doubleday] says, "but they sold in health food stores and local bookshops that weren't counted...."

No matter how scrupulous the editors of the bestseller lists are, no matter how elaborate their procedures, they still have to depend on the figures they get from bookstores, and that's where the system is weakest. Regional lists are especially vulnerable to the method that Elissa Rabellino, an editor of the *Los Angeles Times*'s list, describes as "looking at the piles and counting the ones that have gone down the most." One editor who used to work in a bookstore... remembers employees calling out the titles of books they liked." But even publications that solicit the number of copies sold have no way of knowing whether the figures reported are accurate. There can be any number of titles selling enough to be good prospects for the bottom of the list, and an exact ranking is often hard to come by.... No matter how conscientious booksellers are, the temptations to estimate rather than count and to submit the number of books

continued on page 200

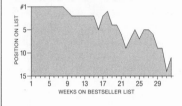

FIRST DATE AT #1: March 9, 1986
TOTAL WEEKS AT #1: 8

The Bourne Supremacy

Robert Ludlum

RANDOM HOUSE

The second book in the Bourne trilogy did half as well as the first, at least as far as time at #1 is concerned. In Ludlum's sixth #1 novel, our hero foils a plot to seize Hong Kong and bring China into conflict with the West.

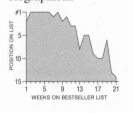

FIRST DATE AT #1: May 4, 1986
TOTAL WEEKS AT #1: 6

A Perfect Spy

John le Carré

KNOPF

The fifth of le Carré's seven #1 bestsellers also had his fifth longest stay at #1. It is a lighthearted story of a British secret agent and his flamboyant con man father, thought to be vaguely autobiographical.

FIRST DATE AT #1: June 8, 1986
TOTAL WEEKS AT #1: 1

I'll Take Manhattan

Judith Krantz

CROWN

Krantz's fourth and last #1 book, published eight years after her first, entered the list at #2, but reached #1 for just one week. It is a novel about the affairs and adventures of a rich and beautiful woman as she conquers the world of magazine publishing in New York.

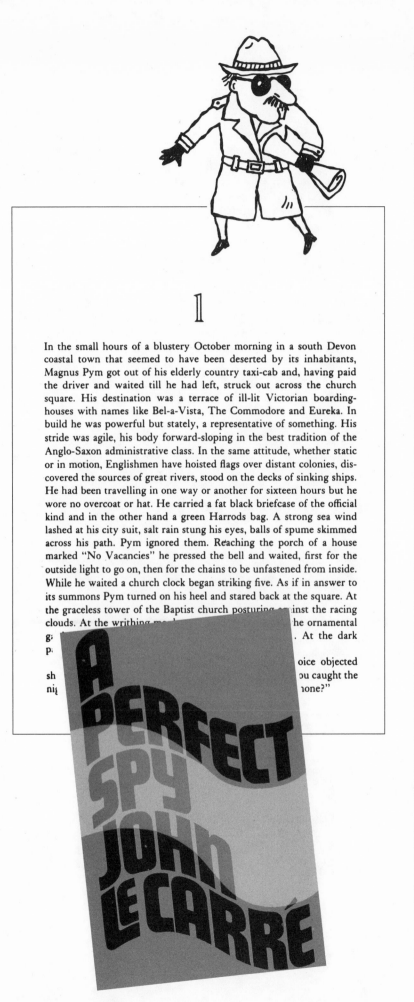

1

In the small hours of a blustery October morning in a south Devon coastal town that seemed to have been deserted by its inhabitants, Magnus Pym got out of his elderly country taxi-cab and, having paid the driver and waited till he had left, struck out across the church square. His destination was a terrace of ill-lit Victorian boarding-houses with names like Bel-a-Vista, The Commodore and Eureka. In build he was powerful but stately, a representative of something. His stride was agile, his body forward-sloping in the best tradition of the Anglo-Saxon administrative class. In the same attitude, whether static or in motion, Englishmen have hoisted flags over distant colonies, discovered the sources of great rivers, stood on the decks of sinking ships. He had been travelling in one way or another for sixteen hours but he wore no overcoat or hat. He carried a fat black briefcase of the official kind and in the other hand a green Harrods bag. A strong sea wind lashed at his city suit, salt rain stung his eyes, balls of spume skimmed across his path. Pym ignored them. Reaching the porch of a house marked "No Vacancies" he pressed the bell and waited, first for the outside light to go on, then for the chains to be unfastened from inside. While he waited a church clock began striking five. As if in answer to its summons Pym turned on his heel and stared back at the square. At the graceless tower of the Baptist church posturing ___inst the racing clouds. At the writing ___ ___ ___ he ornamental g___ ___. At the dark p___

sh___ ___oice objected ___ou caught the ni___ ___one?"

199

FIRST DATE AT #1: November 30, 1986

TOTAL WEEKS AT #1: 3

A Day in the Life of America

Collins

On May 2, 1986, 200 photographers took the pictures of America that are reproduced without comment in this book, the only #1 bestseller other than the Bible with no author given. The only coffee-table book to become a #1 bestseller (unless we include *Gnomes*), it rose quickly to #1, remained there for three weeks before Christmas, and disappeared almost immediately thereafter, the fastest ascent and decline of any of the #1 books.

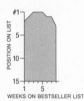

FIRST DATE AT #1: February 1, 1987

TOTAL WEEKS AT #1: 14

A Season on the Brink

John Fennstein

MACMILLAN

Sportswriter Fennstein spent an entire season with Indiana University basketball coach Bobby Knight and his nationally ranked team. This journal chronicles that season, and is the only non-baseball sports book ever to make #1.

continued from page 198

ordered rather than the number sold must be hard to resist. . . .

One objection to bestseller lists persistently raised . . . by religious publishers is that evangelical books are routinely excluded. . . . Dr. Francis Schaeffer's *A Christian Manifesto,* "A serious book about civil disobedience and the history of our country," had outsold *Jane Fonda's Workout Book* by a margin of two to one, [Cal] Thomas asserted, "but Jane was No. 1 on the *New York Times*'s bestseller list and Dr. Schaeffer was relegated to ignominious oblivion."

"I don't know anything about that book," Clymer testily retorts, but he notes that Robert H. Schuller's *Tough Times Never Last, But Tough People Do!* published by Thomas Nelson, one of the major religious houses, had been listed as fifth on the hardcover nonfiction list early in September. (Within a week, it had vanished from the list, never to be seen again.)

. . . What bestseller lists have to do with literature is another story. Glancing over one *Times* list recently, I noted in the hardcover nonfiction category two "literary" titles—William Least Heat Moon's *Blue Highways* and Russell Baker's *Growing Up*—and two that qualify as "serious": *In Search of Excellence* . . . and William Manchester's *The Last Lion.* But how-to books preponderated: *Creating Wealth, The F-Plan Diet, How to Live to Be 100—Or More, How to Satisfy a Woman Every Time.*

The fiction list had the usual James Michener and Stephen King, and four titles that even a snobbish literary critic would consider respectable: Judith Rossner's *August,* Umberto Eco's *The Name of the Rose,* John le Carré's *The Little Drummer Girl,* and Nora Ephron's *Heartburn.* Titles I could do without included *Return of the Jedi* and a book called *Who Killed the Robins Family?* said to have been "created" by Bill Adler and written by Thomas Chastain (I wonder how a "created" book differs from one merely written). . . .

Whatever its imperfections, the bestseller list is seen in the trade as a valuable institution, good for business because it sells books. "The audience demands it and the book industry demands it," Art Seidenbaum, editor of the *Los Angeles Times* book supplement says. "Who are we to complain about what's popular as long as we can say what's good." ■

CHAPTER I

Major Joe Makatozi stepped into the sunlight of a late afternoon. The first thing he must remember was the length of the days at this latitude. His eyes moved left and right.

About three hundred yards long, a hundred yards wide, three guard towers to a side, two men in each. A mounted machine gun in each tower. Each man armed with a submachine gun.

He walked behind Lieutenant Suvarov, and two armed guards followed him.

Five barracklike frame buildings, another under construction, prisoners in four of the five buildings but not all the cells occupied.

He had no illusions. He was a prisoner, and when they had extracted the information they knew he possessed, he would be killed. There was a cool freshness in the air like that from the sea, but he was far from any ocean. His first impression was, he believed, the right one. He was somewhere in the vicinity of Lake Baikal, in Siberia.

A white line six feet inside the barbed wire, the limit of approach for prisoners. The fence itself was ten feet high, ~~twenty~~ ...rawn, *electrified wire. From the* ...e forest, perhaps fifty yards.

...e but his captors. There would be ...feelers. Whatever happened now ...had one asset. They had no idea ...l taken prisoner.

...e was shown was much like a

5

FIRST DATE AT #1: June 22, 1986
TOTAL WEEKS AT #1: 4

Last of the Breed
Louis L'Amour
BANTAM

L'Amour didn't make #1 until the very end of his career. Then he made it twice in a year, but only once with a western. He scored for the first time with this adventure thriller, his 86th published book, about a United States Air Force major in Siberia. (L'Amour was 42 when his first was published.)

FIRST DATE AT #1: July 20, 1986
TOTAL WEEKS AT #1: 4

Wanderlust
Danielle Steel
DELACORTE

Steel returns to #1 for the third of her 10 appearances with this tale of a rich orphan who comes of age as she travels the world.

FIRST DATE AT #1: August 17, 1986
TOTAL WEEKS AT #1: 6

Red Storm Rising
Tom Clancy
PUTNAM

Had Clancy's first book, *The Hunt for Red October*, made #1, it would have set a record for the smallest publisher with a #1 book. It climbed as high as #2. Then the author switched from the tiny Naval Institute Press and Putnam published this book about how the Soviets start World War Three without resorting to the use of nuclear weapons and the West struggles to stop them.

FIRST DATE AT #1: May 10, 1987
TOTAL WEEKS AT #1: 3

Communion
Whitley Strieber
MORROW

Professional writer Strieber (*The Wolfen*) believes he was visited and carried off by "intelligent non-humans" (aliens from outer space), who regularly visit our planet. The *Times* believed him at least to the extent of listing his book in the nonfiction section. Strieber told *Contemporary Authors* that he works "like a maniac. I work from nine in the morning until six o'clock at night, with half an hour for lunch. And I work six or seven days a week. I've worked as long as six months without taking a day off."

FIRST DATE AT #1: May 17, 1987
TOTAL WEEKS AT #1: 5

Love, Medicine and Miracles
Bernie S. Siegel
HARPER

Siegel is a surgeon who believes that patients with a happy and upbeat frame of mind are much more likely to survive and recover from serious illnesses. In this book he makes a case for the importance of the patient's state of mind and emotions. In a unique pattern, this book rose quickly to #1 for only a week, bounced up and down for eight months, dropped from the list for a few weeks, then roared back into the top five and spent four more weeks at #1 before it disappeared entirely.

There were three small people standing beside the bed, their outlines clearly visible in the glow of the burglar-alarm panel. They were wearing blue coveralls and standing absolutely still.

They were familiar figures, not the fierce, huge-eyed feminine being I have described before, but rather the more dwarflike ones, stocky and solidly built, with gray, humanoid faces and glittering, deep-set eyes. They were the ones I felt were "the good army" when they took me on December 26.

I thought to myself, *My God, I'm completely conscious and they're just standing there.* I thought that I could turn on the light, perhaps even get out of bed. Then I tried to move my hand, thinking to flip the switch on my bedside lamp and see the time.

I can only describe the sensation I felt when I tried to move as like pushing my arm through electrified tar. It took every ounce of attention I possessed to get any movement at all. I marshaled my will and brought my attention into the sharpest possible focus. Simply moving my arm did not work. I had to order the movement, to labor at it. All the while they stood there.

I struggled, bit by bit clawing closer and closer to that lamp. I turned my head, fighting a pressure that felt as if a sheath of lead had been draped over me, and saw the light switch in the dark. I watched my hand move slowly closer, and finally felt the switch under my finger. I clicked it. Nothing. Tried again. Still nothing.

The electricity was off. The burglar alarm was still working because it had battery backup—but app███ them, as they had entered the house w███

When I turned my head back I conf███ I thought afterward that I did not kno███ I still don't, so I am just going to plu███

Beside my bed and perhaps two███ enough to see it plainly without my███ the thin ones, the type I have calle███ right, though. Its eyes were like b███

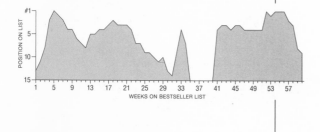

Seven Records that Stephen King Can Still Set

It is too late for him to be the youngest author with a #1 bestseller (Françoise Sagan did that at 19), and barring a Leland Gaunt-like shape-changing episode, he is unlikely to ever be the tallest (probably John K. Galbraith at 6′8″). These seven opportunities are still available, however:

1. **First person ever with a #1 fiction and a #1 nonfiction book at the same time.** Dr. Seuss missed it by four years, and that is the closest anyone has come.

2. **First person with a #1 and a #2 fiction book at the same time.** Fulghum has done it on the nonfiction side, and King missed by only one week few years ago.

3. **Shortest title.** He once held the record with *Cujo,* then improved on it with *It,* but now he's tied with Katherine Hepburn's *Me.* There have been one-letter titles on the list (Thomas Pynchon's *V* and John Updike's *S,* for instance, but none has ever reached #1.

4. **Most total weeks at #1.** He still has over 100 weeks to go to catch James Michener, but that is well within reach.

5. **Longest total weeks for a single title.** Norman Vincent Peale's 98 weeks for *The Power of Positive Thinking* seems like an untouchable record—but so did Bob Beamon's 29-foot long jump, Babe Ruth's 60 homers in a season, and Joe DiMaggio's 56-game hitting streak. Two of the three are now history, and someday, maybe even Peale.

6. **Longest title.** Easy enough to create one. But would a title with 58 or more letters (that would be the record) be memorable enough to sell enough?

7. **Oldest author.** George Burns was nearly 93 when his *Gracie* reached #1. If King can keep going for 48 more years, he has a shot at it.

FIRST DATE AT #1: September 14, 1986
TOTAL WEEKS AT #1: 14

It
Stephen King
VIKING

King's eighth (or ninth counting the Bachman book) #1 book remained at #1 the longest of any of them. *It* made its debut at #1 and remained there for 14 of the next 18 weeks, before beginning a fairly steep decline. *It* was the first two-letter title to make #1, and only the second ever, along with Katherine Hepburn's *Me.*

FIRST DATE AT #1: November 23, 1986
TOTAL WEEKS AT #1: 4

Whirlwind
James Clavell
MORROW

Five years after *Noble House,* Clavell returns to #1 with a story of life and adventures in Iran during the turbulent months following the Shah's departure.

FIRST DATE AT #1: June 7, 1987

TOTAL WEEKS AT #1: 10

The Closing of the American Mind

Allan Bloom

SIMON & SCHUSTER

If Las Vegas took bets on the odds on which books would reach #1 on the *New York Times* list, the early odds on Professor Bloom's book would have been astronomical. Nonetheless, this scholarly critique of liberal arts education over the past 25 years struck a respondent chord in the height of the Reagan era, and spent nearly five months as the #1 or #2 bestseller. Bloom, Professor of Philosophy and Political Science at the University of Chicago, had written an article on this subject for *The National Review* and was encouraged by his friend Saul Bellow to expand it into book length.

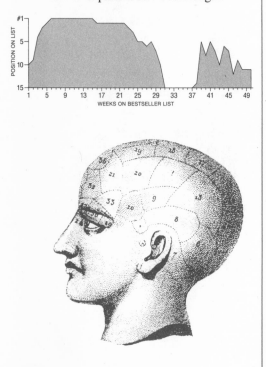

Mixed Bookseller Reaction to Revised NYT Bestseller List

Publishers Weekly, March 2, 1984

For booksellers who plan on displays, promotions or discounts based on the *New York Times* bestseller listings, the first appearance of the revised format on January 1 [1984] marked a day for strategy change. Or did it? How significant was *NYT's* addition of two new lists—Advice, How-to and Miscellaneous, in both paperback and hardcover categories? What is the retail impact, now that mass market and trade paperbacks compete for bestseller ranking?

PW asked a sampling of booksellers around the country for their views on the subject and found responses that ranged from "It's a smart move" to "foolish clutter which is decreasing importance of the list as a whole." Of the 33 stores surveyed, seven believed the revision an improvement over the old system—but 10 booksellers thought it a change for the worse; among this group, opinions tended to be more vehement. But not all respondents in the survey took a strong stance: slightly less than half either expressed indifference to the change, or noted that they could see both benefits and drawbacks.

The adjective which occurred most frequently in the booksellers' comments was "confusing," but it appears that it is primarily a retailer and not a consumer problem. More than 50% of the stores surveyed regularly post the *New York Times* list. "There hasn't been any vast outcry," said one buyer, adding "but customers seem to find it an unnecessary move."

[Some felt that] the removal of self-help books from the nonfiction list would free up places for what they consider "general nonfiction." Says Harriet Mosher of MacBeans Bookshop in Brunswick, Me., "It's nice to see serious nonfiction on the list where humor and how-to books had dominated."

...*PW* also asked the booksellers whether the changes in the list had any effect on bestseller display or other in-store promotions. Several note that they have simply expanded their existing displays to accommodate the added titles...On the other hand, [Lynn] Clark at the Bookworm in Jackson [says] "The logical answer is to build a new display, but I don't want to do that just for the *New York Times*." ∎

Pen Name Answers

Françoise Quoirez = Françoise Sagan
(*Bonjour Tristesse*)

Edward Everett Tanner = Patrick Dennis
(*Auntie Mame*)

John Donaldson Voelker = Robert Traver
(*Anatomy of a Murder*)

David Cornwell = John le Carré
(*The Spy Who Came in from the Cold,* etc.)

George G. Goodman = Adam Smith
(*The Money Game*)

Joan Terry Garrity = J
(*The Sensuous Woman*)

Theodore S. Geisel = Dr. Seuss
(*You're Only Old Once,* etc.)

James Alfred Wight = James Heriot
(*All Things Bright and Beautiful,* etc.)

FIRST DATE AT #1: February 1, 1987
TOTAL WEEKS AT #1: 1

The Eyes of the Dragon
Stephen King

VIKING

This book written by King for his daughter may be the only children's book to make #1, although proponents of Dr. Seuss and *Watership Down* could disagree. It is the only fiction book that came to the list as #1 but remained there only for one week, the poorest showing of all of King's 16 #1s (but then *Carrie, Christine, The Shining*, and a few others didn't make #1 at all). With this and *It*, King missed having simultaneous #1 and #2 books by only one week, the closest any fiction author has come to that achievement.

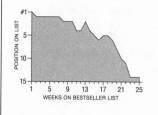

FIRST DATE AT #1: February 8, 1987
TOTAL WEEKS AT #1: 7

Windmills of the Gods
Sidney Sheldon

MORROW

The fifth of Sheldon's seven #1 best-sellers, was the first to enter the list at #1. The plot revolves around the nightmarish experiences which befall a woman and her family after she is appointed as Ambassador to Rumania.

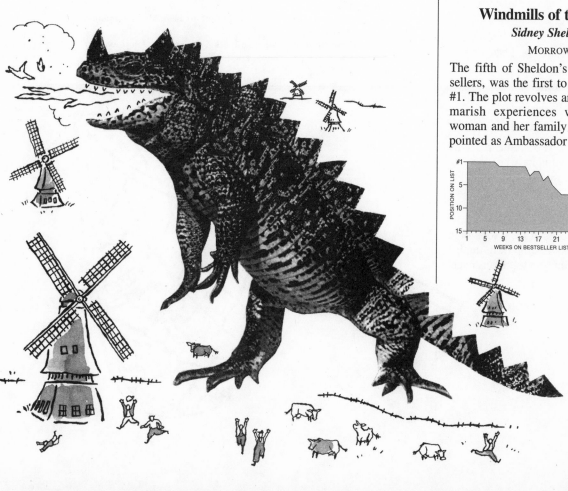

205

FIRST DATE AT #1: August 16, 1987
TOTAL WEEKS AT #1: 9

Spycatcher
Peter Wright

VIKING

This book got the kind of free publicity a publisher can only dream of, when it was banned before publication in Great Britain because the government feared that the memoirs of this former senior member of the British secret service would jeopardize the integrity of Britain's spy network. Even reviews were prohibited. Injunctions were also obtained in Australia and New Zealand. Immediately published in dozens of other countries, the book became a big hit. After four years of legal maneuvering, the courts in England finally ruled in favor of the author and publisher, and the book could at last be published there. In April, 1992, Prime Minister Major confessed that Britain really did have a secret service.

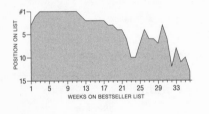

FIRST DATE AT #1: October 18, 1987
TOTAL WEEKS AT #1: 4

Veil
Bob Woodward

SIMON & SCHUSTER

Woodward's sixth #1 bestseller received a great deal of publicity when the late William Casey's family denied that the CIA chief had made some deathbed confessions or revelations to Woodward. Interest in the book was intense at first, but after four weeks at #1, it took only another six weeks to drop from the list entirely, one of the shortest spans ever.

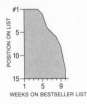

We swept through the archway at the front of the magnificent, triumphalist FBI mausoleum. We were met by Al Belmont, the head of FBI domestic intelligence, and his deputy, Bill Sullivan, who handled the Communist desk. (Sullivan was found dead in the mid-1970s while shooting duck in New England. He is thought to have been murdered.) Belmont was a tough, old-fashioned "G-Man," as FBI men were once known, who had been with the Bureau from its earliest times. Sullivan was the brains to Belmont's brawn (but Belmont was no fool); both believed in the virtues of the stiletto rather than the Magnum. Belmont had many enemies, but I always got along with him. Like me, he had suffered a difficult childhood. His father was shot in a street brawl, and his mother worked day and night to save enough to put him through law school. Hard work and unswerving loyalty to "the old man" brought him to the top of the FBI.

But for all the outward toughness, and the seniority of their positions, both men were cowed by Hoover. Such unswerving loyalty was, I felt, positively unnatural. Of course, they admired Hoover for his achievements in the early years, when he turned a corrupt and incompetent organization into an efficient and feared crime-fighting force. But everyone knew Hoover suffered from God disease, and it seemed odd to me that they never acknowledged the fact, even privately.

I discussed the Tisler affair and the technical implications of RAFTER with both men for most of the day, until it was time to meet Hoover. We trooped down a maze of corridors, past an endless procession of Identikit young FBI officers, well scrubbed, very fit, well suited, closely cropped, and vacant-looking. The FBI offices always reminded me of sanitary clinics. Antiseptic white tiles shone everywhere. Workmen were always busy, constantly repainting, cleaning, and polishing. The obsession with hygiene reeked of an unclean mind.

Hoover's room was the last of four interconnecting offices. Belmont knocked, and entered the room. Hoover stood behind his desk, dressed in a piercing blue suit. He was taller and slimmer than he appeared in photographs, with wrinkled flesh which hung off his face in small drapes. He greeted me with a firm and joyless handshake.

Belmont began to describe the reason for my visit, but Hoover cut him off sharply.

"I've read the report, Al. I want to hear Mr. Wright tell me about it."

Hoover fixed me with coal-black eyes, and I began to outline the discovery of RAFTER. Almost at once, he interrupted me.

LOUIS L'AMOUR

THE HAUNTED MESA

THE HAUNTED MESA

"I'm an old man, boy. I seen the sun set over that red rock country many's the time. I seen men go into that country who never came back. I've knowed others who come back stark ravin' mad, memory gone an' their wits along with it.

"There's another world over there somewheres. At least there's a way to get to it. Like them Spanish men in their iron suits. They *seen* the Seven Cities of Cibola. They *really* seen 'em! They weren't lookin' at any pueblos with the sun on 'em. They just happened to see through the veil. Somehow it was open then and they seen right through and never got over what they seen!

"They are there, boy! I seen 'em, too! But there's evil over there, evil like you an' me can't even imagine. It was that ancient evil that drove the cliff dwellers into this world, comin' through, as they said it, a hole in the ground.

"In their kivas, their ceremonial centers, there's what they call a *sipapu*. It's a hole in the floor that symbolizes how they escaped from the evil. But that evil is still over there, son, an' don't you forget it!"

That had been a long time ago, and Mike Raglan had told the story to no one, not even to Erik Hokart. Yet he had warned Erik about the country. He had advised him to forget it, to choose any other place, but Hokart would not listen.

Later, on that same early trip, he had mentioned the mesa to Jack. "No Man's Mesa," the old miner said. "We camp near there tomorrow night, if we're lucky." He shook his head. "There's not much in the way of roads—some trails and wagon routes the Navajos use. I been through the a-horseback but never with a car. You may have to go ahead an' scout a route, roll rocks out of the way first. It's mighty rough country."

"Know anything about that mesa?"

Jack was a long time in replying. Finally he shrugged. "Just a big chunk of rock, talus slopes, sheer rock around the rim. Kind of out-of-the-way and nobody pays it much mind."

Indicating one of Jack's Paiute friends, Mike suggested: "Ask him if he knows anything about it."

11

FIRST DATE AT #1: March 29, 1987
TOTAL WEEKS AT #1: 9

Fine Things
Danielle Steel
DELACORTE

Steel's fourth #1 book reached the top only 10 weeks after number three left the list. *Fine Things* is a sort of coming-of-age novel which follows the changes in the life of a child of the 1960s as he grows, changes, and finally comes to terms with life in the 1980s.

FIRST DATE AT #1: May 31, 1987
TOTAL WEEKS AT #1: 1

The Haunted Mesa
Louis L'Amour
BANTAM

One of the prolific western author's last works, his 89th book addressed the real-life mystery of the Indian cave dwellers who disappeared many centuries ago. When L'Amour died in 1988 he left behind detailed outlines for more than 50 novels. He felt that "a writer should go ahead and write his books and say what he has to say; if he paid attention to the critics, he'd soon be writing for them instead of for the audience."

FIRST DATE AT #1: November 15, 1987
TOTAL WEEKS AT #1: 2

The Great Depression of 1990
Ravi Batra
SIMON & SCHUSTER

The subtitle is: *Why it's got to happen—How to protect yourself.* Dr. Raveendra Batra has subsequently explained that he meant the depression would *begin* in 1990, but would not necessarily be called that until later. The Oklahoma economist's book of dire predictions rose and fell like the out-of-control stock market it warned about, but it did make #1 for two weeks. Milton Friedman stated that economic safeguards make a depression impossible. Batra responded: "All I can say is, look at the forecasting record. He has elegant and eloquent theories, but what's the use of such eloquence if your forecasts are consistently wrong."

FIRST DATE AT #1: December 6, 1987
TOTAL WEEKS AT #1: 6

Time Flies
Bill Cosby
DOUBLEDAY

On the occasion of his 50th birthday, the television star muses about life, counting his blessings and his losses. His first #1, *Fatherhood,* remained at the top more than four times as long. Around this time, Mikhail Gorbachev's book, *Perestroika* reached the lower levels of the *Times* list.

TIME FLIES

Lead Us Not into McDonald's

Unsure of what to put into my mouth besides a cigar, I now go wandering through the culinary minefields of America, trying to avoid the steps that might be lethal. You will pardon the mixed metaphor—at fifty, I cannot keep both my appointments and my metaphors straight—but these minefields are constantly calling to me:

Come, clog your arteries at Wendy's!
Come, set up your bypass at Burger King!
Come, get your Kentucky Fried triglycerides!
Come, meet your maker at Bar-B-Q!

The temptations are international, for the Chinese are also trying to turn off my circulation. Oh, for the days when MSG meant only Madison Square Garden! At times, of course, I cannot resist the call of the Chinese restaurant; but at such times, I have to turn away ... everything succulent and say to the wa... menu from the Long
M...

BILL COSBY
TIME FLIES
INTRODUCTION BY ALVIN F. POUSSAINT, M.D.

FIRST DATE AT #1: June 7, 1987
TOTAL WEEKS AT #1: 7

Misery

Stephen King

VIKING

For the 5th straight time, King entered the list at #1, this time with a writer's nightmare about an author, injured in a car accident, who is held captive and forced to write romance novels by a psychotic fan. King told an interviewer that he begins with certain ideas and a sense of direction, but no plot outline. "I'm never sure where the story's going or what's going to happen with it. It's a discovery." Typically, he does his research *after* his writing. "I develop the soul of a true debater . . . and find out the things that support my side." "I just want to scare people," King told another interviewer. "I'm very humble about that. . . . Naturally I'll try to terrify you first, and if that doesn't work, I'll try to horrify you, and if I can't make it there, I'll try to gross you out. I'm not proud. . . . So if somebody wakes up screaming because of what I wrote, I'm delighted. If he merely tosses his cookies, it's still a victory, but on a lesser scale. I suppose the ultimate triumph would be to have somebody drop dead of a heart attack. . . . I'd say, 'Gee that's a shame,' but part of me would be thinking, Jesus, that really *worked*."

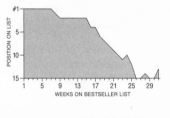

FIRST DATE AT #1: July 26, 1987
TOTAL WEEKS AT #1: 8

Presumed Innocent

Scott Turow

FARRAR, STRAUS

Attorney Turow had the first of his two #1s with a procedural police thriller and murder mystery set in a complex and corrupt world of big-city lawyers and politicians.

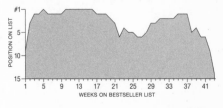

In the 32nd District the normal turmoil of a police station is concealed. About seven years ago now, while we were in the midst of our investigation, one of the Night Saints entered the station with a sawed-off in his windbreaker. It was nuzzled against his chest like a baby protected from a chilly breeze, and as a result, he merely had to lower the zipper slightly before placing the muzzle beneath the chin of the unfortunate desk officer, a twenty-eight-year-old guy named Jack Lansing, who had continued writing some report. The young man with the shotgun, who was never identified, is reported to have smiled and then blown off Jack Lansing's face.

Since then, the cops of this station house have dealt with the public from behind six inches of bulletproof glass, carrying on conversations through a radio system which sounds as if the signal must have been bounced first off the moon. There are public areas where the complainants, the victims, the police groupies loiter, but once you pass beyond the four-inch-thick metal door, with its electronic bolt, there is almost sterility. Prisoners are in a block downstairs, and are never permitted, for any purpose, above that level. Upstairs, so much of the usual turbulence has been removed that it feels a little like an insurance agency. The working cops' desks are in an open area that could pass for any other large office, the guys with

NONFICTION

FIRST DATE AT #1: January 17, 1988
TOTAL WEEKS AT #1: 13

Trump: The Art of the Deal
Donald Trump with Tony Schwartz
RANDOM HOUSE

Trump's first book rose to #1 in its fifth week, and remained there for a quarter of 1988, with another half the year in the top five. The New York entrepreneur discusses his career and the business style that got him there. The *Times* reviewer called it "An entertaining exercise in self-congratulations." Trump told *Newsweek* magazine, "There is no one my age who has accomplished more."

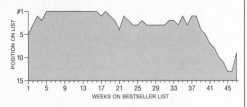

FIRST DATE AT #1: May 15, 1988
TOTAL WEEKS AT #1: 2

Moonwalk
Michael Jackson
DOUBLEDAY

Dr. Jackson (he was awarded an honorary doctorate by Fisk University) is one of the few Grammy winners also to write a #1 *New York Times* bestseller (Dr. William Cosby is another). Jackson's autobiography reached #1 in its second week on the list, but by the 12th week it was gone entirely, one of the fastest descents of any book.

You Want a Bestseller? Start with the Independents and Work Up
From The Tome Machine by David Blum
New York Magazine, October 24, 1988

"The only logical explanation for [*The Closing of the American Mind*] showing up on the [*New York Times*] list as early as it did," says one nonfiction editor, "is that it did incredibly well at a few bookstores that the *New York Times* weighs heavily in its survey."

Are we to believe that to get on the *Times* list, you need only buy a pile of books at a handful of East Coast outlets? Does this mean that you can go out on the day of a rave review, buy 200 copies, and sit back—confident that you will appear on the list? Was the conventional wisdom—that you need to sell 50,000 books to have a bestseller—something a clever publisher could get around?

"We have ways," Adam Clymer says rather slyly, "of making quite sure that won't happen."

Clymer, as assistant to the executive editor, is the guardian of the *New York Times* bestseller list. Before that, he was the paper's chief political correspondent.... The system used by the *Times* is top secret, but this much Clymer could explain.

First of all, the *Times* collects sales figures from the same 2,000 bookstores every week, including the major chains as well as "many" independent bookstores—most of which now keep computerized records. Then the *Times* takes the raw numbers and "weights" the independent bookstores more heavily, ostensibly to balance the sheer volume of the chains' sales. It all sounds vaguely similar to the reapportionment of congressional seats after each census. The weighting, too, is kept confidential. Which stores are weighted most is also a secret.

I checked with some publishing sources who think they have a pretty good idea which independent bookstores the *Times* weights most heavily—and where to start if you're trying to outfox Adam Clymer. In New York, it's the mighty Shakespeare & Company—with its two-story home on the West Side and a new East Village outlet—and Endicott Booksellers, a small but equally prestigious Columbus Avenue store. In Boston, go to the Harvard Cooperative bookstore. In Washington, Kramerbooks. The Tattered Cover in Denver is closely watched, as is Cody's in Berkeley, Powell's in Portland, and Oxford Books in Atlanta.

This is probably as good a place as any to mention William Peter Blatty. He's the author of *The Exorcist*. He also wrote another book you probably don't remember called *Legion*. It wasn't on the *New York Times* bestseller list at first, but Blatty thought it should have been. His $3 million suit against the *Times* was dismissed. The only important point raised by Blatty is that it's possible to sell lots of books at B. Dalton and still not make it onto the all-important *Times* list—because of the weighting of independent stores.

You want a bestseller? Start with the independents and work up. ∎

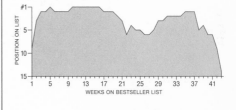

She s... ...g so poorly. She felt ... and all she wanted to do was put ...head down and sleep all day long. It was depressing to feel that lousy. But two days later she knew why. The test results came back, and the doctor did not suggest antibiotics. She was pregnant. He had done a routine pregnancy test, and a VDRL too, checking her for syphilis. When she heard the news she felt she would rather have had the latter than the former. She put the phone down in shock, staring around her office. She knew exactly whose it was. He was the only man she had slept with in two years, and she hadn't used any precautions and neither had he. It had never occurred to her, she didn't have any to use. He was only the second man she'd ever slept with in her adult life, since the tragedies of her youth. And now she was pregnant.

There was only one solution to the problem. And she called the doctor back within the hour and made the appointment. She left her office at lunchtime in a state of shock, and went home to think about the predicament she was in. Should she tell him? Should she not? Would he laugh? Would he figure it was exclusively her problem? And what about the abortion? Was it wrong? Was it a sin? A part of her wanted to be rid of it instantly, and another part of her remembered Axie as a baby, and little Megan again . . . that sweet smell of powder and the silky hair nestled in her arms at night. She remembered the little noises she made before she went to sleep at night, and suddenly Hilary thought she couldn't do it. She had already lost two children she loved, how could she kill this one? Perhaps this was God's way of making it up to her, of making it all right again, of giving her back one of the babies she had lost, of filling the empty years ahead of her with more than just work . . . and the baby would be so beautiful with a father like Bill Brock, and he need never

FIRST DATE AT #1: August 2, 1987
TOTAL WEEKS AT #1: 5

Patriot Games
Tom Clancy
PUTNAM

A year after his first time at #1, Clancy returns with his hero, Dr. Jack Ryan of the CIA, to battle international terrorists in England, Ireland, and America. When *Contemporary Authors* asked the former insurance agent about the massive amount of research that seems to go into his books, he said, "The most time I have spent researching any of my books was three weeks and that was for *Patriot Games*. I do go after the information before I start writing. I know where it is. When I get to a part where I need to look something up, I can simply pick up the book and look it up."

FIRST DATE AT #1: October 25, 1987
TOTAL WEEKS AT #1: 5

Kaleidoscope
Danielle Steel
DELACORTE

Steel's second #1 of the year and her fifth overall, *Kaleidoscope* follows three sisters separated by fate and the lawyer whose mission it is to find and reunite them. Steel told *Contemporary Authors* that she does some writing every day when working on a first draft and a second draft, but works less steadily on book outlines to make time for her family life. She does all her typing herself, using a 1948 metal-body manual typewriter.

FIRST DATE AT #1: May 29, 1988
TOTAL WEEKS AT #1: 4

For the Record
Donald T. Regan

HARCOURT

As with David Stockman's book, people were eager to see what nasty things the former secretary of the treasury and White House chief of staff might have to say about the Reagans, especially after Nancy allegedly fired him. Even revelations about Reagan's reliance on an astrologer couldn't keep the book afloat for long. To critics who said he should have waited until Reagan was out of office before publishing this book, Regan said "They had dismissed me. Why, then, should I wait." To substantiate his claim that the book was not written to make money, Regan promised all proceeds from its sale would go to charity. No other #1 author has been so generous.

DONALD T. REGAN

facts. He said I had to know them or the entire scheduling process would collapse. Deaver came to see me and explained the mystery. I thought at first that he was joking, but he made it plain that he was not.

Deaver told me that he had been dealing with astrological input for a long time. Mrs. Reagan's dependence on the occult went back at least as far as her husband's governorship, when she had depended on the advice of the famous Jeane Dixon. Subsequently she had lost confidence in Dixon's powers. But the First Lady seemed to have absolute faith in the clairvoyant talents of the woman in San Francisco.

Apparently Deaver had ceased to think that there was anything remarkable about this long-established floating seance; Mike is a born chamberlain, and to him it was simply one of many little problems in the life of a servant of the great.

"Humor her," Deaver advised. "At least this astrologer is not as kooky as the last one."

As I discovered in my turn, there was no choice *but* to humor the First Lady in this matter. But the President's schedule is the single most potent tool in the White House, because it determines what the most powerful man in the world is going to do and when he is going to do it. By humoring Mrs. Reagan we gave her this tool—or, more accurately, gave it to an unknown woman in San Francisco who believed that the zodiac controls events and human behavior and that she could read the secrets of the future in the movements of the planets.

(Apparently she couldn't always do so. On one occasion the First Lady explained that there would be a longer delay than usual in choosing a date for some Presidential appearance or other. "I can't reach my Friend," Mrs. Reagan said. "Her mother died suddenly." I sympathized, but also wondered why this sad event should have come as a surprise to a clairvoyant.)

Mrs. Reagan talked to her Friend mostly on Saturday afternoons, from Camp David. The First Lady once complained to me in budgetary terms about revisions in the schedule.

"I wish you'd make up your mind," she said testily. "It's costing me a lot of money, calling up my Friend with all these changes."

· 74 ·

A Decade of Megasellers

by Daisy Mayles
Publishers Weekly, **January 5, 1990**

The term "megasellers" is an '80s word coined specifically to describe the new breed of hard-cover bestsellers, those with seven-figure unit sales—numbers that in previous decades would be applied only to mass market paper-backs. Of course, there were exceptions. In the '70s, *The Living Bible* and *Jonathan Livingston Seagull* sold over the two-million mark. But the latter was called a "publishing phenomenon," and the Bible, especially a new edition, often sells in huge numbers. In the '80s, 13 novels and 12 non-fiction titles went over the one-million sales mark.

What sets apart the million-copy sales of hardcovers during the '80s is not only the increased numbers of titles that achieved those lofty watersheds, but that these huge sales became the expected norm for a work of fiction by a name writer with an established track record, and also for celebrity biographies and books about popular culture. First print-ings, author advances and promo-tional and advertising budgets scaled new heights—all feeding the frenzied and often unrealistic ex-pectations that these books would sell in mass market-like quantities. As the decade would wind down, publishers began to sound more realistic and prudent, talking about lower first printings and author ad-vances—necessary reactions af-ter some of those titles published as megasellers behaved like mass market paperbacks in another re-spect: returns [books sent back for refund] exceeding 30%.

Checking the list of works that comprise *PW's* top 25 fiction titles, we can quickly spot novelists who led the numbers parade. Ten of the 13-million-copy novelists were by three writers—Stephen King, Danielle Steel, and Tom Clancy. How strong were the sales of these three authors at the dawn of the '80s? King's first bestseller on a hardcover list was *The Dead Zone* which, in 1979, finished in the #6 spot with sales of 175,000 copies for that year. Compare that with his 1987 performance—three books among the top 10 of the year, including *The Tommy-knockers* in first place, with one million-plus sales. Steel's sales also gained considerable pace in the '80s. Her first hardcover success was in 1981 when *Remembrances* sold over 127,000. In 1987, two of her novels placed among the top 15 for the year [and sold over 1 million copies each]....

A more eclectic group com-prises the top 25 nonfiction titles of the '80s, but a few familiar themes run throughout. The country's ob-session with health and fitness; idol-ization of celebrity figures, both in business and entertainment; and general money matters all figure extensively among the top 25 books. One can also see the pub-lishing strength of mass market players in what was predominantly a hardcover game during the '70s; Bantam's five nonfiction titles and the two from Warner Books make up almost 30% of the nonfiction list.

The excessive influence of the broadcast medium and Hollywood can also be noted in the top 25 nonfiction books. *Frugal Gourmet* Jeff Smith's popularity was cer-tainly enhanced by his ongoing PBS television series; Carl Sagan's *Cosmos* was helped by his 13-part PBS series; Lee Iacocca's TV ad spots for Chrysler raised his public visibility; as did Erma Bombeck's humorous spots on *Good Morning America;* and Bill Cosby's books were catapulted onto the national charts by his lead-ing television sitcom....

The list does not include dic-tionaries, but if it had, the #1 spot would have been claimed by Merriam Webster's *Webster's Ninth New Collegiate Dictionary,* with sales of more than 6.4 million since its release in 1983. ∎

FIRST DATE AT #1: November 29, 1987
TOTAL WEEKS AT #1: 8

The Tommyknockers
Stephen King
PUTNAM

King's third #1 of the year came out a few weeks after Steel's latest and knocked her from the #1 spot in its first week. When a young writer finds mys-terious artifacts buried in the woods, she unwittingly triggers strange and ter-rible changes in her isolated Maine town. King says that each time he publishes a book, "I feel like a trapper caught by the Iroquois. They're all lined up with tomahawks, and the idea is to run through with your head down, and ev-erybody gets to take a swing...."

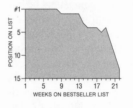

FIRST DATE AT #1: January 24, 1988
TOTAL WEEKS AT #1: 8

The Bonfire of the Vanities
Tom Wolfe
FARRAR, STRAUS

Wolfe had been on the list a number of times before, but never at #1. In this novel, a successful Wall Street bond trader is arrested for hit-and-run driving in the south Bronx, and must face the criminal justice system. Wolfe told the *Times,* "Having said that the novelists weren't doing a good job" he was curi-ous to see what would happen if he became one. After *Bonfire* became a #1 bestseller, Wolfe issued a "literary mani-festo" in *Harpers* urging novelists to "abandon the esoteric literary experi-ments that have characterized fiction for much of the 20th century and use real-ism to chronicle the bizarre and as-tounding world around them."

FIRST DATE AT #1: June 26, 1988
TOTAL WEEKS AT #1: 19

A Brief History of Time
Stephen Hawking
BANTAM

The brilliant British scientist's guide to understanding space, time, and the laws of physics is not only first among all the #1 bestsellers alphabetically, but the most enduring science book ever, with well over two years on the list—more than four months at #1. The subtitle is: *From the big bang to the black holes.* A critic for *New York Magazine* suggested that "Hawking means well, but in the end he has written what amounts to a graduate school textbook, albeit a breezy one." Hawkins replied by citing the large number of intelligent letters he has received, while admitting "I am sure some people bought my book just to have on the . . . coffee table, but I think that is true of all serious books, including the Bible and Shakespeare." At this time, *The Boz,* by a football player of that nickname, rose rapidly to #2, but did not displace Hawking. *The Lives of John Lennon* came onto the list at #2, but only declined from there.

POSITION ON LIST — #1, 5, 10, 15

WEEKS ON BESTSELLER LIST — 1 5 9 13 17 21 25 29 33 37 41 45 49 53 57 61 65 69 73 77 81 85 89 93 97 101 105 109

The Tome Machine
Hawking the Great Unread Books of Our Time
by David Blum
New York Magazine, October 24, 1988

Here are a few laws of theoretical physics that Stephen W. Hawking neglects to mention in his runaway No. 1 bestseller, *A Brief History of Time:*

▶ It takes an infinite amount of time to get from the beginning of the book to the end.

▶ The less you understand the ideas in the book, the more intelligent you will feel while trying to read it.

▶ The book defies *Newton's Philosophiae Naturalis Principia Mathematica,* in that it will not fall from the No. 1 position on the *New York Times* bestseller list.

▶ If you start reading the book after the sun has reached the highest point of its arc, you will be sound asleep within two pages.

At first I was made to feel a little nervous about trying to explain the recent success of intellectual books on the *Times* bestseller list—which, I suspected, had to do with something other than the desire of millions of Americans to contemplate the Heisenberg uncertainty principle.

"You'd better be *very, very* careful," a top book executive told me rather sternly. "Industry people keep lists, too. Make fun of their books and your name goes right on them."

Are they *that* sensitive? Yes, it seems—because readers don't want to be told they bought a book for any but the most noble of motives.

"Look, people buy this kind of book for two reasons," explained a top New York book editor who has handled several nonfiction bestsellers. "One reason is autodidactic. The other is snob appeal. If you want a hit book, you've got to appeal to one thing or the other. And if you want a huge hit book, you need both."

Right away, I knew this was going to be tough, since I didn't even know what "autodidactic" means. (It means "self-taught.")

The other bestsellers are nearly as famous. *The Closing of the American Mind,* a treatise on the nation's intellectual crisis . . . reached the No. 1 spot and stayed on the list for almost a year. . . . And we should not forget last year's *Cultural Literacy* by E. D. Hirsch, Jr. His idea was to make us feel guilty about not reading books so that we would buy his.

I can't say conclusively whether intelligent people are *reading* these books. I can only refer you to an unscientific poll taken in 1985 by Michael Kinsley, the very smart editor of *The New Republic.* A colleague inserted slips of paper three quarters of the way through 70 books in Washington stores, offering $5 to anyone who called to say he'd reached that point. . . . Five months later, he hadn't gotten a single call. Kinsley concluded, "These books don't exist to be read. They exist to be gazed at, browsed through, talked about. They exist, above all, to be reviewed." Meaning that these books go directly from bag to shelf with no intermediate stops.

As for comprehension—well, at the Tattered Cover Book Store in Denver, where twenty copies of Hawking's book have been sold each week, buyer Louise Haggerty has been polling her customers. "So far, I've asked more than 100 people," she says, "and nobody understands it. There's a local book club in town that read it, and none of them understood it, either. But the thing is, nobody seems to mind. They just want to own it."

When I refer to bestsellers, I don't mean books on the *Publishers Weekly* or B. Dalton bestseller list, for the simple reason that they mean nothing compared with the Big Kahuna: the *New York Times* bestseller list . . . .

What exactly is so important about being on the *Times* list? Well, aside from the fact that it means more books are sold and there's a larger pile of cash to divide up among the interested parties, it has grown to become perhaps the most important marketing tool in publishing. . . . Bestsellers get pushed, pushed, pushed. Some chains . . . offer a bigger discount on *Times* bestsellers, and others display them more prominently. Either way, it is of critical importance for a publisher to land a book on the list.

"Once you're on the bestseller list for a little bit," explained Louise Haggerty, "you're probably going to stay there for a little bit longer."

You know what she means.

It used to be different. Before the explosion of chain bookstores and the mass-marketing of hardcovers in the '80s, it seemed likely that book buyers willing to pay $10 or $15 for a brand new hardcover would actually be reading their purchases. As a result, the early bestseller lists became the repository for intellectual challenges—and a reward for writers who took difficult subjects and made them easy to grasp. That, for instance, explains how in 1927, copies of Will Durant's *The Story of Philosophy* were practically flying out of bookstores.

In the twentieth century, there seem to be two types of "intellectual" books. One is books of knowledge and challenge, to which the works of Will Durant and Stephen Hawking belong—fitting clearly under a specific discipline like history, philosophy, or science. The other is the point-of-view book, of which Bloom's extended essay is only the most current example. Any of these can either zoom to the top of the bestseller list or languish forever on the shelves of university bookstores.

Until recently, the bestseller list was considered a fairly reliable measure of quality in intellectual reading; we didn't look at it and wonder, How did that book get there? But the chains now sell to vast numbers of people without regard to quality of prose, let alone consistency of thought. . . .

Today, things are much simpler. Buying a book is the literary equivalent of contributing to a political campaign. When you spend money for Allan Bloom's book, you're saying, "I agree with you." (Or at least, you're agreeing with what you know from the reviews and publicity.) It really doesn't matter anymore whether you read it or not; the debate about Bloom has been overshadowed by his celebrity (which made him worthy of a profile in *People*).

And that's why academics with neither the insights of Galbraith nor the flashy concepts of Reich are rushing to find agents and publishers for their increasingly unreadable manuscripts. They're going straight to the bookshelf anyway—so how good do they have to be?

. . . How did a book as complex and incomprehensible as *A Brief History of Time* end up as the likely bestselling nonfiction book of the year?

The simple answer, I believe, is that Bantam Books is perhaps the top student of bestseller strategy in American publishing. And it knew that the only way to guarantee a bestseller in this case was to exploit the illness of Stephen Hawking to promote his book—in a way that is at best irrelevant and at worst shameful. . . .

continued on page 217

FIRST DATE AT #1: March 20, 1988
TOTAL WEEKS AT #1: 8

The Icarus Agenda
Robert Ludlum
RANDOM HOUSE

Ludlum checks in with his biannual #1 hit in 1988, as he did in 1978, 1980, 1982, 1984, and 1986. This one hinges on a congressman's secret dealings with a band of terrorists.

FIRST DATE AT #1: May 15, 1988
TOTAL WEEKS AT #1: 7

Zoya
Danielle Steel
DELACORTE

The story of one woman's journey from St. Petersburg during the Russian Revolution to Paris in the 1920s to contemporary New York, it is alphabetically the last of all the #1 bestsellers. Gabriel Garcia Marquez' *Love in the Time of Cholera* rose rapidly to #2 on the list, but never made it past Steel and Michener to #1.

FIRST DATE AT #1: July 3, 1988
TOTAL WEEKS AT #1: 5

Alaska
James Michener
RANDOM HOUSE

Using the by-now familiar Michener approach, this story of the 49th state is told by weaving together centuries of history with fictional stories. This is the most recent of Michener's nine #1 bestsellers and the one with the shortest time at #1.

215

FIRST DATE AT #1: July 3, 1988

TOTAL WEEKS AT #1: 2

Talking Straight

Lee Iacocca
with Sonny Kleinfeld

BANTAM

Further stories, anecdotes, and business advice from the man whose name is an acronym for "I Am Chairman Of Chrysler Corporation of America." Like so many sequels in this genre, *Talking Straight*'s time at the top was a tiny fraction of the time of its predecessor (1/19th to be precise). This is Iacocca's second #1 and *Times* reporter Sonny Kleinfeld's first and only.

FIRST DATE AT #1: November 20, 1988

TOTAL WEEKS AT #1: 2

The Last Lion

William Manchester

LITTLE, BROWN

Manchester returns to #1 after 22 years with the second volume (the first didn't make it) of his biography of Winston Churchill, covering the years from 1932 to 1940.

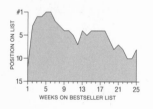

THE LAST LION
Winston Spencer Churchill
1874 VISIONS OF GLORY 1932

William Manchester

Earlier, Irwin had urged Churchill to update his views on India by talking to some members of the congress. Winston had replied: "I am quite satisfied with my views on India, and I don't want them disturbed by any bloody Indians." Since leaving Bangalore in 1899 he had taken little interest in the subcontinent. He seems to have been unaware that the Simon Commission and all that followed were the consequences of a pledge made by Lloyd George in 1917, defining England's aim in India as "the granting of self-governing institutions with a view to the progressive realisation of responsible Government in India as an integral part of the British Empire." But although Winston had seldom thought of the Raj, his feelings about it were strong. No Englishman was more persuaded of Queen Victoria's wisdom in saying, "I think it very unwise to give up what we hold." Indeed, that summed up his attitude toward the entire Empire. He considered it, among other things, a matter of national self-interest. To Churchill, Amery observed, "England is still the starting point and the ultimate object of policy." The Empire gave Britain its prestige; it made Britain the world's most powerful nation. Without its imperial possessions the country would be merely an obscure island lying off the European continent. England deprived of its imperial possessions would, for him, be like Samson shorn of his hair or Antaeus without his feet on earth. Moreover, his vision of India, in particular, was crowned by a romantic nimbus. It was the magic land he had known as an impressionable young cavalry officer, a realm of rajas' palaces, the Taj, shikar, bazaars, fakirs, temples, shrines, and howdahs, a symbol of imperial splendor and proud glory, Britian's most priceless possession. To yield it, he said, would be "a hideous act of self-mutilation."[267]

Many, including some who were close to him, concluded that he lived in the past, a "mid-Victorian," as Amery called him in August 1929, "steeped in the politics of his father's period, and unable ever to get the modern view." Certainly Churchill often quoted pronouncements about the subcontinent made long ago by men now deep in their graves. One of them, indeed, was Lord Randolph: "Our rule in India is, as it were, a sheet of oil spread out over and keeping free from storms a vast and profound ocean of humanity." Another was Lord Morley: "There is a

from page 215

Hawking means well—he tries hard to write in layman's prose, and he even throws in an exclamation point here and there—but in the end, he has written what amounts to a graduate school textbook, albeit a breezy one.

Like everyone else, I admire Hawking for the courage it took to write *A Brief History of Time.* For the past two decades he has suffered the horribly debilitating effects of Lou Gehrig's disease, and cannot move or speak without help. He is assisted at all times by nurses, and his condition will likely never improve.

But Bantam knew that if it could sell that compelling story to the critics and the media, and thus sell the book to the independent-bookstore clientele—heavily influenced by coverage and reviews and word of mouth—Hawking might manage to edge onto the bestseller list. And once there, he and Bantam would become a part of that self-perpetuating cycle of success that bestsellerdom creates. With any luck, the momentum would grow so quickly that Hawking would become a phenomenon. How confident was Bantam of his potential? A little more than Simon & Schuster was of Allan Bloom's. Bantam reportedly gave Hawking an advance of around $500,000. But after spending that kind of money, it wasn't going to take any chances, and that's where the exploitation of Hawking's illness began.

Nearly a third of the book's cover is taken up by a striking photograph of Hawking in his wheelchair. Then there's the dust-jacket copy: "From the vantage point of the wheelchair where he has spent the last 20 years trapped by Lou Gehrig's disease," Bantam's promoters have written, "Professor Hawking himself has transformed our view of the universe."

Does the universe look different from a wheelchair? Is Bantam saying that Hawking's disease has

made him a better physicist? And is there *anything* in the book itself to suggest how relevant his illness is to theoretical physics?

Still, Bantam seems intent on pushing this aspect of his story. Its P.R. people sent over a couple of videocassettes of Hawking on the morning interview shows. I watched with the requisite amount of amazement as Hawking went through the arduous process of speaking through a computer. It was incredibly moving, and there is no question that he has shown tremendous strength.

"You can't separate the book from the man," explains Linda Grey, Bantam's publisher. "I found his personal story compelling and believe that people associate him with courage as well as brilliance."

So it's not enough to be just plain brilliant. At least not if you want to be published by Bantam. And in the process, it doesn't really matter if the book's publishers even understand it. "I can't claim to understand all of it, of course, Linda Grey says. But certainly most of it."

This marketing strategy may seem subtle to the average reader, but not to those who know about Bantam's huge success with other nonfiction works that show the author prominently on the cover, such as the Lee Iacocca, Chuck Yeager, and Geraldine Ferraro books. But those are autobiographies; this is science. This is an almost unprecedented exploitation of a nonfiction author. I defy Bantam to name another nonfiction book in America —*any* nonfiction book other than autobiography—with a picture of its author on the front cover. Even Carl Sagan, whose books on cosmology and the universe and whose wide TV exposure have made him a widely recognizable face, has never had his own photograph on the front of a book.

Obviously all this marketing is designed to assuage the consumer's fear that the book will have

continued on page 219

FIRST DATE AT #1: August 7, 1988
TOTAL WEEKS AT #1: 12

The Cardinal of the Kremlin
Tom Clancy
PUTNAM

Clancy's longest stay at #1 came with the third of his five #1 books, in which the CIA's Jack Ryan rushes to the rescue of a Russian military officer who is also the highest-ranking U.S. secret agent in the Soviet Union.

FIRST DATE AT #1: October 30, 1988
TOTAL WEEKS AT #1: 3

The Queen of the Damned
Anne Rice
KNOPF

Rice has written many popular vampire books, but her only #1 was this the third volume of her vampire chronicles. This 6,000 year history also includes *Interview with a Vampire* and *The Vampire Lestat.* Rice, who is married to a poet, told *Contemporary Authors* that for her "writing is the grand passion, the activity which makes my life worthwhile. . . . At home we are perpetually in the atmosphere of clicking typewriters, booklined walls, passionate conversation. . . . It is a rich and marvelous life."

FIRST DATE AT #1: December 4, 1988
TOTAL WEEKS AT #1: 4

Gracie
George Burns
PUTNAM

At 92, Burns becomes the oldest author ever to have a #1 book with his loving remembrance of Gracie Allen, his late wife and show business partner for many years.

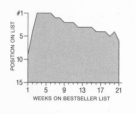

FIRST DATE AT #1: January 1, 1989
TOTAL WEEKS AT #1: 34

All I Really Need to Know I Learned in Kindergarten
Robert Fulghum
VILLARD

The second biggest #1 book in 23 years (only *Iacocca* stayed at #1 longer), Fulghum's inspirational essays about ordinary life came from nowhere to dominate the list for all of 1989 and much of 1990.

1

For forty years my act consisted of one joke. And then she died.

Her real name was Grace Ethel Cecile Rosalie Allen. Gracie Allen. But for those forty years audiences in small-time and big-time vaudeville houses and movie theaters and at home listening to their radios or watching television knew her, and loved her, simply as Gracie. Just Gracie. She was on a first-name basis with America. Lovable, confused Gracie, whose Uncle Barnum Allen had the water drained from his swimming pool before diving one hundred feet into it because he knew how to dive but didn't know how to swim, and who once claimed to have grown grapefruits that were so big it took only eight of them to make a dozen, Gracie, who confessed to cheating on her driver's test by copying from the car in front of her, who decided that horses must be deaf because she saw so few of them at concerts, wh___ ___ted making ice cubes with

from page 217

no value to him—that it is, perhaps, too complex for him to understand. But the fact is that several critics have called *A Brief History of Time* eminently readable, a book for the layman. And there are moments, particularly in the beginning, when a college-educated reader will be reminded of principles first learned in physics class and long since forgotten.

Still, critics have frequently mentioned Hawking's illness in their reviews. *Newsweek* put him on the cover in his wheelchair; inside, one headline said, "Confined to his wheelchair, unable even to speak, physicist Stephen Hawking seeks the grand unification theory that will explain the universe."

Yes, it was certainly courageous of Hawking to write this book, even appropriate for the media to write about his condition—but it was the ultimate act of opportunism for Bantam to use his illness as a sales pitch on the cover. Bantam does not want me to forget that I am writing about a man with a disease.

We will never know where this book would have been on the bestseller list—or whether it would have been there at all—had Bantam sold *A Brief History of Time* merely as a breakthrough in scientific thought, an intellectual challenge to the reading public. Perhaps the saddest thing is that Hawking seems content to let it happen. I wasn't surprised to learn that he wants his next book to be an autobiography. And it will not surprise me to find it at the top of the bestseller list. ∎

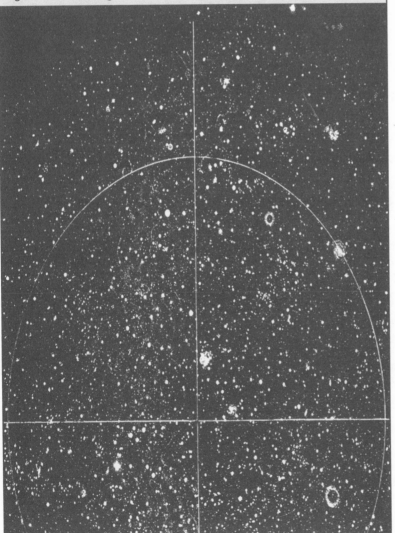

FIRST DATE AT #1: November 20, 1988
TOTAL WEEKS AT #1: 11

The Sands of Time
Sidney Sheldon
MORROW

In the sixth of Sheldon's seven #1 books, four nuns become trapped in a struggle between the Spanish army and Basque separatists.

FIRST DATE AT #1: February 5, 1989
TOTAL WEEKS AT #1: 3

Midnight
Dean R. Koontz
PUTNAM

Koontz makes the first of his four consecutive annual first-week-in-February appearances at #1 with his 51st book, a tale of inexplicable deaths and strange horrors that take over a once idyllic California town. Koontz told *Contemporary Authors* that he began writing as a child, "for both reading and writing provided much needed escape from the poverty in which we lived and from my father's frequent fits of alcohol-induced violence. I started selling my work while I was still in college," a dozen science fiction novels by the age of 25. He abandoned that genre in 1972 for the suspense world. The fact that a thriller by Stephen Coonts (*Final Flight*) was on the list at the same time probably confused a few people.

FIRST DATE AT #1: February 12, 1989

TOTAL WEEKS AT #1: 2

Blind Faith

Joe McGinnis

PUTNAM

McGinnis returns to #1 exactly 20 years after *The Selling of the President* with a detailed description and analysis of the 1984 murder of a New Jersey woman and the family tragedy that investigators uncovered.

FIRST DATE AT #1: May 21, 1989

TOTAL WEEKS AT #1: 7

A Woman Named Jackie

C. David Heymann

LYLE STUART/CARROLL PUBLISHING

The most recent Kennedy book to reach #1, Clemens David Heymann's fifth book is a biography of Jacqueline Kennedy Onassis, and like most political "insider" books, it reached #1 quickly, and stayed on the list for 22 weeks. Heymann told *Contemporary Authors* that he detests "literary cliques and professional ass kissing. There are too many writers and too many books and not enough people who read. There are also too many newspapers and magazines—too many words in the world, floating about on meaningless sheets of paper." Heymann was fishing columnist for *Diversion Magazine* and has written for *Cosmopolitan, New Republic, Paris Match, Redbook, Saturday Review, Vanity Fair*, and many others.

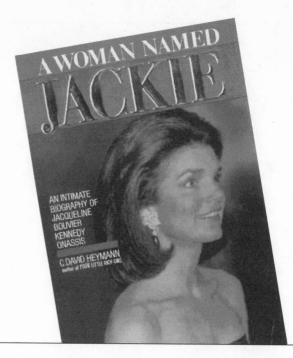

A *Woman Named Jackie*   625

establish friendships but I think everybody feels, without exception, that there's also a loner quality and a remoteness there."

Jackie's cousin John Davis, whose family portraits of the Bouviers and the Kennedys annoyed Jackie immensely, received similar treatment. "That didn't bother me at all," said Davis. "What did disturb me was that she also punished my mother."

Jackie's treatment of Maude Davis and Michelle Putnam, her father's twin sisters, was blatantly cruel. Demonstrating her hostility toward John, she failed to show up in Connecticut at the eightieth birthday party of her aunts, an affair attended by all other members of the family. She then compounded the insult by inviting neither aunt to Caroline's wedding. When Michelle Putnam died in September 1987, Jackie attended the funeral at St. Vincent Ferrer in New York, but barely spoke to Maude Davis and not at all to John.

"She not only didn't speak to John, she refused to shake his hand," said Marianne Strong, who also attended the funeral. "I don't think I've ever seen anything like it before. She shook everybody else's hand. She looked through John; around him, behind him, but not at him. In her eyes he didn't exist."

Jackie's fickleness emerged in other instances as well. She donated money to Channel 13, New York's public television station, but refused to give to the Jewish Opera in Tel Aviv when solicited by Maurice Tempelsman's cousin, Rose Schreiber. She went to Albany to protest a bill removing landmark status from religious properties (a case centered on whether St. Bartholomew's Church in New York should be permitted to erect a residential tower atop its main office). She refused, however, to take part in a symposium on Women and the Constitution sponsored by four other former First Ladies at the Jimmy Carter Presidential Center in Atlanta, Georgia. She campaigned vociferously against Mort Zuckerman's plans to construct 58- and 68-story skyscrapers at Columbus Circle (they would "cast a long shadow over Central Park"), but she said not a word when the Kennedy family announced its intention to build a Merchandise Mart hi-rise at Times Square, putting dozens of small merchants out of business. She attended Marietta Tree's dinner for art dealer Harriet Crawley and the Opening Night Gala of the Martha Graham Dance Company's 61st season, while declining invitations to scores of other dinners and opening night galas. She traveled to Cambridge, Massachusetts, for the dedica-

1

'To be born again,' sang Gibreel Farishta tumbling from the heavens, 'first you have to die. Ho ji! Ho ji! To land upon the bosomy earth, first one needs to fly. Tat-taa! Taka-thun! How to ever smile again, if first you won't cry? How to win the darling's love, mister, without a sigh? Baba, if you want to get born again . . .' Just before dawn one winter's morning, New Year's Day or thereabouts, two real, full-grown, living men fell from a great height, twenty-nine thousand and two feet, towards the English Channel, without benefit of parachutes or wings, out of a clear sky.

'I tell you, you must die, I tell you, I tell you,' and thusly and so beneath a moon of alabaster until a loud cry crossed the night, 'To the devil with your tunes,' the words hanging crystalline in the iced white night, 'in the movies you only mimed to playback singers, so spare me these infernal noises now.'

Gibreel, the tuneless soloist, had been cavorting in moonlight as he sang his impromptu gazal, swimming in air, butterfly-stroke, breast-stroke, bunching himself into a ball, spreadeagling himself against the almost-infinity of the almost-dawn, adopting heraldic postures, rampant, couchant, pitting levity against gravity. Now he rolled happily towards the sardonic voice. 'Ohé, Salad baba, it's you, too good. What-ho, old Chumch.' At which the other, a fastidious shadow falling headfirst in a grey suit with all the jacket buttons done up, arms by his sides, taking for granted the im-probability of the bowler hat on his head, pulled a nickname-hater's face. 'Hey, Spoono,' Gibreel yelled, eliciting a second inverted wince, 'Proper London, bhai! Here we come! Those bastards down there won't know what hit them. Meteor or lightning or vengeance of God. Out of thin air, baby. *Dharrraaammm!* Wham, na? What an entrance, yaar. I swear: splat.'

3

FIRST DATE AT #1: February 26, 1989
TOTAL WEEKS AT #1: 4

Star
Danielle Steel
DELACORTE

Eight weeks after *Zoya* left the list, Steel is back again with her seventh #1 in which a man and a woman cross paths on the road to stardom, one bound for Washington, the other for Hollywood. Steel is one of the few authors who does not do promotional tours. "About once every two years they drag me out of mothballs for a TV show, but that's about it. For one thing, I can't travel. I don't leave my children readily. . . . I did the Donahue show once, but I flew there late the night before the show and came home at lunchtime afterward. . . . I know I need to do promotions, but I don't like it very much. And I am very shy. I'll do magazine things if they can come to me."

FIRST DATE AT #1: March 26, 1989
TOTAL WEEKS AT #1: 9

The Satanic Verses
Salman Rushdie
VIKING

In Rushdie's novel, two emigrés from Bombay enact the roles of good and evil in contemporary London. The Ayatollah Kholmeni, angered by its portrayal of Muhammed, condemned the book as blasphemous and offered a $1 million reward to anyone who murdered the author and the publisher. Whatever else this may have done, it propelled the book onto and to the top of the *New York Times* bestseller list in short order. Rushdie, a Muslim, pointed out that in Islam, Muhammed "is not granted divine status, but the text is." Since all the profane scenes take place only in the main character's dreams, readers have suggested that the blasphemy could be taken as a manifestation of his insanity.

FIRST DATE AT #1: July 2, 1989
TOTAL WEEKS AT #1: 1

Summer of '49
David Halberstam
MORROW

Sixteen years after his book on Vietnam reached #1, Halberstam returns briefly with a look at the year the Yankees and the Boston Red Sox fought it out down to the very last day for the American League pennant.

FIRST DATE AT #1: July 16, 1989
TOTAL WEEKS AT #1: 5

It's Always Something
Gilda Radner
SIMON & SCHUSTER

The late actress and comedian describes her battle with ovarian cancer in this, her only book. The title was her father's favorite expression, and she made it famous through her *Saturday Night Live* character, Roseanne Roseannadanna. In the book, she says she "had always dreamed of being a writer since I was a little girl. I had written poetry and short stories—my impressions of the world.... In college, I found my mouth was mightier than my pen ... but inside there was an introspective poet who never was patient enough to write and wait for a response." Radner died on May 20th, eight weeks before her book reached #1. Around this time another "Roseanne," this one Barr/Arnold, zoomed into the #2 spot with a book about herself, but that one never reached #1.

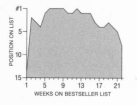

GILDA RADNER

Suddenly, not only did I have the room laughing, but I felt my thumb going up into the air like Roseanne Roseannadanna. There I was at The Wellness Community, and I was getting laughs about cancer and I was loving it. At the end of the meeting a lot of the women came up to me asking questons like "What kind of chemo are you on?" "What happened when your hair fell out?" And I saw they were looking to me for answers or leadership. I tried to help and say what I felt. Then one of the women also said that she was a comedy writer and she had some material and would I read it—a three-hundred-page screenplay. But another woman who was there said, "Hey, look what she is going through right now—this maybe isn't the right time to bring that up."

The woman who wanted to give me the material understood. It was wonderful because this other woman protected me, and I realized you just have to speak up and say, "Don't cross this boundary." What happened in subsequent weeks was some kind of strange balance about being funny, being Gilda Radner, and being someone going through cancer. I found a way to tell my cancer story and get laughs from it. They started to use me for balance at the meetings after someone had told something really sad. They'd say, "Gilda, would you like to speak?" Jack or I would come in to lift the room back up. I love to make people laugh, and at The Wellness Community I'd found my role again. It didn't matter there that I was Gilda Radner. It wasn't my reputation. It was who I was and who I always have been—someone who is funny.

You know that joke about the optimist who says, "If the house is full of shit there must be a pony somewhere"? Sometimes when I was wandering around and I

145

W A T E R   1 3 3

Indeed, the third mate was fairly flying across the forward deck and around a group of mechanics lazily batting a volleyball back and forth over the net.

She added, "He doesn't look happy."

Slava disappeared below and Arkady thought he could hear the reverberations of his Reeboks as they ran up three flights. In Olympic time the third mate emerged on the top deck and pushed into the crane cabin. "What is this about another assistant?" Slava gasped. "And why are you calling me to meet you? Who's in charge?"

"You are," Arkady said. "I thought we might have some fresh air and privacy here. A rare combination."

The crane cabin was the ultimate in privacy because the windows, broken and repaired with washers and pins like crockery, sloped in and forced intimacy whenever more than one person was inside. Still, the view could not be beat.

Natasha said, "Comrade Renko thinks I can be helpful."

"I've cleared Comrade Chaikovskaya with the fleet electrical engineer and the captain," Arkady said. "But since you are in charge, I thought that you should know. Also, I have to make a list of Zina's effects."

"We did that," Slava said. "We saw her old clothes, we examined the body. Why aren't you looking for a suicide note?"

"Victims rarely leave them. It will be very suspicious if that's the first thing we find."

Natasha laughed, then cleared her throat. Since she took up half the cabin, it was hard for her to be subtle.

"And what are you going to be doing?" Slava glared at her.

"Gathering information."

Slava laughed bitterly. "Great. Stirring up more trouble. I can't

---

FIRST DATE AT #1: May 28, 1989
TOTAL WEEKS AT #1: 2

While My Pretty One Sleeps
Mary Higgins Clark
SIMON & SCHUSTER

The murder of a gossip writer causes turmoil in the high-fashion industry of New York. Clark had been faced with the need to support her five children after her husband's untimely death. She began writing short stories for women's magazines. Her first book was a biography of George Washington called *Aspire to the Heavens*. Most book stores put it in the religion section, and sales were dismal.

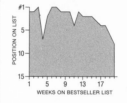

FIRST DATE AT #1: June 11, 1989
TOTAL WEEKS AT #1: 10

The Russia House
John le Carré
KNOPF

The first #1 spy thriller set in a post-glasnost world, le Carré's sixth #1 book shows how espionage was forced to adapt as the Iron Curtain crumbled.

FIRST DATE AT #1: August 6, 1989
TOTAL WEEKS AT #1: 2

Polar Star
Martin Cruz Smith
RANDOM HOUSE

In his second #1 bestseller, Smith moves the venue from a Moscow park to a mysterious fish factory boat plying the northern Pacific waters, watched closely by Russian and American spies.

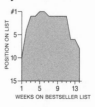

FIRST DATE AT #1: November 26, 1989
TOTAL WEEKS AT #1: 3

My Turn
Nancy Reagan with William Novak
RANDOM HOUSE

It was a short turn for the former first lady, whose recollections of her life in the White House displayed the very fast rise and decline typical of most "insider" political books.

FIRST DATE AT #1: January 7, 1990
TOTAL WEEKS AT #1: 3

It Was On Fire When I Lay Down On It
Robert Fulghum
VILLARD

More or less a continuation of *All I Really Need to Know I Learned in Kindergarten,* Fulghum's second book reached #2 on October 15, 1989 while the first book was still at #1, the first and only time in the list's history that the same author had the #1 and #2 books at the same time. This went on for three more weeks, then *It Was On Fire* became #1, pushing *Kindergarten* into second place. Around this time, Erma Bombeck had her first non-#1 in years, with her tragicomic *I Want to Grow Hair, I Want to Go to Boise,* and a book of actor Jimmy Stewart's poetry spent some time on the list.

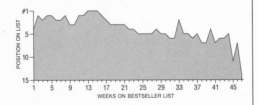

47

that one of

warmth and
g her about
h two of our
ging parents,
as helpful and
came to view
of therapist.

her as a friend. I now see ....

My relationship with Joan Quigley began as a crutch, one of several ways I tried to alleviate my anxiety about Ronnie. Within a year or two, it had become a habit, something I relied on a little less but didn't see the need to change. While I was never certain that Joan's astrological advice was helping to protect Ronnie, the fact is that nothing like March 30 ever happened again.

Was astrology one of the reasons? I don't *really* believe it was, but I don't *really* believe it wasn't. But I do know this: It didn't hurt, and I'm not sorry I did it.

Joan and I had talked several times when she finally said, "Why don't you let me know when the president plans to go out? I could tell you if those are good days or bad days." Well, I thought, what's the harm in that? And so once or twice a month I would talk with Joan (sometimes by appointment, sometimes not). I would have Ronnie's schedule in front of me, and what I wanted to know was very simple: Were specific dates safe or dangerous? If, for example, Ronnie was scheduled to give a speech in Chicago on May 3, should he leave Washington that morning, or was he better off flying out on the previous afternoon?

People seem to be fascinated by the logistics of all this, but it was really quite simple. As with other friends, I placed the calls to Joan myself, on .... ll me back, the White House and .... nd of mine, and put the ca ....

When J .... specific dates, I would, if .... vas in charge of Ronnie's .... made. Beginning in 1985, I .... gan, who became

Longest Winning Streak

Putnam is the only publisher to have at least one #1 book in each of the last eight years (1984 to 1991). Knopf is the next best, with at least one in each of the last four years. Villard has one for each of the last three years: the three Fulghum books. And no one else has more than two.

Long Stays and Short Stays

1980 is a watershed year, with regard to total length of stay on the *New York Times* list, especially for fiction books. Before 1980, there were 34 books that had been on the list (not just at #1) for a year or more. Since 1980, there has only been one (*Bonfire of the Vanities*).

And at the short end of the list, before 1980 only one work of fiction was on the list for less than 20 weeks. But since 1980, 18 books have been on and off in a relative flash.

Fiction Books that Were on the List for More than One Year

NUMBER OF BOOKS PUBLISHED BEFORE 1980

34

NUMBER OF BOOKS PUBLISHED AFTER 1980

1

Fiction Books that Were on the List for Less than 20 Weeks

NUMBER OF BOOKS PUBLISHED BEFORE 1980

1

NUMBER OF BOOKS PUBLISHED AFTER 1980

18

FIRST DATE AT #1: September 3, 1989
TOTAL WEEKS AT #1: 9

Clear and Present Danger
Tom Clancy
PUTNAM

Eleven months after *The Cardinal of the Kremlin,* Clancy is back at #1 with Jack Ryan's coming to the rescue of Americans fighting the drug lords of Colombia. Clancy says he has "titles and plotlines for books in the future. I'm hoping one of them won't be OBE— overtaken by events—which is a good possibility. I'm in the thriller business. There's probably always going to be something exciting to write about."

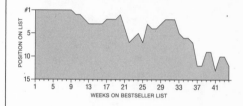

FIRST DATE AT #1: November 5, 1989
TOTAL WEEKS AT #1: 5

The Dark Half
Stephen King
VIKING

A writer of horror stories decides to "kill off" his pseudonym, but the pseudonym takes on a life of its own and goes on a murderous rampage in the 12th of King's 16 #1 bestsellers. King admits to a strong fear of the dark. "I don't like the dark. . . . There's a lot of mystery in the world, a lot of dark, shadowy corners we haven't explored yet. We shouldn't be too smug about dismissing out of hand everything we can't understand. The dark can have *teeth*, man."

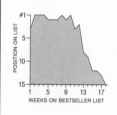

FIRST DATE AT #1: February 4, 1990
TOTAL WEEKS AT #1: 9

Megatrends 2000

John Naisbitt
and Patricia Aburdene

MORROW

Just seven years after *Megatrends* told us what to expect in the 1980s, Naisbitt, now writing with his wife, tells us what to expect in the 1990s and beyond in the way of political, economic, and social developments. The sequel remained at #1 one week longer than the original.

FIRST DATE AT #1: March 11, 1990
TOTAL WEEKS AT #1: 1

Barbarians at the Gate

Bryan Burrough
and John Helyar

HARPER

The story of the 1988 battle for control of RJR Nabisco.

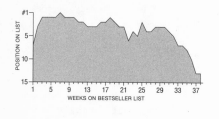

FIRST DATE AT #1: April 8, 1990
TOTAL WEEKS AT #1: 2

Means of Ascent

Robert A. Caro

KNOPF

This detailed look at Lyndon Johnson's seven-year pursuit of a seat in the U.S. Senate, which he won in 1948 by 87 votes out of millions cast, is the first of a proposed three volume series on LBJ.

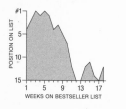

226

46

ence to "scrubbing repeatedly promised the mud and blood." up my draft number indeed, at least partly he had had the foresi (And, naturally, since a Lieutenant Commander, scrubbing the deck of ship—or performing any other function of an ordinary sailor—was not a possibility, either.) He could, of course, have torn up the commission and obtained a draft number (or could have enlisted), but he did not do that.

What he did do, in obedience to orders that he himself had a hand in drafting, was to spend the first five months of the war trying to further his political future, while ensconcing himself in precisely the type of bureaucratic "safe, warm naval berth" he had promised to avoid. For five months, he delayed and stalled, making no serious attempt to get into combat while having what his sidekick John Connally was to call "a lot of fun." And when, after six months of the war had passed, he finally did enter a combat zone—when he no longer had any choice, when "for the sake of political future" he *had* to get into a combat zone, and get there fast—he went not to fight (in the trenches or anywhere else), but to observe. Despite flying more than 20,000 miles to reach that combat zone and return home, the only brush he had with the war there was to fly as an observer on a single mission, at the conclusion of which he left the combat zone on the next plane out.

Nevertheless, although Lyndon Johnson had avoided being at the scene of a battle as long as he could, once he was at it, his conduct was bold and courageous, nonchalant in the face of danger. If he had gone to the Southwest Pacific only so that he could later claim to have been in the war—and if he had been in that war for only one day—still, for that day he had been not a politician but a warrior. Ambition may have governed his war service as it governed his entire life, but, as had always been the case, in the service of that ambition he had done whatever he had to do.

NOTHING ABOUT JOHNSON'S WAR SERVICE, however, was more revealing than the way he came to portray it.

A great storyteller, he had a great story to tell, and he made the most of it. Hardly had he arrived back in Washington when he began telling it to journalists, inviting them to lunch, scheduling interviews, one after the other, with the AP, the UP, INS, *Time* magazine and Texas newspapers. Edwin Weisl, the counsel not only for Paramount but for Hearst News-

FIRST DATE AT #1: November 19, 1989
TOTAL WEEKS AT #1: 6

Daddy
Danielle Steel
DELACORTE

The last time Steel and King faced off at about the same time, his book displaced hers. This time Steel's eighth knocks off King's 12th. But the two would change places four times in the ensuing weeks. *Daddy* is the story of a man whose safe and predictable world is threatened by unexpected crises. This is Steel's 21st published book in nine years. Early in her career, Steel identified Jacqueline Susann as a model, but in later years she clarified that. "It is just that when I was very young she was the most successful novelist, and I wanted to be as successful as she. But I didn't have any desire to emulate her work."

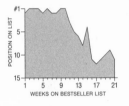

FIRST DATE AT #1: February 4, 1990
TOTAL WEEKS AT #1: 2

The Bad Place
Dean R. Koontz
PUTNAM

For the second year in a row, Koontz reaches #1 during the first week in February, this time with a tale of a troubled sleepwalker who hires a detective to discover the causes and the consequences of his behavior. Thomas Pynchon's *Vineland* rose to #2 at this time, but no further.

The snowflakes fell in big white clusters, clinging together like a drawing in a fairy tale, just like in the books Sarah used to read to the children. She sat at the typewriter, looking out the window, watching snow cover the lawn, hanging from the trees like lace, and she completely forgot the story she'd been chasing around in her head since early that morning. It was so damn picturesque. So pretty. Everything was pretty here. It was a storybook life in a storybook town, and the people around her seemed like storybook people. They were exactly what she had never wanted to become, and now she was one of them, and had been for years. And probably always would be. Sarah Mac-Cormick, the rebel, the assistant editor of the *Crimson,* the girl who had graduated from Radcliffe in 1969 at the top of her class and knew she was different, had become one of them. Overnight. Or almost. In truth, it had taken almost twenty years. And now she was Sarah Watson. Mrs. Oliver Wendell Watson. She lived in Purchase, New York, in a beautiful house they almost owned, after fourteen

◈ 1 ◈

FIRST DATE AT #1: April 29, 1990
TOTAL WEEKS AT #1: 19

Men at Work
George Will

MACMILLAN

In the first extended #1 hit of the '90s, a Pulitzer Prize-winning syndicated political columnist and baseball enthusiast describes the craft of baseball as it is practiced by a manager and three players. Will says that baseball is "one of the few virtuous pursuits left in today's society." Around this time, actor Kirk Douglas made both the fiction and nonfiction lists with his autobiography *The Ragman's Son* and his novel *Dance With the Devil*, but neither came near #1.

FIRST DATE AT #1: September 9, 1990
TOTAL WEEKS AT #1: 2

Trump: Surviving at the Top
*Donald Trump
with Charles Leerhsen*

RANDOM HOUSE

Surviving at the Top didn't. It spent the shortest total time on the *New York Times* bestseller list of any #1 book, seven weeks from start to finish. Trump's empire was in chaos by the time the book came out, and the reading public had begun to lose interest in The Donald, his business, and his personal affairs.

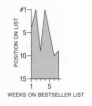

FIRST DATE AT #1: February 18, 1990

TOTAL WEEKS AT #1: 3

Devices and Desires

P. D. James

KNOPF

The first classic British mystery to reach #1 since Agatha Christie, Phyllis Dorothy James White's low-key hero, Adam Dalgliesh of the London police, helps to solve a series of killings on the remote Norfolk coast, in the shadow of a controversial power station. James began writing after 19 years as a hospital administrator.

FIRST DATE AT #1: March 4, 1990

TOTAL WEEKS AT #1: 5

Oh, the Places You'll Go

Dr. Seuss

RANDOM HOUSE

With this children's book for adults (or perhaps *vice versa*), Dr. Seuss becomes the fourth of five authors who have had a #1 bestseller on both the fiction and the nonfiction lists. This book had the most unusual pattern of any #1 bestseller, rising quickly to #1, declining slowly for a year, zooming up to #1 again, declining for a year, and then, inexplicably, raising to #1 for a third time in its third year on the list. Dr. Seuss died in 1991.

The Ultimate Achievement

#1 on Fiction and #1 on Nonfiction at the Same Time

No one has yet come close. Of those five authors who have been #1 on both lists, the appearances were far apart. Closest was Dr. Seuss, whose #1 fiction came four years after his nonfiction. Irving Wallace missed by five years, John Steinbeck by ten, William Styron by eleven, and Ernest Hemingway by fourteen.

FIRST DATE AT #1: September 16, 1990
TOTAL WEEKS AT #1: 1

Darkness Visible
William Styron
RANDOM HOUSE

The author of *Sophie's Choice* and *Nat Turner* becomes the fifth and most recent author to have both a fiction and a nonfiction #1 bestseller, with this very personal memoir of a period of severe depression.

FIRST DATE AT #1: September 30, 1990
TOTAL WEEKS AT #1: 1

Millie's Book
Millie, as told to Barbara Bush
MORROW

The purported memoirs of the Bush's English springer spaniel, about life in the White House. This is the third book by a first lady to reach #1 on the list, following Eleanor Roosevelt and Nancy Reagan. It is also the first nonfiction book since the first week of the list in 1942 to enter at #1, but not remain there the following week.

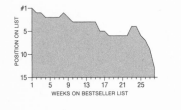

DARKNESS VISIBLE

A MEMOIR OF MADNESS

WILLIAM STYRON

MILLIE'S BOOK

AS DICTATED TO BARBARA BUSH

King Versus Everyone Else

TOTAL NUMBER OF #1 BOOKS

Danielle Steel has a good chance of taking the lead early on in the next millennium, but she is the only one. It seems unlikely that anyone else could have more #1 books, at least during King's lifetime. Here are the projections for the eight currently working members of the Big Nine:

AUTHOR	PROJECTED NUMBER OF #1 BESTSELLERS IF IF THEY KEEP GOING AS LONG AS MICHENER
Danielle Steel	64
Stephen King	59
Tom Clancy	45
Robert Ludlum	27
Bob Woodward	18
John le Carré	15
Sidney Sheldon	12
James Michener	9

TOTAL NUMBER OF WEEKS AT #1

In 1992, Michener has a huge lead over all the others: 207 weeks at #1, compared to 100 for King, 52 for Steel, etc. Even though King, Steel, and Clancy have many fewer weeks, they are also nearly four decades younger than Michener. If they each continue writing at their present pace, and appearing at #1 at their present average number of weeks, here is how things will look in the year 2032 when King, Steel, and Clancy will all be as old as Michener is in 1992:

	PROJECTED NUMBER OF WEEKS AT #1
James Michener	207
Danielle Steel	341
Tom Clancy	351
Stephen King	408

However, if Robert Fulghum were to continue at his present rate, based on the averages of his first three (perhaps skewed since *Kindergarten* outperformed the other two by ten to one), he would be undisputed leader by Michener-age.

Robert Fulghum	429

FIRST DATE AT #1: March 18, 1990
TOTAL WEEKS AT #1: 5

The Bourne Ultimatum
Robert Ludlum
RANDOM HOUSE

Ludlum's eighth and most recent #1 bestseller is the third in the Bourne series. It describes the dramatic consequences when a professor's previous association with Vietnamese terrorists catches up with him.

FIRST DATE AT #1: April 22, 1990
TOTAL WEEKS AT #1: 4

September
Rosamunde Pilcher
ST. MARTIN'S

The Shell Seekers was an extremely popular book that never made #1, but the Scottish author's next, her 25th book, entered the list in the #1 spot. It is a slow-moving tale of life in a small Scottish town, where a September dance brings guests from various parts of the world to encounter often unexpected destinies. Pilcher told *Publishers Weekly* she began her writing career under the name Jane Fraser, doing "sort of mimsy little love stories for Mills and Boon." Her agent, while dining with the president of St. Martin's, was asked, "Have you got a light romantic writer we could publish for women?" "Yes, I have," she replied, and "it all started from there."

FIRST DATE AT #1: October 7, 1990
TOTAL WEEKS AT #1: 4

By Way of Deception

*Victor Ostrovsky
and Claire Hoy*

ST. MARTIN'S

The first author is a former secret agent for Mossad, the Israeli spy service. This controversial book, very briefly on the list, is a chronicle of the operations of Mossad, in the Middle East and worldwide.

FIRST DATE AT #1: November 11, 1990
TOTAL WEEKS AT #1: 3

The Civil War

*Geoffrey Ward
with Ric and Ken Burns*

KNOPF

Based on a popular public television series, the book chronicles the Civil War, from Fort Sumter to Appomattox, in words and pictures.

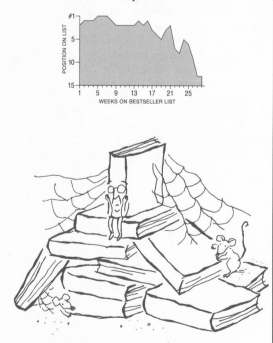

The Ten Most Recently Published #1 FICTION Books That Are Now Out of Print

TITLE	AUTHOR	DATE AT #1
The Hotel New Hampshire	John Irving	9/27/81
Oliver's Story	Erich Segal	4/10/77
Looking for Mr. Goodbar	Judith Rossner	8/3/75
Once Is Not Enough	Jacqueline Susann	5/6/73
The Word	Irving Wallace	5/4/72
The Love Machine	Jacqueline Susann	6/22/69
The Chosen	Chaim Potok	10/1/67
The Arrangement	Elia Kazan	3/26/67
Valley of the Dolls	Jacqueline Susann	5/8/66
The Glass Blowers	Daphne du Maurier	5/5/63

The Ten Most Recently Published #1 NONFICTION Books That Are Now Out of Print

TITLE	AUTHOR	DATE AT #1
Veil	Bob Woodward	10/18/87
Mayor	Edward I. Koch	2/26/84
Never Say Diet	Richard Simmons	3/8/81
Crisis Investing	Douglas Casey	9/21/80
Donahue	Phil Donahue	3/23/80
The Ends of Power	H. R. Haldeman	3/26/78
The Book of Lists	David Wallechinsky, et al.	7/24/77
Doris Day: Her Own Story	A. E. Hotchner	3/14/76
Power!	Michael Korda	11/23/75
Bring on the Empty Horses	David Niven	11/30/75

**OF THE 50 MOST RECENT #1 BOOKS
THAT ARE NOW OUT OF PRINT
78% ARE NONFICTION.**

**OF THE 50 OLDEST #1 BOOKS THAT ARE
STILL IN PRINT 58% ARE FICTION.**

**THE EVIDENCE IS CLEAR THAT NONFICTION
IS MUCH MORE LIKELY TO GO
OUT OF PRINT THAN FICTION**

1

THEY HAD BEEN MARRIED for thirty-one years, and the following spring, full of resolve and a measure of hope, he would marry again. But that day, on a late afternoon near the end of March, Mr. Alejandro Stern had returned home and, with his attaché case and garment bag still in hand, called out somewhat absently from the front entry for Clara, his wife. He was fifty-six years old, stout and bald, and never particularly good-looking, and he found himself in a mood of intense preoccupation.

For two days he had been in Chicago—that city of rough souls—on behalf of his most difficult client. Dixon Hartnell was callous, self-centered, and generally scornful of his lawyers' advice; worst of all, representing him was a permanent engagement. Dixon was Stern's brother-in-law, married to Silvia, his sister, Stern's sole living immediate relation and the enduring object of his affections. For Dixon, of course, his feelings were hardly as pure. In the early years, when Stern's practice amounted to little more than the decorous hustling of clients in the hallways of the misdemeanor courts, serving Dixon's unpredictable needs

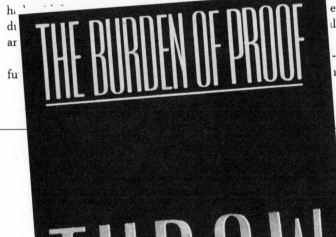

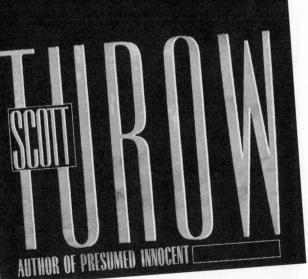

FIRST DATE AT #1: May 13, 1990
TOTAL WEEKS AT #1: 4

The Stand
Stephen King
DOUBLEDAY

When *The Stand* was published in 1978, the less-famous King had less clout, and his publisher cut hundreds of pages from the manuscript. The book did not reach #1. Twelve years later, the book was reissued as King originally wrote it, and it entered the list at #1. After most of the population of America has been killed by a plague, the forces of good and evil compete for those who remain.

FIRST DATE AT #1: June 17, 1990
TOTAL WEEKS AT #1: 11

The Burden of Proof
Scott Turow
FARRAR, STRAUS

An attorney tries to unravel the mystery of his wife's suicide while defending his wheeler-dealer brother-in-law. Bucking the trend toward declining results, Turow's second #1 bestseller was in the #1 position three weeks longer than his first, *Presumed Innocent.*

FIRST DATE AT #1: December 2, 1990
TOTAL WEEKS AT #1: 8

A Life on the Road
Charles Kuralt

PUTNAM

With this account of adventures traveling around the country producing television news features, Kuralt becomes the first news person since Dan Rather 15 years earlier to reach #1. For years, Kuralt and a crew of three (camera, sound, electrician) drove 50,000 miles each year in search of feature stories that "acknowledge the whole world isn't in flames, that people go on living their lives in spite of big black headlines." Most of the ideas for the three or four minute features came from viewer mail. Asked to pick the most inconsequential, Kuralt remembered the man who could hold 30 eggs in one hand.

FIRST DATE AT #1: January 27, 1991
TOTAL WEEKS AT #1: 11

Iron John
Robert Bly

ADDISON-WESLEY

The prominent poet and guru of the new men's movement reached #1 for the first time with his book about male rites of passage as practiced in various cultures around the world and over time. The *Times Literary Supplement (London)* once referred to Bly's style as "heavy simplicity.... For years Mr. Bly has been writing poems so transparent that... they tend to go in one eye and out the other.... Mr. Bly's vocabulary is drab. When he attempts a greater resonance the words fail him."

King Versus Steel

Stephen King has 16 #1 bestsellers and Danielle Steel has ten. They are almost exactly the same age (born five weeks apart in 1947), but King's first #1 bestseller reached the list almost five years sooner than Steel's. King has been producing #1 bestsellers at the rate of one every 9.5 months, while Steel's rate is just a little faster: one every 8.9 months. If nothing else were to change, Steel would catch King in the year 2006, when they would each have their 31st #1 book. Then she would slowly pull ahead, so that when they are both the age that James Michener is now, King would have 59 #1 books and Steel would have 64.

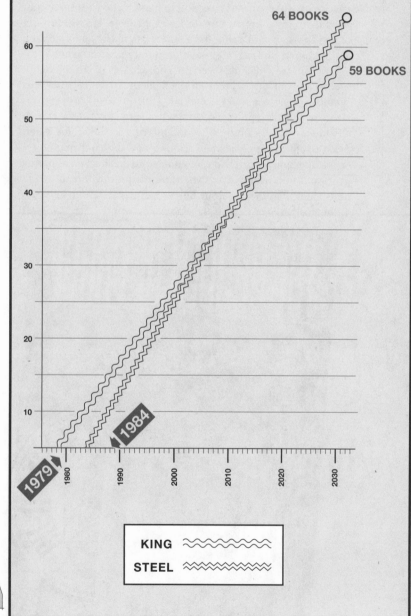

Chapter One

Ioannina, Greece—July 1948

She woke up screaming every night and it was always the same dream. She was in the middle of a lake in a fierce storm and a man and a woman were forcing her head under the icy waters, drowning her. She awakened each time panicky, gasping for breath, soaked with perspiration.

She had no idea who she was and she had no memory of the past. She spoke English—but she did not know what country she was from or how she had come to be in Greece, in the small Carmelite convent that sheltered her.

As time went by, there were tantalizing flashes of memory, glimpses of vague *[...]* ral images that came *[...]* them, to hold them *[...]* nexpected moments, *[...]* r with confusion. *[...]* uestions. The Car-

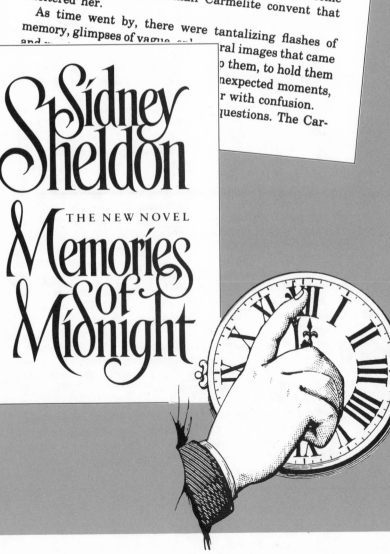

Sidney Sheldon

THE NEW NOVEL

Memories of Midnight

FIRST DATE AT #1: September 2, 1990
TOTAL WEEKS AT #1: 2

Memories of Midnight
Sidney Sheldon
MORROW

In Sheldon's seventh, most recent, and shortest-surviving #1, an American woman is haunted by a cunning and vengeful Greek tycoon. Before 1989, the word "midnight" had never appeared on a #1 book. But Sheldon's was the second in a short time, and it lost the #1 spot to a third.

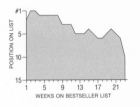

FIRST DATE AT #1: September 16, 1990
TOTAL WEEKS AT #1: 5

Four Past Midnight
Stephen King
VIKING

King's third #1 collection of shorter works joined the list when *The Stand* was at #6, the first time King had two books on the list at the same time. This is King's fifteenth #1 book. (His *Needful Things* reached the list the week after *Scarlett* and hovered at #2 or #3 position for many weeks, but never made it to the top.) Fantasy writer Orson Scott Card told *Contemporary Authors* that in 50 years, King will be "regarded as the dominant literary figure of the time. A lot of us feel that way." David Streitfeld of the *Washington Post* said "King has passed beyond bestsellerdom into a special sort of nirvana reserved for him alone."

FIRST DATE AT #1: February 10, 1991
TOTAL WEEKS AT #1: 1

The Prize

Daniel Yergin

SIMON & SCHUSTER

The Cambridge Ph.D.'s book about the role that oil has played in world history, from the mid-nineteenth century to the present day, quickly rose to #1, then rapidly disappeared. Irving Wallace came close to having a #1 with the same title 20 years earlier.

FIRST DATE AT #1: March 17, 1991
TOTAL WEEKS AT #1: 1

And the Sea Will Tell

Vincent Bugliosi
with Bruce Henderson

NORTON

After several popular crime stories that didn't make #1, including *Helter Skelter*, the Charles Manson story, former Manson prosecutor Bugliosi got there with his account of a bizarre and enigmatic 1974 murder case involving two American couples on a Pacific island.

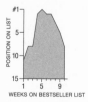

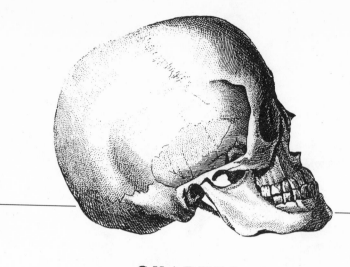

CHAPTER 1

Maui, Hawaii
April 1, 1974

It had rained during the night, one of those warm tropical showers that leaves the air heavy and sweet. A steady breeze born far out at sea kissed the shore at sunrise, rustling the coconut palms. The clouds, like the folks around these parts in no hurry to move on, scattered slowly as the sun rose out of the ocean and washed the sky with bold streaks of light. A few arcs of rainbow loitered above, offering promise for the new day.

Hawaii's locals make a clear distinction between themselves and haoles, the sunburned tourists from the mainland. It is less a term of contempt than bemused pity. On the scenically spectacular island of Maui, most of these visitors pick up their rental cars at Kahului Airport and drive directly to Kaanapali Beach on the western coast, where they stay in glitzy resort hotels, down premixed Mai Tais served by waitresses in synthetic grass skirts, and tap their toes to the canned melodies of Don Ho. Haoles just don't know any better.

The real soul of Maui is manifest on the south shore, with its endless stretches of blinding white beaches. The sun-bleached dunes roll up to wide verdant fields of pineapple and sugar cane. Herds of cattle graze contentedly on the grassy slopes of the West Maui mountains. Majestic Haleakala, the highest point on the island, is a two-mile-high peak topped with a massive volcanic crater, a dramatic reminder that this is a land of sudden, violent change.

At Maalaea Bay boat harbor, Charlie, the winch operator, was working a squeaky crank that unwound a cable still wet from the rain. "Never thought I'd live to see the day this old gal went back in the water," he offered to anyone within earshot as he controlled the speed with which a trailer bearing a thirty-foot wooden sailboat rolled down a launching ramp.

Boat launchings were hardly uncommon hereabouts, but a small crowd of locals had gathered to watch this particular one. These folks and a few hundred other kindred souls lived aboard boats in the bay. Most were dreamers who collected sea charts, atlases, and books about faraway places, yearning to pull up anchor and sail away, just like the excited young couple whose boat was now the center of attention. But few would do so.

17

Shortest Time on the List

Of all the books that were #1 bestsellers for at least one week, none spent a shorter total time on the list than Donald Trump's second compendium of anecdotes and advice, *Trump: Surviving at the Top*. The list of losers amongst the winners includes the otherwise grandly successful authors (Bob Woodward, John le Carré, Arthur Hailey); non-mainstream authors (Michael Jackson, Nancy Reagan), and a host of others.

TITLE	WEEKS ON LIST	AUTHOR	WEEKS AT #1
Trump: Surviving at the Top	7	Donald Trump	2
A Day in the Life of America	8	(no author)	3
The Ends of Power	9	H. R. Haldeman	2
And the Sea Will Tell	10	Vincent Bugliosi	1
By Way of Deception	10	Victor Ostrovsky	4
Dark Vision	10	William Styron	1
For the Record	10	Donald Regan	4
Veil	10	Bob Woodward	4
Midnight	11	Dean Koontz	3
Moonwalk	11	Michael Jackson	2
Nancy Reagan	11	Kitty Kelley	5
The Prize	12	Daniel Yergin	1
The Secret Pilgrim	12	John le Carré	2
The Seeress of Kell	12	David Eddings	3
The Triumph of Politics	12	David Stockman	2
You'll Never Eat Lunch in This Town Again	12	Julia Phillips	3
My Turn	13	Nancy Reagan	3
The Ides of March	13	Thornton Wilder	2
Polar Star	14	Martin Cruz Smith	2
The Bad Place	14	Dean Koontz	2
Cold Fire	15	Dean Koontz	3
Devices and Desires	15	P. D. James	3
Heir to the Empire	15	Timothy Zahn	1
Wired	15	Bob Woodward	4
Day of Infamy	16	Walter Lord	3
First Among Equals	17	Jeffrey Archer	2
Heartbeat	17	Danielle Steel	8
Honor Thy Father	17	Gay Talese	1
Queen of the Damned	17	Ann Rice	3
Roosevelt in Retrospect	17	John Gunther	5
Star	17	Danielle Steel	4
The Coming Battle of Germany	17	William Ziff	4
The Dark Half	17	Stephen King	5
The Kitchen God's Wife	17	Amy Tan	7
The Little Princesses	17	Marion Crawford	1
While My Pretty One Sleeps	17	Mary Higgins Clark	2
Hold the Dream	18	Barbara T. Bradford	1
Means of Ascent	18	Robert Caro	2
Power!	18	Michael Korda	1
Summer of '49	18	David Halberstam	1
Blind Faith	19	Joe McGinnis	2
Lucky	19	Jackie Collins	2
Overload	19	Arthur Hailey	2
The Russia House	19	John le Carré	10

FIRST DATE AT #1: October 21, 1990
TOTAL WEEKS AT #1: 13

The Plains of Passage
Jean M. Auel
CROWN

Bookstores began taking orders for the long-awaited third volume in Auel's saga of life in the Ice Age well before the publication date, so it is little wonder it entered the list at #1, displacing Stephen King. This volume chronicles a young couple's trek on a horseback across Ice Age Europe.

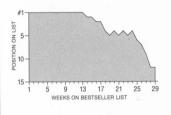

FIRST DATE AT #1: January 20, 1991
TOTAL WEEKS AT #1: 2

The Secret Pilgrim
John le Carré
KNOPF

Le Carré's most recent and shortest stay at #1 comes 27 years after his first appearance. In the book, a British secret service agent, on the eve of his retirement, recalls his three decades as a spy.

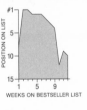

FIRST DATE AT #1: April 7, 1991
TOTAL WEEKS AT #1: 3

You'll Never Eat Lunch in This Town Again

Julia Phillips

RANDOM HOUSE

The Academy Award-winning film producer writes about her experiences with life in Hollywood.

FIRST DATE AT #1: April 28, 1991
TOTAL WEEKS AT #1: 5

Nancy Reagan

Kitty Kelley

SIMON & SCHUSTER

The unauthorized and nasty biography of the former first lady received immense prepublication publicity, entered the list at #1, stayed there for five weeks, then declined rapidly and was gone after six more weeks. The pattern is very similar to Kelley's earlier #1 unauthorized biography of Frank Sinatra, complete with prepublication legal threats.

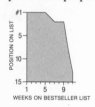

FIRST DATE AT #1: June 2, 1991
TOTAL WEEKS AT #1: 5

The Commanders

Bob Woodward

SIMON & SCHUSTER

Woodward's sixth #1 nonfiction bestseller takes a close look at how the president and his high military commanders made their pre-Desert Storm decisions during the first two years of the George Bush administration.

The Great Battle of 1991–1992

If one were working at a Publishing Research Laboratory, the ideal experiment one might conjure up would be to have a "blockbuster" book from each of the eight currently-active members of the "Big Nine" best-selling authors appear on the same day, then stand back and see what happens to the *New York Times* list.

Never in the fifty-year history of the list have we come closer to such a situation than in the final months of 1991 and the start of 1992. There have been occasions in the past where two big books were battling for position at the same time, notably *The Caine Mutiny* and *From Here to Eternity* in 1951 (they alternated between #1 and #2 for over a year), and on two occasions when a Stephen King and a Danielle Steel emerged within weeks of one another. (Once the Steel displaced the King; the other time, the reverse.)

The Great Battle of 1991–1992 began with Tom Clancy's *The Sum of All Fears,* which came to the list in the #1 position on August 25, 1991. Three weeks later, Alexandra Ripley's *Scarlett* joined the list at #1, displacing Clancy. And then, over the next few weeks, new novels by no less than six former #1 authors would emerge: Stephen King *(Needful Things),* Danielle Steel *(No Greater Love),* Sidney Sheldon *(The Doomsday Conspiracy),* Ken Follett, Garrison Keillor, and Barbara Taylor Bradford. As well, there was perennial also-ran Dick Francis, and the late Dr. Seuss still on the list with *Oh, the Places You'll Go!* after nearly two years.

The people at the Publishing Research Lab must be thinking, "If only it weren't for *Scarlett*...." The opportunity to observe the eddies and currents with seven former #1 authors all coming to the list about the same time would be fascinating. And yet the data skewed, because *Scarlett* has sat atop the list the entire time, and jockeying for #2 rather than #1 may be an entirely different ballgame. ■

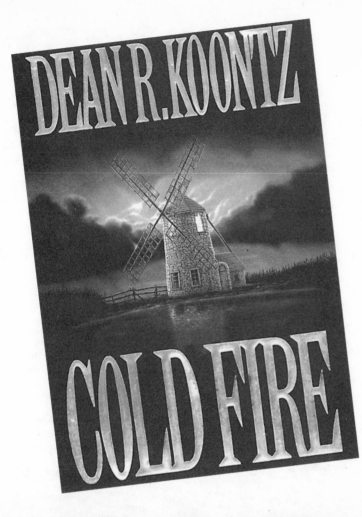

FIRST DATE AT #1: February 3, 1991
TOTAL WEEKS AT #1: 3

Cold Fire
Dean R. Koontz
PUTNAM

For a third consecutive year, Koontz checks into the #1 spot during the first week in February, this time with the story of a despondent reporter who finds hope and then romance as she trails a good samaritan.

FIRST DATE AT #1: February 24, 1991
TOTAL WEEKS AT #1: 8

Heartbeat
Danielle Steel
DELACORTE

Steel's ninth #1 bestseller revolves around a chance meeting between a man and a woman, both of whom have successful careers in television. Their encounter has far-reaching results, enabling them both to solve their romantic problems.

BY AND ABOUT #1 AUTHORS:

"In an age when doomsayers are to be heard in every corner of the land, I find great hope in our species and in the future we will surely make for ourselves. I have no patience whatsoever for misanthropic fiction, of which there is too much these days. In fact, that is one reason why I do not wish to have the 'horror novel' label applied to my books even when it is sometimes accurate; too many current horror novels are misanthropic, senselessly bleak, and I do not wish to be lumped with them. . . . Very little if any great and long-lasting fiction has been misanthropic. I strongly believe that, in addition to entertaining, it is the function of fiction to explore the way we live, reinforce our noble traits, and suggest ways to improve the world where we can. If a writer is misanthropic . . . then he has a one-book message and he might as well quit writing."

—Dean Koontz

FIRST DATE AT #1: July 21, 1991
TOTAL WEEKS AT #1: 4

Chutzpah
Alan M. Dershowitz

LITTLE, BROWN

The well-known law professor takes a look at the Jews in America's past, present, and future. The youngest tenured professor in the history of Harvard Law School, Dershowitz, was known for taking unpopular, even somewhat scandalous cases. As attorney for some of the people described in the 1991 #1 bestseller *Den of Thieves,* he attempted to block the book's publication, then bought full-page ads in newspapers nationwide to attack its credibility.

FIRST DATE AT #1: August 25, 1991
TOTAL WEEKS AT #1: 1

Parliament of Whores
P. J. O'Rourke

ENTREKIN

The conservative political humorist explains the workings of the Federal government in a book disguised as a civics text. He compares George Bush to Captain Kangaroo, and shows why God is a Republican but Santa Claus is a Democrat. The poet and former editor-in-chief of the *National Lampoon* told *Contemporary Authors,* "I write because I don't know how to do anything else." The *Times* reviewer calls it "a bracing cruise around our democratic institutions. For those who might be offended by hearing Marilyn Quayle described as a 'Cape buffalo' or Michael Dukakis as 'Pinchgut Micky,' there's always the op-ed page."

Epilogue: The Past and the Future 349

The visit left me not only with poignant memories of my Orthodox youth but with complex thoughts about the future of Judaism and of my Jewishness. During our week together, I felt as Jewish as any of my friends. Indeed, among the group, I had come from the most observant background. Ironically, the one who had come from the least observant background was now the most Orthodox. As it was in our youth, the levels of observance are as much a function of local community mores as of theological belief. But now it was different, because each of us had relocated to his current com———— its different mores. Living in West Hem————
plying with a certain le————
sachuse————

350 CHUTZPAH

The week with my boyhood friends on Martha's Vineyard reminded me of how quickly life passes. It was just yesterday that we were taunting our teachers in elementary school. And now, half a lifetime later, we are still full of chutzpah, but a bit less certain about our answers. I hope to retain some of those irreverent qualities of youth — some of the Brooklyn chutzpah — as I continue to confront the eternal questions inherent in being a Jewish American and an American Jew.

As I have thought about these questions and how my friends and I are continuing to struggle with them, I find myself pondering a Jewish future that has always defied prognostication. I began this book by pointing to the profound yet entirely unpredictable changes in the nature of Jewish life, death, and existence over the past century. In the spirit of chutzpah, I end it by offering some tentative predictions about the near future of the American Jewish condition. Not even a chutzpahnik would venture to prophesy our long-term future.

We will continue to live in that most uncomfortable of temporal zones, "the meantime." Jewish life in America will neither be as secure as we would like it, nor as insecure as it has historically been. Although we will continue to witness the external indica of primitive anti-Semitism — the swastika graffiti, the hate mail, and the verbal slurs — this will not reflect mainstream attitudes. Some mainstream figures, like Patrick Buchanan, will continue to be insensitive to Jewish concerns, but such insensitivity will diminish rather than enhance their general influence. Buchanan will remain influential *despite* his anti-Semitism, not *because* of it. Social and economic anti-Semitism will continue to abate, as Jews become more like other groups. Anti-Semitism will become less acceptable among black leaders as they learn — and as we help teach them — that insensitivity to Jewish concerns is fatal to electoral success in many parts of the country. Black politicians who are sensitive to Jewish concerns will continue to be elected with Jewish support, and black politicians who are anti-Semitic or who court anti-Semitic support will continue to be defeated with Jewish opposition.

The greatest challenges to the survival of the Jewish people will take place in Israel, as American support for the Jewish state vacillates. It will become more acceptable, politically, for American office seekers to be "evenhanded" on Israel. And American "evenhandedness," in the face of European and third world support for the PLO, can prove disastrous to Israeli security. The physical threat — as distinguished

FIRST DATE AT #1: April 21, 1991
TOTAL WEEKS AT #1: 3

The Seeress of Kell
David Eddings
DEL REY-BALLANTINE

While the first four were popular, the fifth and final volume of Edding's ongoing fantasy saga, *The Malloreon*, finally broke through to #1, the first of its genre to do so. It tells the story of Belgarion, the Child of Light, accompanied by his wife Ce'Nedra and members of his shape-changing family heading to his long-awaited meeting with Zandramas, Child of the Dark, with the fate of the planet at stake.

FIRST DATE AT #1: May 12, 1991
TOTAL WEEKS AT #1: 6

Loves Music, Loves to Dance
Mary Higgins Clark
SIMON & SCHUSTER

Two years after her first #1 book, Clark returns with the frightening story of two Manhattan women whose research into personals advertising leads them into a trap set by the "dancing shoe" serial killer. When one woman is murdered, her friends seeks to meet the men she dated in hopes of finding the killer.

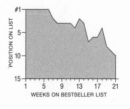

THE HIGH PLACES OF KORIM

The burning red clouds overhead erupted with [...] hideously twinned beast came at them. "Spread out!" [...] "Silk! Tell them what to do!" He drew a deep breath as [...] lightning streaked down from the roiling red sky above to crash against the sides of the terraced pyramid with earth-shattering claps of thunder. "Let's go!" Garion cried to Zakath as he once more drew Iron-grip's sword. But then he paused, dumbfounded. Poledra, as calmly as she would if crossing a meadow, approached the awful monstrosity.

"Thy Master is the Lord of Deception, Mordja," she said to the suddenly immobilized creature before her, "but it is time for deceit to end. Thou wilt speak only truth. What is thy purpose here? What is the purpose of all of thy kind in this place?"

The Demon Lord, frozen within the form of the dragon, snarled its hatred as it twisted and writhed, attempting to break free.

"Speak, Mordja," Poledra commanded. Did *anyone* have that kind of power?

"I *will* not." Mordja spat out the words.

"Thou wilt," Garion's grandmother said in a dreadfully quiet voice.

Mordja shrieked then, a shriek of total agony.

"What is thy purpose?" Poledra insisted.

"I serve the King of Hell!" the demon cried.

"And what is the purpose of the King of Hell here?"

"He would possess the stones of power," Mordja howled.

"And why?"

"That he may break his chains, the chains in which accursed UL bound him long ere any of this was made."

"Wherefore hast thou then aided the Child of Dark, and wherefore didst thy foe Nahaz aid the Disciple of Torak? Didst not thy Master know that each of them sought to raise a God? A God which would even more securely bind *him*?"

"What they sought was of no moment," Mordja snarled. "Nahaz and I contended with each other, in truth, but our contention was *not* on behalf of mad Urvon or sluttish Zandramas. In the instant that either of them gained Sardion would the King of Hell reach forth with my hands—or with the hands of Nahaz—and seize the stone. Then, using its power, would the one of us or the other wrest Cthrag Yaska from the Godslayer and deliver both stones to our Master. In the instant

283

FIRST DATE AT #1: September 1, 1991
TOTAL WEEKS AT #1: 1

When You Look Like Your Passport Photo, It's Time to Go Home

Erma Bombeck

HARPER

Bombeck's first three #1 books averaged 16 weeks at the top spot, but her fourth only remained for one week before it was displaced by the one-two punch of Fulghum and Hepburn. While humorously describing her travels through a dozen countries, she also finds time to question the whole concept of travel. "What were we doing poking into other people's lives and cultures? Swatting their flies, worshipping at their shrines in our stocking feet, and lugging home Indonesian art to hang over our Santa Fe sofa?"

FIRST DATE AT #1: September 8, 1991
TOTAL WEEKS AT #1: 2

Uh-Oh

Robert Fulghum

VILLARD

Like his first two #1 bestsellers, Fulghum's third in three years, subtitled "Some observations from both sides of the refrigerator door" offers advice on how to turn unfortunate surprises ("Uh-Oh") into triumphs. The bride who develops uncontrollable hiccups during the ceremony parlays the hysterically-laughing congregation into a more merry wedding. Being panned by *Time* and named one of *People* magazine's worst books of 1991 did not seem to have any effect on its long stay on the list, although only two weeks at #1.

242

Erma Bombeck

My husband, a former history teacher, is disposed to read every single sign on every single exhibit in every single museum. If there is a button to activate a voice, he will push it. If there is a guide who will explain how paint dries, he will listen. If there is a mountaintop where he can view Islamic graffiti, he will scale it.

I gave Stonehenge ten minutes.

It's not that I don't respect age. I respect anything that has been through children and is still standing. A mother cannot view the Acropolis without observing that if just once the Athens jousting team had won the city championship, they would have trashed that site in ten minutes and there would be nothing left to see. It's just that you have to pay such exorbitant prices. I didn't mind taking a train ride to see Machu Picchu in Peru, a cable car to visit Masada in Israel, or a cab ride to walk among Jordan's Roman ruins at Gerash. But those are exceptions. Most trips to antiquity are death marches. I spent a half day crawling up a mountain of cinders in Indonesia to do what? To stare into a hole called Krakatau. It looked exactly like the big hole I stared into in Italy called Vesuvius. The problem is I don't see a volcano all year. Then for two weeks, that's all I see, and I get burned out.

Same with museums. Same with churches. Same with ruins.

My husband and I do not look for the same things on the... is focused, asks questions about the ...the cathedral was size o...

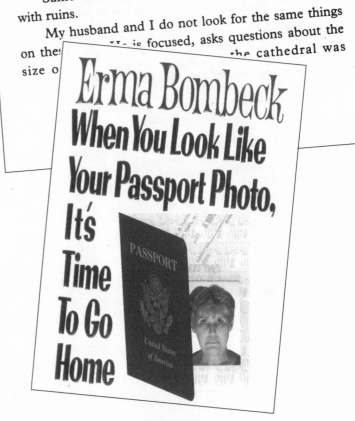

Youngest and Oldest #1 Authors Today

If all the 356 authors were alive on the 50th anniversary of the list (August 9, 1992) and assembled in he same room, the youngest one present would be Michael Jackson (34 years old), and the oldest would be Bernard Baruch (122 years old).

The youngest and oldest people in the room would be:

YOUNGEST		OLDEST	
Michael Jackson	34	Bernard Baruch	122
Amy Wallace	37	Somerset Maugham	118
Amy Tan	40	Winston Churchill	117
Timothy Zahn	41	Harry Overstreet	116
Ken Follett	43	Lloyd C. Douglas	115
Richard Simmons	44	Harry E. Fosdick	114
Joan D. Vinge	44	James F. Byrnes	113
David Wallechinsky	44	Douglas MacArthur	112
P. J. O'Rourke	44	Sholem Asch	111
Stephen King	44	Eleanor Roosevelt	107
Danielle Steel	45	Kenneth Roberts	107
Salman Rushdie	45	Sinclair Lewis	107
Tom Clancy	45	Thomas B. Costain	107
David Stockman	45	Francis Keyes	107
Gilda Radner	46	Samuel Shellabarger	104
Priscilla Presley	46	Dale Carnegie	103
Douglas Casey	46	Ben Ames Williams	103

FIRST DATE AT #1: June 30, 1991
TOTAL WEEKS AT #1: 1

Heir to the Empire
Timothy Zahn
BANTAM

The "Star Wars" galaxy is in jeopardy, threatened by new dangers from an unknown source. The author of the second "Star Wars" book to reach #1 (after Vinge's *Return of the Jedi*), Zahn told *Contemporary Authors* that he "began writing science fiction as a hobby while working toward my Ph.D. in physics.... After my first story sale in December, 1978, I began to consider the possibility of perhaps taking a year off sometime after getting my degree and writing full time. Seven months later... my thesis adviser died suddenly....I decided that my trial writing year had merely arrived earlier than I'd expected it to."

FIRST DATE AT #1: July 7, 1991
TOTAL WEEKS AT #1: 7

The Kitchen God's Wife
Amy Tan
PUTNAM

A Chinese-American matriarch tells the harrowing story of her life in what may quite possibly be the first #1 bestseller by a person of Asian ancestry. Tan's earlier novel, *The Joy Luck Club*, was on the *Times* list, but never reached #1. In an article called "Angst & the Second Novel," Tan says she is "glad that I shall never again have to write a Second Book." After a friend suggested that most writers go on to write lousy second books, Tan "decided that whatever those writers had lacked—confidence, stamina, vision, sharp red pencils—I would stock in extra portions."

243

FIRST DATE AT #1: September 22, 1991
TOTAL WEEKS AT #1: 12

Me

Katherine Hepburn

KNOPF

Five strong Hollywood woman have written #1 bestsellers about their lives: Tallulah Bankhead, Lauren Bacall, Shelley Winters, Gilda Radner, and now Katherine Hepburn. These memories of her life before, with, and after Spencer Tracy are subtitled *Stories of My Life*. Without the subtitle, this becomes one of the only two two-letter #1 titles, along with Stephen King's *It*.

FIRST DATE AT #1: November 3, 1991
TOTAL WEEKS AT #1: 7

Den of Thieves

James B. Stewart

SIMON & SCHUSTER

How the junk bond kings plundered and created havoc on Wall Street. Michael Milken is depicted as the pivotal figure in "the greatest criminal conspiracy the financial world has never known." Alan Dershowitz, himself at #1 on the list a month earlier, was retained by Milken to orchestrate an attack on the integrity of this book, including full-page anti-book advertisements in daily newspapers. The author is an attorney who became front page editor of the *Wall Street Journal*. While *Business Week* found the book "not without flaws," the *Times* declared that it "should, must be read by every American who gives a damn about this country."

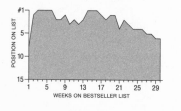

Short #1 Titles

THE SHORTEST ONE-WORD TITLES

It	Stephen King
Me	Katherine Hepburn
1876	Gore Vidal
Burr	Gore Vidal
Cujo	Stephen King
Star	Danielle Steel
Uh-Oh	Robert Fulghum
Veil	Bob Woodward
Zoya	Danielle Steel

THE SHORTEST TWO-WORD TITLES

QBVII	Leon Uris
Act One	Moss Hart
His Way	Kitty Kelley
My Turn	Nancy Reagan
The Robe	Lloyd C. Douglas
The Wall	John Hersey
The Word	Irving Wallace
Up Front	Bill Mauldin

THE SHORTEST THREE-WORD TITLES

Men at Work	George Will
Men in Love	Nancy Friday
East of Eden	John Steinbeck
For 2¢ Plain	Harry Golden
Good as Gold	Joseph Heller
Ship of Fools	Katherine Ann Porter
Summer of '49	David Halberstam
The 900 Days	Harrison Salisbury

Another Day, Lots of Dollars as Scarlett Returns to Tara

by Esther B. Fein
New York Times, **October 3, 1991**

Frankly, it appears readers do give a damn. Again. Hundreds of thousands of people have been stampeding bookstores around the country to buy *Scarlett,* the sequel to *Gone With the Wind* that has soared so quickly to the top of the bestseller list that even its publisher is astonished.

A million copies of the book have been printed, though the book has been in the stores barely a week, and orders are coming in so furiously, the publisher says he is printing 50,000 copies a day and shipping directly from the bindery to bookstores. . . .

"We've been astonished by the reaction," said Laurence J. Kirshbaum, president of Warner Books, which paid $4.94 million for the rights to the sequel that Margaret Mitchell said she would never write, but that her heirs decided to publish. . . .

Booksellers, other publishers, and the editor in charge of compiling the *Times* list said they could not remember when another book moved in and out of bookstores at this pace. The *New York Times* does not reveal the sales figures it collects weekly from more than 3,000 bookstores across the country, but a spokesman at the newspaper said that "*Scarlett* had sold more than 10 times as many copies as *Sum of All Fears,* a novel by Tom Clancy that was pushed into the No. 2 slot.

Scarlett also sold more than twice as many copies in the first week as Mr. Clancy's book and Kitty Kelley's *Nancy Reagan: The Unauthorized Biography* in the first week, and they are two of the biggest sellers so far this year. "We've checked our files and we have not been able to come up with anything this dramatic in the dozen years since we've computerized our bestseller list," the *Times* spokesman said. "It's a fascinating event. . . ."

The conventional wisdom in book publishing is that any big seller is good for the business because it brings people into bookstores and, hopefully, those people will buy other books as well. But with *Scarlett* selling at $24.95, the high end of fiction hardcovers . . . booksellers and publishers are wondering what effect its success will have on the two other works by major authors that have been published at the same time: Norman Mailer's *Harlot's Ghost,* which at $30 set a new high for popular fiction, and Stephen King's *Needful Things* ($24.95). . . .

Macmillan Publishing Company, which has had the rights to *Gone With the Wind* since it was first published in 1936, printed 55,000 copies of the book to coincide with the publication of *Scarlett,* but the company has gone back to press three times and so far as printed more than 100,000 copies of the original.

The last time *Gone With the Wind* appeared on the bestseller list was 1986, when it had a five-week run on the 50th anniversary of the book's publication. A spokesman for the *New York Times Book Review* could recall only one recent example of a classic that reappeared on the list: George Orwell's *1984* which was a bestseller for a while in, predictably, 1984. ■

FIRST DATE AT #1: August 25, 1991
TOTAL WEEKS AT #1: 7

The Sum of All Fears
Tom Clancy
PUTNAM

Clancy's fifth and most recent #1 book arrived at the top seven weeks before *Scarlett,* but was immediately knocked out of #1 by that southern belle. Clancy tells the story of a band of middle-eastern terrorists who edge the world to the brink of war by exploding a nuclear device at the Super Bowl in Denver. (His terrorists are all familiar with *Black Sunday!*) In a *Washington Post* article, Clancy says, "I'm not that good a writer. I do a good action scene. I handle technology well. I like to think that I do a fair —fairer—job of representing the kind of people that we have in the Navy . . . portraying them the way they really are. Beyond that, I'll try to . . . improve what needs improving."

FIRST DATE AT #1: October 13, 1991
TOTAL WEEKS AT #1: 16

Scarlett
Alexandra Ripley
WARNER

The Margaret Mitchell estate selected Ripley, author of three previous southern novels, to write the sequel to *Gone with the Wind.* The long-awaited book entered the list at #1 where it remained four months despite many poor reviews (*Time* said, "Frankly, it's not worth a damn"), promptly displaced Tom Clancy and held off the most recent efforts from previous #1 authors Stephen King, Danielle Steel, Sidney Sheldon, Ken Follett, Garrison Keillor, and Barbara Taylor Bradford.

FIRST DATE AT #1: December 1, 1991
TOTAL WEEKS AT #1: 1

Under Fire

Oliver North and William Novak

HARPER

Subtitled "An American Story," this is the former Marine colonel's autobiography, including his account of the Iran-Contra scandal and his allegation that Reagan knew everything about the arms-for-hostages scandal. This is Novak's third #1 "with" appearance. In this instance, the existence of the project remained a total secret from the press and public until a week before publication. Once a week for more than a year, Novak would fly to Washington under an assumed name to meet with North.

FIRST DATE AT #1: February 9, 1992
TOTAL WEEKS AT #1: 13

Revolution from Within

Gloria Steinem

LITTLE, BROWN

The *Times* called the book a "thick compilation of self-help techniques mixed with feminist fundamentals . . . an assertion of self-esteem as the driving force of the feminist movement and, indeed, of all social change. . . ." The original title was *The Bedside Book of Self-Esteem*; now its subtitle is "A book of self-esteem." *Newsweek* reports that Steinem "says she has lots more books to write before she will be ready to do an autobiography," but suggests that "Her career has been a thousand times more inspirational than the . . . canned benevolence she offers here."

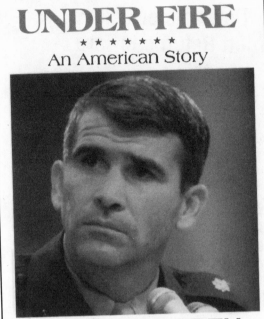

UNDER FIRE

★ ★ ★ ★ ★ ★

An American Story

OLIVER L. NORTH
with William Novak

...ORTH

...ned that he hadn't told the
...ed the temperature. But it
...n," said the press, extend-
...know. According to the polls,
...people still found it diffi-

...ught so, too. ...resident Reagan *did* know.

And now, five years later, I am even more convinced: *President Reagan knew everything.*

True, he didn't learn about the "diversion" from me—at least not directly. In all my time in Washington, I never met alone with him, and the only time we talked privately on the phone was the day I was fired. John Poindexter insisted that *he* didn't tell the President either, because Poindexter wanted him to have "plausible deniability." At the hearings, Poindexter said, "I made a very deliberate decision not to ask the President, so that I could insulate him from the decision and provide some future deniability for the President if it ever leaked out."

Even if that's true, I find it hard to believe that the President didn't know.

Here's why. The contras were not the only beneficiary of the arms sales to Iran. Part of the residuals were to be used for other projects, including several counterterrorist operations and various plans involving the release of the hostages. Because these activities were so sensitive, I made sure to get explicit permission for each one. Every time one of these projects came up, whether or not the particular plan was actually carried out in the end (and not all of them were), I wrote a memo or a computer message to Admiral Poindexter outlining how the money would be used. It was always my belief that these memos were passed up the line to the President, because... type generally were. In fact... April 1986...

"For me, writing is the only thing that passes the three tests of metier: (1) when I'm doing it, I don't feel that I should be doing something else instead; (2) it produces a sense of accomplishment and, once in a while, pride; and (3) it's frightening."

—Gloria Steinem

Mr. Consistency

Dean Koontz has reached #1 in fiction four times during the first week of February in 1989, 1990, 1991, and 1992, where he remained for two to four weeks each time: *Midnight, The Bad Place, Cold Fire,* and *Hideaway.*

SHORTEST LAST NAMES

The pseudonymous "J" could be considered to have a one-letter surname. Otherwise, the shortest last names have been three letters, in the cases of:

Bly   Eco   Hoy   Tan

LONGEST LAST NAMES

Three #1 authors have 12-letter last names:

Hammarskjold   Shellabarger   Wallechinsky

Four more have 11-letter last names, including the only hyphenated author, André Schwarz-Bart:

Auchincloss   Schlesinger
Schwarz-Bart   Silverstein

SHORTEST COMPLETE NAMES

The only six-letter #1 author is Amy Tan. At seven letters, we have:

Bob Hope   P. D. James   Cy Janos
Dr. Seuss   W. L. White

Fourteen #1 authors have an 8-letter combined name.

LONGEST COMPLETE NAMES

The longest name (without including middle names) belongs to Alexander deSeversky, at 19 letters. There are three 18-letter names:

Elizabeth Chevalier
Samuel Shellabarger
Immanuel Velikovsky

FIRST DATE AT #1: February 2, 1992
TOTAL WEEKS AT #1: 4

Hideaway
Dean R. Koontz
PUTNAM

For the fourth consecutive year, a Dean Koontz comes out of nowhere to rise rapidly to #1 during the first week of February. Hatch Harrison is resuscitated after drowning but now he has visions linking his mind with a deranged killer trying to get to Hell by assembling a collection of corpses hidden deep beneath an abandoned theme park.

FIRST DATE AT #1: March 1, 1992
TOTAL WEEKS AT #1: 2

Rising Sun
Michael Crichton
PUTNAM

After coming close half a dozen times (*The Andromeda Strain, Terminal Man, Jurassic Park*), Dr. Crichton finally reached #1 with his sociological thriller about an American detective's attempt to solve a murder, finding himself up against immensely powerful Japanese overlords who control government, business, the press, and the universities. By his third year at Harvard Medical School, Crichton had published several thrillers under the name John Lange, and decided to be a writer, not a practicing physician. He confirmed this during a postgraduate year at the Salk Institute, where he determined that "These people were professionals of a very high order, and I was a pottering amateur."

FIRST DATE AT #1: May 10, 1992
TOTAL WEEKS AT #1: 1

Give War a Chance
P. J. O'Rourke

ATLANTIC MONTHLY

The subtitle of this collection of previously-published articles is "Eyewitness accounts of mankind's struggle against tyranny, injustice and alcohol-free beer." The conservative columnist writes that "I have often been called a Nazi, and, although it is unfair, I don't let it bother me. I don't let it bother me for one simple reason. No one has *ever* had a fantasy about being tied to a bed and sexually ravished by someone dressed as a liberal."

FIRST DATE AT #1: June 7, 1992
TOTAL WEEKS AT #1: 4

The Silent Passage
Gail Sheehy

RANDOM HOUSE

A decade and a half after *Passages,* Sheehy returns to #1 with this book subtitled "Menopause." She suggests that for more than 80% of women, menopause is fear, depression, hot flashes, and a loss of libido. She acknowledges that it is not such a big deal in some societies ("The Japanese language does not even have a word for hot flashes."), and that there is a body of research suggesting that most women have little trauma or regret traceable to menopause. In the end, she discovers that menopause is a passage and an opportunity for spiritual growth.

The Longest One-Word Titles

Reminiscences	Douglas MacArthur
Andersonville	MacKinlay Kantor
Kaleidoscope	Danielle Steel
Civilisation	Kenneth Clark
Firestarter	Stephen King
Wanderlust	Danielle Steel
Megatrends	John Naisbitt
Fatherhood	Bill Cosby
Chesapeake	James Michener
Centennial	James Michener

FIRST DATE AT #1: March 15, 1992
TOTAL WEEKS AT #1: 11

The Pelican Brief
John Grisham
DOUBLEDAY

Louisiana law student Darby Shaw solves the mystery of the murder of two Supreme Court justices. Her legal brief sets off an elaborate series of adventures. While Grisham's first #1 bestseller, *The Firm,* was well-reviewed almost everywhere, some critics felt that he didn't play fair with his readers here, by failing to provide a plausible explanation for the events of the book. As *Newsweek* put it, "Grisham keeps the pages turning but, in the end, badly breaches the thrillermeister-reader contract."

FIRST DATE AT #1: May 17, 1992
TOTAL WEEKS AT #1: 4

Jewels
Danielle Steel
DELACORTE

Steel's tenth #1 book tells the story of Sarah, an ambitious young woman who survives personal tragedy and the Nazi death camps to become a wealthy financier and jewelry dealer. The book remained at #1 for four weeks before being displaced by the resurgent Dr. Seuss. Steel's local paper, the *San Francisco Chronicle* was not enthralled. "Steel means well," they wrote, "but she always skims the surface of her own story, drawing characters from a kind of literary central casting, and plots, it seems, from silent films." The prolific Ms. Steel also published nine juvenile books during 1989–1990, including *Marina's New School, Max's New Baby,* and *Martha's New Puppy.*

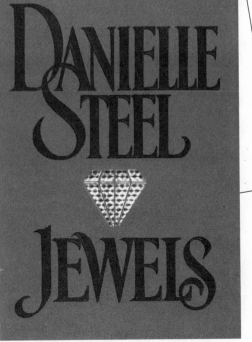

Jewels

wide sapphire bracelet, set with a diamond clasp, and a ruby necklace and earrings that were really stunning. And a huge ruby brooch at Van Cleef in the shape of a rose.

"My God, William . . . I feel so guilty." She knew he had spent an absolute fortune, but he didn't seem to mind it. And the jewelry he had bought her was fabulous and she loved it. "Just don't be silly!" He brushed it off as an ordinary event. "That is promise me we won't leave the room again for two days. That is the tax I will demand of you each time we go shopping."

"Don't you like to shop?" She looked briefly disappointed, he had seemed such a good sport about it the summer before.

"I love it. But I'd rather make love to my wife."

"Oh that . . ." She laughed, and addressed his needs the moment they went back to their room at the Ritz. They went shopping repeatedly after that. He bought her beautiful clothes at Jean Patou, and a fabulous leopard coat at Dior, and an enormous string of pearls at Mouboussin, which she wore every hour of every day after that. They even managed to go to the Louvre, and on their second week there, they went to tea with the Duke and Duchess of Windsor. And Sarah had to admit that William was right. Although she'd been predisposed to dislike her, she actua[...] extremely charming. And he was a lovely [...]mely kind when you got [...] people he kr[...] them at first[...] draw an unf[...] was quick t[...] faintly emb[...] was no que[...] utmost aff[...]

"Damn[...] to the hou[...] could sti[...]

249

FIRST DATE AT #1: July 5, 1992
TOTAL WEEKS AT #1: 6

Diana: Her True Story

Andrew Morton

SIMON & SCHUSTER

In the summer of 1992, three books on the unhappy life of Diana, Princess of Wales, reached the *Times* list at about the same time, but only British columnist Morton's version, based on interviews with friends and family members, and describing a series of suicide attempts, rose to #1, where it remained as the list closed out its first 50 years.

FIRST DATE AT #1: July 19, 1992

TOTAL WEEKS AT #1: 4

Gerald's Game

Stephen King

VIKING

King's previous book, *Needful Things,* was his first in a long time that did not reach #1. But he comes roaring back with his sixteenthth #1 book. Gerald Burlingame's "game" is kinky sex. His wife Jessie, handcuffed to the bedposts, accidentally kills him, then suffers increasingly and horribly for the next 28 hours. Many reviewers agreed with *Publishers Weekly* that while the book is "one of the best-written stories King has ever published, it will offend many through sheer bad taste," especially in the detailed descriptions of an earlier incestual relationship. The book entered the list at #1, and, fittingly for the man with the most #1 bestsellers ever, remained there as the *Times* list completed its first half century.

AUTHOR INDEX

TITLE INDEX